MICROECONOMICS

Custom Edition for the University of Pennsylvania

THIRD EDITION

Robert S. Pindyck
Massachusetts Institute of Technology

Daniel L. Rubinfeld
University of California, Berkeley

 SIMON & SCHUSTER CUSTOM PUBLISHING

Microeconomics, Third Edition
by Robert S. Pindyck and Daniel L. Rubinfeld
Copyright © 1989, 1992, 1995
by Prentice-Hall, Inc.
Simon & Schuster Company/A Viacom Company
Upper Saddle River, New Jersey 07458

This special edition published in cooperation with
Simon & Schuster Custom Publishing.

Printed in the United States of America

10   9   8   7   6   5   4   3

ISBN 0–536–58999–2

BA 97063

 SIMON & SCHUSTER CUSTOM PUBLISHING
160 Gould Street/Needham Heights, MA 02194
Simon & Schuster Education Group

To our daughters

Maya, Talia, and Shira   Sarah and Rachel

CONTENTS

Preface

For students who care about how the world works, microeconomics is one of the most relevant and interesting subjects they study. A good grasp of microeconomics is vital for managerial decision making, for designing and understanding public policy, and more generally for appreciating how a modern economy functions.

We wrote this book, *Microeconomics*, because we believe that students need to be exposed to the new topics that have come to have a central role in microeconomics over the past few years—topics such as game theory and competitive strategy, the roles of uncertainty and information, and the analysis of pricing by firms with market power. We also felt that students need to be shown how microeconomics can be used as a tool for decision making. Microeconomics is an exciting and dynamic subject, but students need to be given an appreciation of its relevance and usefulness. They want and need a good understanding of how microeconomics can actually be used outside the classroom.

To respond to these needs, our book provides a fresh treatment of microeconomic theory that stresses its relevance and application to both managerial and public-policy decision making. This applied emphasis is accomplished by including more than eighty extended examples that cover such topics as the analysis of demand, cost, and market efficiency, the design of pricing strategies, investment and production decisions, and public policy analysis. Because of the importance that we attach to these examples, they are included in the flow of the text, rather than being "boxed" or screened. (A list of the examples is included in the table of contents on pages xv–xvii.)

The coverage in *Microeconomics* incorporates the dramatic changes that have occurred in the field in recent years. There is growing interest in game theory and the strategic interactions of firms (Chapters 12 and 13), in the role and implications of uncertainty and asymmetric information (Chapters 5 and 17), in the pricing strategies of firms with market power (Chapters 10 and 11), and in the design of policies to deal efficiently with externalities such as environmental pollution (Chapter 18). These topics, which are missing or barely covered in most books, receive prominent attention here.

That the coverage in *Microeconomics* is comprehensive and up-to-date does not mean that it is "advanced" or difficult. We have worked hard to make the exposition clear and accessible as well as lively and engaging. We believe that the study of microeconomics should be enjoyable and stimulating. We hope that our book reflects this. Except for appendices and footnotes, *Microeconomics* uses no calculus. As a result, it should be suitable for students with a broad range of backgrounds. (Those sections that are more demanding are marked with an asterisk and can be easily omitted.)

Changes in the Second Edition

The second edition of *Microeconomics* contained a number of important changes and additions. Chapters 3 and 4 on Consumer Demand, and Chapters 6 and 7 on the Theory of the Firm, were heavily revised. The coverage of these important core topics was more comprehensive and much more clear and accessible. We reorganized and rewrote some of the material on oligopoly in Chapter 12; we began with an introductory discussion of the Nash Equilibrium, and then used this concept as a framework for analyzing the Cournot model and models of price competition. Less extensive revisions were also made in the other chapters of the book. In addition, a number of new examples were added, and many of the book's existing examples were revised and updated.

We also added new material throughout the book. Chapter 1 discussed the extent of a market and the meaning of a market price. Chapter 3 included coverage of revealed preference, Chapter 4 discussed Engel curves, and in Chapters 8 and 10 we expanded our coverage of profit maximization and output choice. In Chapter 11 we added a new section on advertising. Chapter 13 was considerably expanded, with new material on game theory and its application not only to the competitive strategies of firms, but also to the strategic trade policies of nations. Chapter 16 discussed comparative advantage and international trade explicitly. In Chapter 17 we added a new section on incentive design in vertically integrated firms. Finally, in response to a heightened interest in environmental issues, we expanded our coverage in Chapter 18 of externalities and the design of public policies to deal with them.

Changes in the Third Edition

The third edition of *Microeconomics* contains a number of important changes and additions. Chapters 3 and 4 on Consumer Demand, and Chapters 6, 7, and 8 on the Theory of the Firm and Competitive Supply have been rewritten with an eye toward greater clarity and accessibility. New material has been added in several places, including Hicksian substitution effects in Chapter 4, and an analysis of recycling in Chapter 18. Less extensive revisions were also made in other chapters of the book. Finally, a number of new examples have been added, and many of the book's existing examples have been revised and updated.

Alternative Course Designs

Microeconomics offers instructors substantial flexibility in course design. For a one-quarter or one-semester course stressing the basic core material, we would suggest using the following chapters and sections of chapters: 1, 2, 3, 4.1–4.4, 6.1–6.5, 7.1–7.4, 8, 9.1–9.4, 10.1–10.4, 11.1–11.3, 12.1–12.2, 12.5–12.6, 14, 15.1–15.4, 18.1–18.2, and 18.5. A somewhat more ambitious course might also include parts of Chapters 5 and 16, and additional sections in Chapters 6, 7, 9, 10, and 12. To emphasize uncertainty and market failure, an instructor should also include substantial parts of Chapters 5 and 17.

Depending on one's interests and the goals of the course, other sections could be added or used to replace the materials listed above. A course that emphasized modern pricing theory and business strategy would include all of Chapters 10, 11, 12, and 13, and the remaining sections of Chapter 15. A course in managerial economics might also include the Appendices to Chapters 4, 7, and 11, as well as the Appendix on regression analysis at the end of the book. A course that emphasized welfare economics and public policy should include Chapter 16 and additional sections of Chapter 18.

Finally, we want to stress that those sections or subsections which are more demanding and/or are peripheral to the core material have been marked with an asterisk. These sections can easily be omitted without detracting from the flow of the book.

Supplementary Materials

Instructional aids of an exceptionally high quality are available to instructors and students using this book. The *Instructor's Manual* was written by Gilbert White of Michigan State University, Geoffrey Rothwell of Stanford University, and Valerie Suslow of the University of Michigan. It provides answers to all of the Questions for Review and the Exercises that appear at the end of the chapters, as well as a summary of the key points in each chapter and a series of teaching suggestions. It is available from the publisher on request, as is a separate *Test Bank*, written by Dennis Muraoka and Judith Roberts of California State University at Long Beach. The *Study Guide*, by Valerie Suslow of the University of Michigan and Jonathan Hamilton of the University of Florida, provides a wide variety of review materials and exercises for students. The *Study Guide* can be purchased separately. Finally, Arthur Lewbel of Brandeis University has developed MICRO-EX, an innovative software package that extends many of the examples, and reinforces an understanding of the concepts and their application by allowing the student to easily work through a variety of simulation exercises. This software is also available for separate purchase. Please contact your Prentice Hall sales representative for information on availability of all supplementary materials.

Acknowledgments

Since this text has been the outgrowth of years of experience in the classroom, we owe a debt of gratitude to our students and to the colleagues with whom we often discuss microeconomics and its presentation. We have also had the help of capable research assistants, including Walter Athier, Phillip Gibbs, Jamie Jue, Kathy O'Regan, Karen Randig, Subi Rangan, and Deborah Senior. Kathy Hill helped with the art, while Assunta Kent, Mary Knott, and Dawn Elliott Linahan provided secretarial assistance with the first edition. We especially want to thank Lynn Steele and Jay Tharp, who provided considerable editorial support for the second edition. Mark Glickman and Steve Wiggins assisted with the examples in the third edition, while Andrew Guest, Jeanette Sayre, and Lynn Steele provided valuable editorial support.

Writing this book has been a painstaking and enjoyable process. At each stage we received exceptionally fine guidance from teachers of microeconomics throughout the country. After the first draft of the first edition of this book had been edited and reviewed, it was discussed at a two-day focus group meeting in New York. This provided an opportunity to get ideas from instructors with a variety of backgrounds and perspectives. We would like to thank the following focus group members for advice and criticism: Carl Davidson of Michigan State University; Richard Eastin of the University of Southern California; Judith Roberts of California State University, Long Beach; and Charles Strein of the University of Northern Iowa. We would also like to thank all those who reviewed the first edition at each stage of its evolution:

Ted Amato, University of North Carolina, Charlotte
John J. Antel, University of Houston
Kerry Back, Northwestern University
Jeremy Bulow, Stanford University
Larry A. Chenault, Miami University
Jacques Cremer, Virginia Polytechnic Institute and State University
Carl Davidson, Michigan State University
Arthur T. Denzau, Washington University
Richard V. Eastin, University of Southern California
William H. Greene, New York University
George Heitman, Pennsylvania State University
George E. Hoffer, Virginia Commonwealth University
Robert Inman, The Wharton School, University of Pennsylvania
B. Patrick Joyce, Michigan Technological University
Leonard Lardaro, University of Rhode Island
Peter Linneman, University of Pennsylvania
R. Ashley Lyman, University of Idaho
Wesley A. Magat, Duke University
Anthony M. Marino, University of Southern Florida
Michael J. Moore, Duke University

Daniel Orr, Virginia Polytechnic Institute and State University
Judith Roberts, California State University, Long Beach
Geoffrey Rothwell, Stanford University
Edward L. Sattler, Bradley University
Charles T. Strein, University of Northern Iowa
Michael Wasylenko, Syracuse University
Lawrence J. White, New York University

We had a good deal of feedback and assistance in the development of the second edition. We would like to thank the following reviewers of the second edition for the extremely valuable advice they provided:

Dale Ballou, University of Massachusetts, Amherst
Henry Chappel, University of South Carolina
John Coupe, University of Maine at Orono
Richard Eastin, University of Southern California
Otis Gilley, Louisiana Tech University
John Gross, University of Wisconsin at Milwaukee
Jonathan Hamilton, University of Florida
Claire Hammond, Wake Forest University
James Hartigan, University of Oklahoma
Robert Inman, The Wharton School, University of Pennsylvania
Joyce Jacobsen, Rhodes College
Richard Mills, University of New Hampshire
Julianne Nelson, Stern School of Business, New York University
Michael Podgursky, University of Massachusetts, Amherst
Charles Ratliff, Davidson College
Nestor Ruiz, University of California, Davis
Valerie Suslow, University of Michigan
David Vrooman, St. Lawrence University

We would like to thank a thoughtful and talented group of reviewers whose comments and ideas have greatly improved this third edition:

Jack Adams, University of Arkansas, Little Rock
William Baxter, Stanford University
James A. Brander, University of British Columbia
Charles Clotfelter, Duke University
Kathryn Combs, California State University, Los Angeles
Richard Corwall, Middlebury College
Tran Dung, Wright State University
Carl E. Enomoto, New Mexico State University
Ray Farrow, Seattle University
Gary Ferrier, Southern Methodist University
David Kaserman, Auburn University

Michael Kende, INSEAD, France
Anthony Krautman, DePaul University
James MacDonald, Rensselaer Polytechnical Institute
David Mills, University of Virginia, Charlottesville
Jennifer Moll, Fairfield University
Sharon J. Pearson, University of Alberta Edmonton
Ivan P'ng, University of California, Los Angeles
Roger Sherman, University of Virginia
Abdul Turay, Radford University
Robert Whaples, Wake Forest University
Arthur Woolf, University of Vermont
Chiou-nan Yeh, Alabama State University
Joseph Ziegler, University of Arkansas, Fayetteville

Apart from the formal review process, we are especially grateful to Jean Andrews, Paul Anglin, J. C. K. Ash, Ernst Berndt, George Bittlingmayer, Severin Borenstein, Paul Carlin, Whewon Cho, Setio Angarro Dewo, Frank Fabozzi, Joseph Farrell, Jonathan Hamilton, Robert Inman, Joyce Jacobsen, Stacey Kole, Jeannette Mortensen, John Mullahy, Krishna Pendakur, Jeffrey Perloff, Ivan P'ng, A. Mitchell Polinsky, Judith Roberts, Geoffrey Rothwell, Garth Saloner, Joel Schrag, Daniel Siegel, Thomas Stoker, David Storey, and James Walker, who were kind enough to provide comments, criticisms, and suggestions as our manuscript developed.

Finally, we wish to express our sincere thanks for the extraordinary effort those at Macmillan and Prentice Hall made in the development of our book. Throughout the writing of the first edition, Bonnie Lieberman provided invaluable guidance and encouragement; Ken MacLeod kept the progress of the book on an even keel; Gerald Lombardi provided masterful editorial assistance and advice; and John Molyneux ably oversaw the book's production.

In the development of the second edition, we were fortunate to have the encouragement and support of David Boelio, and the organizational and editorial help of two Macmillan editors, Caroline Carney and Jill Lectka. The second edition also benefitted greatly from the superb development editing of Gerald Lombardi, and from John Travis, who managed the book's production.

Jill Lectka and Denise Abbott were our editors for the third edition, and we benefitted greatly from their input. We also want to thank Valerie Ashton, John Sollami, and Sharon Lee for their superb handling of the production of the third edition.

R.S.P.
D.L.R.

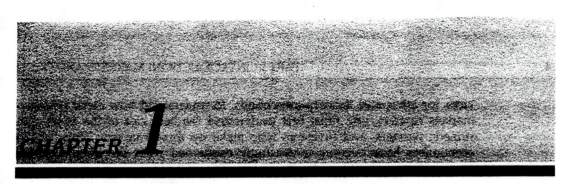

Preliminaries

*E*conomics is divided into two main branches: microeconomics and macroeconomics. Microeconomics deals with the behavior of individual economic units. These units include consumers, workers, investors, owners of land, business firms—in fact, any individual or entity that plays a role in the functioning of our economy.[1] Microeconomics explains how and why these units make economic decisions. For example, it explains how consumers make purchasing decisions and how their choices are affected by changing prices and incomes. It also explains how firms decide how many workers to hire and how workers decide where to work and how much work to do.

Another important concern of microeconomics is how economic units interact to form larger units—markets and industries. Microeconomics helps us to understand, for example, why the American automobile industry developed the way it did and how producers and consumers interact in the market for automobiles. It explains how automobile prices are determined, how much automobile companies invest in new factories, and how many cars are produced each year. By studying the behavior and interaction of individual firms and consumers, microeconomics reveals how industries and markets operate and evolve, why they differ from one another, and how they are affected by government policies and global economic conditions.

By contrast, macroeconomics, the other major branch of economics, deals with aggregate economic quantities, such as the level and growth rate of national output, interest rates, unemployment, and inflation. But the boundary between macroeconomics and microeconomics has become less and less distinct in recent years. The reason is that macroeconomics also involves the analysis of markets—for example, the aggregate markets for goods and ser-

---

[1] The prefix *micro-* is derived from the Greek word meaning "small." However, many of the individual economic units that we will study are small only in relation to the U.S. economy as a whole. For example, the annual sales of General Motors, IBM, or Exxon are larger than the gross national products of many countries.

vices, for labor, and for corporate bonds. To understand how these aggregate markets operate, one must first understand the behavior of the firms, consumers, workers, and investors who make up these markets. Thus, macroeconomists have become increasingly concerned with the microeconomic foundations of aggregate economic phenomena, and much of macroeconomics is actually an extension of microeconomic analysis.

1.1 *The Use and Limitations of Microeconomic Theory*

Like any science, economics is concerned with the *explanation* and *prediction* of observed phenomena. Why, for example, do firms tend to hire or lay off workers when the prices of raw materials needed in the production process change? How many workers are likely to be hired or laid off by a firm or an industry if the price of raw materials increases by, say, 10 percent?

In economics, as in other sciences, explanation and prediction are based on *theories*. Theories are developed to explain observed phenomena in terms of a set of basic rules and assumptions. The theory of the firm, for example, begins with a simple assumption—firms try to maximize their profits. The theory uses this assumption to explain how firms choose the amounts of labor, capital, and raw materials that they use for production, as well as the amount of output they produce. It also explains how these choices depend on the *prices* of inputs, such as labor, capital, and raw materials, as well as the price the firm can receive for its output.

Economic theories are also the basis for making predictions. Thus, the theory of the firm tells us whether a firm's output level will increase or decrease in response to an increase in wage rates or a decrease in the price of raw materials. With the application of statistical and econometric techniques, theories can be used to construct *models*, from which quantitative predictions can be made. A model is a mathematical representation, based on economic theory, of a firm, a market, or some other entity. For example, we might develop a model of a particular firm and use it to predict by *how much* the firm's output level will change as a result of, say, a 10 percent drop in the price of raw materials.[2]

No theory, whether it be in economics, physics, or any other science, is perfectly correct. The usefulness and validity of a theory depend on whether it succeeds in explaining and predicting the set of phenomena that it is intended to explain and predict. Consistent with this goal, theories are continually tested against observation. As a result of this testing, theories are often modified or

---

[2] Statistics and econometrics also let us measure the *accuracy* of our predictions. For example, suppose we predict that a 10 percent drop in the price of raw materials will lead to a 5 percent increase in output. Are we sure that the increase in output will be exactly 5 percent, or might it be between 3 and 7 percent? Quantifying the accuracy of a prediction can be as important as the prediction itself.

refined and occasionally even discarded. The process of testing and refining theories is central to the development of economics as a science.

When evaluating a theory, it is important to keep in mind that it is invariably imperfect. This is the case in every branch of science. For example, in physics, Boyle's law relates the volume, temperature, and pressure of a gas.[3] The law is based on the assumption that individual molecules of a gas behave as though they were tiny, elastic billiard balls. Physicists today know that gas molecules do not, in fact, always behave like billiard balls, and partly because of this, Boyle's law breaks down under extremes of pressure and temperature. Nonetheless, under most conditions it does an excellent job of predicting how the temperature of a gas will change when the pressure and volume change, and it is therefore an essential tool for engineers and scientists.

The situation is much the same in economics. For example, firms do not maximize their profits all the time. Perhaps because of this, the theory of the firm has had only limited success in explaining certain aspects of firms' behavior, such as the timing of capital investment decisions. Nonetheless, the theory does explain a broad range of phenomena regarding the behavior, growth, and evolution of firms and industries, and so it has become an important tool for managers and policymakers.[4]

1.2 *Positive versus Normative Analysis*

Microeconomics deals with both *positive* and *normative* questions. Positive questions have to do with explanation and prediction, normative questions with what ought to be. Suppose the U.S. government imposes a quota on the import of foreign cars. What will happen to the price of cars and to their production and sales? What impact will this have on American consumers? On workers in the automobile industry? These questions are all in the realm of positive analysis. Positive analysis is central to microeconomics. As we explained above, theories are developed to explain phenomena, are tested against observations, and are used to construct models from which predictions are made.

The use of economic theory for prediction is important both for the managers of firms and for public policy. Suppose the federal government is considering raising the tax on gasoline. The tax would affect the price of gasoline,

---

[3] Robert Boyle (1627–1691) was a British chemist and physicist who discovered experimentally that pressure (P), volume (V), and temperature (T) were related in the following way: $PV = RT$, where R is a constant. Later, physicists derived this relationship as a consequence of the kinetic theory of gases, which describes the movement of gas molecules in statistical terms.

[4] A recent study shows that the managers of large American corporations make increasing use of microeconomic concepts. See Giuseppe A. Forgionne, "Economic Tools Used by Management in Large American Operated Corporations," *Business Economics* 19 (April 1984): 5–17.

consumers' preferences for small or large cars, the amount of driving that people do, and so on. To plan sensibly, oil companies, automobile companies, producers of automobile parts, and firms in the tourist industry would all want to know how large the various effects of this tax will be. Government policymakers would also need quantitative estimates of the effects of the tax. They would want to determine the costs imposed on consumers (perhaps broken down by income categories); the effects on profits and employment in the oil, automobile, and tourist industries; and the amount of tax revenue likely to be collected each year.

Sometimes we want to go beyond explanation and prediction to ask questions, such as "What is best?" This involves *normative* analysis, which is also important both for managers of firms and for designers of new public policies. Again, consider a new tax on gasoline. Automobile companies would want to determine the best (profit-maximizing) mix of large and small cars to produce once the tax is in place, or how much money should be invested to make cars more fuel-efficient. For policymakers, the primary issue is likely to be whether this tax is in the public interest. The same policy objectives (say, an increase in tax revenues and a decrease in our dependence on imported oil) might be met more cheaply with a different kind of tax, such as a tariff on imported oil.

Normative analysis is not only concerned with alternative policy options; it also involves the design of particular policy choices. For example, suppose it has been decided that a gasoline tax is desirable. Balancing costs and benefits, we then ask what is the optimal size of the tax?

Normative analysis is often supplemented by value judgments. For example, a comparison between a gasoline tax and an oil import tariff might conclude that the gasoline tax is easier to administer but has a greater impact on lower-income consumers. At that point society must make a value judgment, weighing equity against economic efficiency.[5] When value judgments are involved, microeconomics cannot tell us what the best policy is. However, it can clarify the trade-offs and thereby help to illuminate and sharpen the debate.

EXAMPLE 1.1 UNEMPLOYMENT AND THE LABOR FORCE PARTICIPATION OF WOMEN

Women's participation in the labor force has increased rapidly since World War II, from a rate of 31.4 percent in 1950 to 57.8 percent in 1992. (A person participates in the labor force by either working or looking for work.) Why has the rate of labor force participation by women grown? What are the policy im-

---

[5] Most of the value judgments involving economic policy boil down to just this trade-off—equity versus economic efficiency. This conflict and its implications are discussed clearly and in depth in Arthur M. Okun, *Equality and Efficiency: The Big Tradeoff* (Washington, D.C.: Brookings Institution, 1975).

plications of this growth? Microeconomic theory applied to labor markets helps us address these positive and normative questions.

In this example, we will focus on the relationship between the unemployment rate and labor force participation of married women. (The unemployment rate is the number of unemployed people divided by the number of people in the labor force.) Anyone who is unemployed or has dropped out of the labor force because he or she could not find suitable work is a cause for concern in our society. When the unemployment rate decreases, it is important to know whether that decrease is the result of economic policies that reduce the number of unemployed, or because people have stopped looking for a job. Microeconomic theory predicts that a change in the unemployment rate can have two conflicting effects on the rate of labor force participation of married women.

The *additional-worker effect* says that a higher unemployment rate will lead to a *higher* labor force participation rate for married women because previously unemployed wives are forced to enter the labor force to support their families when their husbands are unemployed. If high unemployment means less work for a husband, the likelihood that his wife will enter the labor force will increase.

By contrast, the *discouraged-worker effect* says that a higher unemployment rate will lead to a *lower* labor force participation rate because people who might otherwise look for work will become discouraged and drop out of the labor force. The higher the unemployment rate, the less likely a woman will be to try to find a job.

These two effects work in opposite directions. Which is more important? One way to find out is to examine data that relate the labor force participation rate for married women to the overall unemployment rate for different cities in the United States. A statistical analysis of the data for large cities shows that higher unemployment rates are associated with *lower* labor force participation rates. Specifically, for every 1 percent increase in the overall unemployment rate, the labor force participation rate of married women falls by 1.4 percent. Thus, the data indicate that the discouraged-worker effect is more important than the additional-worker effect.

In this particular case, the evidence is strong—and has been supported by more sophisticated analyses.[6] The policy implications are also clear—decreasing unemployment rates for married women that are associated with lower labor force participation rates should *not* be viewed as improvements in social welfare. They may be masking serious social problems that must be directly confronted.

---

[6] See Tim Maloney, "Employment Constraints and the Labor Supply of Married Women," *The Journal of Human Resources* 22 (1987): 51–61.

1.3 *Why Study Microeconomics?*

We think that after reading this book, you will have no doubt about the importance and broad applicability of microeconomics. In fact, one of our major goals is to show you how to apply microeconomic principles to actual decision-making problems. Nonetheless, some extra motivation early on never hurts. Here are two examples that show the use of microeconomics in practice and also provide a preview of the book.

Corporate Decision Making: Ford Introduces the Taurus

In late 1985 Ford introduced the Taurus—a newly designed, aerodynamically styled, front-wheel-drive automobile. The car was a huge success at the time and helped Ford almost to double its profits by 1987. The design and efficient production of this car involved not only some impressive engineering advances, but a lot of economics as well.

First, Ford had to think carefully about how the public would react to the Taurus' design. Would consumers be swayed by the styling and performance of the car? How strong would demand be initially, how fast would it grow, and how would demand depend on the price Ford charged? Understanding consumer preferences and trade-offs and predicting demand and its responsiveness to price were essential parts of the Taurus program. (We discuss consumer preferences and demand in Chapters 3, 4, and 5.)

Next, Ford had to be concerned with the cost of the car. How high would production costs be, and how would this depend on the number of cars Ford produced each year? How would union wage negotiations or the prices of steel and other raw materials affect costs? How much and how fast would costs decline as managers and workers gained experience with the production process? And to maximize profits, how many cars should Ford plan to produce each year? (We discuss production and cost in Chapters 6 and 7 and the profit-maximizing choice of output in Chapter 8.)

Ford also had to design a pricing strategy for the car and consider how its competitors would react to this strategy. For example, should Ford charge a low price for the basic stripped-down version of the car but high prices for individual options, such as air conditioning and power steering? Or would it be more profitable to make these options "standard" items and charge a high price for the whole package? Whatever prices Ford chose, how were its competitors likely to react? Would GM and Chrysler try to undercut Ford by lowering prices? Might Ford be able to deter GM and Chrysler from lowering prices by threatening to respond with its own price cuts? (We discuss pricing in Chapters 10 and 11 and competitive strategy in Chapters 12 and 13.)

The Taurus program required a large investment in new capital equipment, and Ford had to consider the risks involved and the possible outcomes. Some of this risk was due to uncertainty over the future price of gasoline (higher gasoline prices would shift demand to smaller cars), and some was due to uncertainty over the wages that Ford would have to pay its workers. What would happen if world oil prices doubled or tripled again, or if the government imposed a new tax on gasoline? How much bargaining power would the unions have, and how might this affect wage rates? How should Ford take these uncertainties into account when making its investment decisions? (Commodity markets and the effects of taxes are discussed in Chapters 2 and 9. Labor markets and union power are discussed in Chapter 14. Investment decisions and the role of uncertainty are discussed in Chapters 5 and 15.)

Ford also had to worry about organizational problems. Ford is an integrated firm—separate divisions produce engines and parts, then assemble finished cars. How should the managers of the different divisions be rewarded? What price should the assembly division be charged for engines it receives from another division? Should all the parts be obtained from the upstream divisions, or should some of them be purchased from outside firms? (We discuss internal pricing and organizational incentives for the integrated firm in Chapters 11 and 17.)

Finally, Ford had to think about its relationship to the government and the effects of regulatory policies. For example, the Taurus had to meet federal emission standards, and production line operations had to comply with health and safety regulations. How were these regulations and standards likely to change over time? How would they affect the company's costs and profits? (We discuss the role of government in limiting pollution and promoting health and safety in Chapter 18.)

Public Policy Design: Automobile Emission Standards

In 1970, the federal Clean Air Act imposed strict tailpipe emission standards on new automobiles. These standards have become increasingly stringent, so that if the program reaches its desired goal in the 1990s, the 1970 levels of nitrogen oxides, hydrocarbons, and carbon monoxide emitted by automobiles will be reduced by roughly 90 percent.

The design of a program like the Clean Air Act involves a careful analysis of the ecological and health effects of auto emissions. But it also involves a good deal of economics. First, the government has to evaluate the monetary impact of the program on consumers. The emission standards affect the cost both of purchasing a car (catalytic converters would be necessary, which would raise the cost of cars) and of operating it (gas mileage would be lower, and the catalytic converters would have to be repaired and maintained). Consumers ultimately bear much of this added cost, so it is important to know how it affects their standards of living. This requires an analysis of consumer preferences and demand. For example, would consumers drive less and spend more of their income on other goods? If so, would they be nearly as well off? (Consumer preferences and demand are discussed in Chapters 3 and 4.)

To answer these questions, the government needs to determine how the standards would affect the cost of producing cars. Might automobile producers use other materials to produce cars, so that cost increases would be small? (Production and cost are discussed in Chapters 6 and 7.) Then the government needs to know how the changes in production costs affect the level of production and the prices of new automobiles—are the additional costs absorbed or passed on to consumers in the form of higher prices? (Output determination is discussed in Chapter 8, and pricing in Chapters 10 through 13.)

Finally, the government needs to ask why the problems related to air pollution are not solved by our market-oriented economy. The answer is that much of the cost of air pollution is external to the firm. If firms do not find it in their self-interest to deal with auto emissions adequately, then what is the best way to alter their incentives? Should standards be set, or is it more economical to impose air pollution fees? How do we decide what people will pay to clean up the environment when there is no explicit market for clean air? Is the political process likely to solve these problems? The ultimate question is whether the auto emissions control program makes sense on a cost-benefit basis. Are the aesthetic, health, and other benefits of clean air worth the higher cost of automobiles? (These problems are discussed in Chapter 18.)

These are just two examples of how microeconomics can be applied; you will see more applications throughout this book. Many of these applications deal with markets and prices. These two words are a part of our everyday language, but it is important to be clear about their meaning.

1.4 *What Is a Market?*

We can divide individual economic units into two broad groups according to function—*buyers* and *sellers*. Buyers include consumers, who purchase goods and services, and firms, which buy labor, capital, and raw materials that they use to produce goods and services. Sellers include firms, which sell their goods and services; workers who sell their labor services; and resource owners, who rent land or sell mineral resources to firms. Clearly, most people and most firms act as both buyers and sellers, but we will find it helpful to think of them as simply buyers when they are buying something, and sellers when they are selling something.

Together, buyers and sellers interact to form *markets*. *A market is a collection of buyers and sellers that interact, resulting in the possibility for exchange.* Note that a market includes more than an industry. An *industry* is a collection of firms that sell the same or closely related products. In effect, an industry is the supply side of the market.

Markets are at the center of economic activity, and many of the most interesting questions and issues in economics concern how markets work. For example, why do only a few firms compete with one another in some markets, while in other markets a great many firms compete? Are consumers necessarily better off if there are many firms? If so, should the government intervene in markets with only a few firms? Why have prices in some markets risen or fallen rapidly, while in other markets prices have hardly changed at all? And which markets offer the best opportunities for an entrepreneur thinking of going into business?

Competitive Versus Noncompetitive Markets

In this book we study the behavior of both competitive and noncompetitive markets. A *perfectly competitive market* has many buyers and sellers, so that no single buyer or seller has a significant impact on price. Most agricultural markets are close to being perfectly competitive. For example, thousands of farmers produce wheat, which thousands of buyers purchase to produce flour and other products. As a result, no single farmer and no single buyer can significantly affect the price of wheat.

Many other markets are competitive enough to be treated as if they were perfectly competitive. The world market for copper, for example, contains a few dozen major producers. That is enough for the impact on price to be negligible if any one producer goes out of business. The same is true for many other natural resource markets, such as those for coal, iron, tin, or lumber.

Other markets containing only several producers may still be treated as competitive for purposes of analysis. For example, the airline industry in the United States contains several dozen firms, but most routes are served by only a few firms. Nonetheless, competition among those firms is often (but not always!) fierce enough, so that for some purposes (but not others) the market can be treated as competitive. Finally, some markets contain many producers but are *noncompetitive*; that is, individual firms can affect the price of the product. The world oil market is one example; since the early 1970s, the market has been dominated by the OPEC cartel. (A *cartel* is a group of producers that acts collectively.)

Market Price

Markets provide the possibility of transactions between buyers and sellers. Quantities of a good are sold at specific prices. In a perfectly competitive market, a single price—the *market price*—will usually prevail. The price of wheat in Kansas City and the price of gold in New York are two examples. These prices are also usually easy to measure. For example, you can find the price of corn, wheat, or gold each day in the business section of a newspaper.

In markets that are not perfectly competitive, different firms might charge different prices for the same product. This might happen because one firm is trying to win customers from its competitors, or because customers have brand loyalties that allow some firms to charge higher prices than their competitors. For example, two brands of laundry detergent might be sold in the same supermarket at different prices. Or, two supermarkets in the same town might be selling the same brand of laundry detergent at different prices. In cases like this, when we refer to the market price, we will mean the price averaged across brands or supermarkets.

The market prices of most goods will fluctuate over time, and for many goods the fluctuations can be rapid. This is particularly true for goods sold in competitive markets. The stock market, for example, is highly competitive—there are typically many buyers and sellers for any one stock. As anyone who has invested in the stock market knows, the price of any particular stock fluctuates from minute to minute and can rise or fall substantially during a single day. Similarly, the prices of commodities such as wheat, soybeans, coffee, oil, gold, silver, or lumber can also rise or fall dramatically in a day or a week.

The Extent of a Market

The *extent of a market* refers to its *boundaries*, both *geographic* and in terms of the *range of products* to be included in it. When we refer to the market for gasoline, for example, we must be clear about its geographic boundaries. Are we referring to downtown Los Angeles, southern California, or the entire United States? And we must also be clear about the range of products we are referring to. Should regular octane and high octane premium gasoline be included in the same market? Leaded and unleaded gasoline? Gasoline and diesel fuel?

For some goods, it makes sense to talk about a market only in terms of very restrictive geographic boundaries. Housing is a good example. Most people who work in downtown Chicago will look for housing within commuting distance of that city. They will not look at homes that are 200 or 300 miles away, even though those homes might be much cheaper. And homes (together with the land they are sitting on) 200 miles away cannot easily be moved closer to Chicago. Hence the housing market in Chicago is separate and distinct from, say, the housing markets in Cleveland, Houston, Atlanta, or Philadelphia. Retail gasoline markets, on the other hand, are less limited geographically, but are still regional because of the expense of shipping gasoline long distances. Thus the market for gasoline in southern California is distinct from the market in northern Illinois.

Gold, on the other hand, is bought and sold in a world market. The reason is that the cost of transporting gold is small relative to its value. Thus if the price of gold in New York were substantially lower than the price in Zurich, people would buy gold in New York and sell it at a profit in Zurich. (This is called *arbitrage*, and the people who engage in it are called *arbitrageurs*. It is the possibility of arbitrage that prevents the prices of gold in New York and Zurich from differing significantly.)

When discussing a market, we must also be clear about the range of products that we mean to include in it. For example, there is a market for 35-millimeter single lens reflex (SLR) cameras, and many brands compete in that market. But what about Polaroid instant cameras? Should they be considered part of the same market? Probably not, because they are used for different purposes, and so do not compete with SLR cameras. Gasoline is another example. Regular and premium octane gasolines might be considered part of the same market because most consumers can use either in their cars. Diesel fuel, however, is not part of this market because cars that use regular gasoline cannot use diesel fuel, and vice versa.[7]

1.5 Real Versus Nominal Prices

We often want to compare the price of a good today with what it was in the past or is likely to be in the future. To make such a comparison meaningful, we need to measure prices relative to the overall price level. In absolute terms, the price of a dozen eggs is many times higher today than it was 50 years ago, but relative to prices overall, it is actually lower. Therefore, we must be careful to correct for inflation when comparing prices across time. This means measuring prices in *real* rather than *nominal* terms.

The *nominal price* of a good (sometimes called its "current dollar" price) is just its absolute price. For example, the nominal price of a quart of milk was about 40 cents in 1970, about 65 cents in 1980, and about 90 cents in 1993. These are the prices you would have seen in supermarkets in those years. The *real price* of a good (sometimes called its "constant dollar" price) is the price relative to an aggregate measure of prices.

The aggregate measure most often used is the Consumer Price Index (CPI). The CPI is calculated by the U.S. Bureau of Labor Statistics and is published monthly. It records how the cost of a large market basket of goods purchased by a "typical" consumer in some base year changes over time. (Currently the base year is 1983.) Percentage changes in the CPI measure the rate of inflation in the economy.[8]

After correcting for inflation, was milk more expensive in 1993 than in 1970? To find out, let's calculate the 1993 price of milk in terms of 1970 dollars. The

---

[7] How can we determine the extent of a market? Since the market is where the price of a good is established, one approach focuses on market prices. We ask whether product prices in different geographic regions (or for different product types) are approximately the same, or whether they tend to move together. If either is the case, we place them in the same market. For a more detailed discussion, see George J. Stigler and Robert A. Sherwin, "The Extent of the Market," *Journal of Law and Economics* 27 (Oct. 1985): 555–585.

[8] Because the market basket is fixed, the CPI can tend to overstate inflation. The reason is that when the prices of some goods rise substantially, consumers will shift some of their purchases to goods whose prices have not risen as much, and the CPI ignores this.

CPI was 38.8 in 1970 and rose to about 144 in 1993.[9] (There was considerable inflation in the United States during the 1970s and early 1980s.) In 1970 dollars the price of milk was therefore

$$\frac{38.8}{144} \times \$0.90 = \$0.26$$

In real terms the price of milk was lower in 1993 than it was in 1970. Put another way, the nominal price of milk went up by about 125 percent, but the CPI went up 271 percent, so that milk prices fell relative to inflation.

In this book we will usually be concerned with real rather than nominal prices because consumer choices involve an analysis of how one price compares with another. These relative prices can most easily be evaluated if there is a common basis of comparison. Stating all prices in real terms achieves this objective. Thus, even though we will often measure prices in dollars, we will be thinking in terms of the real purchasing power of those dollars.

In 1970 Grade A eggs cost about 61 cents a dozen. In the same year, the average annual cost of a college education in a private four-year college, including room and board, was about $2,530. By 1990 the price of eggs had risen to 95 cents a dozen, and the average cost of a college education was $12,800. In real terms, were eggs more expensive in 1990 than in 1970? Had a college education become more expensive?

Table 1.1 shows the nominal price of eggs, the nominal cost of a college education, and the CPI for 1970–1990. (The CPI is based on 1983 = 100.) Also shown are the *real* prices of eggs and a college education in 1970 dollars, calculated as follows:

$$\text{Real price of eggs in 1975} = \frac{CPI_{1970}}{CPI_{1975}} \times \text{nominal price in 1975,}$$

$$\text{Real price of eggs in 1980} = \frac{CPI_{1970}}{CPI_{1980}} \times \text{nominal price in 1980,}$$

and so forth.

The table shows clearly that the real cost of a college education rose (by 62 percent) during this period, while the real cost of eggs fell (by 56 percent). It is these relative changes in the prices of eggs and college that are important for the choices that consumers must make, not the fact that both eggs and college cost more in dollars today than they did in 1970.

---

[9] Two good sources of data on the national economy are the *Economic Report of the President* and the *Statistical Abstract of the United States.* Both are published annually and are available from the U.S. Government Printing Office.

TABLE 1.1   The Real Prices of Eggs and of a College Education

	1970	1975	1980	1985	1990	1993
Nominal Prices						
Grade A Eggs	$0.61	$0.77	$0.84	$0.80	$0.95	$1.01
College Education	$2530	$3403	$4912	$8156	$12,800	$15,212
Consumer Price Index	38.8	53.8	82.4	107.6	130.2	144.0
Real Prices ($1970)						
Grade A Eggs	$0.61	$0.56	$0.40	$0.29	$0.28	$0.27
College Education	$2530	$2454	$2313	$2941	$3814	$4099

In the table, we calculated real prices in terms of 1970 dollars, but we could have just as easily calculated them in terms of the dollars of some other base year. For example, suppose we want to calculate the real price of eggs in *1980 dollars*. Then:

$$\text{Real price of eggs in 1975} = \frac{CPI_{1980}}{CPI_{1975}} \times \text{nominal price in 1975,}$$

$$\text{Real price of eggs in 1985} = \frac{CPI_{1980}}{CPI_{1985}} \times \text{nominal price in 1985,}$$

and so forth. By going through the calculations, you can check that in terms of 1980 dollars, the real price of eggs was $1.30 in 1970, $1.18 in 1975, 84 cents in 1980, 61 cents in 1985, 60 cents in 1990, and 58 cents in 1993. You can also check that the percentage declines in real price are the same no matter which base year we use.

Summary

1. Microeconomics is concerned with the decisions made by small economic units—consumers, workers, investors, owners of resources, and business firms. It is also concerned with the interaction of consumers and firms to form markets and industries.

2. Microeconomics relies heavily on the use of theory, which can (by simplification) help to explain how economic units behave and predict what that behavior will be in the future. Models are mathematical representations of theory that can help in this explanation and prediction process.

3. Microeconomics is concerned with positive questions that have to do with the explanation and prediction of phenomena. But microeconomics is also important for normative analy-

sis, in which we ask what choices are best—for a firm or for society as a whole. Normative analyses must often be combined with individual value judgments because issues of equity and fairness as well as of economic efficiency may be involved.

4. A *market* refers to a collection of buyers and sellers who interact and to the possibility for sales and purchases that results. Microeconomics involves the study of both perfectly competitive markets in which no single buyer or seller has an impact on price and noncompetitive markets in which individual entities can affect price.

5. The market price is established by the interaction of buyers and sellers. In a perfectly competitive market, a single price will usually prevail. In markets that are not perfectly competitive, different sellers might charge different prices. Then the market price refers to the average prevailing price.

6. When discussing a market, we must be clear about its extent in terms both of its geographic boundaries and of the range of products to be included in it. Some markets (e.g., housing) are highly localized, whereas others (e.g., gold) are worldwide.

7. To eliminate the effects of inflation, we measure real (or constant dollar) prices, rather than nominal (or current dollar) prices. Real prices use an aggregate price index, such as the CPI, to correct for inflation.

Questions for Review

1. What is the difference between a market and an industry? Are there interactions among firms in different industries that you might describe as taking place within a single market?

2. It is often said that a good theory is one that can in principle be refuted by an empirical, data-oriented study. Explain why a theory that cannot be evaluated empirically is not a good theory.

3. In Example 1.1, both the additional-worker and the discouraged-worker theories are economic in nature, because they reflect the responses of married women to the economic conditions that their husbands face in the market. Could it be that both theories are correct, but that the additional-worker theory applies to certain households, and the discouraged-worker theory applies to others? If so, how might you figure out which theory applies to whom?

4. Which of the following two statements involves positive economic analysis and which normative? How do the two kinds of analysis differ?

    a. Gasoline rationing (allocating to each individual a maximum amount of gasoline that can be purchased each year) is a poor social policy because it interferes with the workings of the competitive market system.

    b. Gasoline rationing is a policy under which more people are made worse off than are made better off.

5. Suppose the price of unleaded regular octane gasoline were 20 cents per gallon higher in New Jersey than in Oklahoma. Do you think there would be an opportunity for arbitrage (i.e., that firms could buy gas in Oklahoma and then sell it at a profit in Jersey)? Why or why not?

6. In Example 1.2, what economic forces explain why the real price of eggs has fallen, while the real price of a college education has increased? How have these changes affected consumer choices?

7. Suppose that the Japanese yen rises against the U.S. dollar; that is, it now takes more dollars to buy any given amount of Japanese yen. Explain why this simultaneously increases the real price of Japanese cars for U.S. consumers and lowers the real price of U.S. automobiles for Japanese consumers.

CHAPTER 2

The Basics of Supply and Demand

One of the best ways to appreciate the relevance of economics is to begin with the basics of supply and demand. Supply-demand analysis is a fundamental and powerful tool that can be applied to a wide variety of interesting and important problems. To name a few: understanding and predicting how changing world economic conditions affect market price and production; evaluating the impact of government price controls, minimum wages, price supports, and production incentives; and determining how taxes, subsidies, tariffs, and import quotas affect consumers and producers.

We begin with a review of how supply and demand curves are used to describe the market mechanism. Without government intervention (e.g., through the imposition of price controls or some other regulatory policy), supply and demand will come into equilibrium to determine the market price of a good and the total quantity produced. What that price and quantity will be depends on the particular characteristics of supply and demand. And how price and quantity vary over time depends on how supply and demand respond to other economic variables, such as aggregate economic activity and labor costs, which are themselves changing.

We will therefore discuss the characteristics of supply and demand and how those characteristics may differ from one market to another. Then we can begin to use supply and demand curves to understand a variety of phenomena—why the prices of some basic commodities have fallen steadily over a long period, while the prices of others have experienced sharp gyrations; why shortages occur in certain markets; and why announcements about plans for future government policies or predictions about future economic conditions can affect markets well before those policies or conditions become reality.

Besides understanding *qualitatively* how market price and quantity are determined and how they can vary over time, it is also important to learn how they can be analyzed *quantitatively*. We will see how simple "back of the envelope" calculations can be used to analyze and predict evolving market conditions, and how markets respond both to domestic and international macroeconomic fluctuations and to the effects of government interventions. We will try to convey this understanding through simple examples and by urging you to work through some exercises at the end of the chapter.

2.1 *The Market Mechanism*

Let us begin with a brief review of the basic supply-demand diagram as shown in Figure 2.1. The vertical axis shows the price of a good, P, measured in dollars per unit. This is the price that sellers receive for a given quantity supplied and that buyers will pay for a given quantity demanded. The horizontal axis shows the total quantity demanded and supplied, Q, measured in number of units per period.

The *supply curve S* tells us how much producers are willing to sell for each price that they receive in the market. The curve slopes upward because the higher the price, the more firms are usually able and willing to produce and sell. For example, a higher price may enable existing firms to expand production in the short run by hiring extra workers or by having existing workers

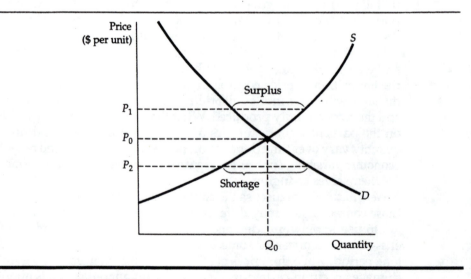

FIGURE 2.1   **Supply and Demand.**   The market clears at price P_0 and quantity Q_0. At the higher price P_1 a surplus develops, so price falls. At the lower price P_2 there is a shortage, so price is bid up.

work overtime (at greater cost to the firm), and in the long run by increasing the size of their plants. A higher price may also attract into the market new firms that face higher costs because of their inexperience and that therefore would have found entry into the market uneconomical at a lower price.

The *demand curve D* tells us how much consumers are willing to buy for each price per unit that they must pay. It slopes downward because consumers are usually ready to buy more if the price is lower. For example, a lower price may encourage consumers who have already been buying the good to consume a larger quantity, and it may enable other consumers who previously might not have been able to afford the good to begin buying it.

The two curves intersect at the *equilibrium*, or *market-clearing*, price and quantity. At this price P_0, the quantity supplied and the quantity demanded are just equal (to Q_0). The *market mechanism* is the tendency in a free market for the price to change until the market clears (i.e., until the quantity supplied and the quantity demanded are equal). At this point there is neither shortage nor excess supply, so there is also no pressure for the price to change further. Supply and demand might not *always* be in equilibrium, and some markets might not clear quickly when conditions change suddenly, but the *tendency* is for markets to clear.

To understand why markets tend to clear, suppose the price were initially above the market clearing level, say, P_1 in Figure 2.1. Then producers would try to produce and sell more than consumers were willing to buy. A surplus would accumulate, and to sell this surplus or at least prevent it from growing, producers would begin to lower their prices. Eventually price would fall, quantity demanded would increase, and quantity supplied would decrease until the equilibrium price P_0 was reached.

The opposite would happen if the price were initially below P_0, say, at P_2. A shortage would develop because consumers would be unable to purchase all they would like at this price. This would put upward pressure on price as consumers tried to outbid one another for existing supplies and producers reacted by increasing price and expanding output. Again, the price would eventually reach P_0.

When we draw and use supply and demand curves, we are assuming that at any given price, a given quantity will be produced and sold. This makes sense only if a market is at least roughly *competitive*. By this we mean that both sellers and buyers should have little *market power* (i.e., little ability *individually* to affect the market price). Suppose instead that supply were controlled by a single producer—a monopolist. In this case there would no longer be a simple one-to-one relationship between price and quantity supplied. The reason is that a monopolist's behavior depends on the shape and position of the demand curve. If the demand curve shifted in a particular way, it might be in the monopolist's interest to keep the quantity fixed but change the price, or keep the price fixed and change the quantity. (How this could occur is explained in Chapter 10.) So when we work with supply and demand curves, we implicitly assume that we are referring to a competitive market.

2.2 *Shifts in Supply and Demand*

Supply and demand curves tell us how much competitive producers and consumers are willing to sell and buy as functions of the price they receive and
pay. But supply and demand are also determined by other variables besides
price. For example, the quantity that producers are willing to sell depends not
only on the price they receive, but also on their production costs, including
wages, interest charges, and costs of raw materials. And in addition to price,
quantity demanded depends on the total disposable income available to consumers, and perhaps on other variables as well. Later we will want to determine how changes in economic conditions or tax or regulatory policy affect
market prices and quantities. To do this, we must understand how supply and
demand curves shift in response to changes in such variables as wage rates,
capital costs, and income.

Let's begin with the supply curve S in Figure 2.2. This curve shows how
much producers are willing to sell as a function of market price. For example,
at a price P_1, the quantity produced and sold would be Q_1. Now suppose the
cost of raw materials *falls*. How does this affect supply?

Lower raw material costs, indeed lower costs of any kind, make production
more profitable, encouraging existing firms to expand production and enabling
new firms to enter the market and produce. So if the market price stayed constant at P_1, we would expect to observe a greater supply of output than be-

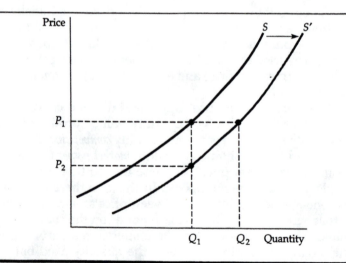

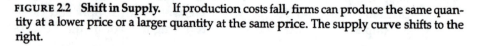

FIGURE 2.2   Shift in Supply.   If production costs fall, firms can produce the same quantity at a lower price or a larger quantity at the same price. The supply curve shifts to the
right.

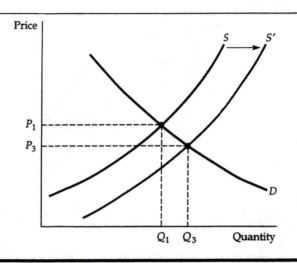

FIGURE 2.3   **New Equilibrium Following Shift in Supply.**   When the supply curve shifts to the right, the market clears at a lower price P_3 and a larger quantity Q_3.

fore. In Figure 2.2 this is shown as an increase from Q_1 to Q_2. Output increases no matter what the market price happens to be, *so the entire supply curve shifts to the right*, which is shown in the figure as a shift from S to S'.

Another way of looking at the effect of lower raw material costs is to imagine that the quantity produced stays fixed at Q_1 and consider what price firms would require to produce this quantity. Because their costs are lower, the price they would require would also be lower—P_2 in Figure 2.2. This will be the case no matter what quantity is produced. Again, we see in the figure that the supply curve must shift to the right.

Of course, neither price nor quantity will always remain fixed when costs fall. Usually both will change as the new supply curve comes into equilibrium with the demand curve. This is illustrated in Figure 2.3, where the supply curve has shifted from S to S' as it did in Figure 2.2. As a result, the market price drops (from P_1 to P_3), and the total quantity produced increases (from Q_1 to Q_3). This is just what we would expect: Lower costs result in lower prices and increased sales. (And indeed, gradual decreases in costs resulting from technological progress and better management are an important driving force behind economic growth.)

Now let's turn to Figure 2.4 and the demand curve labeled D. How would an *increase in disposable income* affect demand?

With greater disposable income, consumers can spend more money on any good, and some consumers will do so for most goods. If the market price were held constant at P_1, we would therefore expect to see an increase in quantity demanded, say, from Q_1 to Q_2. This would happen no matter what the market price was, so that the result would be a *shift to the right of the entire demand*

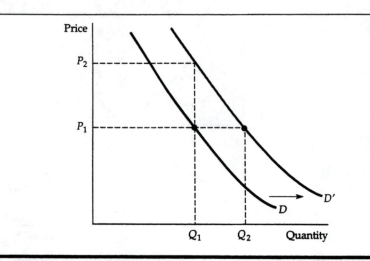

FIGURE 2.4   Shift in Demand.   The demand for a product depends on its price but may also depend on other variables, such as income, the weather, and the prices of other goods. For most products, demand increases when income rises. A higher income level shifts the demand curve to the right.

curve. In the figure, this is shown as a shift from D to D'. Alternatively, we can ask what price consumers would pay to purchase a given quantity Q_1. With greater disposable income, they should be willing to pay a higher price, say, P_2 instead of P_1 in Figure 2.4. Again, *the demand curve will shift to the right.*

In general, neither price nor quantity remains constant when disposable income increases. A new price and quantity result after demand comes into equilibrium with supply. As shown in Figure 2.5, we would expect to see consumers pay a higher price P_3 and firms produce a greater quantity Q_3 as a result of an increase in disposable income.

Changes in the prices of related goods also affect demand. For example, copper and aluminum are substitute goods. Because one can often be substituted for the other in industrial use, the demand for copper will increase if the price of aluminum increases. Automobiles and gasoline, on the other hand, are complementary goods (i.e., they tend to be used together). Therefore a decrease in the price of gasoline increases the demand for automobiles. So the shift to the right of the demand curve in Figure 2.5 could also have resulted from an increase in the price of a substitute good or from a decrease in the price of a complementary good.

In most markets both the demand and supply curves shift from time to time. Consumers' disposable incomes change as the economy grows (or contracts, during economic recessions). The demands for some goods shift with the seasons (e.g., fuels, bathing suits, umbrellas), with changes in the prices of related goods (an increase in oil prices increases the demand for natural gas), or sim-

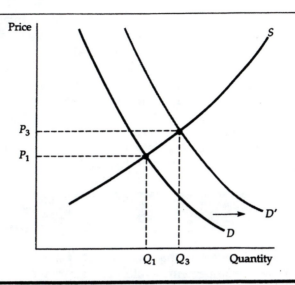

FIGURE 2.5   New Equilibrium Following Shift in Demand.   When the demand curve shifts to the right, the market clears at a higher price P_3 and a larger quantity Q_3.

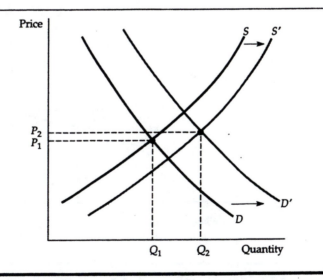

FIGURE 2.6   New Equilibrium Following Shifts in Supply and Demand.   Supply and demand curves shift over time as market conditions change. In this example, rightward shifts of the supply and demand curves lead to slightly higher price and a much larger quantity. In general, changes in price and quantity depend on the amount by which each curve shifts and the shape of each curve.

ply with changing tastes. Similarly wage rates, capital costs, and the prices of raw materials also change from time to time, which shifts supply.

Supply and demand curves can be used to trace the effects of these changes. In Figure 2.6, for example, shifts to the right of both supply and demand result in a slightly higher price (from P_1 to P_2) and a much larger quantity (from Q_1 to Q_2). In general, price and quantity will change depending both on how much the supply and demand curves shift and on the shapes of those curves. To predict the sizes and directions of such changes, we must be able to quantitatively characterize the dependence of supply and demand on price and other variables. We will turn to this in the next section.

In Example 1.2 we saw that from 1970 to 1993, the real (constant dollar) price of eggs fell by 56 percent, while the real price of a college education rose by

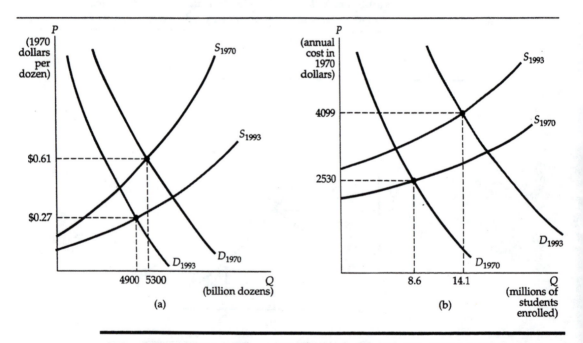

FIGURE 2.7a **Market for Eggs.**   The supply curve for eggs shifted down as production costs fell, and the demand curve shifted to the left as consumer preferences changed. As a result, the real price of eggs fell sharply, and egg consumption fell slightly.

FIGURE 2.7b **Market for College Education.**   The supply curve for a college education shifted up as the costs of equipment, maintenance, and staffing rose. The demand curve shifted to the right as a growing number of high school graduates desired a college education. As a result, both price and enrollments rose sharply.

62 percent. What caused this large decline in egg prices and large increase in the price of college?

We can understand these price changes by examining the behavior of supply and demand for each good, as shown in Figure 2.7. For eggs, the mechanization of poultry farms sharply reduced the cost of producing eggs, shifting the supply curve downward over this period. At the same time, the demand curve for eggs shifted to the left as a more health (and cholesterol) conscious population changed its eating habits, tending to avoid eggs. As a result, not only did the real price of eggs decline sharply, but total annual consumption fell somewhat (from 5300 billion dozen to 4900 billion dozen).

For college, supply and demand shifted in the opposite directions. Increases in the costs of equipping and maintaining modern classrooms, laboratories, and libraries, along with increases in faculty salaries, pushed the supply curve up. At the same time, the demand curve shifted to the right as a larger and larger percentage of a growing number of high school graduates decided that a college education was essential. Thus, despite the increase in price, 1993 found over 14 million students enrolled in college degree programs, compared to 8.6 million in 1970.

The early 1970s was a period of public concern about the earth's natural resources. Groups like the Club of Rome predicted that our energy and mineral resources would soon be depleted, so that prices would skyrocket and bring an end to economic growth.[1] But these predictions ignored basic microeconomics. The earth does indeed have only a finite amount of minerals, such as copper, iron, and coal. Yet during the past century, the prices of these and most other minerals have declined or remained roughly constant relative to overall prices. For example, Figure 2.8 shows the price of iron in real terms (adjusted for inflation), together with the quantity of iron consumed from 1880 to 1985. (Both are shown as an index, with 1880 = 1.) Despite short-term variations in price, no significant long-term increase has occurred, even though annual consumption is now about 20 times greater than in 1880. Similar patterns hold for other mineral resources, such as copper, oil, and coal.[2]

---

[1] See, for example, Dennis Meadows et al., *The Limits to Growth* (New York: Potomac Associates, 1972). This book and others like it struck a resonant chord in the public consciousness. Unfortunately these studies ignored such basic economic phenomena as cost reduction resulting from technical progress, experience, and economies of scale, and substitution of alternative resources (including nondepletable ones) in response to higher prices. For a discussion of these issues, see Julian L. Simon, *The Ultimate Resource* (Princeton, N.J.: Princeton University Press, 1981).

[2] The data in Figure 2.8 are from Robert S. Manthy, *Natural Resource Commodities—A Century of Statistics* (Baltimore: Johns Hopkins University Press, 1978), supplemented after 1973 with data from the U.S. Bureau of Mines.

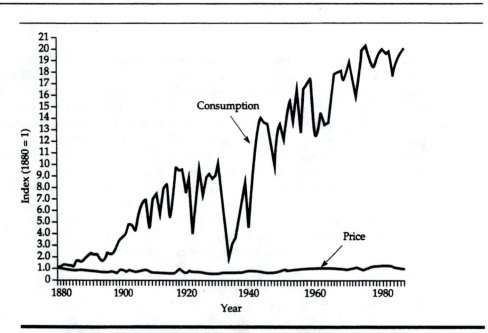

FIGURE 2.8   Consumption and Price of Iron, 1880–1985.   Annual consumption has increased about twentyfold, but the real (inflation-adjusted) price has not changed much.

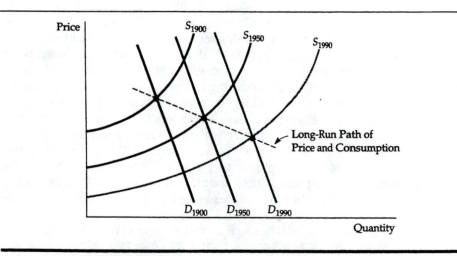

FIGURE 2.9   Long-Run Movements of Supply and Demand for Mineral Resources. Demand for most resources has increased dramatically over the past century, but prices have fallen or risen only slightly in real (inflation-adjusted) terms because cost reductions have shifted the supply curve to the right just as dramatically.

The demands for these resources grew along with the world economy. (These shifts in the demand curve are illustrated in Figure 2.9.) But as demand grew, production costs fell. This was due first to the discovery of new and bigger deposits, which were cheaper to mine, and then to technical progress and the economic advantage of mining and refining on a large scale. As a result, the supply curve shifted to the right over time. Over the long term, these shifts in the supply curve were greater than the shifts in the demand curve, so that price often fell, as shown in Figure 2.9.

This is not to say that the prices of copper, iron, and coal will decline or remain constant forever—these resources are *finite*. But as their prices begin to rise, consumption will likely shift at least in part to substitute materials. For example, copper has already been replaced in many applications by aluminum, and more recently in electronic applications by fiber optics. (See Example 2.6 for a more detailed discussion of copper prices.)

EXAMPLE 2.3   THE MARKET FOR WHEAT

Wheat is an important agricultural commodity, and the market for it has been studied extensively by agricultural economists. During the 1980s, changes in the wheat market had major implications for American farmers and for U.S. agricultural policy. To understand what happened, let us examine the behavior of supply and demand.

From statistical studies, we know that for 1981 the supply curve for wheat was approximately as follows:[3]

$$Supply: Q_S = 1800 + 240P$$

where price is measured in dollars per bushel and quantities are in millions of bushels per year. These studies also indicate that in 1981 the demand curve for wheat was

$$Demand: Q_D = 3550 - 266P$$

By setting supply equal to demand, we can determine the market-clearing price of wheat for 1981:

$$Q_S = Q_D$$

$$1800 + 240P = 3550 - 266P$$

$$506P = 1750$$

$$P = \$3.46 \text{ per bushel}$$

---

[3] For a survey of statistical studies of the demand and supply of wheat and an analysis of evolving market conditions, see Larry Salathe and Sudchada Langley, "An Empirical Analysis of Alternative Export Subsidy Programs for U.S. Wheat," *Agricultural Economics Research* 38, No. 1 (Winter 1986). The supply and demand curves in this example are based on the studies they survey.

The demand for wheat has two components—domestic demand (i.e., demand by U.S. consumers) and export demand (i.e., demand by foreign consumers). By the mid-1980s, the domestic demand for wheat had risen only slightly (due to modest increases in population and income), but export demand had fallen sharply. Export demand had dropped for several reasons. First and foremost was the success of the Green Revolution in agriculture—developing countries like India that had been large importers of wheat became increasingly self-sufficient. On top of this, the increase in the value of the dollar against other currencies made U.S. wheat more expensive abroad. Finally, European countries adopted protectionist policies that subsidized their own production and imposed tariff barriers against imported wheat. In 1985, for example, the demand curve for wheat was

$$\text{Demand: } Q_D = 2580 - 194P$$

(The supply curve remained more or less the same as in 1981.)

Now we can again equate supply and demand and determine the market-clearing price for 1985:

$$1800 + 240P = 2580 - 194P$$

$$P = \$1.80 \text{ per bushel}$$

We see, then, that the major shift in export demand led to a sharp drop in the market-clearing price of wheat—from $3.46 in 1981 to $1.80 in 1985.

Was the price of wheat actually $3.46 in 1981, and did it actually fall to $1.80 in 1985? No—consumers paid about $3.70 in 1981 and about $3.20 in 1985. Furthermore, in both years American farmers received more than $4 for each bushel they produced. Why? Because the U.S. government props up the price of wheat and pays subsidies to farmers. We discuss exactly how this is done and evaluate the costs and benefits for consumers, farmers, and the federal budget in Chapter 9.

2.3 Elasticities of Supply and Demand

We have seen that the demand for a good depends on its price, as well as on consumer income and on the prices of other goods. Similarly, supply depends on price, as well as on variables that affect production cost. For example, if the price of coffee increases, the quantity demanded will fall, and the quantity supplied will rise. Often, however, we want to know *how much* supply or demand will rise or fall. How sensitive is the demand for coffee to its price? If price increases by 10 percent, how much will demand change? How much will demand change if income rises by 5 percent? We use *elasticities* to answer questions like these.

An elasticity is a measure of the sensitivity of one variable to another. Specifically, it is a number that tells us *the percentage change that will occur in one variable in response to a 1 percent change in another variable.* For example, the *price elasticity of demand* measures the sensitivity of quantity demanded to price changes. It tells us what the percentage change in the quantity demanded for a good will be following a 1 percent increase in the price of that good.

Let's look at this in more detail. Denoting quantity and price by Q and P, we write the price elasticity of demand as

$$E_p = (\%\Delta Q)/(\%\Delta P)$$

where $\%\Delta Q$ simply means "percentage change in Q" and $\%\Delta P$ means "percentage change in P."[4] But the percentage change in a variable is just the absolute change in the variable divided by the original level of the variable. (If the Consumer Price Index were 200 at the beginning of the year and increased to 204 by the end of the year, the percentage change—or annual rate of inflation—would be $4/200 = .02$, or 2 percent.) So we can also write the price elasticity of demand as[5]

$$E_p = \frac{\Delta Q/Q}{\Delta P/P} = \frac{P}{Q}\frac{\Delta Q}{\Delta P} \qquad (2.1)$$

The price elasticity of demand is usually a negative number. When the price of a good increases, the quantity demanded usually falls, so $\Delta Q/\Delta P$ (the change in quantity for a change in price) is negative, and therefore E_p is negative.

When the price elasticity is greater than 1 in magnitude, we say that demand is *price elastic* because the percentage decline in quantity demanded is greater than the percentage increase in price. If the price elasticity is less than 1 in magnitude, demand is said to be *price inelastic.* In general, the elasticity of demand for a good depends on the availability of other goods that can be substituted for it. When there are close substitutes, a price increase will cause the consumer to buy less of the good and more of the substitute. Demand will then be highly price elastic. When there are no close substitutes, demand will tend to be price inelastic.

Equation (2.1) says that the price elasticity of demand is the change in quantity associated with a change in price ($\Delta Q/\Delta P$) times the ratio of price to quantity (P/Q). But as we move down the demand curve, $\Delta Q/\Delta P$ may change, and the price and quantity will always change. Therefore, the price elasticity of demand must be measured *at a particular point on the demand curve* and will generally change as we move along the curve.

This is easiest to see for a *linear* demand curve, that is, a demand curve of the form

$$Q = a - bP$$

---

[4] The symbol Δ is the Greek capital letter delta; it means "the change in." So ΔX means "the change in the variable X," say, from one year to the next.

[5] In terms of infinitesimal changes (letting the ΔP become very small), $E_p = (P/Q)(dQ/dP)$.

As an example, consider the demand curve

$$Q = 8 - 2P$$

For this curve, $\Delta Q/\Delta P$ is constant and equal to -2 (a ΔP of 1 results in a ΔQ of -2). However, the curve does *not* have a constant elasticity. Observe from Figure 2.10 that as we move down the curve, the ratio P/Q falls, and therefore the elasticity decreases in magnitude. Near the intersection of the curve with the price axis, Q is very small, so $E_p = -2(P/Q)$ is large in magnitude. When $P = 2$ and $Q = 4$, $E_p = -1$. And at the intersection with the quantity axis, $P = 0$ so $E_p = 0$.

Because we draw demand (and supply) curves with price on the vertical axis and quantity on the horizontal axis, $\Delta Q/\Delta P = $ (1/slope of curve). As a result, for any price and quantity combination, the steeper the slope of the curve, the less elastic demand is. Figures 2.11a and b show two special cases. Figure 2.11a shows a demand curve that is *infinitely elastic*. There is only a single price P^* at which consumers will buy the good; for even the smallest increase in price above this level, quantity demanded drops to zero, and for any decrease in price, quantity demanded increases without limit. The demand curve in Figure 2.11b, on the other hand, is *completely inelastic*. Consumers will buy a fixed quantity Q^*, no matter what the price.

We will also be interested in elasticities of demand with respect to other variables besides price. For example, demand for most goods usually rises when

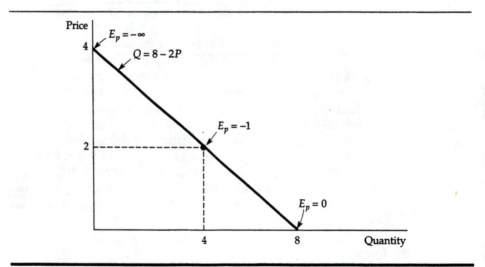

FIGURE 2.10   Linear Demand Curve.   The price elasticity of demand depends not only on the slope of the demand curve, but also on the price and quantity. The elasticity therefore varies along the curve as price and quantity change. Slope is constant for this linear demand curve. Near the top, price is high and quantity is small, so the elasticity is large in magnitude. The elasticity becomes smaller as we move down the curve.

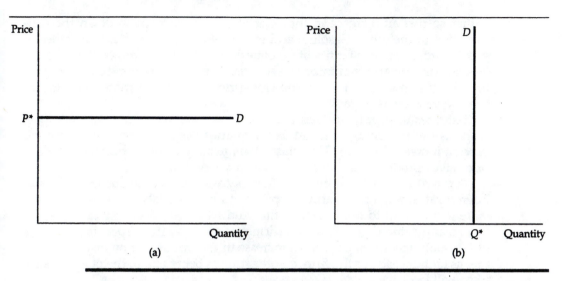

FIGURE 2.11a   Infinitely Elastic Demand.   For a horizontal demand curve, $\Delta Q/\Delta P$ is infinite. (A tiny change in price leads to an enormous change in demand.) The elasticity of demand is therefore infinite.

FIGURE 2.11b   Completely Inelastic Demand.   For a vertical demand curve, $\Delta Q/\Delta P$ is zero. The quantity demanded is the same no matter what the price, so the elasticity of demand is zero.

aggregate income rises. The *income elasticity of demand* is the percentage change in the quantity demanded Q resulting from a 1 percent increase in income I:

$$E_I = \frac{\Delta Q/Q}{\Delta I/I} = \frac{I}{Q}\frac{\Delta Q}{\Delta I} \qquad (2.2)$$

The demand for some goods is also affected by the prices of other goods. For example, because butter and margarine can easily be substituted for each other, the demand for each depends on the price of the other. A *cross-price elasticity of demand* refers to the percentage change in the quantity demanded for a good that results from a 1 percent increase in the price of another good. So the elasticity of demand for butter with respect to the price of margarine would be written as

$$E_{Q_bP_m} = \frac{\Delta Q_b/Q_b}{\Delta P_m/P_m} = \frac{P_m}{Q_b}\frac{\Delta Q_b}{\Delta P_m} \qquad (2.3)$$

where Q_b is the quantity of butter and P_m is the price of margarine.

In this example of butter and margarine, the cross-price elasticities will be positive because the goods are *substitutes*—they compete in the market, so a rise in the price of margarine, which makes butter cheaper relative to margarine than it was before, leads to an increase in the demand for butter. (The demand curve for butter will shift to the right, so its price will rise.) But this is not always the case. Some goods are *complements*; they tend to be used together, so that an increase in the price of one tends to push down the consumption of the other. Gasoline and motor oil are an example. If the price of gasoline goes up, the quantity of gasoline demanded falls—motorists will drive less. But the demand for motor oil also falls. (The entire demand curve for motor oil shifts to the left.) Thus, the cross-price elasticity of motor oil with respect to gasoline is negative.

Elasticities of supply are defined in a similar manner. The *price elasticity of supply* is the percentage change in the quantity supplied resulting from a 1 percent increase in price. This elasticity is usually positive because a higher price gives producers an incentive to increase output.

We can also refer to elasticities of supply with respect to such variables as interest rates, wage rates, and the prices of raw materials and other intermediate goods used to manufacture the product in question. For example, for most manufactured goods, the elasticities of supply with respect to the prices of raw materials are negative. An increase in the price of a raw material input means higher costs for the firm, so other things being equal, the quantity supplied will fall.

2.4 *Short-Run Versus Long-Run Elasticities*

When analyzing demand and supply, it is important to distinguish between the short run and the long run. In other words, if we ask how much demand or supply changes in response to a change in price, we must be clear about *how much time is allowed to pass before measuring the changes in the quantity demanded or supplied*. If we allow only a short time to pass, say, one year or less, then we are dealing with short-run demand or supply. In general, short-run demand and supply curves look very different from their long-run counterparts.

Demand

For many goods, demand is much more price elastic in the long run than in the short run. One reason is that people take time to change their consumption habits. For example, even if the price of coffee rises sharply, the quantity demanded will fall only gradually as consumers slowly begin to drink less of it. Another reason is that the demand for a good might be linked to the stock of another good, which changes only slowly. For example, the demand for gasoline is much more elastic in the long run than in the short run. A sharply higher price of gasoline reduces the quantity demanded in the short run by causing motorists to drive less, but it has its greatest impact on demand by inducing consumers to buy smaller and more fuel-efficient cars. But the stock of cars changes only slowly, so that the quantity of gasoline demanded falls only slowly. Figure 2.12a shows short-run and long-run demand curves for goods such as these.

On the other hand, for some goods just the opposite is true—demand is more elastic in the short run than in the long run. These goods (automobiles, refrigerators, televisions, or the capital equipment purchased by industry) are *durable*, so that the total stock of each good owned by consumers is large relative to the annual production. As a result, a small change in the total stock that consumers want to hold can result in a large percentage change in the level of purchases. Suppose, for example, that price goes up 10 percent, causing the total stock of the good consumers want to hold to drop 5 percent. Initially, this will cause purchases to drop much more than 5 percent. But eventually, as the stock depreciates (and units must be replaced), demand will increase again, so that in the long run the total stock of the good owned by consumers will be about 5 percent less than before the price increase.

Automobiles are an example. (Annual U.S. demand—new car purchases—is about 7 to 10 million, but the stock of cars is around 70 million.) If automo-

durable goods are the opposite more inelastic in the long run [handwritten marginal note]

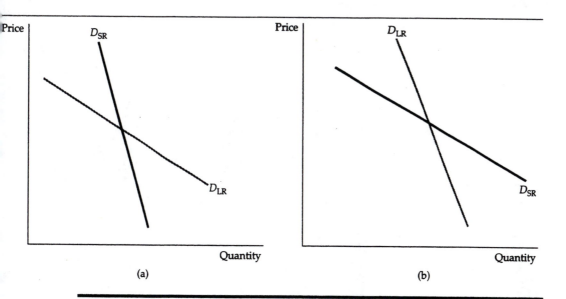

(a)   (b)

FIGURE 2.12a   **Gasoline: Short-Run and Long-Run Demand Curves.**   In the short run, an increase in price has only a small effect on the demand for gasoline. Motorists may drive less, but they will not change the kind of car they are driving overnight. In the longer run, however, they will shift to smaller and more fuel-efficient cars, so the effect of the price increase will be larger. Demand is therefore more elastic in the long run than in the short run.

FIGURE 2.12b   **Automobiles: Short-Run and Long-Run Demand Curves.**   The opposite is true for automobile demand. If price increases, consumers initially defer buying a new car, so that annual demand falls sharply. In the longer run, however, old cars wear out and must be replaced, so that annual demand picks up. Demand is therefore less elastic in the long run than in the short run.

bile prices rise, many people will delay buying new cars, and the quantity demanded will fall sharply (even though the total stock of cars that consumers want to hold falls only a small amount). But eventually, old cars wear out and have to be replaced, so demand picks up again. As a result, the long-run change in the quantity demanded is much smaller than the short-run change. Figure 2.12b shows demand curves for a durable good like automobiles.

Income elasticities also differ from the short run to the long run. For most goods and services—foods, beverages, fuel, entertainment, etc.—the income elasticity of demand is larger in the long run than in the short run. For example, consider the behavior of gasoline consumption during a period of strong economic growth when aggregate income rises by 10 percent. Eventually people will increase their gasoline consumption—they can afford to take more trips and perhaps own a larger car. But this change in consumption takes time, and initially demand increases only a small amount. Thus, the long-run elasticity will be larger than the short-run elasticity.

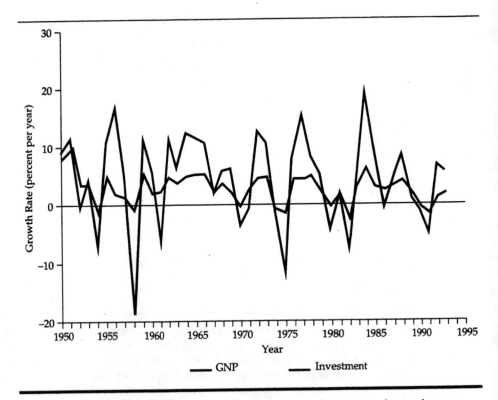

FIGURE 2.13   GNP and Investment in Durable Equipment.   Annual growth rates are compared for GNP and investment in durable equipment. The short-run GNP elasticity of demand is larger than the long-run elasticity for long-lived capital equipment, so changes in investment in equipment magnify changes in GNP. Hence, capital goods industries are considered "cyclical."

For a durable good, the opposite is true. Again, consider automobiles. If aggregate income rises by 10 percent, the stock of cars that consumers will want to hold will also rise, say, by 5 percent. But this means a much larger increase in *current purchases* of cars. (If the stock is 70 million, a 5 percent increase is 3.5 million, which might be about 50 percent of normal demand in a single year.) Eventually consumers succeed in building up the stock of cars, after which new purchases are largely to replace old cars. (These new purchases will still be greater than before because with a larger stock of cars outstanding, more cars need to be replaced each year.) Clearly, the short-run income elasticity of demand will be much larger than the long-run elasticity.

Because the demands for durable goods fluctuate so sharply in response to short-run changes in income, the industries that produce these goods are very vulnerable to changing macroeconomic conditions, and in particular to the business cycle—recessions and booms. Hence, these industries are often called

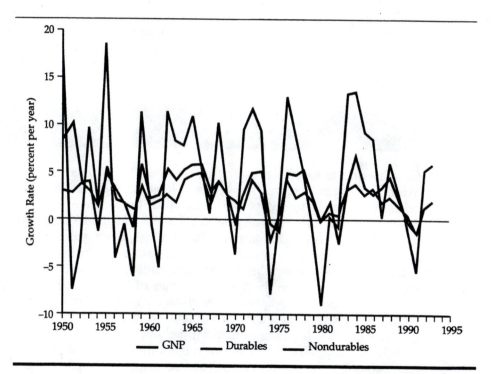

FIGURE 2.14   **Consumption of Durables Versus Nondurables.** Annual growth rates are compared for GNP, consumer expenditures on durable goods (automobiles, appliances, furniture, etc.), and consumer expenditures on nondurable goods (food, clothing, services, etc.). The stock of durables is large compared with annual demand, so short-run demand elasticities are larger than long-run elasticities. Like capital equipment, industries that produce consumer durables are "cyclical" (i.e., changes in GNP are magnified). This is not true for nondurables.

cyclical industries—their sales tend to magnify cyclical changes in gross national product (GNP) and national income.

Figures 2.13 and 2.14 illustrate this. Figure 2.13 plots two variables over time, the annual real (inflation-adjusted) rate of growth of GNP, and the annual real rate of growth of investment in producers' durable equipment (i.e., machinery and other equipment purchased by firms). Note that the durable equipment series follows the same pattern as the GNP series, but the changes in GNP are magnified. For example, in 1961–1966 GNP grew by at least 4 percent each year. Purchases of durable equipment also grew but by much more (over 10 percent in 1963–1966). On the other hand, during the recessions of 1974–1975, 1982, and 1991, equipment purchases fell by much more than GNP.

Figure 2.14 also shows the real rate of growth of GNP, and in addition, the annual real rates of growth of spending by consumers on durable goods (automobiles, appliances, etc.), and on nondurable goods (food, fuel, clothing, etc.). Note that both consumption series follow GNP, but only the durable goods series tends to magnify the changes in GNP. Changes in consumption of nondurables are roughly the same as changes in GNP, but changes in consumption of durables are usually several times larger. It should be clear from this why companies such as General Motors and General Electric are considered "cyclical"—sales of cars and of electrical appliances are strongly affected by changing macroeconomic conditions.

Gasoline and automobiles exemplify some of the different characteristics of demand discussed above. They are complementary goods—an increase in the price of one tends to reduce the demand for the other. And their respective dynamic behaviors (long-run versus short-run elasticities) are just the opposite from each other—for gasoline the long-run price and income elasticities are larger than the short-run elasticities; for automobiles the reverse is true.

There have been a number of statistical studies of the demands for gasoline and automobiles. Here we report estimates of price and income elasticities from two studies that emphasize the dynamic response of demand.[6] Table 2.1 shows price and income elasticities of demand for gasoline in the United States for the short run, the long run, and just about everything in between.

Note the large differences between the long-run and the short-run elasticities. Following the sharp increases that occurred in the price of gasoline with the rise of the OPEC cartel in 1974, many people (including executives in the automobile and oil industries) claimed that the demand for gasoline would

[6] The study of gasoline demand is in Robert S. Pindyck, *The Structure of World Energy Demand* (Cambridge, Mass.: MIT Press, 1979). The estimates of automobile demand elasticities are based on the article by Saul H. Hymans, "Consumer Durable Spending: Explanation and Prediction," *Brookings Papers on Economic Activity* 1 (1971): 173–199.

Elasticity	Years Following Price or Income Change					
	1	2	3	5	10	20
Price	−0.11	−0.22	−0.32	−0.49	−0.82	−1.17
Income	0.07	0.13	0.20	0.32	0.54	0.78

not change much—that demand was not very elastic. Indeed, for the first year after the price rise, they were right—the quantity demanded did not change much. But demand did eventually change. It just took time for people to alter their driving habits and to replace large cars with smaller and more fuel-efficient ones. This response continued after the second sharp increase in oil prices that occurred in 1979–1980. It is partly because of this that OPEC could not maintain oil prices above $30 per barrel, and prices fell.

Table 2.2 shows price and income elasticities of demand for automobiles. Note that the short-run elasticities are much larger than the long-run elasticities. It should be clear from the income elasticities why the automobile industry is so highly cyclical. For example, GNP fell by nearly 3 percent in real (inflation-adjusted) terms during the 1982 recession, but automobile sales fell by about 8 percent in real terms.[7] Auto sales recovered, however, during 1983–1985. Auto sales also fell by about 8 percent during the 1991 recession (when GNP fell 2 percent), but began to recover in 1993.

Elasticity	Years Following Price or Income Change					
	1	2	3	5	10	20
Price	−0.20	−0.93	−0.75	−0.55	−0.42	−0.40
Income	3.00	2.33	1.88	1.38	1.02	1.00

Supply

Elasticities of supply also differ from the long run to the short run. For most products, long-run supply is much more price elastic than short-run supply

---

[7] This includes imports, which were capturing a growing share of the U.S. market. Domestic auto sales fell by even more.

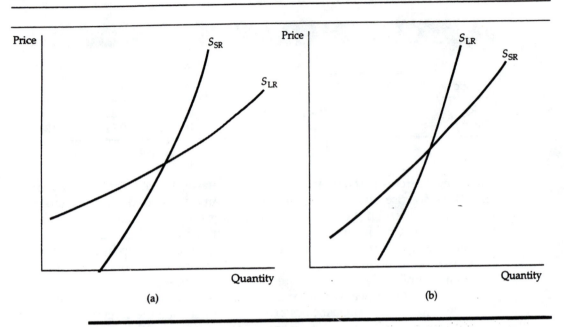

(a)   (b)

FIGURE 2.15a   **Primary Copper: Short-Run and Long-Run Supply Curves.**   Like most goods, supply is more elastic in the long run. If price increases, firms would like to produce more but are limited by capacity constraints in the short run. In the longer run, they can add to capacity and produce more.

FIGURE 2.15b   **Secondary Copper: Short-Run and Long-Run Supply Curves.**   If price increases, there is a greater incentive to convert scrap copper into new supply, so initially secondary supply (i.e., supply from scrap) increases sharply. But later, as the stock of scrap falls, secondary supply contracts. Secondary supply is therefore less elastic in the long run than in the short run.

because firms face *capacity constraints* in the short run and need time to expand their capacity by building new production facilities and hiring workers to staff them. This is not to say that supply will not increase in the short run if price goes up sharply. Even in the short run, firms can increase output by using their existing facilities more hours per week, paying workers to work overtime, and hiring some new workers immediately. But firms will be able to expand output much more given the time to expand their facilities and hire a larger permanent work force.

For some goods and services, short-run supply is completely inelastic. Rental housing in most cities is an example. In the very short run, because there is only a fixed number of rental units, an increase in demand only pushes rents up. In the longer run, and without rent controls, higher rents provide an incentive to renovate existing buildings and construct new ones, so that the quantity supplied increases.

For most goods, however, firms can find ways to increase output even in the short run, if the price incentive is strong enough. The problem is that be-

TABLE 2.3   Supply of Copper

Price Elasticity of:	Short-run	Long-run
Primary supply	0.20	1.60
Secondary supply	0.43	0.31
Total supply	0.25	1.50

cause of the constraints that firms face, it is costly to increase supply rapidly, so that it may require a large price increase to elicit a small short-run increase in supply. We discuss these characteristics of supply in more detail in Chapter 8, but for now it should be clear why for many goods, short-run and long-run supply curves resemble those in Figure 2.15a. (The figure refers to the supply of primary [newly mined] copper, but it could also apply to many other goods.)

For some goods, supply is more elastic in the short run than in the long run. Such goods are durable and can be recycled as part of supply if price goes up. An example is the *secondary supply* of metals (i.e., the supply from *scrap metal*, which is often melted down and refabricated). When the price of copper goes up, it increases the incentive to convert scrap copper into new supply, so that initially secondary supply increases sharply. But eventually the stock of good-quality scrap will fall, making the melting, purifying, and refabricating more costly, so that secondary supply will contract. Thus the long-run price elasticity of secondary supply is smaller than the short-run elasticity.

Figures 2.15a and 2.15b show short-run and long-run supply curves for primary (production from the mining and smelting of ore) and secondary copper production. Table 2.3 shows estimates of the elasticities for each component of supply, and then for total supply, based on a weighted average of the component elasticities.[8] Because secondary supply is only about 20 percent of total supply, the price elasticity of total supply is larger in the long run than in the short run.

EXAMPLE 2.5   THE WEATHER IN BRAZIL AND THE PRICE OF COFFEE IN NEW YORK

Subfreezing weather occasionally destroys or damages many of Brazil's coffee trees. Because Brazil produces much of the world's coffee, the result is a decrease in the supply of coffee and a sharp run-up in its price. A dramatic example of this occurred in July 1975, when a frost destroyed most of

---

[8] These estimates were obtained by aggregating the regional estimates reported in Franklin M. Fisher, Paul H. Cootner, and Martin N. Baily, "An Econometric Model of the World Copper Industry," *Bell Journal of Economics* 3 (Autumn 1972): 568–609.

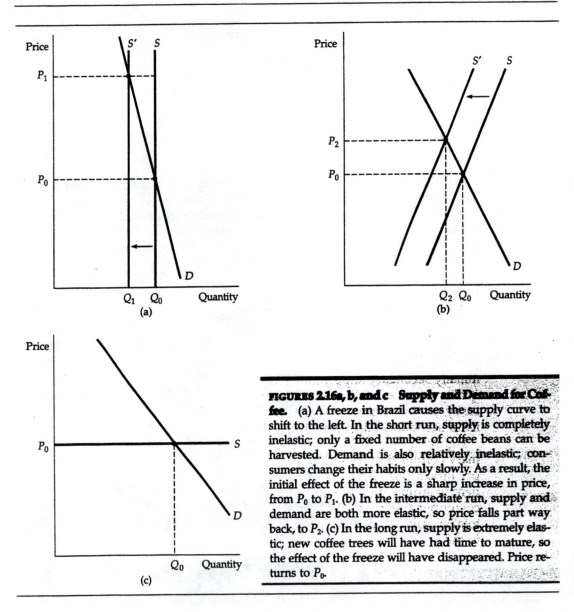

FIGURES 2.16a, b, and c   Supply and Demand for Coffee. (a) A freeze in Brazil causes the supply curve to shift to the left. In the short run, supply is completely inelastic; only a fixed number of coffee beans can be harvested. Demand is also relatively inelastic; consumers change their habits only slowly. As a result, the initial effect of the freeze is a sharp increase in price, from P_0 to P_1. (b) In the intermediate run, supply and demand are both more elastic, so price falls part way back, to P_2. (c) In the long run, supply is extremely elastic; new coffee trees will have had time to mature, so the effect of the freeze will have disappeared. Price returns to P_0.

Brazil's 1976–1977 coffee crop. (Remember that it is winter in Brazil when it is summer in the northern hemisphere.) The spot price of a pound of coffee in New York went from 68 cents in 1975 to $1.23 in 1976, and then to $2.70 in 1977.

The run-up in price following a freeze is usually short-lived, however. Within a year price begins to fall, and within three or four years it returns to its prefreeze level. For example, in 1978 the price of coffee in New York fell to

$1.48 per pound, and by 1983 it had fallen in real (inflation-adjusted) terms to within a few cents of its prefreeze 1975 price.[9]

Coffee prices behave this way because both demand and supply (especially supply) are much more elastic in the long run than in the short run. Figures 2.16a, 2.16b, and 2.16c show this. Note that in the very short run (within one or two months after a freeze), supply is completely inelastic; there are simply a fixed number of coffee beans, some of which have been damaged by the frost. Demand is also relatively inelastic. As a result of the frost, the supply curve shifts to the left, and price increases sharply, from P_0 to P_1.

In the intermediate run, say, one year after the freeze, both supply and demand are more elastic, supply because existing trees can be harvested more intensively (with some decrease in quality), and demand because consumers have had time to change their buying habits. The intermediate-run supply curve also shifts to the left, but price has come down from P_1 to P_2. The quantity supplied has also increased somewhat from the short run, from Q_1 to Q_2. In the long run, price returns to its normal level; coffee growers have had time to replace the trees damaged by the freeze. The long-run supply curve, then, simply reflects the cost of producing coffee, including the costs of land, of planting and caring for the trees, and of a competitive rate of profit.

---

*2.5 Understanding and Predicting the Effects of Changing Market Conditions

We have discussed the meaning and characteristics of supply and demand, but our treatment has been largely qualitative. To use supply and demand curves to analyze and predict the effects of changing market conditions, we must begin to attach numbers to them. For example, to see how a 50 percent reduction in the supply of Brazilian coffee may affect the world price of coffee, we need to write down actual supply and demand curves and then calculate how those curves will shift, and how price will then change.

In this section we will see how to do simple "back of the envelope" calculations with linear supply and demand curves. Although they are often an approximation to more complex curves, we use linear curves because they are the easiest to work with. It may come as a surprise, but one can do some in-

---

[9] During 1980, however, prices temporarily went just above $2.00 per pound as a result of export quotas imposed under the International Coffee Agreement (ICA). The ICA is essentially a cartel agreement implemented by the coffee-producing countries in 1968. It has been largely ineffective and in most years has had little impact on price. We discuss cartel pricing in detail in Chapter 12.

formative economic analyses on the back of a small envelope with a pencil and a pocket calculator.

First, we must learn how to "fit" linear demand and supply curves to market data. (By this we do not mean statistical fitting in the sense of linear regression or other statistical techniques, which we discuss later in the book.) Suppose we have two sets of numbers for a particular market. First are the price and quantity that generally prevail in the market (i.e., the price and quantity that prevail "on average," or when the market is in equilibrium, or when market conditions are "normal"). We call these numbers the equilibrium price and quantity, and we denote them by P^* and Q^*. Second are the price elasticities of supply and demand for the market (at or near the equilibrium), which we denote by E_S and E_D, as before.

These numbers might come from a statistical study done by someone else; they might be numbers that we simply think are reasonable; or they might be numbers that we want to try out on a "what if" basis. What we want to do is *write down the supply and demand curves that fit (i.e., are consistent with) these numbers.* Then we can determine numerically how a change in a variable such as GNP, the price of another good, or some cost of production will cause supply or demand to shift and thereby affect the market price and quantity.

Let's begin with the linear curves shown in Figure 2.17. We can write these curves algebraically as

$$\text{Demand:} \qquad Q = a - bP \qquad\qquad (2.4a)$$

$$\text{Supply:} \qquad Q = c + dP \qquad\qquad (2.4b)$$

The problem is to choose numbers for the constants a, b, c, and d. This is done, for supply and for demand, in a two-step procedure:

Step One: Recall that each price elasticity, whether of supply or demand, can be written as

$$E = (P/Q)(\Delta Q/\Delta P)$$

where $\Delta Q/\Delta P$ is the change in quantity demanded or supplied resulting from a small change in price. For linear curves, $\Delta Q/\Delta P$ is constant. From equations (2.4a) and (2.4b), we see that $\Delta Q/\Delta P = d$ for supply, and $\Delta Q/\Delta P = -b$ for demand. Now, let's substitute these values for $\Delta Q/\Delta P$ into the elasticity formula:

$$\text{Demand:} \qquad E_D = -b(P^*/Q^*) \qquad\qquad (2.5a)$$

$$\text{Supply:} \qquad E_S = d(P^*/Q^*) \qquad\qquad (2.5b)$$

where P^* and Q^* are the equilibrium price and quantity for which we have data and to which the curves will be fit. Because we have numbers for E_S, E_D, P^*, and Q^*, we can substitute these numbers in equations (2.5a) and (2.5b) and solve for b and d.

Step Two: Since we now know b and d, we can substitute these numbers, as well as P^* and Q^*, into equations (2.4a) and (2.4b) and solve for the remaining constants a and c. For example, we can rewrite equation (2.4a) as

$$a = Q^* + bP^*$$

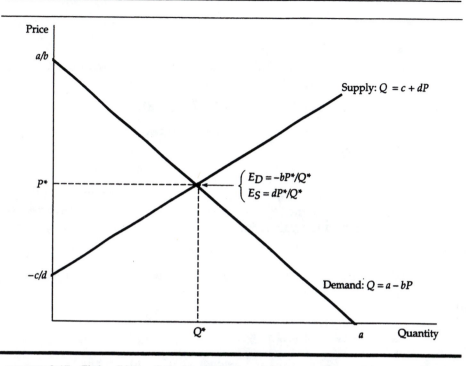

FIGURE 2.17   **Fitting Linear Supply and Demand Curves to Data.**   Linear supply and
demand curves provide a convenient tool for analysis. Given data for the equilibrium
price and quantity P^* and Q^*, and estimates of the elasticities of demand and supply
E_D and E_S, we can calculate the parameters c and d for the supply curve, and a and b for
the demand curve. (In the case drawn here, $c < 0$.) The curves can then be used to analyze the behavior of the market quantitatively.

and then use our data for Q^* and P^*, together with the number we calculated
in Step One for b, to obtain a.

Let's do this for a specific example—long-run supply and demand for the
world copper market. The relevant numbers for this market are as follows:[10]
quantity $Q^* = 7.5$ million metric tons per year (mmt/yr); price $P^* = 75$ cents
per pound; elasticity of supply $E_S = 1.6$; elasticity of demand $E_D = -0.8$. (The
price of copper has fluctuated during the past decade between 50 cents and
more than $1.30, but 75 cents is a reasonable average price for 1980–1990.)

We begin with the supply curve equation (2.4b) and use our two-step procedure to calculate numbers for c and d. The long-run price elasticity of supply is 1.6, $P^* = .75$, and $Q^* = 7.5$.

Step One: Substitute these numbers in equation (2.5b) to determine d:

[10] The supply elasticity is for total supply, as shown in Table 2.3. The demand elasticity is a regionally
aggregated number based on Fisher, Cootner, and Baily, "An Econometric Model." Quantities refer
to what was then the non-Communist world market.

$$1.6 = d(0.75/7.5) = 0.1d,$$

so that $d = 1.6/0.1 = 16$.

Step Two: Substitute this number for d, together with the numbers for P^* and Q^*, into equation (2.4b) to determine c:

$$7.5 = c + (16)(0.75) = c + 12,$$

so that $c = 7.5 - 12 = -4.5$. We now know c and d, so we can write our supply curve:

Supply: $Q = -4.5 + 16P$

We can now follow the same steps for the demand curve equation (2.4a). An estimate for the long-run elasticity of demand is -0.8. First, substitute this number, and the values for P^* and Q^*, in equation (2.5a) to determine b:

$$-0.8 = -b(0.75/7.5) = -0.1b$$

so that $b = 0.8/0.1 = 8$. Second, substitute this value for b and the values for P^* and Q^* in equation (2.4a) to determine a:

$$7.5 = a - (8)(0.75) = a - 6,$$

so that $a = 7.5 + 6 = 13.5$. Thus, our demand curve is

Demand: $Q = 13.5 - 8P$

To check that we have not made a mistake, set supply equal to demand and calculate the equilibrium price that results:

$$\text{Supply} = -4.5 + 16P = 13.5 - 8P = \text{Demand}$$

$$16P + 8P = 13.5 + 4.5,$$

or $P = 18/24 = 0.75$, which is indeed the equilibrium price we began with.

We have written supply and demand so that they depend only on price, but they could easily depend on other variables as well. For example, demand might depend on income as well as price. We would then write demand as

$$Q = a - bP + fI \tag{2.6}$$

where I is an index of aggregate income or GNP. (For example, I might equal 1.0 in a base year and then rise or fall to reflect percentage increases or decreases in aggregate income.)

For our copper market example, a reasonable estimate for the long-run income elasticity of demand is 1.3. For the linear demand curve (2.6), we can then calculate f by using the formula for the income elasticity of demand: $E = (I/Q)(\Delta Q/\Delta I)$. Taking the base value of I as 1.0, we have

$$1.3 = (1.0/7.5)(f)$$

so $f = (1.3)(7.5)/(1.0) = 9.75$. Finally, substituting the values $b = 8$, $f = 9.75$, $P^* = 0.75$, and $Q^* = 7.5$ into (2.6), we can calculate that a must equal 3.75.

We have seen how to fit linear supply and demand curves to data. Now, to see how these curves can be used to analyze markets, look at Example 2.6 on the behavior of copper prices and Example 2.7 on the world oil market.

After reaching a level of about $1.00 per pound in 1980, the price of copper fell sharply to about 60 cents per pound in 1986. In real (inflation-adjusted) terms, this price was even lower than during the Great Depression 50 years earlier. Only in 1988–1989 did prices recover somewhat, as a result of strikes by miners in Peru and Canada that disrupted supplies. Figure 2.18 shows the behavior of copper prices in 1965–1993 in both real and nominal terms.

The world-wide recessions of 1980 and 1982 contributed to the decline of copper prices; as mentioned above, the income elasticity of copper demand is about 1.3. But copper demand did not pick up as the industrial economies re-

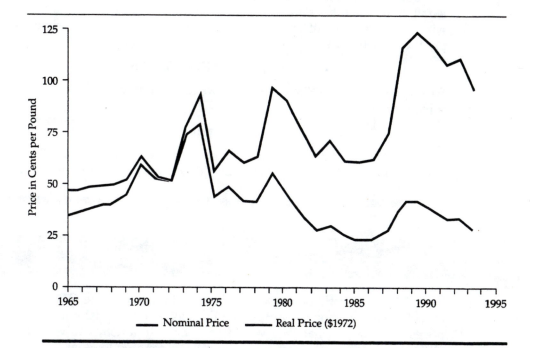

FIGURE 2.18   Copper Prices 1965–1993.   Copper prices are shown in both nominal (no adjustment for inflation) and real (inflation-adjusted) terms. In real terms copper prices declined steeply from the early 1970s through the mid-1980s as demand fell. In 1988–1990 copper prices rose in response to supply disruptions caused by strikes in Peru and Canada, but prices later fell after the strikes ended.

covered during the mid-1980s. Instead, the 1980s saw the beginning of a deep decline in the demand for copper.

This decline occurred for two reasons. First, a large part of copper consumption is for the construction of equipment for electric power generation and transmission. But by the late 1970s, the growth rate of electric power generation had fallen dramatically in most industrialized countries. (For example, in the United States the growth rate fell from over 6 percent per annum in the 1960s and early 1970s to less than 2 percent in the late 1970s and 1980s.) This meant a big drop in what had been a major source of copper demand. Second, in the 1980s other materials, such as aluminum and fiber optics, were increasingly substituted for copper.

Copper producers are concerned about the possible effects of further declines in demand, particularly as strikes end and supplies increase. Declining demand will depress prices; to find out how much, we can use the linear supply and demand curves that we just derived. Let us calculate the effect on price of a 20 percent decline in demand. Since we are not concerned here with the effects of GNP growth, we can leave the income term fI out of demand.

We want to shift the demand curve to the left by 20 percent. In other words, we want the quantity demanded to be 80 percent of what it would be otherwise for every value of price. For our linear demand curve, we simply multiply the right-hand side by 0.8:

$$Q = (0.8)(13.5 - 8P) = 10.8 - 6.4P$$

Supply is again $Q = -4.5 + 16P$. Now we can equate supply and demand and solve for price:

$$16P + 6.4P = 10.8 + 4.5$$

or $P = 15.3/22.4 = 68.3$ cents per pound. A decline in demand of 20 percent therefore implies a drop in price of roughly 7 cents per pound, or 10 percent.

EXAMPLE 2.7   THE WORLD OIL MARKET ON THE BACK OF AN ENVELOPE

Since 1974, the world oil market has been dominated by the OPEC cartel. By collectively restraining output, OPEC succeeded in pushing world oil prices well above what they would have been in a competitive market. OPEC producers could do this because they accounted for a large fraction of world oil production (about two-thirds in 1974).

We discuss OPEC's pricing strategy in more detail in Chapter 12 as part of our analysis of cartels and the behavior of cartelized markets. But for now, let's see how simple linear supply and demand curves (and the back of a small envelope) can be used to predict what should happen, in the short and longer run, following a cutback in production by OPEC.

This example is set in 1973–1974, so all prices are measured in 1974 dollars (which, because of inflation, were worth much more than today's dollars). Here are some rough figures: 1973 world price = $4 per barrel, world demand and total supply = 18 billion barrels per year (bb/yr), 1973 OPEC supply = 12 bb/yr and competitive (non-OPEC) supply = 6 bb/yr. And here are price elasticity estimates consistent with linear supply and demand curves:[11]

	Short-run	Long-run
World Demand:	−0.05	−0.40
Competitive Supply:	0.10	0.40

You should verify that these numbers imply the following for demand and competitive supply in the *short run:*

$$\text{Short-run Demand:} \qquad D = 18.9 - 0.225P$$

$$\text{Short-run Competitive Supply:} \quad S_C = 5.4 + 0.15P$$

Of course, *total* supply is competitive supply *plus* OPEC supply, which we take as constant at 12 bb/yr. Adding this 12 bb/yr to the competitive supply curve above, we obtain the following for total short-run supply:

$$\text{Short-run Total Supply:} \quad S_T = 17.4 + 0.15P$$

You should check that demand and total supply are equal at a price of $4 per barrel.

You should also verify that the corresponding demand and supply curves for the *long run* are

$$\text{Long-run Demand:} \qquad D = 25.2 - 1.8P$$

$$\text{Long-run Competitive Supply:} \quad S_C = 3.6 + 0.6P$$

$$\text{Long-run Total Supply:} \qquad S_T = 15.6 + 0.6P$$

Again, you can check that supply and demand equate at a price of $4.

Now let's calculate what should happen if OPEC cuts production by one-fourth, or 3 bb/yr. For the *short-run,* just subtract 3 from total supply:

$$\text{Short-run Demand:} \qquad D = 18.9 - 0.225P$$

$$\text{Short-run Total Supply:} \quad S_T = 14.4 + 0.15P$$

By equating this total supply with demand, we can see that in the short run, the price should rise to $12 per barrel, which in fact it did. Figure 2.19 illustrates the shift in supply and its effect on price. The initial equilibrium is at

---

[11] These elasticities are larger when price is higher. For the sources of these numbers and a more detailed discussion of OPEC oil pricing, see Robert S. Pindyck, "Gains to Producers from the Cartelization of Exhaustible Resources," *Review of Economics and Statistics* 60 (May 1978): 238–251, and James M. Griffin and David J. Teece, *OPEC Behavior and World Oil Prices* (London: Allen & Unwin, 1982).

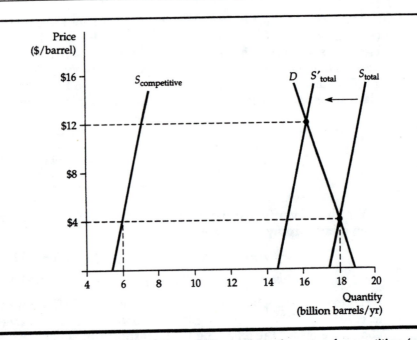

FIGURE 2.19   OPEC Production Cut.   Total supply is the sum of competitive (non-OPEC) supply and the 12 billion barrels per year of OPEC supply. These are short-run supply and demand curves. If OPEC reduces its production, the supply curve will shift to the left. In the short run, price will increase sharply.

the intersection of S_{total} and D. After the drop in OPEC production, the equilibrium occurs where S'_{total} and D cross.

In the *long run*, however, things will be different. Because both demand and competitive supply are more elastic in the long run, a one-fourth cut in production by OPEC will no longer support a $12 price. By subtracting 3 from the long-run total supply function and equating with long-run demand, we can see that the price will be only $5.25. This is $1.25 above the old $4 price but much lower than $12.

We would therefore expect to see a sharp increase in price, followed by a gradual decline, as demand falls and competitive supply rises in response to price. And this is what did occur, at least until 1979. But during 1979–1980 the price of oil again rose dramatically. What happened? The Iranian Revolution and the outbreak of the Iran–Iraq war. By cutting about 1.5 bb/yr from Iranian production and nearly 1 bb/yr from Iraqi production, the revolution and war allowed oil prices to continue to increase, and consequently they were a blessing for the other members of OPEC.

Yet even though the Iran–Iraq war dragged on, by 1986 oil prices had fallen much closer to competitive levels. This was largely due to the long-run response of demand and competitive supply. As demand fell and competitive supply expanded, OPEC's share of the world market fell to about one-third, as compared with almost two-thirds in 1973.

2.6 *Effects of Government Intervention— Price Controls*

In the United States and most other industrial countries, markets are rarely free of government intervention. Besides imposing taxes and granting subsidies, governments often regulate markets (even competitive markets) in a variety of ways. Here we will see how to use supply and demand curves to analyze the effects of one common form of government intervention: price controls. Later, in Chapter 9, we examine the effects of price controls and other forms of government intervention and regulation in more detail.

Figure 2.20 illustrates the effects of price controls. Here P_0 and Q_0 are the equilibrium price and quantity that would prevail without government regulation. The government, however, has decided that P_0 is too high and has mandated that the price can be no higher than a maximum allowable *ceiling price*, denoted by P_{max}. What is the result? At this lower price, producers (particularly those with higher costs) will produce less, and supply will be Q_1. Consumers, on the other hand, will demand more at this low price; they would like to purchase the quantity Q_2. So demand exceeds supply, and a shortage develops, known as *excess demand*. The amount of excess demand is $Q_2 - Q_1$.

This excess demand sometimes takes the form of queues, as when drivers lined up to buy gasoline during the winter of 1974 and the summer of 1979. (In both instances, the gasoline lines were the result of price controls; the government prevented domestic oil and gasoline prices from rising along with world oil prices.) Sometimes it takes the form of curtailments and supply rationing, as with natural gas price controls and the resulting gas shortages of the mid-1970s, when industrial consumers of gas had their supplies cut off, forcing factories to close. And sometimes it spills over to other markets, where it artificially increases demand. For example, natural gas price controls caused potential buyers of gas to use oil instead.

Some people gain and some lose from price controls. As Figure 2.20 suggests, producers lose—they receive lower prices, and some leave the industry. Some but not all consumers gain. Consumers who can purchase the good at a lower price are clearly better off, but those who have been "rationed out" and cannot buy the good at all are worse off. How large are the gains to the winners, how large are the losses to the losers, and do the total gains exceed the total losses? To answer these questions we need a method to measure the

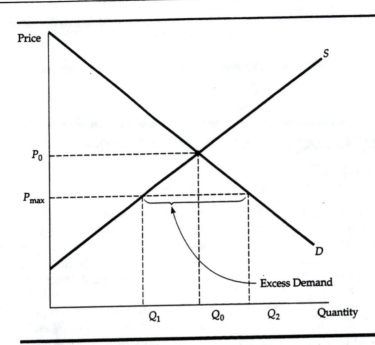

FIGURE 2.20   **Effects of Price Controls.**   Without price controls the market clears at the equilibrium price and quantity P_0 and Q_0. If price is regulated to be no higher than P_{max}, supply falls to Q_1, demand increases to Q_2, and a shortage develops.

gains and losses from price controls and other forms of government intervention. We discuss such a method in Chapter 9.

In 1954, the federal government began regulating the wellhead price of natural gas. Initially the controls were not binding; the ceiling prices were above those that cleared the market. But in about 1962, these ceiling prices did become binding, and excess demand for natural gas developed and slowly began to grow. In the 1970s, this excess demand, spurred by higher oil prices, became severe and led to widespread curtailments. Ceiling prices were far below those that would have prevailed in a free market.[12]

[12] This regulation began with the Supreme Court's 1954 decision requiring the then Federal Power Commission to regulate wellhead prices on natural gas sold to interstate pipeline companies. These price controls were largely removed during the 1980s, under the mandate of the Natural Gas Policy Act of 1978. For a detailed discussion of natural gas regulation and its effects, see Paul W. MacAvoy and Robert S. Pindyck, *The Economics of the Natural Gas Shortage* (Amsterdam: North-Holland, 1975), R. S. Pindyck, "Higher Energy Prices and the Supply of Natural Gas," *Energy Systems and Policy* 2 (1978): 177–209, and Arlon R. Tussing and Connie C. Barlow, *The Natural Gas Industry* (Cambridge, Mass.: Ballinger, 1984).

To analyze the impact of these price controls, we will take 1975 as a case in point. Based on econometric studies of natural gas markets and the behavior of those markets as controls were gradually lifted during the 1980s, the following data describe the market in 1975. The free market price of natural gas would have been about $2.00 per mcf (thousand cubic feet), and production and consumption would have been about 20 Tcf (trillion cubic feet). The average price of oil (including both imports and domestic production), which affects both supply and demand for natural gas, was about $8/barrel.

A reasonable estimate for the price elasticity of supply is 0.2. Higher oil prices also lead to more natural gas production because oil and gas are often discovered and produced together; an estimate of the cross-price elasticity of supply is 0.1. As for demand, the price elasticity is about -0.5, and the cross-price elasticity with respect to oil price is about 1.5. You can verify that the following linear supply and demand curves fit these numbers:

$$\textit{Supply:} \quad Q = 14 + 2P_G + .25P_O$$

$$\textit{Demand:} \quad Q = -5P_G + 3.75P_O$$

where Q is the quantity of natural gas (in Tcf), P_G is the price of natural gas (in dollars per mcf), and P_O is the price of oil (in dollars per barrel). You can also verify, by equating supply and demand and substituting $8.00 for P_O, that these supply and demand curves imply an equilibrium free market price of $2.00 for natural gas.

The regulated price of gas in 1975 was about $1.00 per mcf. Substituting this price for P_G in the supply function gives a quantity supplied (Q_1 in Figure 2.20) of 18 Tcf. Substituting for P_G in the demand function gives a demand (Q_2 in Figure 2.20) of 25 Tcf. Price controls thus created an excess demand of $25 - 18 = 7$ Tcf, which manifested itself in the form of widespread curtailments.

Price regulation was a major component of U.S. energy policy during the 1960s and 1970s, and it continued to influence the evolution of natural gas markets in the 1980s. In Example 9.1 of Chapter 9, we show how to measure the gains and losses that result from natural gas price controls.

Summary

1. Supply-demand analysis is a basic tool of microeconomics. In competitive markets, supply and demand curves tell us how much will be produced by firms and how much will be demanded by consumers as a function of price.

2. The market mechanism is the tendency for supply and demand to equilibrate (i.e., for price to move to the market-clearing level), so that there is neither excess demand nor excess supply.

3. Elasticities describe the responsiveness of supply and demand to changes in price, income, or other variables. For example, the price elasticity of demand measures the percentage change in the quantity demanded resulting from a 1 percent increase in price.

4. Elasticities pertain to a time frame, and for most goods it is important to distinguish between short-run and long-run elasticities.

5. If we can estimate, at least roughly, the supply and demand curves for a particular market, we can calculate the market-clearing price by equating supply and demand. Also, if we know how supply and demand depend on other economic variables, such as income or the prices of other goods, we can calculate how the market-clearing price and quantity will change as these other variables change. This is a means of explaining or predicting market behavior.

6. Simple numerical analyses can often be done by fitting linear supply and demand curves to data on price and quantity and to estimates of elasticities. For many markets such data and estimates are available, and simple "back of the envelope" calculations can help us understand the characteristics and behavior of the market.

Questions for Review

1. Suppose that unusually hot weather causes the demand curve for ice cream to shift to the right. Why will the price of ice cream rise to a new market-clearing level?

2. Use supply and demand curves to illustrate how each of the following events would affect the price of butter and the quantity of butter bought and sold: (a) an increase in the price of margarine; (b) an increase in the price of milk; (c) a decrease in average income levels.

3. Suppose a 3 percent increase in the price of corn flakes causes a 6 percent decline in the quantity demanded. What is the elasticity of demand for corn flakes?

4. Why do long-run elasticities of demand differ from short-run elasticities? Consider two goods: paper towels and televisions. Which is a durable good? Would you expect the price elasticity of demand for paper towels to be larger in the short run or in the long run? Why? What about the price elasticity of demand for televisions?

5. Explain why for many goods, the long-run price elasticity of supply is larger than the short-run elasticity.

6. Suppose the government regulates the prices of beef and chicken and sets them below their market-clearing levels. Explain why shortages of these goods will develop and what factors will determine the sizes of the shortages. What will happen to the price of pork? Explain briefly.

7. In a discussion of tuition rates, a university official argues that the demand for admission is completely price inelastic. As evidence she notes that while the university has doubled its tuition (in real terms) over the past 15 years, neither the number nor quality of students applying has decreased. Would you accept this argument? Explain briefly. (Hint: The official makes an assertion about the demand for admission, but does she actually observe a demand curve? What else could be going on?)

8. Use supply and demand curve shifts to illustrate the effect of the following events on the market for apples. Make clear the direction of the change in both price and quantity sold.

a. Scientists find that an apple a day does indeed keep the doctor away.
b. The price of oranges triples.
c. A drought shrinks the apple crop to one-third its normal size.

d. Thousands of college students abandon the academic life to become apple pickers.
e. Thousands of college students abandon the academic life to become apple growers.

Exercises

1. Consider a competitive market for which the quantities demanded and supplied (per year) at various prices are given as follows:

Price ($)	Demand (millions)	Supply (millions)
60	22	14
80	20	16
100	18	18
120	16	20

a. Calculate the price elasticity of demand when the price is $80. When the price is $100.
b. Calculate the price elasticity of supply when the price is $80. When the price is $100.
c. What are the equilibrium price and quantity?
d. Suppose the government sets a price ceiling of $80. Will there be a shortage, and if so, how large will it be?

2. Refer to Example 2.3 on the market for wheat. Suppose that in 1985 the Soviet Union had bought an additional 200 million bushels of U.S. wheat. What would the free market price of wheat have been and what quantity would have been produced and sold by U.S. farmers?

3. The rent control agency of New York City has found that aggregate demand is $Q_D = 100 - 5P$, with quantity measured in tens of thousands of apartments, and price, the average monthly rental rate, measured in hundreds of dollars. The agency also noted that the increase in Q at lower P results from more three-person families coming into the city from Long Island and demanding apartments. The city's board of realtors acknowledges that this is a good demand estimate and has shown that supply is $Q_S = 50 + 5P$.

a. If both the agency and the board are right about demand and supply, what is the free market price? What is the change in city population if the agency sets a maximum average monthly rental of $100, and all those who cannot find an apartment leave the city?
b. Suppose the agency bows to the wishes of the board and sets a rental of $900 per month on all apartments to allow landlords a "fair" rate of return. If 50 percent of any long-run increases in apartment offerings comes from new construction, how many apartments are constructed?

4. Much of the demand for U.S. agricultural output has come from other countries. From Example 2.3, total demand is $Q = 3,550 - 266P$. In addition, we are told that domestic demand is $Q_D = 1,000 - 46P$. Domestic supply is $Q = 1,800 + 240P$. Suppose the export demand for wheat falls by 40 percent.

a. U.S. farmers are concerned about this drop in export demand. What happens to the free market price of wheat in the United States? Do the farmers have much reason to worry?
b. Now suppose the U.S. government wants to buy enough wheat each year to raise the price to $3.00 per bushel. Without export demand, how much wheat would the government have to buy each year? How much would this cost the government?

5. In Example 2.6 we examined the effect of a 20 percent decline in copper demand on the price of copper, using the linear supply and demand curves developed in Section 2.5. Suppose the long-run price elasticity of copper demand were −0.4 instead of −0.8.

a. Assuming, as before, that the equilibrium price and quantity are $P^* = 75$ cents per pound and $Q^* = 7.5$ million metric tons per year, derive the linear demand curve consistent with the smaller elasticity.

b. Using this demand curve, recalculate the effect of a 20 percent decline in copper demand on the price of copper.

6. Example 2.7 analyzes the world oil market. Using the data given in that example,

a. Show that the short-run demand and competitive supply curves are indeed given by

$$D = 18.9 - 0.225P$$
$$S_C = 5.4 + 0.15P$$

b. Show that the long-run demand and competitive supply curves are indeed given by

$$D = 25.2 - 1.8P$$
$$S_C = 3.6 + 0.6P$$

c. Use this model to calculate what would happen to the price of oil in the short run *and* the long run if OPEC were to cut its production by 6 billion barrels per year.

7. Refer to Example 2.8, which analyzes the effects of price controls on natural gas.

a. Using the data in the example, show that the following supply and demand curves did indeed describe the market in 1975:

Supply: $Q = 14 + 2P_G + 0.25P_O$

Demand: $Q = -5P_G + 3.75P_O$

where P_G and P_O are the prices of natural gas and oil, respectively. Also, verify that if the price of oil is $8.00, these curves imply a free market price of $2.00 for natural gas.

b. Suppose the regulated price of gas in 1975 had been $1.50 per million cubic feet, instead of $1.00. How much excess demand would there have been?

c. Suppose that the market for natural gas had *not* been regulated. If the price of oil had increased from $8 to $16, what would have happened to the free market price of natural gas?

CHAPTER *4*

Individual and Market Demand

4.3 *Market Demand*

So far we have discussed the demand curve for an individual consumer. But where do *market demand* curves come from? In this section we show how market demand curves can be derived as the sum of the individual demand curves of all consumers in a particular market.

From Individual to Market Demand

To keep things simple, let's assume that only three consumers (*A*, *B*, and *C*) are in the market for coffee. Table 4.2 tabulates several points on each of these

---

[3] Of course, some consumers (those who spend little on gasoline) will be better off after receiving the rebate, while others (those who spend a lot on gasoline) will be worse off.

TABLE 4.2   Determining the Market Demand Curve

(1) Price ($)	(2) Individual A (units)	(3) Individual B (units)	(4) Individual C (units)	(5) Market (units)
1	6	10	16	32
2	4	8	13	25
3	2	6	10	18
4	0	4	7	11
5	0	2	4	6

consumers' demand curves. The market demand, column (5), is found by adding columns (2), (3), and (4) to determine the total quantity demanded at every price. For example, when the price is $3, the total quantity demanded is 2 + 6 + 10, or 18.

Figure 4.9 shows these same three consumers' demand curves for coffee (labeled D_A, D_B, and D_C). In the graph, the market demand curve is the *horizontal summation* of the demands of each of the consumers. We sum horizontally to find the total amount that the three consumers will demand at any given price. For example, when the price is $4, the quantity demanded by the market (11 units) is the sum of the quantity demanded by A (no units), by B (4 units), and by C (7 units). Because all the individual demand curves slope downward, the market demand curve will also slope downward. However, the market demand curve need not be a straight line, even though each of the individual demand curves is. In Figure 4.9, for example, the market demand curve is *kinked* because one consumer makes no purchases at prices the other consumers find inviting (those above $4).

Two points should be noted. First, the market demand curve will shift to the right as more consumers enter the market. Second, factors that influence the demands of many consumers will also affect the market demand. Suppose, for example, that most consumers in a particular market earn more income, and as a result, increase their demands for coffee. Because each consumer's demand curve shifts to the right, so will the market demand curve.

The aggregation of individual demands into market demands is not just a theoretical exercise. It becomes important in practice when market demands are built up from the demands of different demographic groups or from consumers located in different areas. For example, we might obtain information about the demand for home computers by adding independently obtained information about the demands of (i) households with children, (ii) households without children, and (iii) single individuals. Or we might determine the U.S. demand for natural gas by aggregating the demands for natural gas of the major regions (East, South, Midwest, Mountain, and West, for example).

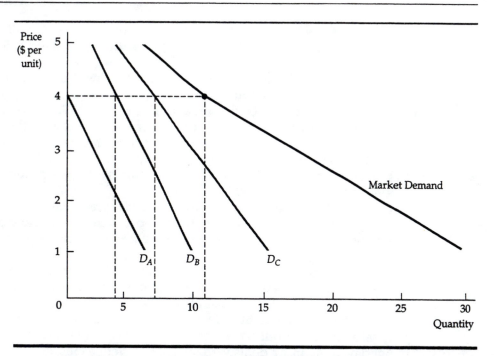

FIGURE 4.9   Summing to Obtain a Market Demand Curve. The market demand curve is obtained by summing the consumers' demand curves D_A, D_B, and D_C. At each price, the quantity of food demanded by the market is the sum of the quantity demanded by each consumer. For example, at a price of $4, the quantity demanded by the market (11 units) is the sum of the quantity demanded by A (no units), by B (4 units), and by C (7 units).

Point and Arc Elasticities of Demand

Recall from Chapter 2 that the price elasticity of demand measures the percentage change in the quantity demanded resulting from a percentage change in price at any point on a demand curve. Denoting the quantity of a good by Q and its price by P, the *point elasticity of demand* is:

$$E_P = \frac{\Delta Q/Q}{\Delta P/P} = \frac{\Delta Q/\Delta P}{Q/P} \tag{4.1}$$

(Here Δ means "a change in" so $\Delta Q/Q$ is the percentage change in Q.)

When demand is inelastic (i.e., E_P is less than 1 in magnitude), the quantity demanded is relatively unresponsive to changes in price. As a result, the total expenditure on the product increases when the price increases. Suppose, for example, that a family currently uses 1000 gallons of gasoline a year when the price is $1 per gallon. Suppose, in addition, that the family's price elasticity of demand for gasoline is -0.5. Then if the price of gasoline increases to $1.10 (a 10 percent increase), the consumption of gasoline falls to 950 gallons (a 5 percent decrease). Total expenditures on gasoline, however, will increase from $1000 (1000 gallons × $1 per gallon) to $1045 (950 gallons × $1.10 per gallon).

In contrast, when demand is elastic (E_P is greater than 1 in magnitude), the total expenditure on the product decreases as the price goes up. Suppose that a family buys 100 pounds of chicken a year, at a price of $2 per pound, and that the price elasticity of demand for chicken is −1.5. Then if the price of chicken increases to $2.20 (a 10 percent increase), the family's consumption of chicken falls to 85 pounds a year (a 15 percent decrease). Total expenditures on chicken will fall as well, from $200 (100 pounds × $2 per pound) to $187 (85 pounds × $2.20 per pound).

If the elasticity of demand is −1 (the *unit elastic* case), total expenditure remains the same after a price change. Then a price increase leads to a decrease in quantity demanded that is just sufficient to leave the total expenditure on the good unchanged.

Table 4.3 summarizes the relationship between elasticity and expenditure. It is useful to review the table from the point of view of the seller of the good rather than the buyer. When demand is inelastic, a price increase leads only to a small decrease in quantity demanded, so that the total revenue received by the seller increases. But when demand is elastic, a price increase leads to a large decline in quantity demanded, and total revenue falls.

There are times when we want to calculate a price elasticity over some portion of the demand curve rather than at a point. Suppose, for example, that we are concerned with a portion of a demand curve in which the price of a product increases from $10 to $11, while the quantity demanded falls from 100 to 95. How should we calculate the price elasticity of demand? We can calculate that $\Delta Q = -5$, and $\Delta P = 1$, but what values do we use for P and Q in the formula $E_P = (\Delta Q/\Delta P)(P/Q)$?

If we use the lower price of $10, we find that $E_P = (-5)(^{10}\!/\!_{100}) = -0.50$. However, if we use the higher price, we find that $E_P = (-5)(^{11}\!/\!_{95}) = -0.58$. The difference between the two elasticities is not large, but it is discomforting to have two choices, neither of which is obviously preferable to the other. To solve this problem when we are dealing with large price changes, we use the *arc elasticity* of demand:

$$E_P = (\Delta Q/P)(\overline{P}/\overline{Q}) \qquad\qquad (4.2)$$

TABLE 4.3   Price Elasticity and Consumer Expenditures

Demand	If Price Increases, Expenditures	If Price Decreases, Expenditures
Inelastic	Increase	Decrease
Unit elastic	Are unchanged	Are unchanged
Elastic	Decrease	Increase

where $\overline{P}$ is the *average* of the two prices and $\overline{Q}$ is the *average* of the two quantities.

In our example, the average price is $10.50 and the average quantity is 97.5 so the arc elasticity is $E_P = (-5)(^{10.5}\!/_{97.5}) = -0.54$. The arc elasticity will always lie somewhere (but not necessarily halfway) between the two point elasticities calculated at the lower and the higher prices.

In Chapter 2 (Example 2.2), we discussed the two components of the demand for wheat—domestic demand (by U.S. consumers) and export demand (by foreign consumers). Let us see how the world demand for wheat in 1981 can be obtained by aggregating the domestic and foreign demands. The domestic demand for wheat is given by the equation $Q_{DD} = 1000 - 46P$, where Q_{DD} is the number of bushels (in millions) demanded domestically, and P is the price in dollars per bushel. Export demand is given by $Q_{DE} = 2550 - 220P$, where Q_{DE} is the number of bushels (in millions) demanded from abroad. As shown in Figure 4.10, the domestic demand for wheat, given by AB, is relatively price

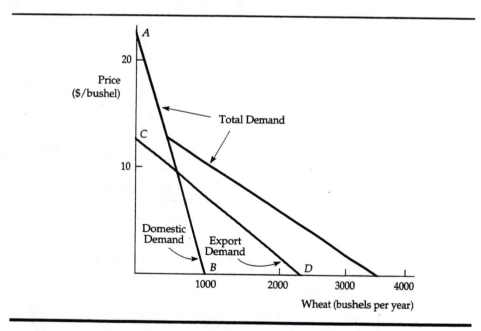

FIGURE 4.10   **The Aggregate Demand for Wheat.**   The total world demand for wheat is the horizontal sum of the domestic demand AB and the export demand CD. Even though each individual demand curve is linear, the market demand curve is kinked, reflecting that there is no export demand when the price of wheat is greater than $12 per bushel.

inelastic. In fact, statistical studies have shown that the price elasticity of domestic demand is about -0.2. However, export demand, given by CD, is more price elastic, with an elasticity of demand of -0.4 to -0.5. Export demand is more elastic than domestic demand because many poorer countries that import U.S. wheat turn to other grains and foodstuffs if wheat prices rise.[4]

To obtain the world demand for wheat, we set the left-hand side of each demand equation equal to the quantity of wheat (the variable on the horizontal axis). Then we add the right-hand side of the equations. Therefore, $Q_D = Q_{DD} + Q_{DE} = (1000 - 46P) + (2550 - 220P) = 3550 - 266P.$

At all prices above C, there is no export demand, so world demand and domestic demand are identical. However, below C, there is both domestic and export demand. As a result, demand is obtained by adding the quantity demanded of domestic wheat and export wheat at each price level. As the figure shows, the world demand for wheat is kinked. The kink occurs at the price level C above which there is no export demand.

EXAMPLE 4.4　THE DEMAND FOR HOUSING

A family's demand for housing depends on the age and status of the household making the purchasing decision. One approach to housing demand is to relate the number of rooms per house for each household (the quantity demanded) to an estimate of the price of an additional room in a house and to the household's family income.[5] (Prices of rooms vary across the United States

TABLE 4.4　Price and Income Elasticities of the Demand for Rooms

Group	Price Elasticity	Income Elasticity
Single individuals	-0.14	0.19
Married, Head of household age less than 30, 1 child	-0.22	0.07
Married, Head age 30–39, 2 or more children	0	0.11
Married, Head age 50 or older, 1 child	-0.08	0.18

---

[4] For a survey of statistical studies of demand and supply elasticities and an analysis of the U.S. wheat market, see Larry Salathe and Sudchada Langley, "An Empirical Analysis of Alternative Export Subsidy Programs for U.S. Wheat," *Agricultural Economics Research* 38, No. 1 (Winter 1986).

[5] See Mahlon Strazheim, *An Econometric Analysis of the Urban Housing Market* (New York: National Bureau of Economic Research, 1975), Chapter 4.

because of differences in construction costs.) Table 4.4 lists some of the price and income elasticities obtained for different demographic groups.

In general, the elasticities show that the size of houses that consumers demand (as measured by the number of rooms) is relatively insensitive to differences in either income or price. However, differences among subgroups of the population are important. For example, married families with young heads of households have a price elasticity of −0.22, substantially greater than married households with older household heads. Presumably, families buying houses are more price sensitive when the parents and their children are younger and the parents may plan on having more children. Among married households, the income elasticity of demand for rooms also increases with age, which tells us that older households buy larger houses than younger households.

Price and income elasticities of demand for housing also depend on where people live.[6] Demand in the central cities is substantially more price elastic than the suburban elasticities. Income elasticities, however, increase as one moves farther from the central city. Thus, poorer (on average) central city residents (who live where the price of land is relatively high) are more price sensitive in their housing choices than their wealthier suburban counterparts.

4.4 *Consumer Surplus*

Consumers buy goods because the purchase makes them better off. *Consumer surplus* measures how much better off individuals in the aggregate are by being able to buy a good in the market. Because different consumers value consumption of particular goods differently, the maximum amount they are willing to pay for those goods also differs. *Consumer surplus is the difference between what a consumer is willing to pay for a good and what the consumer actually pays when buying it.* Suppose, for example, that a student would have been willing to pay $13 for a rock concert ticket, even though she had to pay only $12. The $1 that she saved is her consumer surplus.[7] When we add the consumer sur-

---

[6] See Allen C. Goodman and Masahiro Kawai, "Functional Form, Sample Selection, and Housing Demand," *Journal of Urban Economics* 20 (Sept. 1986): 155–167.

[7] Measuring consumer surplus in dollars involves an implicit assumption about the shape of the consumers' indifference curves—that a consumer's marginal utility associated with increases in income remains constant within the range of income in question. In many cases, this is a reasonable assumption, although it might be suspect when large changes in income are involved. See Robert D. Willing, "Consumer Surplus Without Apology," *American Economic Review* 65 (1976): 589–597.

pluses of all consumers who buy a good, we obtain a measure of the aggregate consumer surplus.

Consumer surplus can be calculated easily if we know the demand curve. To see the relationship between demand and consumer surplus, examine the individual demand curve for concert tickets shown in Figure 4.11.[8] Drawing the demand curve to look more like a stepladder than a straight line allows us to measure the value that this consumer obtains from buying tickets.

When deciding how many tickets to buy, the student might calculate as follows: The first ticket costs $14 but is worth $20. This $20 valuation is obtained by using the demand curve to find the maximum amount that the student will pay for each additional ticket ($10 is the maximum this student will pay for the first ticket). The ticket is worth purchasing because it generates $6 of surplus value above and beyond the cost of the purchase. The second ticket is also worth buying because it generates a surplus of $5 ($19 − $14). The third

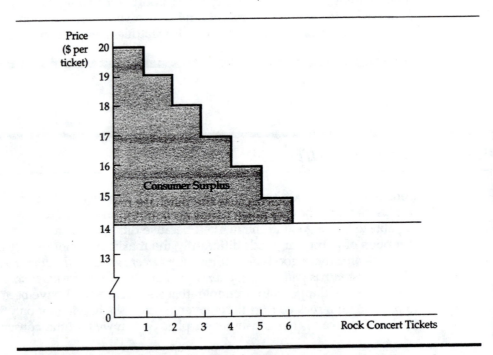

FIGURE 4.11   Consumer Surplus.   Consumer surplus is the total benefit from the consumption of a product, net of the total cost of purchasing it. In this figure the consumer surplus associated with 6 concert tickets (purchased at $14 per ticket) is given by the red-shaded area.

---

[8] The following discussion applies to an individual demand curve, but a similar argument would also apply to a market demand curve.

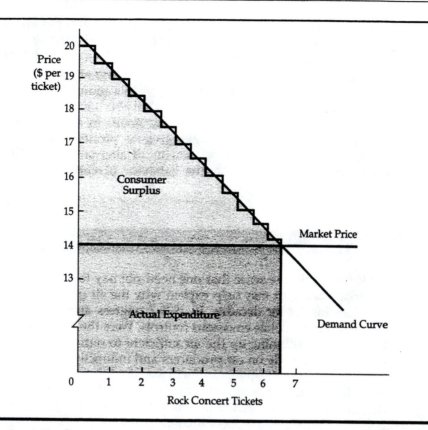

FIGURE 4.12   Consumer Surplus Generalized.   When the units of consumption of a good (here, tickets) are small, the consumer surplus can be measured by the area under the demand curve and above the line representing the purchase price of the good. In the figure the consumer surplus is given by the red-shaded triangle.

ticket generates a surplus of $4. However, the fourth generates a surplus of only $3, the fifth a surplus of $2, and the sixth a surplus of just $1. The student is indifferent about purchasing the seventh ticket (since it generates zero surplus) and prefers not to buy any more than that, as the value of each additional ticket is less than its cost.

In Figure 4.11, consumer surplus is obtained by adding the excess values or surpluses for all units purchased. In this case, consumer surplus = $6 + $5 + $4 + $3 + $2 + $1 = $21.

In a more general case, the stepladder demand curve can be easily transformed into a straight-line demand curve by making the units of the good smaller and smaller. In Figure 4.12, the stepladder is drawn when half tickets are sold (two students share a ticket), and the stepladder begins to approximate the straight-line demand curve. We use such demand curves as approximations and correspondingly use the triangle in Figure 4.12 to measure consumer surplus. When the demand curve is not a straight line, the consumer surplus is measured by the area below the demand curve and above the price line.[9] To calculate the aggregate consumer surplus in a market, we simply find the area below the *market* demand curve and above the price line.

Consumer surplus has important applications in economics. When added over many individuals, consumer surplus measures the aggregate benefit that consumers obtain from buying goods in a market. When we combine consumer surplus with the aggregate profits that producers obtain, we can evaluate the costs and benefits of alternative market structures and of public policies that alter the behavior of consumers and firms in those markets.

Air is free in the sense that one need not pay to breathe it. Yet the absence of a market for air may help explain why the air quality in some cities has been deteriorating for decades. In 1970 Congress amended the Clean Air Act to tighten automobile emissions controls. Were these controls worth it? Were the benefits of cleaning up the air sufficient to outweigh the costs that would be imposed directly on car producers and indirectly on car buyers?

To answer this question, Congress asked the National Academy of Sciences to evaluate these emissions controls in a cost-benefit study. The benefits portion of that study examined how much people value clean air, using empirically determined estimates of the demand for clean air.

Although there is no explicit market for clean air, people do pay more to buy houses where the air is clean than they pay to buy comparable houses in areas with dirtier air. This information was used to estimate the demand for clean air.[10] Detailed data for house prices among neighborhoods of Boston and Los Angeles were compared with the levels of various air pollutants, while the effects of other variables that might affect house value were taken into account statistically. The study determined a demand curve for clean air that looked approximately like that shown in Figure 4.13.

The horizontal axis measures the amount of *air pollution reduction*, and the vertical axis measures the increased value of a home associated with those pollution reductions. For example, consider the demand for cleaner air of a homeowner in a city in which the air is rather dirty, as exemplified by a level of nitrogen oxides (NOX) of 10 parts per 100 million (pphm). If the family were

---

[9] In the demand curve drawn in Figure 4.12, the consumer surplus is $21⅛, a close approximation to the $21 previously determined. This demand curve involves a maximum price of $20.50 and a quantity sold of 6½. In this case, the triangle has a base of 6½, a height of $6.50, and an area of $21⅛.

[10] The results are summarized in Daniel L. Rubinfeld, "Market Approaches to the Measurement of the Benefits of Air Pollution Abatement," in Ann Friedlaender, ed., *The Benefits and Costs of Cleaning the Air* (Cambridge, MA: M.I.T. Press, 1976): 240–273.

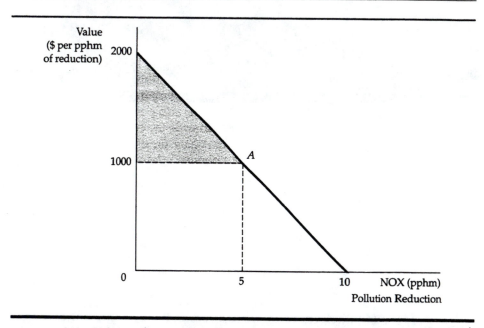

FIGURE 4.13 Valuing Cleaner Air. The shaded area gives the consumer surplus generated when air pollution is reduced by 5 parts per 100 million of nitrogen oxide at a cost of $1000 per part reduced. The surplus is created because most consumers are willing to pay more than $1000 for each unit reduction of nitrogen oxide.

required to pay $1000 for each 1 pphm reduction in air pollution, it would choose A on the demand curve to obtain a pollution reduction of 5 pphm.

How much is a 50 percent, or 5 pphm, reduction in pollution worth to the typical family just described? We can measure this value by calculating the consumer surplus associated with reducing air pollution. Since the price for this reduction is $1000 per unit, the family would pay $5000. However, the family values all but the last unit of reduction by more than $1000. As a result, the shaded area in Figure 4.13 gives the value of the cleanup (above and beyond the payment). Since the demand curve is a straight line, the surplus can be calculated from the area of the triangle whose height is $1000 ($2000 − $1000) and whose base is 5 pphm. Therefore, the value to the household of the pollution reduction is $2500.

A complete benefit-cost analysis would use a measure of the total benefit of the cleanup (the benefit per household times the number of households). This could be compared with the total cost of the cleanup to determine whether such a project were worthwhile. We will discuss clean air further in Chapter 18 when we describe the tradeable emissions permits that were introduced by the Clean Air Act of 1990.

CHAPTER 6

Production

In the last three chapters, we focused on the demand side of the market—the preferences and behavior of consumers. Now we turn to the supply side and examine the behavior of producers. We will see how firms can organize their production efficiently and how their costs of production change as input prices and the level of output change. We will also see that there are strong similarities between the optimizing decisions of firms and those of consumers—understanding consumer behavior will help us understand producer behavior.

The theory of production and cost is central to the economic management of the firm. Just consider some of the problems that a company like General Motors faces regularly. How much assembly-line machinery and how much labor should it use in its new automobile plants? If it wants to increase production, should it hire more workers, or should it also construct new plants? Does it make more sense for one automobile plant to produce different models, or should each model be manufactured in a separate plant? What should GM expect its costs to be during the coming year, and how are these costs likely to change over time and be affected by the level of production? These questions apply not only to business firms, but also to other producers of goods and services, such as governments and nonprofit agencies.

In this chapter we study the firm's production technology—the physical relationship that describes how inputs (such as labor and capital) are transformed into outputs (such as cars and televisions). We do this in several steps. First, we show how the production technology can be represented in the form of a production function—a compact description that facilitates the analysis. Then, we use the production function to show how the firm's output changes when first one and then all the inputs are varied. We will be particularly concerned with the scale of the firm's operation. Are there technological advantages that make the firm more productive as its scale increases?

6.1 *The Technology of Production*

In the production process, firms turn *inputs*, which are also called *factors of production*, into *outputs* (or products). For example, a bakery uses inputs that include the labor of its workers; raw materials, such as flour and sugar; and the capital invested in its ovens, mixers, and other equipment to produce such outputs as bread, cakes, and pastries.

We can divide inputs into the broad categories of labor, materials, and capital, each of which might include more narrow subdivisions. Labor inputs include skilled workers (carpenters, engineers) and unskilled workers (agricultural workers), as well as the entrepreneurial efforts of the firm's managers. Materials include steel, plastics, electricity, water, and any other goods that the firm buys and transforms into a final product. Capital includes buildings, equipment, and inventories.

The relationship between the inputs to the production process and the resulting output is described by a production function. A *production function* indicates the output Q that a firm produces for every specified combination of inputs. For simplicity, we will assume that there are two inputs, labor L and capital K. We can then write the production function as

$$Q = F(K,L) \tag{6.1}$$

This equation relates the quantity of output to the quantities of the two inputs, capital and labor. For example, the production function might describe the number of personal computers that can be produced each year with a 10,000-square-foot plant and a specific amount of assembly-line labor employed during the year. Or it might describe the crop that a farmer can obtain with a specific amount of machinery and workers.

The production function allows for inputs to be combined in varying proportions to produce an output in many ways. For example, wine can be produced in a labor-intensive way by people stomping the grapes, or in a capital-intensive way by machines squashing the grapes. Note that equation (6.1) applies to a *given technology* (i.e., a given state of knowledge about the various methods that might be used to transform inputs into outputs). As the technology becomes more advanced and the production function changes, a firm can obtain more output for a given set of inputs. For example, a new, faster computer chip may allow a hardware manufacturer to produce more high-speed computers in a given period of time.

Production functions describe what is *technically feasible* when the firm operates *efficiently*; that is, when the firm uses each combination of inputs as effectively as possible. Because production functions describe the maximum output feasible for a given set of inputs in a *technically efficient* manner, it follows that inputs will not be used if they decrease output. The presumption that production is always technically efficient need not always hold, but it is reasonable to expect that profit-seeking firms will not waste resources.

6.2 Isoquants

Let's begin by examining the firm's production technology when it uses two inputs and can vary both of them. Suppose, for example, that the inputs are labor and capital, and that they are used to produce food. Table 6.1 tabulates the output achievable for various combinations of inputs.

Labor inputs are listed across the top row, capital inputs down the column on the left. Each entry in the table is the maximum (technically efficient) output that can be produced per time period (say, a year) with each combination of labor and capital used over that time period. (For example, 4 units of labor per year and 2 units of capital per year yield 85 units of food per year.) Reading along each row, we see that output increases as labor inputs are increased, with capital inputs fixed. Reading down each column, we see that output also increases as capital inputs are increased, with labor inputs fixed.

The information contained in Table 6.1 can also be represented graphically using isoquants. *An isoquant is a curve that shows all the possible combinations of inputs that yield the same output.* Figure 6.1 shows three isoquants. (Each axis in the figure measures the quantity of inputs.) These isoquants are based on the data in Table 6.1, but have been drawn as smooth curves to allow for the use of fractional amounts of inputs.

For example, isoquant Q_1 shows all combinations of labor per year and capital per year that together yield 55 units of output per year. Two of these points, A and D, correspond to Table 6.1. At A, 1 unit of labor and 3 units of capital yield 55 units of output; whereas at D, the same output is produced from 3 units of labor and 1 unit of capital. Isoquant Q_2 shows all combinations of inputs that yield 75 units of output and corresponds to the four combinations of

Capital Input	Labor Input				
	1	2	3	4	5
1	20	40	55	65	75
2	40	60	75	85	90
3	55	75	90	100	105
4	65	85	100	110	115
5	75	90	105	115	120

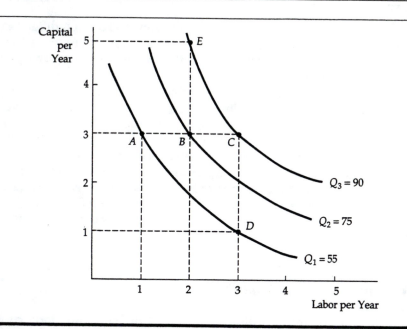

FIGURE 6.1   Production with Two Variable Inputs. Production isoquants show the various combinations of inputs necessary for the firm to produce a given output. A set of isoquants, or isoquant map, describes the firm's production function. Output increases as one moves from isoquant Q_1 (55 units per year) to isoquant Q_2 (75 units per year) and to isoquant Q_3 (90 units per year).

labor and capital italicized in the table (e.g., at B, where 2 units of capital and 3 units of labor are combined). Isoquant Q_2 lies above and to the right of Q_1 because it takes more labor and/or capital to obtain a higher level of output. Finally, isoquant Q_3 shows labor-capital combinations that yield 90 units of output. Point C involves 3 units of labor and 3 units of capital, while Point E involves only 2 units of labor and 5 units of capital. Note that inputs and output are *flows*. The firm uses certain amounts of labor and capital *each year* to produce an amount of output over that year. To simplify, we will frequently ignore the reference to time, and just refer to amounts of labor, capital, and output.

Isoquants are similar to the indifference curves that we used to study consumer theory. Where indifference curves order levels of satisfaction from low to high, isoquants order levels of output. However, unlike indifference curves, each isoquant is associated with a *specific level of output*. By contrast, the numerical labels attached to indifference curves are meaningful only in an ordinal way—higher levels of utility are associated with higher indifference curves, but we cannot measure a specific level of utility the way we can measure a specific level of output with an isoquant.

An *isoquant map* is a set of isoquants, each of which shows the maximum output that can be achieved for any set of inputs. An isoquant map is another way of describing a production function, just as an indifference map is a way of describing a utility function. Each isoquant corresponds to a different level of output, and the level of output increases as you move up and to the right in the figure.

Isoquants show the flexibility that firms have when making production decisions—firms can usually obtain a particular output using various combinations of inputs. It is important for the managers of a firm to understand the nature of this flexibility. For example, fast-food restaurants have recently faced shortages of young, low-wage employees. The companies have responded by automating, for example by adding salad bars or by introducing more sophisticated cooking equipment. They have also recruited older people to fill these positions. As we discuss in Chapters 7 and 8, by taking this flexibility in the production process into account, managers can choose input combinations that minimize cost and maximize profit.

The Short Run Versus the Long Run

It is important to distinguish between the short and long run when analyzing production. The *short run* refers to a period of time in which one or more factors of production cannot be changed. Factors that cannot be varied over this period are called *fixed inputs*. A firm's capital, for example, usually requires time to change—a new factory must be planned and built, machinery and other equipment must be ordered and delivered, all of which can take a year or more. The *long run* is the amount of time needed to make all inputs variable. In the short run, firms vary the intensity with which they utilize a given plant and machinery; in the long run, they vary the size of the plant. All fixed inputs in the short run represent the outcomes of previous long-run decisions based on firms' estimates of what they could profitably produce and sell.

There is no specific time period, such as one year, that separates the short run from the long run. Rather, one must distinguish them on a case-by-case basis. For example, the long run can be as brief as a day or two for a child's lemonade stand, or as long as five or ten years for a petrochemical producer or an automobile manufacturer.

6.3 *Production with One Variable Input (Labor)*

Let's consider the case in which capital is fixed, but labor is variable, so that the firm can produce more output by increasing its labor input. Imagine, for example, that you are managing a clothing plant. You have a fixed amount of equipment, but you can hire more labor or less to sew and to run the machines. You have to decide how much labor to hire and how much clothing to produce. To make the decision, you will need to know how the amount of output Q increases (if at all), as the input of labor L increases.

Table 6.2 gives this information. The first three columns show the amount of output that can be produced in one month with different amounts of labor, and with capital fixed at ten units. (The first column shows the amount of labor, the second the fixed amount of capital, and the third output.) When labor input is zero, output is also zero. Then output increases as labor is increased up to an input of eight units. Beyond that point, total output declines: While initially each unit of labor can take greater and greater advantage of the existing machinery and plant, after a certain point, additional labor is no longer useful and indeed can be counterproductive. (Five people can run an assembly line better than two, but ten people may get in each other's way.)

Average and Marginal Products

The contribution that labor makes to the production process can be described in terms of the average and marginal products of labor. The fourth column in Table 6.2 shows the *average product of labor* AP_L, which is the output per unit of labor input. The average product is calculated by dividing the total output Q by the total input of labor, L. In our example the average product increases initially but falls when the labor input becomes greater than 4. The fifth column shows the *marginal product of labor* MP_L. This is the *additional* output produced as the labor input is increased by one unit. For example, with capital fixed at 10 units, when the labor input increases from 2 to 3, total output increases from 30 to 60, creating an additional output of 30 $(60 - 30)$ units. The marginal product of labor can be written as $\Delta Q/\Delta L$ (i.e., the change in output ΔQ resulting from a one-unit increase in labor input ΔL).

Amount of Labor (L)	Amount of Capital (K)	Total Output (Q)	Average Product (Q/L)	Marginal Product (ΔQ/ΔL)
0	10	0	—	—
1	10	10	10	10
2	10	30	15	20
3	10	60	20	30
4	10	80	20	20
5	10	95	19	15
6	10	108	18	13
7	10	112	16	4
8	10	112	14	0
9	10	108	12	−4
10	10	100	10	−8

Remember that the marginal product of labor depends on the amount of capital used. If the capital input increased from 10 to 20, for example, the marginal product of labor would most likely increase. The reason is that additional workers are likely to be more productive if they have more capital to use. Like the average product, the marginal product first increases then falls, in this case after the third unit of labor.

To summarize:

> Average Product of Labor = Output/Labor Input = Q/L
>
> Marginal Product of Labor = Change in Output/Change in Labor Input = $\Delta Q/\Delta L$

Figure 6.2 plots the information contained in Table 6.2. (We have connected all the points in the figure with solid lines.) Figure 6.2a shows that output increases until it reaches the maximum output of 112; thereafter it diminishes. That portion of the total output is dashed to denote that production past an output of 8 is not technically efficient and therefore is not part of the production function; technical efficiency rules out negative marginal products. Figure 6.2b shows the average and marginal product curves. (The units of the vertical axis have changed from output to output per unit of labor.) Note that the marginal product is always positive when output is increasing, and it is negative when output is decreasing.

It is no coincidence that the marginal product curve crosses the horizontal axis of the graph at the point of maximum total product. This happens because adding a worker to a production line in a manner that slows up the line and decreases total output implies a negative marginal product for that worker.

The average product and marginal product curves are closely related. When the marginal product is greater than the average product, the average product is increasing, as shown between outputs 1 and 4 in Figure 6.2b. For example, suppose that the only employee of an advertising firm can write 10 advertisements per day, so that initially 10 is the average product of labor. Now, a more productive employee is hired who can produce 20 ads per day. The marginal product of labor, 20 ads, is greater than the average, 10. And because both workers combine to produce 30 ads in two days of labor, the new average product has increased to 15 ads.

Similarly, when the marginal product is less than the average product, the average product is decreasing, as shown between outputs 4 and 10 in Figure 6.2b. In our previous example, had the first worker been the more productive of the two, the marginal product of the first worker would have been 20 ads and the marginal product of the second worker 10 ads. Since the marginal product (10 ads) would then be less than the average product (20 ads), the new average product would have fallen to 15 ads.

Because the marginal product is above the average product when the average product is increasing, and below the average product when the average prod-

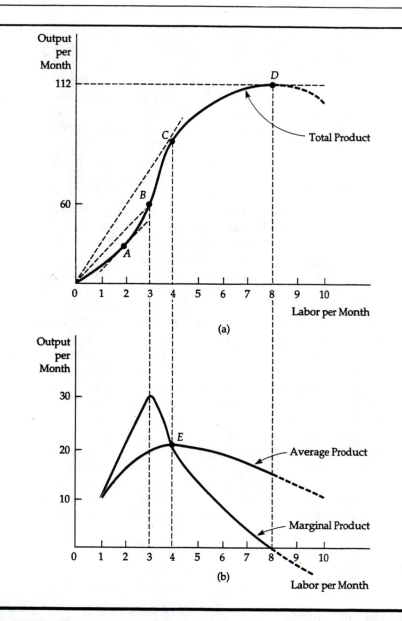

Figure 6.2   Production with One Variable Input.   When all inputs other than labor are fixed, the total product curve in (a) shows the output produced for different amounts of labor input. The average and marginal products in (b) are obtained directly from the total product curve. At point B in (a) the average product of labor is given by the slope of the line from the origin to B.

uct is decreasing, it follows that the marginal product must equal the average product when the average product reaches its maximum. This happens at point E in Figure 6.2b.

The geometric relationship between the total product and the average and marginal product curves is shown in Figure 6.2a. The average product of labor is the total product divided by the quantity of labor input. For example, at B the average product is equal to the output of 60 divided by the input of 3, or 20 units of output per unit of labor input. But this is just the slope of the line running from the origin to B in Figure 6.2a. In general, *the average product of labor is given by the slope of the line drawn from the origin to the corresponding point on the total product curve.*

The marginal product of labor is the change in the total product resulting from an increase of one unit of labor. For example, at A the marginal product is 20 because the tangent to the total product curve has a slope of 20. In general, *the marginal product of labor at a point is given by the slope of the total product at that point.* We can see in Figure 6.2a that the marginal product of labor increases initially, peaks at an input of 3, and then declines as we move up the total product curve to C and D. At D, when total output is maximized, the slope of the tangent to the total product curve is 0, as is the marginal product. Beyond that point, the marginal product becomes negative.

Note the graphical relationship between average and marginal products. At B, the marginal product of labor (the slope of the tangent to the total product curve at B—not shown explicitly) is greater than the average product (dashed line OB). As a result, the average product of labor increases as we move from B to C. At C, the average and marginal products of labor are equal—the average product is the slope of the line from the origin OC, while the marginal product is the tangent to the total product curve at C (note the equality of the average and marginal products at point E in Figure 6.2b). Finally, as we move beyond C toward D, the average marginal product falls below the average product; you can check that the slope of the tangent to the total product curve at any point between C and D is lower than the slope of the line from the origin.

The Law of Diminishing Returns

A diminishing marginal product of labor (and a diminishing marginal product of other inputs) holds for most production processes; the phrase "the law of diminishing returns" is often used to describe this phenomenon. The *law of diminishing returns* states that as the use of an input increases (with other inputs fixed), a point will eventually be reached at which the resulting additions to output decrease. When the labor input is small (and capital is fixed), small increments in labor input add substantially to output as workers are allowed to develop specialized tasks. Eventually, however, the law of diminishing returns applies. When there are too many workers, some workers become ineffective, and the marginal product of labor falls.

The law of diminishing returns usually applies to the short run where at least one input is fixed. However, it can also apply to the long run. Even though all inputs are variable in the long run, a manager may still want to analyze production choices for which one or more inputs are unchanged. Suppose, for example, that only two plant sizes are feasible, and a manager must decide which to build. Then, the manager would want to know when diminishing returns will set in for each of the two options.

Do not confuse the law of diminishing returns with possible changes in the quality of labor as labor inputs are increased (as, for example, if the most highly qualified laborers are hired first, and the least qualified last). In our analysis of production, we have assumed that all labor inputs are of equal quality; diminishing returns result from limitations on the use of other fixed inputs (e.g., machinery), not from declines in worker quality. Also, do not confuse diminishing returns with negative returns. The law of diminishing returns describes a *declining* marginal product, but not necessarily a negative one.

The law of diminishing returns applies to a given production technology. Over time, however, inventions and other improvements in technology may allow the entire total product curve in Figure 6.2a to shift upward, so that more output can be produced with the same inputs. Figure 6.3 illustrates this.

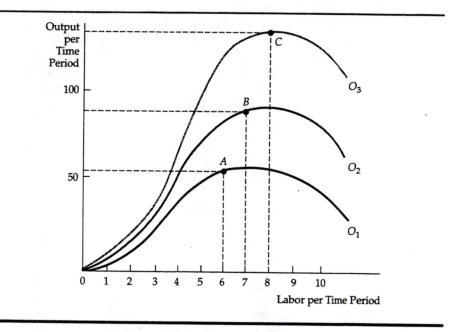

FIGURE 6.3   The Effect of Technological Improvement.   Labor productivity (output per unit of labor) can increase if there are improvements in the technology, even though any given production process exhibits diminishing returns to labor. As we move from point *A* on curve O_1 to *B* on curve O_2 to *C* on curve O_3 over time, labor productivity increases.

Initially the output curve is given by O_1, but improvements in technology may allow the curve to shift upward, first to O_2, and later to O_3.

Suppose that over time as labor is increased in production, technological improvements are also being made. Then, output changes from A (with an input of 6 on curve O_1) to B (with an input of 7 on curve O_2) to C (with an input of 8 on curve O_3). The move from A to B to C relates an increase in labor input to an increase in output and makes it appear that there are no diminishing returns when there are. For inputs greater than 6, each of the individual product curves exhibits diminishing returns to labor.

The shifting of the total product curve hides the presence of diminishing returns, and suggests that they need not have any negative long-run implications for economic growth. In fact, as we discuss in Example 6.1, the failure to account for improvements in technology in the long run led British economist Thomas Malthus wrongly to predict dire consequences from continued population growth.

EXAMPLE 6.1　MALTHUS AND THE FOOD CRISIS

The law of diminishing returns was central to the thinking of economist Thomas Malthus (1766–1834).[1] Malthus believed that the limited amount of land on our globe would not be able to supply enough food as population grew and more laborers began to farm the land. Eventually as both the marginal and average productivity of labor fell and there were more mouths to feed, mass hunger and starvation would result. Fortunately, Malthus was wrong (although he was right about the diminishing returns to labor).

TABLE 6.3　Index of World Food Consumption Per Capita[2]

Year	Index
1948–1952	100
1955	109
1960	115
1965	116
1970	123
1978	128
1987	133
1991	142

[1] Thomas Malthus, *Essay on the Principle of Population*, 1798.

[2] All but the data for 1987 and 1991 appear as Table 4–1 in Julian Simon, *The Ultimate Resource* (Princeton: Princeton University Press, 1981). The original source for all the data is the UN Food and Agriculture Organization, *Production Yearbook,* and *World Agricultural Situation.*

Over the past century, technological improvements have dramatically altered the production of food in most countries (including developing countries, such as India), so that the average product of labor has increased. These improvements include new high-yielding and disease-resistant strains of seeds, better fertilizers, and better harvesting equipment. As Table 6.3 shows, overall food production throughout the world has outpaced population growth more or less continually since the end of World War II.

Some of the increase in food production has been due to small increases in the amount of land devoted to farming. For example, from 1961 to 1975, the percentage of land devoted to agriculture increased from 32.9 percent to 33.3 percent in Africa, from 19.6 percent to 22.4 percent in Latin America, and from 21.9 percent to 22.6 percent in the Far East.[3] However, during the same period the percentage of land devoted to agriculture fell from 26.1 percent to 25.5 percent in North America, and from 46.3 percent to 43.7 percent in Western Europe. Clearly most of the improvement in food output is due to improved technology and not to increases in land used for agriculture.

Hunger remains a severe problem in some areas, such as the Sahel region of Africa, in part because of the low productivity of labor there. Although other countries produce an agricultural surplus, mass hunger still occurs because of the difficulty of redistributing foods from more to less productive regions of the world, and because of the low incomes of those less productive regions.

Labor Productivity

We sometimes measure the average product of labor for an industry or for the economy as a whole; then we refer to the results as *labor productivity*. Because the average product measures output per unit of labor input, it is relatively easy to measure (because total labor input and total output are the only pieces of information you need), and can provide useful comparisons across industries and for one industry over a long period. But productivity is especially important because it determines the real standard of living that a country can achieve for its citizens.

There is a simple link between productivity and the standard of living. In any particular year, the aggregate value of goods and services produced by an economy is equal to the payments made to all factors of production, including wages, rental payments to capital, and profit to firms. But consumers ultimately receive these factor payments, whatever their form. As a result, consumers in the aggregate can increase their rate of consumption in the long run only by increasing the total amount they produce.

[3] See Julian Simon, *The Ultimate Resource*, 83.

TABLE 6.4   Labor Productivity in Developed Countries[4]

	France	West Germany	Japan	United Kingdom	United States
	Output per Person (1990)				
	$17,431	$18,291	$17,634	$15,720	$21,449
Years	Annual Rate of Growth of Labor Productivity (%)				
1960–1973	5.4	4.5	8.6	3.6	2.2
1973–1991	2.5	2.1	2.8	1.8	0.4

As Table 6.4 shows, the level of output per person in the United States in 1990 was substantially higher than in other leading developed nations. But two patterns over the post–World War II period have been disturbing for Americans. First, productivity growth in the United States has been less rapid than productivity growth in most other developed nations. Second, productivity growth in the past two decades has been substantially lower in all developed countries than it has been in the past. Both these patterns can be seen clearly in the table.

Throughout the period 1960 to 1991, the rate of productivity growth in Japan has been the highest, followed by West Germany and France. United States productivity growth has been the lowest, even lower than that of the United Kingdom. How can this slowdown in growth be explained? And why has productivity growth in the United States been lower than elsewhere? The most important source of growth in labor productivity is the growth in the *stock of capital*. An increase in capital means more and better machinery, so that each worker can produce more output for each hour worked. Differences in the rate of growth of capital help to explain much of the data in Table 6.4. The greatest capital growth during the postwar period was in Japan and France, which were rebuilt substantially after World War II. To some extent, therefore, the lower rate of growth of productivity in the United States as compared with Japan, France, and West Germany is the result of these countries catching up after the war.

Productivity growth is also tied to the natural resource sector of the economy. As oil and other resources began to be depleted, output per worker fell somewhat. Environmental regulations (e.g., the need to restore land to its original condition after strip mining for coal) magnified this effect as the public became more concerned with the importance of cleaner air and water.

---

[4] See Angus Maddison, "Growth and Slowdown in Advanced Capitalist Countries," *Journal of Economic Literature* 25 (1987): 649–698. The more recent growth numbers are adjusted based on data from *Industrial Policy in OECD Countries, Annual Review*, 1992, and The Supplement to the *OECD Observer*, 1992, No. 176 (June/July 1992).

These factors explain part, but not all, of productivity growth over time and across different countries. A full understanding of these differences remains an important research problem in economics.

EXAMPLE 6.2   WILL THE STANDARD OF LIVING IN THE UNITED STATES IMPROVE?

Will the standard of living in the United States continue to improve, or will the economy barely keep future generations from being worse off than we are today? The answer depends on the labor productivity of U.S. workers, because the real incomes of U.S. consumers increase only as fast as productivity does.

From 1979 to 1990, productivity growth in the United States was 0.4 percent, the lowest of all major developed countries.[5] What does this mean for the average U.S. worker? In a competitive international economy, this low growth will eventually lead to lower increases in workers' wages; otherwise, higher wages would have to be matched by higher prices. But these higher prices would not be competitive in today's world economy. The result is that workers will have to absorb most of the impact of low productivity growth.

We have seen how slow growth in capital investment leads to low productivity growth. But the decline in productivity growth in the United States has other causes particular to this country. This can best be understood if we look at three major production sectors of the economy. First, during 1945–1965, many workers left farms and entered manufacturing. Agriculture has lower productivity than manufacturing, so the shift created productivity growth. (The ratio of agricultural to industrial productivity was about 0.40 in 1948, and has not changed much since.) By 1965 few people were left on the farms who could move to manufacturing, so this source of growth was exhausted.

Second, the productivity of the U.S. construction sector has declined substantially. There is no consensus about the source of this decline—it may be due in part to problems with nuclear reactor construction, and in part to problems with the interstate highway system. Whatever the cause, construction productivity has fallen and does not seem likely to increase.

Third, the movement of workers into the service sector of the economy has also dampened productivity growth in the United States, since productivity in the service sector is approximately 60 percent of the national average. By 1990, for example, over 35 percent of all hours of work were spent on service industry jobs, with a substantial portion of these hours devoted to nursing and health care and to lawyers and accountants.

Overall, this suggests that much of the slowdown in productivity growth was inevitable, and that not all of it was bad. Nursing care may be a low-productivity industry, but it is one that our society considers important. Other sources of low productivity growth include a relatively inexperienced labor

---

[5] This discussion is based in part on Lester Thurow, "The Productivity Problem," *Technology Review* (1980): 40–51; and Martin N. Baily, "What Has Happened to Productivity Growth," *Science* (Oct. 1986): 443–451.

force due to the postwar baby boom, and the inhibiting effects of government regulations involving health, safety, and the environment. Because the sources of low productivity growth are varied and complex, the standard of living cannot be increased simply by reversing what has happened in the past. But the future need not be bleak. Capital can be increased by tax policies that stimulate investment, and greater and more creative efforts can be made to encourage productivity-enhancing research and development.

6.4 Production with Two Variable Inputs

Now that we have seen the relationship between production and productivity, let's consider the firm's production technology in the long run, where both capital and labor inputs (instead of just labor) are variable. We can examine alternative ways of producing by looking at the shape of a series of isoquants.

Recall that an isoquant describes all combinations of inputs that yield the same level of output. The isoquants shown in Figure 6.4 are reproduced from Figure 6.1; they all slope downward because both labor and capital have positive marginal products. More of either input increases output; so if output is to be kept constant as more of one input is used, less of the other input must be used.

Diminishing Returns

There are diminishing returns to both labor and capital in this example. To see why there are diminishing returns to labor, draw a horizontal line at a particular level of capital, say 3. Reading the levels of output from each isoquant as labor is increased, we note that each additional unit of labor generates less and less additional output. For example, when labor is increased from 1 unit to 2 (from A to B), output increases by 20 (from 55 to 75). However, when labor is increased by an additional unit (from B to C), output increases by only 15 (from 75 to 90). Thus, there are diminishing returns to labor both in the long and short run. Because adding one factor while holding the other factor constant eventually leads to lower and lower increments to output, the isoquant must become steeper, as more capital is added in place of labor, and flatter when labor is added in place of capital.

There are also diminishing returns to capital. With labor fixed, the marginal product of capital decreases as capital is increased. For example, when capital is increased from 1 to 2 and labor is held constant at 3, the marginal product of capital is initially 20 (75 − 55), but the marginal product falls to 15 (90 − 75) when capital is increased from 2 to 3.

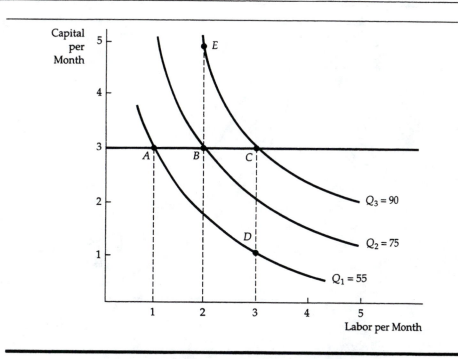

FIGURE 6.4 The Shape of Isoquants.   In the long run when both labor and capital are variable, both factors of production can exhibit diminishing returns. As we move from A to C, there are diminishing returns to labor, and as we move from D to C, there are diminishing returns to capital.

Substitution Among Inputs

With two inputs that can be varied, a manager will want to consider substituting one input for another. The slope of each isoquant indicates how the quantity of one input can be traded off against the quantity of the other, while keeping output constant. When the negative sign is removed, we call the slope the marginal rate of technical substitution (MRTS). The *marginal rate of technical substitution of labor for capital* is the amount by which the input of capital can be reduced when one extra unit of labor is used, so that output remains constant. This is analogous to the marginal rate of substitution (MRS) in consumer theory. Like the MRS, the MRTS is always measured as a positive quantity. In formal terms,

$$MRTS = -\text{Change in Capital Input/Change in Labor Input}$$

$$= -\Delta K/\Delta L \text{ (for a fixed level of } Q)$$

where ΔK and ΔL are small changes in capital and labor along an isoquant.

Note that in Figure 6.5 the MRTS is equal to 2 when labor increases from 1 unit to 2, and output is fixed at 75. However, the MRTS falls to 1 when labor

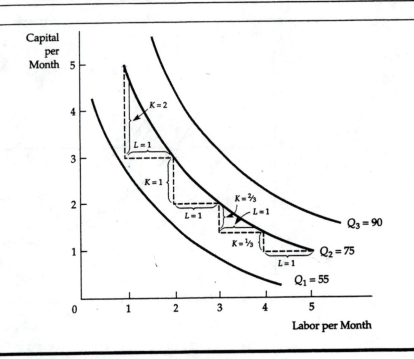

FIGURE 6.5   Marginal Rate of Technical Substitution. Isoquants are downward sloping and convex like indifference curves. The slope of the isoquant at any point measures the marginal rate of technical substitution, the ability of the firm to replace capital with labor while maintaining the same level of output. On isoquant Q_2, the marginal rate of technical substitution falls from 2 to 1 to 2/3 to 1/3.

is increased from 2 units to 3, and then declines to ⅔ and to ⅓. Clearly, as more and more labor replaces capital, labor becomes less productive and capital becomes relatively more productive. So less capital needs to be given up to keep constant the output from production, and the isoquant becomes flatter.

Isoquants are convex—the MRTS diminishes as we move down along an isoquant. The diminishing MRTS tells us that the productivity that any one input can have is limited. As a lot of labor is added to the production process in place of capital, the productivity of labor falls. Similarly, when a lot of capital is added in place of labor, the productivity of capital falls. Production needs a balanced mix of both inputs.

As our discussion has just suggested, the MRTS is closely related to the marginal products of labor MP_L and capital MP_K. To see how, imagine adding some labor and reducing the amount of capital to keep output constant. The addition to output resulting from the increased labor input is equal to the additional output per unit of additional labor (the marginal product of labor) times the number of units of additional labor:

Additional Output from Increased Use of Labor = $(MP_L)(\Delta L)$

Similarly, the decrease in output resulting from the reduction in capital is the loss of output per unit reduction in capital (the marginal product of capital) times the number of units of capital reduction:

Reduction in Output from Decreased Use of Capital = $(MP_K)(\Delta K)$

Because we are keeping output constant by moving along an isoquant, the total change in output must be zero. Thus,

$$(MP_L)(\Delta L) + (MP_K)(\Delta K) = 0$$

Now, by rearranging terms we see that

$$(MP_L)/(MP_K) = -(\Delta K/\Delta L) = MRTS \qquad (6.2)$$

Equation (6.2) tells us that as we move along an isoquant, continually replacing capital with labor in the production process, the marginal product of capital increases and the marginal product of labor decreases. The combined effect of both these changes is for the marginal rate of technical substitution to decrease as the isoquant becomes flatter.

Production Functions—Two Special Cases

Two extreme cases of production functions show the possible range of input substitution in the production process. In the first case, shown in Figure 6.6, inputs to production are *perfectly substitutable* for one another. Here the MRTS is constant at all points on an isoquant. As a result the same output (say Q_3) can be produced with mostly capital (at *A*), mostly labor (at *C*), or a balanced combination of both (at *B*). For example, a toll booth on a road or bridge might be run automatically or manned by a toll collector. Another example is musical instruments, which can be manufactured almost entirely with machine tools or with very few tools and highly skilled labor.

Figure 6.7 illustrates the opposite extreme, the *fixed-proportions production function*. In this case it is impossible to make any substitution among inputs. Each level of output requires a specific combination of labor and capital. Additional output cannot be obtained unless more capital and labor are added in specific proportions. As a result, the isoquants are L-shaped. An example is the reconstruction of concrete sidewalks using jackhammers. It takes one person to use a jackhammer—neither two people and one jackhammer nor one person and two jackhammers is likely to increase production.

In Figure 6.7 points *A*, *B*, and *C* represent technically efficient combinations of inputs. For example, to produce output Q_1, a quantity of labor L_1 and capital K_1 can be used, as at *A*. If capital stays fixed at K_1, adding more labor does not change output. Nor does adding capital with labor fixed at L_1. Thus, on the vertical and the horizontal segments of the L-shaped isoquants, either the

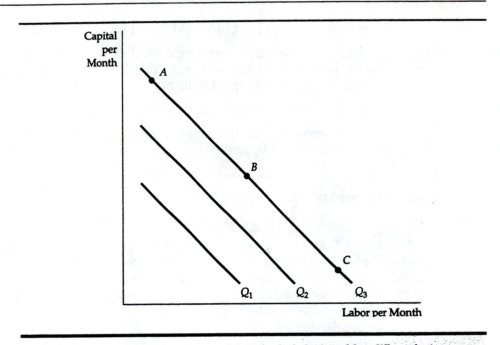

FIGURE 6.6   Isoquants When Inputs Are Perfectly Substitutable. When the isoquants are straight lines, the MRTS is constant. Hence the rate at which capital and labor can be substituted for each other is the same whatever level of inputs is being used.

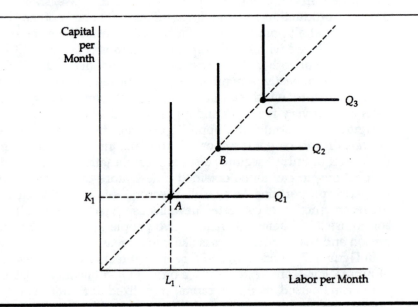

FIGURE 6.7   Fixed-Proportions Production Function. When the isoquants are L-shaped, only one combination of labor and capital can be used to produce a given output. Adding more labor does not increase output, nor does adding more capital alone.

marginal product of capital or the marginal product of labor is zero. Higher output results only when both labor and capital are added, as in the move from input combination A to input combination B.

The fixed-proportions production function describes situations in which the methods of production available to firms are limited. For example, the production of a television show might involve a certain mix of capital (camera and sound equipment, etc.) and labor (producer, director, actors, etc.). To make more television shows, all inputs to production must be increased proportionally. In particular, it would be difficult to increase capital inputs at the expense of labor, since actors are necessary inputs to production (except perhaps for animated films). Likewise, it would be difficult to substitute labor for capital, since filmmaking today requires sophisticated film equipment.

EXAMPLE 6.3 A PRODUCTION FUNCTION FOR WHEAT

Crops can be produced using different methods. Food grown on large farms in the United States is usually produced with a *capital-intensive technology*, which involves substantial investments in capital, such as buildings and equipment, and relatively little input of labor. However, food can also be produced using very little capital (a hoe) and a lot of labor (several people with the patience and stamina to work the soil). One way to describe the agricultural production process is to show one isoquant (or more) that describes the combination of inputs that generates a given level of output (or several output levels). The description that follows comes from a production function for wheat that was estimated statistically.[6]

Figure 6.8 shows one isoquant, associated with the production function, corresponding to an output of 13,800 bushels of wheat per year. The manager of the farm can use this isoquant to decide whether it is profitable to hire more labor or use more machinery. Assume the farm is currently operating at A, with a labor input L of 500 hours and a capital input K of 100 machine-hours. The manager decides to experiment by using fewer hours of machine time. To produce the same crop per year, he finds that he needs to replace this machine time by adding 260 hours of labor.

The results of this experiment tell the manager about the shape of the wheat production isoquant. When comparing points A (where $L = 500$ and $K = 100$) and B (where $L = 760$ and $K = 90$) in Figure 6.8, both of which are on the same isoquant, the manager finds that the marginal rate of technical substitution is equal to 0.04 ($-\Delta K/\Delta L = -(-10)/260 = .04$).

The MRTS tells the manager the nature of the trade-off between adding labor and reducing the use of farm machinery. Because the MRTS is substantially less than 1 in value, the manager knows that when the wage of a laborer is equal to the cost of running a machine, he ought to use more capital. (At

---

[6] The food production function on which this example is based is given by the equation $Q = 100(K^8 L^2)$, where Q is the rate of output in bushels of food per year, K is the quantity of machines in use per year, and L is the number of hours of labor per year.

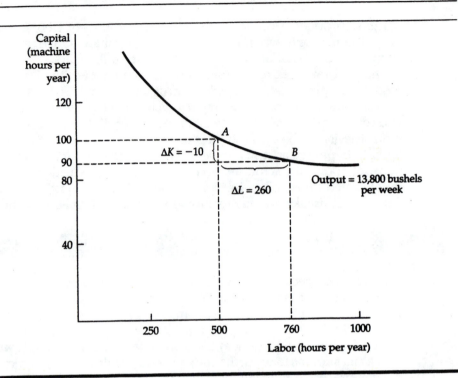

FIGURE 6.8   Isoquant Describing the Production of Wheat.   A wheat output of 13,800 bushels per week can be produced with different combinations of labor and capital. The more capital-intensive production process is shown as point A, and the more labor-intensive process as B. The marginal rate of technical substitution between A and B is 10/260 = 0.04.

his current level of production, he needs 260 units of labor to substitute for 10 units of capital.) In fact, he knows that unless labor is substantially less expensive than the use of a machine, his production process ought to become more capital-intensive.

The decision about how many laborers to hire and machines to use cannot be fully resolved until we discuss the costs of production in the next chapter. However, this example illustrates how knowledge about production isoquants and the marginal rate of technical substitution can help a manager. It also suggests why most farms in the United States and Canada, where labor is relatively expensive, operate in the range of production in which the MRTS is relatively high (with a high capital-to-labor ratio), while farms in developing countries in which labor is cheap operate with a lower MRTS (and a lower capital-to-labor ratio).[7] The exact labor/capital combination to use depends on the input prices, a subject we discuss in Chapter 7.

6.5 *Returns to Scale*

The measure of increased output associated with increases in *all* inputs is fundamental to the long-run nature of the firm's production process. How does the output of the firm change as its inputs are proportionately increased? If output more than doubles when inputs are doubled, there are *increasing returns to scale.* This might arise because the larger scale of operation allows managers and workers to specialize in their tasks and make use of more sophisticated, large-scale factories and equipment. The automobile assembly line is a famous example of increasing returns.

The presence of increasing returns to scale is an important issue from a public policy perspective. If there are increasing returns, then it is economically advantageous to have one large firm producing (at relatively low cost) than to have many small firms (at relatively high cost). Because this large firm can control the price that it sets, it may need to be regulated. For example, increasing returns in the provision of electricity is one reason why we have large, regulated power companies.

A second possibility with respect to the scale of production is that output may double when inputs are doubled. In this case, we say there are *constant returns to scale.* With constant returns to scale, the size of the firm's operation does not affect the productivity of its factors. The average and marginal productivity of the firm's inputs remains constant whether the plant is small or large. With constant returns to scale, one plant using a particular production process can easily be replicated, so that two plants produce twice as much output. For example, a large travel agency might provide the same service per client and use the same ratio of capital (office space) and labor (travel agents) as a small travel agency that services fewer clients.

Finally, output may less than double when all inputs double. This case of *decreasing returns to scale* is likely to apply to any firm with large-scale operations. Eventually, difficulties of management associated with the complexities of organizing and running a large-scale operation may lead to decreased productivity of both labor and capital. Communication between workers and managers can become difficult to monitor and the workplace more impersonal. Thus, the decreasing-returns case is likely to be associated with the problems of coordinating tasks and maintaining a useful line of communication between management and workers. Or it may result because individuals cannot exhibit their entrepreneurial abilities in a large-scale operation.

---

[7] With the production function given in footnote 6, it is not difficult (using calculus) to show that the marginal rate of technical substitution is given by MRTS = (MP_L/MP_K) = $(\frac{1}{4})(K/L)$. Thus, the MRTS decreases as the capital-to-labor ratio falls. For an interesting study of agricultural production in Israel, see Richard E. Just, David Zilberman, and Eithan Hochman, "Estimation of Multicrop Production Functions," *American Journal of Agricultural Economics* 65 (1983): 770–780.

The presence or absence of returns to scale is seen graphically in Figure 6.9. The production process is one in which labor and capital are used as inputs in the ratio of 5 hours of labor to 1 hour of machine time. The ray $0B$ from the origin describes the various combinations of labor and capital that can be used to produce output when the input proportions are kept constant.

At relatively low output levels, the firm's production function exhibits increasing returns to scale, as shown in the range from 0 to A. When the input combination is 5 hours of labor and 1 hour of machine time, 10 units of output are produced (as shown in the lowest isoquant in the figure). When both inputs double, output triples from 10 to 30 units. Then when inputs increase by one-half again (from 10 to 15 hours of labor and 2 to 3 hours of machine time), output doubles from 30 to 60 units.

At higher output levels, the production function exhibits decreasing returns to scale, as shown in the range from A to B. When the input combination increases by one-third, from 15 to 20 hours of labor and from 3 to 4 machine hours, output increases only by one-sixth, from 60 to 70 units. And when inputs increase by one-half, from 20 to 30 hours of labor and from 4 to 6 machine hours, output increases by only one-seventh, from 70 to 80 units.

Figure 6.9 shows that with increasing returns to scale, isoquants become closer and closer to one another as inputs increase proportionally. However,

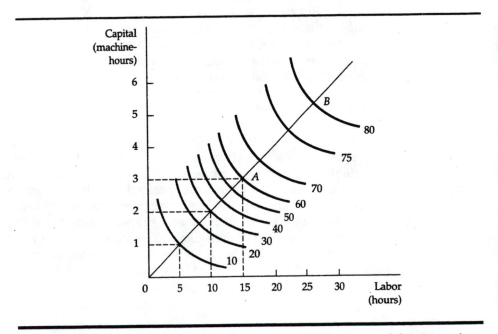

FIGURE 6.9   Returns to Scale.   When a firm's production process exhibits increasing returns to scale as shown by a movement from 0 to A along ray $0B$, the isoquants get closer and closer to one another. However, when there are decreasing returns to scale as shown by a move from A to B, the isoquants get farther apart.

with decreasing returns to scale, isoquants become farther and farther from one another, because more and more inputs are needed. When there are constant returns to scale (not shown in Figure 6.9), isoquants are equally spaced.

Returns to scale vary considerably across firms and industries. Other things equal, the greater the returns to scale, the larger firms in an industry are likely to be. Manufacturing industries are more likely to have increasing returns to scale than service-oriented industries because manufacturing involves large investments in capital equipment. Services are more labor-intensive and can usually be provided as efficiently in small quantities as they can on a large scale.

EXAMPLE 6.4   RETURNS TO SCALE IN THE RAIL INDUSTRY

During most of this century, railroads have grown larger and larger, yet their financial problems have continued to mount.[8] Does this increase in size make good economic sense? If so, why do railroads continue to have difficulty competing with other forms of transportation? We can get some insight into these questions by looking at the economics of rail freight transportation.

To see whether there are increasing returns to scale, we will measure input as *freight density*, the number of tons of railroad freight that are run per unit of time along a particular route. Output is given by the amount of a particular commodity shipped along this route within the specified time. Then we can ask whether the amount that can be shipped increases more than proportionately as we add to freight tonnage. We might expect increasing returns initially because as more freight is shipped, the railroad management can use its planning and organization to design the appropriate scheduling of the freight system efficiently. However, decreasing returns will arise at some point when there are so many freight shipments that scheduling gets difficult and rail speeds are reduced.

Most studies of the railroad industry indicate increasing returns to scale at low and moderate freight densities, but decreasing returns to scale begin to set in after a certain point (called the *efficient density*). Only when the density gets quite large is this phenomenon important, however. One study, for example, indicated increasing returns to scale up to the range of 8 to 10 million tons (per year) per route-mile, a very large freight density.

To see the practical importance of these numbers, we have tabulated the 1980 freight densities of major U.S. railroads in Table 6.5. Some railroads such as Colorado & Southern and Union Pacific have reached or surpassed the point of minimum efficient size (the point at which increasing returns to scale disappear). But many railroads operate at freight densities below this.

---

[8] This example draws on the analysis of railroad freight regulation by Theodore Keeler, *Railroads, Freight, and Public Policy* (Washington D.C.: The Brookings Institution, 1983), Chapter 3.

TABLE 6.5   Freight Densities of Major Railroads (Million Tons Per Route-Mile)

Railroad	Density
Atchison, Topeka & Santa Fe	6.03
Baltimore & Ohio	4.46
Burlington Northern	6.11
Chicago and Northwestern	3.10
Colorado & Southern	10.66
Fort Worth & Denver	6.55
Kansas City Southern	5.96
Missouri Pacific	5.01
Southern Pacific	5.35
Union Pacific	7.87
Western Pacific	3.20

Since most rail companies have not surpassed their optimum size, it appears that growth has been economically advantageous. The financial problems of the railroad industry relate more to competition from other forms of transportation than to the nature of the production process itself.

Summary

1. A *production function* describes the maximum output a firm can produce for each specified combination of inputs.

2. An *isoquant* is a curve that shows all combinations of inputs that yield a given level of output. A firm's production function can be represented by a series of isoquants associated with different levels of output.

3. In the short run, one or more inputs to the production process are fixed, whereas in the long run all inputs are potentially variable.

4. Production with one variable input, labor, can be usefully described in terms of the *average product of labor* (which measures the productivity of the average worker), and the *marginal product of labor* (which measures the productivity of the last worker added to the production process).

5. According to the "law of diminishing returns," when one or more inputs are fixed, a variable input (usually labor) is likely to have a marginal product that eventually diminishes as the level of input increases.

6. Isoquants always slope downward because the marginal product of all inputs is positive. The shape of each isoquant can be described by the marginal rate of technical substitution at each point on the isoquant. The *marginal rate of technical substitution of labor for capital* (MRTS) is the amount by which the input of capital can be reduced when one extra unit of labor is used, so that output remains constant.

7. The standard of living that a country can attain for its citizens is closely related to its level of labor productivity. Recent decreases in the rate of productivity growth in developed countries are due in part to the lack of growth of capital investment.

8. The possibilities for substitution among inputs in the production process range from a production function in which inputs are perfectly substitutable to one in which the proportions of inputs to be used are fixed (a fixed-proportions production function).

9. In the long-run analysis, we tend to focus on the firm's choice of its scale or size of operation. Constant returns to scale means that doubling all inputs leads to doubling output. Increasing returns to scale occurs when output more than doubles when inputs are doubled, whereas decreasing returns to scale applies when output less than doubles.

Questions for Review

1. What is a production function? How does a long-run production function differ from a short-run production function?

2. Why is the marginal product of labor likely to increase and then decline in the short run?

3. Diminishing returns to a single factor of production and constant returns to scale are not inconsistent. Discuss.

4. You are an employer seeking to fill a vacant position on an assembly line. Are you more concerned with the average product of labor or the marginal product of labor for the last person hired? If you observe that your average product is just beginning to decline, should you hire any more workers? What does this situation imply about the marginal product of your last worker hired?

5. Faced with constantly changing conditions, why would a firm ever keep *any* factors fixed? What determines whether a factor is fixed or variable?

6. How does the curvature of an isoquant relate to the marginal rate of technical substitution?

7. Can a firm have a production function that exhibits increasing returns to scale, constant returns to scale, and decreasing returns to scale as output increases? Discuss.

8. Give an example of a production process in which the short run involves a day or a week, and the long run any period longer than a week.

Exercises

1. Suppose a chair manufacturer is producing in the short run when equipment is fixed. The manufacturer knows that as the number of laborers used in the production process increases from 1 to 7, the number of chairs produced changes as follows: 10, 17, 22, 25, 26, 25, 23.

a. Calculate the marginal and average product of labor for this production function.

b. Does this production function exhibit diminishing returns to labor? Explain.

c. Explain intuitively what might cause the marginal product of labor to become negative.

2. Fill in the gaps in the table below.

Quantity of Variable Input	Total Output	Marginal Product of Variable Input	Average Product of Variable Input
0	0	—	—
1	150		
2			200
3		200	
4	760		
5		150	
6			150

3. A political campaign manager has to decide whether to emphasize television advertisements or letters to potential voters in a reelection campaign. Describe the production function for campaign votes. How might information about this function (such as the shape of the isoquants) help the campaign manager to plan strategy?

4. A firm has a production process in which the inputs to production are perfectly substitutable in the long run. Can you tell whether the marginal rate of technical substitution is high or low, or is further information necessary? Discuss.

5. The marginal product of labor is known to be greater than the average product of labor at a given level of employment. Is the average product increasing or decreasing? Explain.

6. The marginal product of labor in the production of computer chips is 50 chips per hour. The marginal rate of technical substitution of hours of labor for hours of machine-capital is $\frac{1}{4}$. What is the marginal product of capital?

7. Do each of the following production functions exhibit decreasing, constant, or increasing returns to scale.

   a. $Q = .5KL$

   b. $Q = 2K + 3L$

8. The production function for the personal computers of DISK, Inc., is given by $Q = 10K^5L^5$, where Q is the number of computers produced per day, K is hours of machine time, and L is hours of labor input. DISK's competitor, FLOPPY, Inc., is using the production function $Q = 10K^6L^4$.

   a. If both companies use the same amounts of capital and labor, which will generate more output?

   b. Assume that capital is limited to 9 machine hours, but labor is unlimited in supply. In which company is the marginal product of labor greater? Explain.

9. In Example 6.3, wheat is produced according to the production function $Q = 100(K^8L^2)$.

   a. Beginning with a capital input of 4 and a labor input of 49, show that the marginal product of labor and the marginal product of capital are both decreasing.

   b. Does this production function exhibit increasing, decreasing, or constant returns to scale?

CHAPTER 7

The Cost of Production

*I*n the last chapter, we examined the firm's production technology—the relationship that shows how factor inputs can be transformed into outputs. Now we will see how the production technology, together with the prices of factor inputs, determine the firm's cost of production.

Given a firm's production technology, managers must decide *how* to produce. As we saw, inputs can be combined in different ways to yield the same amount of output. For example, one can produce a certain output with a lot of labor and very little capital, with very little labor and a lot of capital, or with some other combination of the two. In this chapter we see how the *optimal* (cost-minimizing) combination of inputs is chosen. We will also see how a firm's costs depend on its rate of output, and how these costs are likely to change over time.

We begin by explaining how cost is defined and measured, distinguishing between the concept of cost used by economists, who are concerned about the firm's performance, and by accountants, who focus on the firm's financial statements. We then examine how the characteristics of the firm's production technology affect costs, both in the short run when the firm can do little to change its capital stock, and in the long run when the firm can change all its factor inputs.

We then show how the concept of returns to scale can be modified to apply to the process of producing many different outputs. We also show how cost sometimes falls over time as managers and workers learn from experience, so that the production process becomes more efficient. Finally, we show how empirical information can be used to estimate cost functions and predict future cost.

7.1 *Measuring Cost: Which Costs Matter?*

Before we can analyze how cost is determined, we need to be clear about what we mean by cost and how we measure it. What items should be included as part of a firm's cost? Cost obviously includes the wages a firm pays its workers and the rent it pays for office space. But what if the firm already owns an office building and doesn't have to pay rent? And how should we treat money that the firm spent two or three years ago (and can't recover) for equipment or for research and development? We'll answer these questions in the context of the economic decisions that managers make.

Economic Cost versus Accounting Cost

An economist thinks of cost differently from an accountant, who is concerned with the firm's financial statements. Accountants tend to take a retrospective look at a firm's finances because they have to keep track of assets and liabilities and evaluate past performance. Accounting cost includes depreciation expenses for capital equipment, which are determined on the basis of the allowable tax treatment by the Internal Revenue Service.

Economists—and we hope managers—take a forward-looking view of the firm. They are concerned with what cost is expected to be in the future, and with how the firm might be able to rearrange its resources to lower its cost and improve its profitability. They must therefore be concerned with *opportunity cost*, the cost associated with opportunities that are foregone by not putting the firm's resources to their highest value use.

For example, consider a firm that owns a building, and therefore pays no rent for office space. Does this mean that the cost of office space is zero? Although an accountant would treat this cost as zero, an economist would note that the firm could have earned rent on the office space by leasing it to another company. This foregone rent is an opportunity cost of utilizing the office space and should be included as part of the cost of doing business.

Accountants and economists both include actual outlays, called *explicit costs*, in their calculations. Explicit costs include wages, salaries, and the cost of materials and property rentals. For accountants, explicit costs are important because they involve direct payments by a company to other firms and individuals that it does business with. These costs are relevant for the economist because the cost of wages and materials represents money that could have usefully been spent elsewhere.

Let's take a look at how economic cost can differ from accounting cost in the treatment of wages and economic depreciation. For example, consider an owner who manages her own retail store but chooses not to pay herself a salary. Although no monetary transaction has occurred (and thus would not appear as an accounting cost), the business nonetheless incurs an opportunity cost because the owner could have earned a competitive salary by working elsewhere.

Accountants and economists also treat depreciation differently. When estimating the future profitability of a business, an economist or manager is concerned with the capital cost of plant and machinery. This involves not only the explicit cost of buying and then running the machinery, but also the cost associated with wear and tear. When evaluating past performance, accountants use tax rules that apply to broadly defined types of assets to determine allowable depreciation in their cost and profit calculations. But these depreciation allowances need not reflect the actual wear and tear on the equipment, which is likely to vary asset by asset.

Sunk Costs

Although opportunity cost is often hidden, it should be taken into account when making economic decisions. Just the opposite is true of sunk cost—it is usually visible, but after it has been incurred, it should always be ignored when making future economic decisions.

A *sunk cost* is an expenditure that has been made and cannot be recovered. Because it cannot be recovered, it should not influence the firm's decisions. For example, consider the purchase of specialized equipment designed to order for a plant. We assume the equipment can be used to do only what it was originally designed for and can't be converted for alternative use. The expenditure on this equipment is a sunk cost. Because it has no alternative use, its opportunity cost is zero. Thus it shouldn't be included as part of the firm's costs.[1] The decision to buy this equipment may have been good or bad. It doesn't matter. It's water under the bridge and shouldn't affect the firm's current decisions.

For example, suppose a firm is considering moving its headquarters to a new city. Last year it paid $500,000 for an option to buy a building in the city; the option gives it the right to buy the building at a cost of $5,000,000, so that its total expenditure will be $5,500,000 if it indeed buys the building. Now it finds that a comparable building has become available in the same city at a price of $5,250,000. Which building should it buy? The answer is the original building. The $500,000 option is a cost that has been sunk and that should not affect the firm's current decision. The economic cost of the original property is $5,000,000 to the firm (because the sunk cost of the option is not part of the economic cost), while the newer property has an economic cost of $5,250,000. Of course, if the new building cost $4,750,000, the firm should buy it, and forgo its option.

---

[1] If, on the other hand, the equipment could be put to other use, or be sold or rented to another firm, its current economic cost would be measured by the value from its next most profitable use.

EXAMPLE 7.1   CHOOSING THE LOCATION FOR A NEW LAW SCHOOL BUILDING

The Northwestern University Law School has long been located in Chicago, along the shores of Lake Michigan. However, the main campus of the university is located in the suburb of Evanston. In the mid-1970s, the law school began planning the construction of a new building and needed to decide on an appropriate location. Should it be built on the current site in the city, where it would remain near the downtown law firms? Or should it be moved to Evanston, where it would become physically integrated with the rest of the university?

The downtown location had many prominent supporters. They argued in part that it was cost-effective to locate the new building in the city because the university already owned the land, whereas a large parcel of land would have to be purchased in Evanston if the building were to be built there. Does this argument make economic sense?

No. It makes the common mistake of failing to distinguish accounting costs from economic costs. From an economic point of view, it is very expensive to locate downtown because the opportunity cost of the valuable lakeshore location is high—that property could have been sold for enough money to buy the Evanston land with substantial funds left over.

In the end, Northwestern decided to keep the law school in Chicago. This was a costly decision. It may have been appropriate if the Chicago location was particularly valuable to the law school, but the decision was inappropriate if it was made on the presumption that the downtown land was without cost.

EXAMPLE 7.2   THE OPPORTUNITY COST OF WAITING IN A GASOLINE LINE

As a result of gasoline price controls in the spring of 1980, Chevron gasoline stations in California were required to lower their prices substantially below those of other major gasoline companies.[2] This allowed an experiment to be conducted in which consumers revealed information about the opportunity cost of their time.

In this experiment, 109 customers at one Chevron station and 61 customers at two competing stations nearby were surveyed.[3] The consumers could ei-

---

[2] This special treatment for Chevron stations occurred because these stations were owned and operated by Standard Oil of California. Stations owned by integrated oil companies such as SoCal were affected by the ceiling, but those operated by franchised dealers were not.

[3] The survey was by Robert T. Deacon and Jon Sonstelie, "Rationing by Waiting and the Value of Time: Results from a Natural Experiment," *Journal of Political Economy* 93 (1985): 627–647.

ther buy high-priced gasoline with little or no wait, or wait almost 15 minutes longer to buy lower-priced Chevron gasoline.

Many respondents chose to wait in line for the lower-priced Chevron gasoline, presumably because they valued their time less than the savings they could obtain when they bought the lower-priced gasoline. Suppose, for example, that a motorist could save $0.25 per gallon by waiting for 20 minutes at the Chevron station, and that there would be no wait at the other stations. If she bought ten gallons of gasoline, the total savings would be $2.50. Because she chose to wait in line, the opportunity cost of her time must be less than $2.50 per 20 minutes, or $7.50 per hour. Suppose another person chose to buy gasoline at one of the stations where there was no waiting. Then the opportunity cost of his time must be at least $7.50 per hour. By using this general approach, and by noting that Chevron patrons bought 53 percent more gasoline than the patrons of the other two stations, we can estimate the opportunity cost of waiting time.

Table 7.1 provides some lower- and upper-bound estimates of the opportunity cost of time, in dollars per hour, obtained from the study. Part-time workers displayed the lowest value of time. They could earn additional money working, but that did not conflict with waiting in gas lines because their schedules were flexible. Students' opportunity costs are relatively high because class work is time consuming and because those students who work part time have relatively inflexible schedules and could be working more rather than waiting in gas lines. For all groups, the opportunity cost of time was found to increase with income. This is not surprising; we would expect that the higher the wage one can earn, the greater the opportunity cost of waiting in line to buy lower-priced gas.

This example shows that consumers' as well as firms' decisions are typically based on economic or opportunity cost and not on accounting cost. Everyone would have saved money at the Chevron gas station, and thus made an accounting profit, but many people chose not to because the opportunity cost was too high.

TABLE 7.1   Opportunity Cost of Time

Category	Lower Bound	Upper Bound
Students	$7.15	$10.96
Part-time workers	3.52	5.39
Income $20,000–$30,000	6.51	9.44
Income $30,000–$40,000	8.93	13.70
Income over $40,000	11.26	17.26

7.2 Cost in the Short Run

In the short run, some of the firm's inputs to production are fixed, while others can be varied as the firm changes its output. Various measures of the cost of production can be distinguished on this basis.

Total Cost (TC) The total cost of production has two components: the *fixed cost* FC, which is borne by the firm whatever level of output it produces, and the *variable cost* VC, which varies with the level of output. Depending on circumstances, fixed cost may include expenditures for plant maintenance, insurance, and perhaps a minimal number of employees—this cost remains the same no matter how much the firm produces. Variable cost includes expenditures for wages, salaries, and raw materials—this cost increases as output increases.

Fixed cost does not vary with the level of output—it must be paid even if there is no output. It can be eliminated only by shutting down altogether. (In Chapter 8 we will see that a firm may decide to go out of business and thereby forgo its (future) outlays on fixed costs.)

To decide how much to produce, managers of firms need to know how variable cost increases with the level of output. To address this issue, we need to develop some additional cost measures. We will use a specific example that typifies the cost situation of many firms. After we explain each of the cost concepts, we will describe how they relate to our previous analysis of the firm's production process.

The data in Table 7.2 describe a firm with a fixed cost of $50. Variable cost increases with output, as does total cost. The total cost is the sum of the fixed cost in column (1) and the variable cost in column (2). From the figures given in columns (1) and (2), a number of additional cost variables can be defined.

Marginal Cost (MC) Marginal cost—sometimes called incremental cost—is the increase in cost that results from producing one extra unit of output. Because fixed cost does not change as the firm's level of output changes, marginal cost is just the increase in variable cost that results from an extra unit of output. We can therefore write marginal cost as

$$MC = \Delta VC / \Delta Q$$

Marginal cost tells us how much it will cost to expand the firm's output by one unit. In Table 7.2, marginal cost is calculated from either the variable cost (column 2) or the total cost (column 3). For example, the marginal cost of increasing output from 2 to 3 units is $20 because the variable cost of the firm increases from $78 to $98. (Total cost of production also increases by $20, from $128 to $148. Total cost differs from variable cost only by the fixed cost, which by definition does not change as output changes.)

Average Cost (AC) Average cost is the cost per unit of output. Average total cost (ATC) is the firm's total cost divided by its level of output TC/Q. Thus, the

Rate of Output	Fixed Cost	Variable Cost	Total Cost	Marginal Cost	Average Fixed Cost	Average Variable Cost	Average Total Cost
	(FC) (1)	(VC) (2)	(TC) (3)	(MC) (4)	(AFC) (5)	(AVC) (6)	(ATC) (7)
0	50	0	50	—	—	—	—
1	50	50	100	50	50	50	100
2	50	78	128	28	25	39	64
3	50	98	148	20	16.7	32.7	49.3
4	50	112	162	14	12.5	28	40.5
5	50	130	180	18	10	26	36
6	50	150	200	20	8.3	25	33.3
7	50	175	225	25	7.1	25	32.1
8	50	204	254	29	6.3	25.5	31.8
9	50	242	292	38	5.6	26.9	32.4
10	50	300	350	58	5	30	35
11	50	385	435	85	4.5	35	39.5

average total cost of producing at a rate of five units is $36, $180/5. Basically, average total cost tells us the per-unit cost of production. By comparing the average total cost to the price of the product, we can determine whether production is profitable.

ATC has two components. *Average fixed cost* AFC is the fixed cost (column 1) divided by the level of output, FC/Q. For example, the average fixed cost of producing four units of output is $12.50 ($50/4). Because fixed cost is constant, average fixed cost declines as the rate of output increases. *Average variable cost* (AVC) is variable cost divided by the level of output VC/Q. The average variable cost of producing five units of output is $26, $130 divided by 5.

The Determinants of Short-Run Cost

Table 7.2 shows that variable and total costs increase with output. The rate at which these costs increase depends on the nature of the production process, and in particular on the extent to which production involves diminishing returns to variable factors. Recall from Chapter 6 that diminishing returns to labor occurs when the marginal product of labor is decreasing. If labor is the only variable factor, what happens as we increase the firm's rate of output? To produce more output, the firm has to hire more labor. Then, if the marginal product of labor decreases rapidly as the amount of labor hired is increased (owing to diminishing returns), greater and greater expenditures must be made to produce output at the faster rate. As a result, variable and total costs increase rapidly as the rate of output is increased. On the other hand, if the marginal product of labor decreases only slightly as the amount of labor is increased, costs will not rise so fast when the rate of output is increased.[4]

Let's look at the relationship between production and cost in more detail by concentrating on the costs of a firm that can hire as much labor as it wishes at a fixed wage w. Recall that marginal cost MC is the change in variable cost for a one-unit change in output (i.e., $\Delta VC/\Delta Q$). But the variable cost is the per-unit cost of the extra labor w times the amount of extra labor ΔL. It follows, then, that

$$MC = \Delta VC/\Delta Q = w\Delta L/\Delta Q$$

The marginal product of labor MP_L is the change in output resulting from a one-unit change in labor input, or $\Delta Q/\Delta L$. Therefore, the extra labor needed to obtain an extra unit of output is $\Delta L/\Delta Q = 1/MP_L$. As a result,

$$MC = w/MP_L \qquad (7.1)$$

Equation (7.1) states that in the short run, marginal cost is equal to the price of the input that is being varied divided by its marginal product. Suppose, for example, that the marginal product of labor is 3 and the wage rate is $30 per hour. Then, one hour of labor will increase output by 3 units, so that 1 unit of output will require ⅓ hour of labor, and will cost $10. The marginal cost of producing that unit of output is $10, which is equal to the wage, $30, divided by the marginal product of labor, 3. A low marginal product of labor means that a large amount of additional labor is needed to produce more output, which leads to a high marginal cost. A high marginal product means that the labor requirement is low, as is the marginal cost. More generally, whenever the marginal product of labor decreases, the marginal cost of production increases, and vice versa.[5]

The effect of the presence of diminishing returns in the production process can also be seen by looking at the data on marginal costs in Table 7.2. The marginal cost of additional output is high at first because the first few inputs to production are not likely to raise output much in a large plant with a lot of equipment. However, as the inputs become more productive, the marginal cost decreases substantially. Finally, marginal cost increases again for relatively high levels of output, owing to the effect of diminishing returns.

The law of diminishing returns also creates a direct link between the average variable cost of production and the average productivity of labor. Average variable cost AVC is the variable cost per unit of output, or VC/Q. When L units of labor are used in the production process, the variable cost is wL. Thus,

$$AVC = wL/Q$$

---

[4] We are implicitly assuming that labor is hired in competitive markets, so that the payment per unit of factor used is the same no matter what the firm's output.

[5] With two or more variable inputs, the relationship is more complex, but still the greater the productivity of factors, the less the variable cost that the firm must incur to produce any given level of output.

Recall from Chapter 6 that the average product of labor AP_L is given by the output per unit of input Q/L. As a result

$$AVC = w/AP_L \qquad (7.2)$$

Since the wage rate is fixed from the firm's perspective, there is an inverse relationship between average variable cost and the average product of labor. Suppose, for example, that the average product of labor is 5 and the wage rate is $30 per hour. Then, each hour of labor will increase output on average by 5 units, so that each unit of output will require ⅕ hour of labor, and will cost $6. The average variable cost of producing each unit of output is $6, which is equal to the wage, $30, divided by the average product of labor, 5. A lower marginal product of labor means that a lot of labor is needed to produce the firm's output, which leads to a high average variable cost. A high average product of labor means that the labor required for production is low, as is the average variable cost.

We have seen that with both marginal cost and average variable cost, there is a direct link between the productivity of factors of production and the costs of production. Marginal and average product tell us about the relationship between inputs and output. The comparable cost variables tell us about the budgetary implications of that production information.

The Shapes of the Cost Curves

Figure 7.1 shows two sets of continuous curves that approximate the cost data in Table 7.2. The fixed cost, variable cost, and total cost curves are shown in Figure 7.1a. Fixed cost FC does not vary with output and is shown as a horizontal line at $50. Variable cost VC is zero when output is zero, and then increases continuously as output increases. The total cost curve TC is determined by vertically adding the fixed cost curve to the variable cost curve. Because fixed cost is constant, the vertical distance between the two curves is always $50.

Figure 7.1b shows the corresponding set of marginal and average variable cost curves.[6] Since total fixed cost is $50, the average fixed cost curve AFC falls continuously from $50 toward zero. The shape of the remaining short-run cost curves is determined by the relationship between the marginal and average cost curves. Whenever marginal cost lies below average cost, the average cost curve falls. Whenever marginal cost lies above average cost, the average cost curve rises. And when average cost is at a minimum, marginal cost equals average cost. Marginal and average costs are another example of the average-marginal relationship described in Chapter 6 (with respect to marginal and

---

[6] Because the marginal cost represents the change in cost associated with a change in output, we have plotted the marginal cost curve associated with the first unit of output by setting output equal to ½, for the second unit by setting output equal to 1½, and so on.

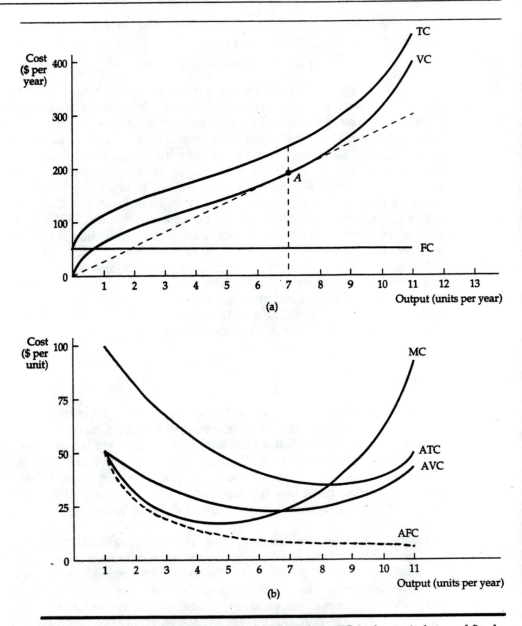

FIGURE 7.1   Cost Curves for a Firm.   In (a) total cost TC is the vertical sum of fixed cost FC and variable cost VC. In (b) average total cost ATC is the sum of average variable cost AVC and average fixed cost AFC. Marginal cost MC crosses the average variable cost and average total cost curves at their minimum points.

average product). For example, at $20 marginal cost is below the average variable cost of $25, and the average is lowered. But when marginal cost is $30, which is greater than average variable cost ($25), the average increases. Finally, when marginal cost ($25) and average cost ($25) are the same, the average variable cost remains unchanged (at $25).

The ATC curve shows the average total cost of production. Since average total cost is the sum of average variable cost and average fixed cost and the AFC curve declines everywhere, the vertical distance between the ATC and AVC curves decreases as output increases. The AVC cost curve achieves its minimum point at a lower output than the ATC curve. This follows because MC = AVC at its minimum point, and MC = ATC at its minimum point. Since ATC is always greater than AVC and the marginal cost curve MC is rising, the minimum point of the ATC curve must lie above and to the right of the minimum point of the AVC curve.

Another way to see the relationship between the total cost curves and the average and marginal cost curves is to consider the ray from origin to point A in Figure 7.1a. In that figure the slope of the ray measures average variable cost (a total cost of $175 divided by an output of 7, or a cost per unit of $25). Since the slope of the VC curve is the marginal cost (it measures the change in variable cost as output increases by one unit), the tangent to the VC curve at A is the marginal cost of production when output is 7. At A this marginal cost of $25 is equal to the average variable cost of $25, since average variable cost is minimized at this output.[7]

Note that the firm's output is measured as a flow; the firm produces a certain number of units *per year*. Hence its total cost is a flow, for example, some number of dollars per year. (Average and marginal costs, however, are measured in dollars *per unit*.) For simplicity, we will often drop the time reference, and refer to total cost in dollars and output in units. But you should remember that a firm's production of output and expenditure of cost occur over some time period. Also, for simplicity, we will often use *cost* (C) to refer to total cost. Likewise, unless noted otherwise, we will use *average cost* (AC) to refer to average total cost.

Marginal and average cost are important concepts. As we will see in Chapter 8, they enter critically into the firm's choice of output level. Knowledge of short-run costs is particularly important for firms that operate in an environment in which demand conditions fluctuate considerably. If the firm is currently producing at a level of output at which marginal cost is sharply increasing, and demand may increase in the future, the firm might want to expand its production capacity to avoid higher costs.

---

[7] The relationships just described hold only approximately when we are describing discrete rather than infinitesimal changes in output. Thus, at an output of 8, average total cost is approximately, but not identically, equal to marginal cost.

7.3 Cost in the Long Run

In the long run, the firm can change all its inputs. In this section we show how to choose the combination of inputs that minimizes the cost of producing a given output. We will also examine the relationship between long-run cost and the level of output.

The Cost-Minimizing Input Choice

Let's begin by considering a fundamental problem that all firms face: *how to select inputs to produce a given output at minimum cost.* For simplicity, we will work with two variable inputs: labor (measured in hours of work per year) and capital (measured in hours of use of machinery per year). We assume that both labor and capital can be hired (or rented) in competitive markets. The price of labor is the wage rate w, and the price of capital is the rental rate for machinery r. We assume that capital is rented rather than purchased, so that we can put all business decisions on a comparable basis. For example, labor services might be hired at a wage of $12,000 per year, or capital might be "rented" for $75,000 per machine per year.

Because capital and labor inputs are hired in competitive factor markets, we can take the price of these inputs as fixed. We can then focus on the firm's optimal combination of factors, without worrying about whether large purchases will cause the price of an input to increase.[8]

The Isocost Line

We begin by looking at the cost of hiring factor inputs, which can be represented by a firm's isocost lines. An *isocost line* includes all possible combinations of labor and capital that can be purchased for a given total cost. To see what an isocost line looks like, recall that the total cost C of producing any particular output is given by the sum of the firm's labor cost wL and its capital cost rK:

$$C = wL + rK \qquad (7.3)$$

For each different level of total cost, equation (7.3) describes a different isocost line. For example, in Figure 7.2, the isocost line C_0 describes all possible combinations of inputs that cost C_0 to purchase.

If we rewrite the total cost equation (7.3) as an equation for a straight line, we get:

[8] This might happen because of overtime or a relative shortage of capital equipment. We discuss the possibility of a relationship between the prices of factor inputs and the quantities demanded by a firm in Chapter 14.

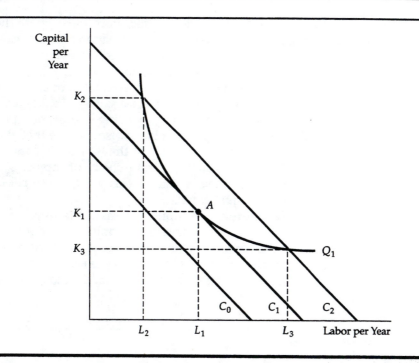

FIGURE 7.2   Producing a Given Output at Minimum Cost. Isocost curves describe the combination of inputs to production that cost the same amount to the firm. Isocost curve C_1 is tangent to isoquant Q_1 at A and shows that output Q_1 can be produced at minimum cost with labor input K_1 and capital input L_1. Other input combinations—L_2, K_2 and L_3, K_3—yield the same output at higher cost.

$$K = C/r - (w/r)L$$

It follows that the isocost line has a slope of $\Delta K/\Delta L = -(w/r)$, which is the ratio of the wage rate to the rental cost of capital. This slope is similar to the slope of the budget line that the consumer faces (because it is determined solely by the prices of the goods in question, whether inputs or outputs). It tells us that if the firm gave up a unit of labor (and recovered w dollars in cost) to buy w/r units of capital at a cost of r dollars per unit, its total cost of production would remain the same. For example, if the wage rate were $10 and the rental cost of capital $5, the firm could replace one unit of labor with two units of capital, with no change in total cost.

Choosing Inputs

Suppose we wish to produce output level Q_1. How can we do this at minimum cost? Look at the firm's production isoquant, labeled Q_1, in Figure 7.2. The problem is to choose the point on this isoquant that minimizes total costs.

Figure 7.2 illustrates the solution to this problem. Suppose the firm were to spend C_0 on inputs. Unfortunately, no combination of inputs can be purchased for expenditure C_0 that will allow the firm to achieve output Q_1. Output Q_1 can be achieved with the expenditure of C_2, however, either by using K_2 units of capital and L_2 units of labor, or by using K_3 units of capital and L_3 units of labor. But C_2 is not the minimum cost. The same output Q_1 can be produced more cheaply than this, at a cost of C_1, by using K_1 units of capital and L_1 units of labor. In fact, isocost line C_1 is the lowest isocost line that allows output Q_1 to be produced. The point of tangency of the isoquant Q_1 and the isocost line C_1 at point A tells us the cost-minimizing choice of inputs, L_1 and K_1, which can be read directly from the diagram. At this point, the slopes of the isoquant and the isocost line are just equal.

When the expenditure on all inputs increases, the slope of the isocost line does not change (because the prices of the inputs have not changed), but the intercept increases. Suppose, however, that the price of one of the inputs, such as labor, were to increase. Then, the slope of the isocost line $-(w/r)$ would increase in magnitude, and the isocost line would become steeper. Figure 7.3

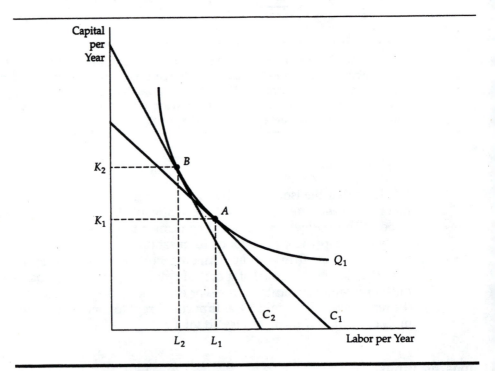

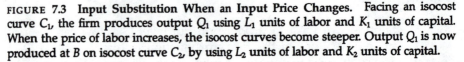

FIGURE 7.3   Input Substitution When an Input Price Changes.   Facing an isocost curve C_1, the firm produces output Q_1 using L_1 units of labor and K_1 units of capital. When the price of labor increases, the isocost curves become steeper. Output Q_1 is now produced at B on isocost curve C_2, by using L_2 units of labor and K_2 units of capital.

shows this. Initially, the isocost line is C_1, and the firm minimizes its costs of producing output Q_1 at A by using L_1 units of labor and K_1 units of capital. When the price of labor increases, the isocost line becomes steeper. The isocost line C_2 reflects the higher price of labor. Facing this higher price of labor, the firm minimizes its cost of producing output Q_1 by producing at B, using L_2 units of labor and K_2 units of capital. The firm has responded to the higher price of labor by substituting capital for labor in the production process.

How does this relate to the firm's production process? Recall that in our analysis of production technology, we showed that the marginal rate of technical substitution MRTS of labor for capital is the negative of the slope of the isoquant, and is equal to the ratio of the marginal products of labor and capital.

$$\text{MRTS} = -\Delta K/\Delta L = \text{MP}_L/\text{MP}_K \tag{7.4}$$

Above, we noted that the isocost line has a slope of $\Delta K/\Delta L = -w/r$. It follows that when a firm minimizes the cost of producing a particular output, the following condition holds:

$$\text{MP}_L/\text{MP}_K = w/r$$

Rewriting this condition slightly,

$$\text{MP}_L/w = \text{MP}_K/r \tag{7.5}$$

Equation (7.5) tells us that when cost is minimized, each dollar of input added to the production process will add an equivalent amount to output. Assume, for example, that the wage rate is $10 and the rental rate on capital is $2. If the firm chooses inputs so that the marginal product of labor and the marginal product of capital are equal to ten, it will want to hire less labor and rent more capital because capital is five times less expensive than labor. The firm can minimize its cost only when the production of an additional unit of output costs the same regardless of which additional input is used.

EXAMPLE 7.3   THE EFFECT OF EFFLUENT FEES ON FIRMS' INPUT CHOICES

Steel plants are often built on or near a river. A river offers readily available, inexpensive transportation for both the iron ore that goes into the production process and the finished steel itself. A river also provides a cheap method of disposing of by-products of the production process, called effluent. For example, a steel plant processes its iron ore for use in blast furnaces by grinding taconite deposits into a fine consistency. During this process, the ore is extracted by a magnetic field as a flow of water and fine ore passes through the plant. One by-product of this process—fine taconite particles—can be dumped in the river at relatively little cost to the firm, whereas alternative removal methods or private treatment plants are relatively expensive.

Because the taconite particles are a nondegradable waste that can harm vegetation and fish, the Environmental Protection Agency (EPA) has imposed an effluent fee—a per-unit fee that the steel firm must pay for the effluent that goes into the river. How should the manager of the firm respond to the imposition of this effluent fee to minimize the costs of production?

Suppose that without regulation the steel firm is producing 2000 tons of steel per month, while using 2000 machine-hours of capital and 10,000 gallons of water (which contains taconite particles when returned to the river). The manager of the firm estimates that a machine-hour costs $40, and dumping each gallon of waste water in the river costs the firm $10. (The total cost of production is therefore $180,000: $80,000 for capital and $100,000 for waste water.) How should the manager respond to an EPA-imposed effluent fee of $10 per gallon of waste water dumped?

Figure 7.4 shows the cost-minimizing response. The vertical axis measures the firm's input of capital in machine-hours per month, and the horizontal axis measures the quantity of waste water in gallons per month. First, consider how the firm produces when there is no effluent fee. Point A represents

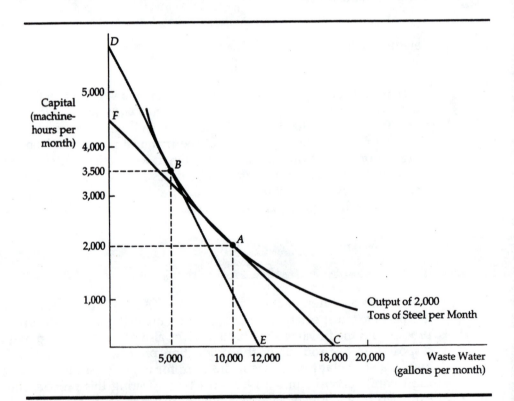

FIGURE 7.4   **The Cost-Minimizing Response to an Effluent Fee.**   When the firm is not charged for dumping its waste water in a river, it chooses to produce a given output using 10,000 gallons of waste water and 2000 machine-hours of capital at A. However, an effluent fee raises the cost of waste water, shifts the isocost curve from FC to DE, and causes the firm to produce at B, with much less effluent.

the input of capital and the level of waste water that allows the firm to produce its quota of steel at minimum cost. Because the firm is minimizing cost, A lies on the isocost line FC, which is tangent to the isoquant. The slope of the isocost line is equal to −$10/$40 = −0.25 because a unit of capital costs four times more than a unit of waste water.

When the effluent fee is imposed, the cost of waste water increases from $10 per gallon to $20, because for every gallon of waste water (which costs $10), the firm has to pay the government an additional $10. The effluent fee increases the cost of waste water relative to capital. To produce the same output at the lowest possible cost, the manager must choose the isocost line with a slope of −$20/$40 = −0.5, which is tangent to the isoquant. In Figure 7.4, DE is the appropriate isocost line, and B gives the appropriate choice of capital and waste water. The move from A to B shows that with an effluent fee the use of an alternative production technology, which emphasizes the use of capital (3500 machine-hours) and uses less waste water (5000 gallons), is cheaper than the original process, which did not emphasize recycling. (The total cost of production has increased to $240,000: $140,000 for capital, $50,000 for waste water, and $50,000 for the effluent fee.)

We can learn two lessons from this decision. First, the more easily factors can be substituted in the production process, that is, the more easily the firm can deal with its taconite particles without using the river for waste treatment, the more effective the fee will be in reducing effluent. Second, the greater the degree of substitution, the less the firm will have to pay. In our example, the fee would have been $100,000 had the firm not changed its inputs. However, the steel company pays only a $50,000 fee by moving production from A to B.

Cost Minimization with Varying Output Levels

In the previous section we saw how a cost-minimizing firm selects a combination of inputs to produce a given level of output. Now we extend this analysis to see how the firm's costs depend on its output level. To do this we determine the firm's cost-minimizing input quantities for each output level, and then calculate the resulting cost.

The cost-minimization exercise yields a result such as that shown in Figure 7.5. Each of the points A, B, C, D, and E represents a tangency between an isocost curve and an isoquant for the firm. The curve which moves upward and to the right from the origin, tracing out the points of tangency, is the firm's *expansion path*. The expansion path describes the combinations of labor and capital that the firm will choose to minimize costs for every output level. So long as the use of both inputs increases as output increases, the curve will look approximately as shown in Figure 7.5. The firm's expansion path shows the lowest long-run total cost of producing each level of output.

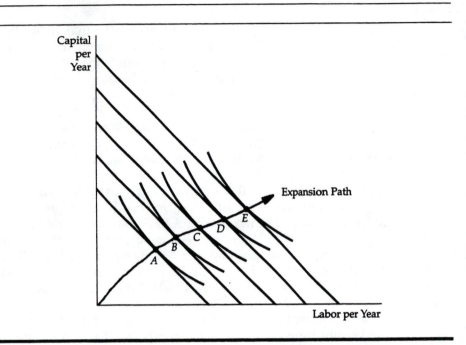

FIGURE 7.5   A Firm's Expansion Path.   The expansion path illustrates the least-cost combinations of labor and capital that can be used to produce each level of output in the long run when both inputs to production can be varied.

7.4 *Long-Run Versus Short-Run Cost Curves*

We saw earlier (see Figure 7.1) that short-run average cost curves are U-shaped. We will see that long-run average cost curves can also be U-shaped, but different economic factors explain the shapes of these curves. In this section, we discuss long-run average and marginal cost curves and highlight the differences between these curves and their short-run counterparts.

The Inflexibility of Short-Run Production

Recall that in the long run all inputs to the firm are variable, because its planning horizon is long enough to allow for a change in plant size. This added flexibility allows the firm to produce at a lower average cost than in the short run. To see why, we might compare the situation in which capital and labor are both flexible to the case in which capital is fixed in the short run.

Figure 7.6 shows the firm's production isoquants. Suppose capital is fixed at a level K_1 in the short run. To produce output Q_1, the firm would minimize costs by choosing labor equal to L_1, corresponding to the point of tangency with the isocost line AB. The inflexibility appears when the firm decides to increase its output to Q_2. If capital were not fixed, it would produce this output with capital K_2 and labor L_2. Its cost of production would be reflected by isocost line CD. However, the fixed capital forces the firm to increase its output by using capital K_1 and labor L_3 at P. Point P lies on the isocost line EF, which represents a higher cost than isocost line CD. The cost of production is higher when capital is fixed because the firm is unable to substitute relatively inexpensive capital for more costly labor when it expands its production.

Long-Run Average Cost

In the long run, the ability to change the amount of capital allows the firm to reduce costs. To see how costs vary as the firm moves along its expansion path

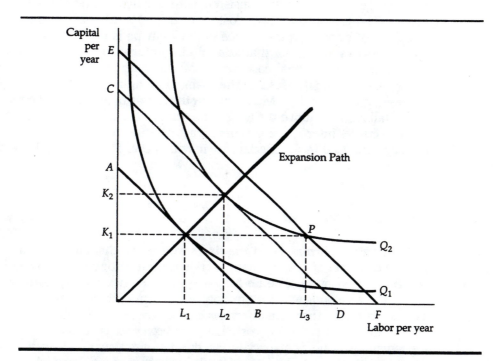

FIGURE 7.6   The Inflexibility of Short-Run Production.   When a firm operates in the short run, its cost of production may not be minimized because of inflexibility in the use of capital inputs. Output is initially at level Q_1. In the short run, output Q_2 can be produced only by increasing labor from L_1 to L_3 because capital is fixed at K_1. In the long run, the same output can be produced more cheaply by increasing labor from L_1 to L_2 and capital from K_1 to K_2.

in the long run, we can look at the long-run average and marginal cost curves.[9] The most important determinant of the shape of the long-run average and marginal cost curves is whether there are increasing, constant, or decreasing returns to scale. Suppose, for example, that the firm's production process exhibits constant returns to scale at all levels of output. Then a doubling of inputs leads to a doubling of output. Because input prices remain unchanged as output increases, the average cost of production must be the same for all levels of output.

Suppose instead that the firm's production process is subject to increasing returns to scale. A doubling of inputs leads to more than a doubling of output. Then the average cost of production falls with output because a doubling of costs is associated with a more than twofold increase in output. By the same logic, when there are decreasing returns to scale, the average cost of production must be increasing with output.

In the last chapter, we saw that in the long run most firms' production technologies first exhibit increasing returns to scale, then constant returns to scale, and eventually decreasing returns to scale. Figure 7.7 shows a typical long-run average cost curve LAC consistent with this description of the production process. The long-run average cost curve is U-shaped, just like the short-run average cost curve, but the source of the U-shape is increasing and decreasing returns to scale, rather than diminishing returns to a factor of production.

The long-run marginal cost curve LMC is determined from the long-run average cost curve; it measures the change in long-run total costs as output is increased incrementally. LMC lies below the long-run average cost curve when LAC is falling, and above the long-run average cost curve when LAC is rising. The two curves intersect at *A*, where the long-run average cost curve achieves its minimum. And in the special case in which LAC is constant, LAC and LMC are equal.

Economies and Diseconomies of Scale

In the long run, it may be in the firm's interest to change the input proportions as the level of output changes. When input proportions do change, the concept of returns to scale no longer applies. Rather, we say that a firm enjoys *economies of scale* when it can double its output for less than twice the cost. Correspondingly, there are *diseconomies of scale* when a doubling of output requires more than twice the cost. The term *economies of scale* includes increasing returns to scale as a special case, but it is more general because it allows input combinations to be altered as the firm changes its level of production. In this more general setting, a U-shaped long-run average cost curve is con-

---

[9] We saw that in the short run the shapes of the average and marginal cost curves were determined primarily by diminishing returns. As we showed in Chapter 6, diminishing returns to each factor are consistent with constant (or even increasing) returns to scale.

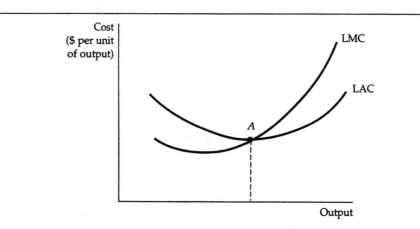

FIGURE 7.7   **Long-Run Average and Marginal Cost.** When a firm is producing at an output at which the long-run average cost LAC is falling, the long-run marginal cost LMC is less than long-run average cost. When long-run average cost is increasing, long-run marginal cost is greater than long-run average cost.

sistent with the firm facing economies of scale for relatively low output levels and diseconomies of scale for higher levels.

Economies of scale are often measured in terms of a cost-output elasticity, E_c. E_c is the percentage change in the average cost of production resulting from a one percent increase in output:

$$E_c = (\Delta C/C)/(\Delta Q/Q) \qquad (7.6)$$

To see how E_c relates to our traditional measures of cost, rewrite equation (7.6) as follows:

$$E_c = (\Delta C/\Delta Q)/(C/Q) = MC/AC \qquad (7.7)$$

Clearly, E_c is equal to one when marginal and average costs are equal; then costs increase proportionately with output, and there are neither economies nor diseconomies of scale (constant returns to scale would apply if input proportions were fixed). When there are economies of scale (costs increase less than proportionately with output), marginal cost is less than average cost (both are declining), and E_c is less than one. Finally, when there are diseconomies of scale, marginal cost is greater than average cost, and E_c is greater than one.

The Relationship Between Short-Run and Long-Run Cost

Figures 7.8 and 7.9 show the relationship between short-run and long-run cost. Assume a firm is uncertain about the future demand for its product and is considering three alternative plant sizes. The short-run average cost curves for

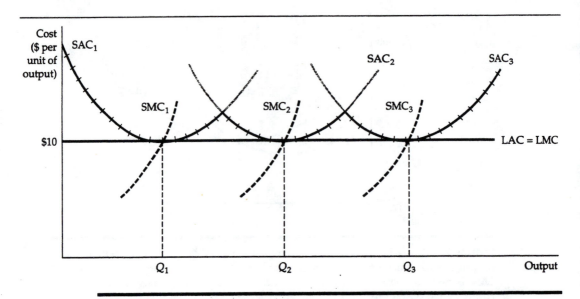

FIGURE 7.8 **Long-Run Cost with Constant Returns to Scale.** The long-run average cost curve LAC, which is identical to the long-run marginal cost curve LMC, is the envelope of the short-run average cost curves (SAC₁, SAC₂, and SAC₃ are shown). With constant returns to scale, the long-run average cost curve consists of the minimum points of the short-run average cost curves.

the three plants are given by SAC_1, SAC_2, and SAC_3 in Figure 7.8. The decision is important because, once built, the firm may not be able to change the plant size for some time.

Figure 7.8 shows the case in which there are constant returns to scale in the long run. If the firm were expecting to produce Q_1 units of output, then it should build the smallest plant. Its average cost of production would be $10; this is the minimum cost because the short-run marginal cost SMC crosses short-run average cost SAC when both equal $10. If the firm is to produce Q_2 units of output, the middle-sized plant is best, and its average cost of production is again $10. If it is to produce Q_3, it moves to the third plant. With only these plant sizes, any production choice between Q_1 and Q_2 will entail an increase in the average cost of production, as will any level of production between Q_2 and Q_3.

What is the firm's long-run cost curve? In the long run, the firm can change the size of its plant, so if it was initially producing Q_1 and wanted to increase output to Q_2 or Q_3, it could do so with no increase in average cost. The long-run average cost curve is therefore given by the cross-hatched portions of the short-run average cost curves because these show the minimum cost of production for any output level. The long-run average cost curve is the *envelope* of the short-run average cost curves—it envelops or surrounds the short-run curves.

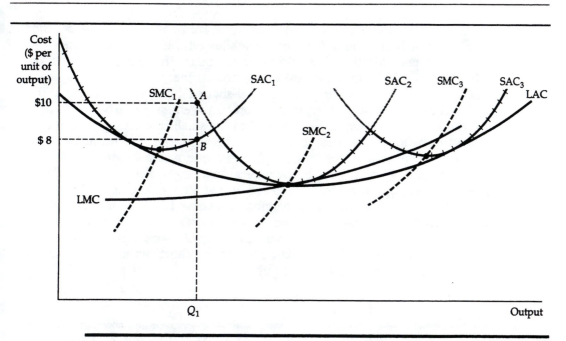

FIGURE 7.9   Long-Run Cost with Economies and Diseconomies of Scale.   The long-run average cost curve LAC is the envelope of the short-run average cost curves (SAC₁, SAC₂, and SAC₃). With economies and diseconomies of scale, the minimum points of the short-run average cost curves do not lie on the long-run average cost curve.

Now suppose there are many choices of plant size, each of which has a short-run average cost curve that has its minimum at the $10 level. Again, the long-run average cost curve is the envelope of the short-run curves. In Figure 7.8 it is the straight line LAC. Whatever the firm wants to produce, it can choose the plant size (and the mix of capital and labor) that allows it to produce that output at the minimum average cost of $10.

With economies or diseconomies of scale, the analysis is essentially the same, but the long-run average cost curve is no longer a horizontal line. Figure 7.9 illustrates the typical case in which three plant sizes are possible; the minimum average cost is lowest for a medium-sized plant. The long-run average cost curve, therefore, exhibits economies of scale initially, but at higher output levels it exhibits diseconomies. Once again, the cross-hatched lines show the envelope associated with the three plants.

To clarify the relationship between the short-run and the long-run cost curves, consider a firm that wants to produce output Q_1 in Figure 7.9. If it builds a small plant, the short-run average cost curve SAC₁ is relevant, so that the average cost of production (at B on SAC₁) is $8. A small plant is a better choice than a medium-sized plant with an average cost of production of $10 ($A$ on curve SAC₂). Point B would, therefore, become one point on the long-run cost function when only three plant sizes are possible. If plants of other sizes could be built, and at least one size allowed the firm to produce Q_1 at less than \$8 per unit, then B would no longer be on the long-run cost curve.

In Figure 7.9, the envelope that would arise if plants of any size could be built is given by the LAC curve, which is U-shaped. Note, once again, that the LAC curve never lies above any of the short-run average cost curves. Also note that the points of minimum average cost of the smallest and largest plants do *not* lie on the long-run average cost curve because there are economies and diseconomies of scale in the long run. For example, a small plant operating at minimum average cost is not efficient because a larger plant can take advantage of increasing returns to scale to produce at a lower average cost.

Finally, note that the long-run marginal cost curve LMC is not the envelope of the short-run marginal cost curves. Short-run marginal costs apply to a particular plant; long-run marginal costs apply to all possible plant sizes. Each point on the long-run marginal cost curve is the short-run marginal cost associated with the most cost-efficient plant.

7.5 *Production with Two Outputs—Economies of Scope*

Many firms produce more than one product. Sometimes a firm's products are closely linked to one another—a chicken farm produces poultry and eggs, an automobile company produces automobiles and trucks, and a university produces teaching and research. Other times, firms produce products that are physically unrelated. In both cases, however, a firm is likely to enjoy production or cost advantages when it produces two or more products. These advantages could result from the joint use of inputs or production facilities, joint marketing programs, or possibly the cost savings of a common administration. In some cases, the production of one product gives an automatic and unavoidable by-product that is valuable to the firm. For example, sheet metal manufacturers produce scrap metal and shavings they can sell.

To study the economic advantages of joint production, let's consider an automobile company that produces two products, cars and tractors. Both products use capital (factories and machinery) and labor as inputs. Cars and tractors are not typically produced at the same plant, but they do share management resources, and both rely on similar machinery and skilled labor. The managers of the company must choose how much of each product to produce. Figure 7.10 shows two *product transformation curves*. Each curve shows the various combinations of cars and tractors that can be produced with a given input of labor and machinery. Curve O_1 describes all combinations of the two outputs that can be produced with a relatively low level of inputs, and curve O_2 describes the output combinations associated with twice the inputs.

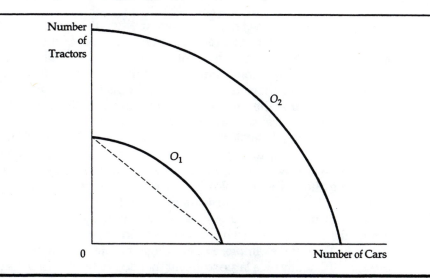

FIGURE 7.10 Product Transformation Curve. The product transformation curve describes the different combinations of two outputs that can be produced with a fixed amount of production inputs. The product transformation curves O_1 and O_2 are bowed out (or concave) because there are economies of scope in production.

The product transformation curve has a negative slope because to get more of one output, the firm must give up some of the other output. For example, a firm that emphasizes car production will devote less of its resources to producing tractors. In this case, curve O_2 lies twice as far from the origin as curve O_1, signifying that this firm's production process exhibits constant returns to scale in the production of both commodities.[10]

If curve O_1 were a straight line, joint production would entail no gains (or losses). One smaller company specializing in cars and another in tractors would generate the same output as the single company that produces both. However, the product transformation curve is bowed outward (or *concave*) because joint production usually has advantages that enable a single company to produce more cars and tractors with the same resources than would two companies producing each product separately. These production advantages involve the joint sharing of inputs. A single management is often able to schedule and organize production and to handle accounting and financial aspects more effectively than separate managements could.

[10] Our discussion would be more complex if it incorporated the possibility of diseconomies or economies of scale. For a more general analysis of economies of scope, see Elizabeth E. Bailey and Ann F. Friedlaender, "Market Structure and Multiproduct Industries: A Review Article," *Journal of Economic Literature* 20 (Sept. 1982): 1024–1048, or John C. Panzar and Robert D. Willig, "Economies of Scope," *American Economic Review* 71 (May 1981): 268–272.

In general, *economies of scope* are present when the *joint output of a single firm is greater than the output that could be achieved by two different firms each producing a single product* (with equivalent production inputs allocated between the two firms). If a firm's joint output is *less* than that which could be achieved by separate firms, then its production process involves *diseconomies of scope*. This could occur if the production of one product somehow conflicted with the production of the second product.

There is no direct relationship between economies of scale and economies of scope. A two-output firm can enjoy economies of scope even if its production process involves diseconomies of scale. Suppose, for example, that manufacturing flutes and piccolos jointly is cheaper than producing both separately. Yet the production process involves highly skilled labor and is most effective if undertaken on a small scale. Likewise, a joint-product firm can have economies of scale for each individual product, yet not enjoy economies of scope. Imagine, for example, a large conglomerate that owns several firms that produce efficiently on a large scale but that do not take advantage of economies of scope because they are administered separately.

The extent to which there are economies of scope can also be determined by studying a firm's costs. If a combination of inputs used by one firm generates more output than two independent firms would produce, then it costs less for a single firm to produce both products than it would cost the independent firms. To measure the degree to which there are economies of scope, we should ask what percentage of the cost of production is saved when two (or more) products are produced jointly rather than individually. Equation (7.8) gives the *degree of economies of scope* (SC) that measures this savings in cost:

$$SC = \frac{C(Q_1) + C(Q_2) - C(Q_1, Q_2)}{C(Q_1, Q_2)} \qquad (7.8)$$

$C(Q_1)$ represents the cost of producing output Q_1, $C(Q_2)$ the cost of producing output Q_2, and $C(Q_1, Q_2)$ the joint cost of producing both outputs. (When the physical units of output can be added, as in the car-tractor example, the expression becomes $C(Q_1 + Q_2)$.) With economies of scope, the joint cost is less than the sum of the individual costs, so that SC is greater than 0. With diseconomies of scope, SC is negative. In general, the larger the value of SC, the greater the economies of scope.

EXAMPLE 7.4 ECONOMIES OF SCOPE IN THE TRUCKING INDUSTRY

Suppose that you are managing a trucking firm that hauls loads of different sizes between cities.[11] In the trucking business, several related but distinct products can be offered depending on the size of the load and the length of

---

[11] This example is based on Judy S. Wang Chiang and Ann F. Friedlaender, "Truck Technology and Efficient Market Structure," *Review of Economics and Statistics* 67 (1985): 250–258.

the haul. First, any load, small or large, can be taken directly from one location to another without intermediate stops. Second, a load can be combined with other loads, which may go between different locations, and eventually be shipped indirectly from its origin to the appropriate destination. And each type of load, partial or full, may involve different lengths of haul.

This raises questions about both economies of scale and economies of scope. The scale question is whether large-scale, small, direct hauls are cheaper and more profitable than individual hauls by small truckers. The scope question is whether a large trucking firm enjoys cost advantages from operating both direct quick hauls and indirect, slower (but less expensive) hauls. Central planning and organization of routes could provide for economies of scope. The key to the presence of economies of scale is the fact that the organization of routes and the types of hauls we have described can be accomplished more efficiently when many hauls are involved. Then it will be more likely that hauls can be scheduled that allow most truckloads to be full, rather than half-full.

Studies of the trucking industry show that economies of scope are present. For example, an analysis of 105 trucking firms in 1976 looked at four distinct outputs: (1) short hauls with partial loads, (2) intermediate hauls with partial loads, (3) long hauls with partial loads, and (4) hauls with total loads. The results indicate that the degree of economies of scope SC was 1.576 for a reasonably large firm. However, the degree of economies of scope falls to 0.104 when the firm becomes very large. Large firms carry sufficiently large truckloads, so there is usually no advantage to stopping at an intermediate terminal to fill a partial load. A direct trip from the origin to the destination is sufficient. Apparently, however, other disadvantages are associated with the management of very large firms, so the economies of scope get smaller as the firm gets bigger. In any event, the ability to combine partial loads at an intermediate location lowers the firm's costs and increases its profitability.

The study suggests, therefore, that to compete in the trucking industry a firm must be large enough to be able to combine loads at intermediate stopping points.

*7.6 Dynamic Changes in Costs— The Learning Curve

Our discussion has suggested one reason a large firm may have a lower long-run average cost than a small firm—increasing returns to scale in production. It is tempting to conclude that firms that enjoy lower average cost over time are growing firms with increasing returns to scale. But this need not be true. In some firms, long-run average cost may decline over time because workers and managers absorb new technological information as they become more experienced at their jobs.

As management and labor gain experience with production, the firm's marginal and average cost of producing a given level of output falls for four reasons. First, workers often take longer to accomplish a given task the first few times they do it. As they become more adept, their speed increases. Second, managers learn to schedule the production process more effectively, from the flow of materials to the organization of the manufacturing itself. Third, engineers, who are initially very cautious in their product designs, may gain enough experience to be able to allow for tolerances in design that save cost without increasing defects. Better and more specialized tools and plant organization may also lower cost. Fourth, suppliers of materials may learn how to process materials required by the firm more effectively and may pass on some of this advantage to the firm in the form of lower materials cost.

As a consequence, a firm "learns" over time as cumulative output increases. Managers use this learning process to help plan production and to forecast future costs. Figure 7.11 illustrates this process, in the form of a learning curve. A *learning curve* describes the relationship between a firm's cumulative output and the amount of inputs needed to produce a unit of output.

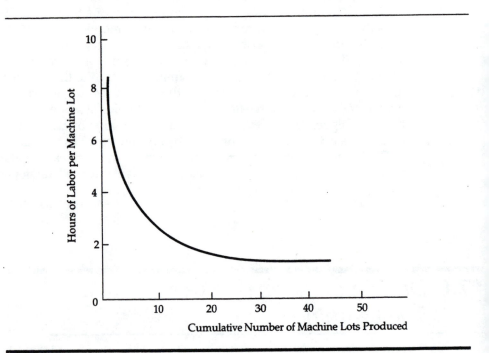

FIGURE 7.11   The Learning Curve.   A firm's cost of production may fall over time as the managers and workers become more experienced and more effective at using the available plant and equipment. The learning curve shows the extent to which the hours of labor needed per unit of output (a machine in this case) fall as the cumulative output (number of machines) produced increases.

Figure 7.11 shows a learning curve for the production of machine tools by a manufacturer.[12] The horizontal axis measures the *cumulative* number of lots of machine tools that the firm has produced (a lot is a group of approximately 40 machines), and the vertical axis the number of hours of labor needed to produce each lot. Labor input per unit of output directly affects the firm's cost of production because the fewer the hours of labor needed, the lower the marginal and average cost of production.

The learning curve in the figure is based on the relationship

$$L = A + BN^{-\beta} \tag{7.9}$$

where N is the cumulative units of output produced, L is the labor input per units of output, and A, B, and β are constants, with A and B positive, and β between 0 and 1. When N is equal to 1, L is equal to $A + B$, so that $A + B$ measures the labor input required to produce the first unit of output. When β equals 0, labor input per unit of output remains the same as the cumulative level of output increases, so there is no learning. When β is positive and N gets larger and larger, L becomes arbitrarily close to A, so that A represents the minimum labor input per unit of output after all learning has taken place.

The larger is β, the more important is the learning effect. With β equal to 0.5, for example, the labor input per unit of output falls proportionally to the square root of the cumulative output. This degree of learning can substantially reduce the firm's production costs as the firm becomes more experienced.

In this machine tool example, the value of β is 0.31. For this particular learning curve, every doubling in cumulative output causes the difference between the input requirement and the minimum attainable input requirement to fall by about 20 percent.[13] As Figure 7.11 shows, the learning curve drops sharply as the cumulative number of lots produced increases to about 20. Beyond an output of 20 lots, the cost savings are relatively small.

Once the firm has produced 20 or more machine lots, the entire effect of the learning curve would be complete, and the usual analysis of cost could be employed. If, however, the production process were relatively new, then relatively high cost at low levels of output (and relatively low cost at higher levels) would indicate learning effects, and not economies of scale. With learning, the cost of production for a mature firm is relatively low irrespective of the scale of the firm's operation. If a firm that produces machine tools in groups (or "lots") knows that it enjoys economies of scale, it should produce its machines in very large lots to take advantage of the lower cost associated with size. If there is a learning curve, the firm can lower its cost by scheduling the production of many lots irrespective of the individual lot size.

Figure 7.12 shows this phenomenon. AC_1 represents the long-run average cost of production of a firm that enjoys economies of scale in production. Thus, the change in production from A to B along AC_1 leads to lower

---

[12] See Werner Z. Hirsch, "Manufacturing Progress Functions," *Review of Economics and Statistics* 34 (May 1952): 143–155.

[13] Because $(L - A) = BN^{-.31}$, one can check that $0.8(L - A)$ is approximately equal to $B(2N)^{-.31}$.

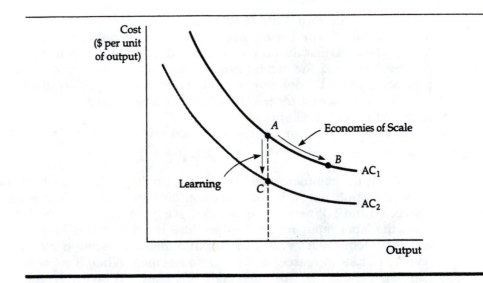

FIGURE 7.12   Economies of Scale Versus Learning.   A firm's average cost of production can decline over time because of growth of sales when increasing returns are present (a move from A to B on curve AC_1), or it can decline because there is a learning curve (a move from A on curve AC_1 to C on curve AC_2).

cost due to economies of scale. However, the move from A on AC_1 to C on AC_2 leads to lower cost due to learning, which shifts the average cost curve downward.

The learning curve is crucial for a firm that wants to predict the cost of producing a new product. Suppose, for example, that a firm producing machine tools knows that its labor requirement per machine for the first 10 machines is 1.0, the minimum labor requirement A is equal to zero, and β is approximately equal to 0.32. Table 7.3 calculates the total labor requirement for producing 80 machines.

Because there is a learning curve, the per-unit labor requirement falls with increased production. As a result, the total labor requirement for producing more and more output increases in smaller and smaller increments. Therefore, a firm looking at the high initial labor requirement will obtain an overly pessimistic view of the business. Suppose the firm plans to be in business for a long time and the total labor requirement for each year's product is 10. In the first year of production, the labor requirement is 10, so the firm's cost will be high as it learns the business. But once the learning effect has taken place, production costs will be lower. After 8 years, the labor requirement will be only 0.51, and per-unit cost will be roughly half what it was in the first year of production. Thus, learning curve effects can be important for a firm deciding whether it is profitable to enter an industry.

TABLE 7.3   Predicting the Labor Requirements of Producing a Given Output

Cumulative Output (N)	Per-Unit Labor Requirement for each 10 units of Output (L)[14]	Total Labor Requirement
10	1.00	10.0
20	.80	18.0 (10.0 + 8.0)
30	.70	25.0 (18.0 + 7.0)
40	.64	31.4 (25.0 + 6.4)
50	.60	37.4 (31.4 + 6.0)
60	.56	43.0 (37.4 + 5.6)
70	.53	48.3 (43.0 + 5.3)
80 and over	.51	53.4 (48.3 + 5.1)

EXAMPLE 7.5   THE LEARNING CURVE IN THE CHEMICAL PROCESSING INDUSTRY

Suppose that as the manager of a firm that has just entered the chemical processing industry you face the following problem: Should you produce a relatively low level of output (and sell at a high price), or should you price your product lower and increase your rate of sales? The second alternative is particularly appealing if there is a learning curve in this industry. Then the increased volume will lower your average production costs over time and increase the firm's profitability.

To decide what to do, you can examine the available statistical evidence that distinguishes the components of the learning curve (learning new processes by labor, engineering improvements, etc.) from increasing returns to scale. A study of 37 chemical products from the late 1950s to 1972 reveals that cost reductions in the chemical processing industry were directly tied to the growth of cumulative industry output, to investment in improved capital equipment, and to a lesser extent to economies of scale.[15] In fact, for the entire sample of chemical products, average costs of production fell at 5.5 percent per year.[16] The study reveals that for each doubling of plant scale, the average cost of production falls by 11 percent. For each doubling of cumulative output, how-

---

[14] The numbers in this column were calculated from the equation $\log(L) = -0.322 \log(N/10)$, where L is the unit labor input and N is cumulative output.

[15] The study was by Marvin Lieberman, "The Learning Curve and Pricing in the Chemical Processing Industries," *RAND Journal of Economics* 15 (1984): 213–228.

[16] The author used the average cost AC of the chemical products, the cumulative industry output X, and the average scale of a production plant Z and estimated the relationship $\log (AC) = -0.387 \log (X) - 0.173 \log (Z)$. The -0.387 coefficient on cumulative output tells us that for every 1 percent increase in cumulative output, average cost decreases 0.387 percent. The -0.173 coefficient on plant size tells us that for every 1 percent increase in plant size, cost decreases 0.173 percent.

ever, the average cost of production falls by 27 percent. The evidence shows clearly that learning effects are more important than economies of scale in the chemical processing industry.[17]

Learning curve effects can be important in determining the shape of long-run cost curves and can thus help guide the firm's manager. The manager can use learning curve information to decide whether a production operation is profitable, and if it is, to plan how large the plant operation and the volume of cumulative output need be before a positive cash flow will result.

*7.7 Estimating and Predicting Cost

A business that is expanding or contracting its operation needs to predict how costs will change as output changes. Estimates of future costs can be obtained from a *cost function*, which relates the cost of production to the level of output and other variables that the firm can control.

Suppose we wanted to characterize the short-run cost of production in the automobile industry. We could obtain data on the number of automobiles Q produced by each car company and relate this information to the variable cost of production VC. The use of variable cost, rather than total cost, avoids the problem of trying to allocate the fixed cost of a multiproduct firm's production process to the particular product being studied.[18]

Figure 7.13 shows a typical pattern of cost and output data. Each point on the graph relates the output of an auto company to that company's variable cost of production. To predict cost accurately, we need to determine the underlying relationship between variable cost and output. Then, if a company expands its production, we can calculate what the associated cost is likely to be. The curve in the figure is drawn with this in mind—it provides a reasonably close fit to the cost data. (Typically, least-squares regression analysis would be used to fit the curve to the data.) But what shape of curve is the most appropriate, and how do we represent that shape algebraically?

One cost function that might be chosen is

$$VC = \alpha + \beta Q \tag{7.10}$$

[17] By interpreting the two coefficients in footnote 16 in light of the levels of the output and plant size variables, one can allocate about 15 percent of the cost reduction to increases in the average scale of plants, and 85 percent to increases in cumulative industry output. (Suppose plant scale doubled, while cumulative output increased by a factor of 5 during the study. Then costs would fall by 11 percent from the increased scale and by 62 percent from the increase in cumulative output.)

[18] If an additional piece of equipment is needed as output increases, then annual rental cost of the equipment should be counted as a variable cost. If, however, the same machine can be used at all output levels, then its cost is fixed and should not be included.

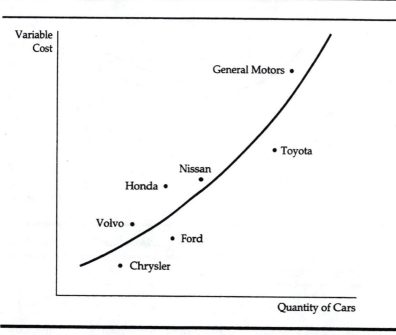

FIGURE 7.13   **Total Cost Curve for the Automobile Industry.**   An empirical estimate of the total cost curve can be obtained by using data for individual firms in an industry. The total cost curve for automobile production is obtained by determining statistically the curve that best fits the points that relate the output of each firm to the total cost of production.

This *linear* relationship between cost and output is easy to use but is applicable only if marginal cost is constant.[19] For every unit increase in output, variable cost increases by β, so marginal cost is constant and equal to β. (α is also a component of variable cost but it varies with factors other than output.)

If we wish to allow for a U-shaped average cost curve and a marginal cost that is not constant, we must use a more complex cost function. One possibility, shown in Figure 7.14, is the *quadratic* cost function, which relates variable cost to output and output squared:

$$VC = \alpha + \beta Q + \gamma Q^2 \qquad\qquad (7.11)$$

This implies a straight-line marginal cost curve of the form $MC = \beta + 2\gamma Q$.[20] Marginal cost increases with output if γ is positive, and decreases with output if γ is negative. Average cost, given by $AC = \alpha/Q + \beta + \gamma Q$, is U-shaped when γ is positive.

---

[19] In statistical cost analyses, other variables might be added to the cost function to account for differences in input costs, production processes, product mix, etc., among firms.

[20] Short-run marginal cost is given by $\Delta TVC/\Delta Q = \beta + \gamma\Delta(Q^2)/\Delta Q$. But $\Delta(Q^2)/\Delta Q = 2Q$. (Check this using calculus or by numerical example.) Therefore, $MC = \beta + 2\gamma Q$.

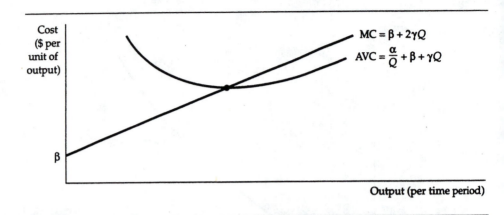

FIGURE 7.14   Quadratic Cost Function.   A quadratic function is useful for either short-run or long-run cost functions when the average cost curve is U-shaped and the marginal cost curve is linear.

If the marginal cost curve is not linear, we might use a *cubic* cost function:

$$VC = \alpha + \beta Q + \gamma Q^2 + \delta Q^3 \qquad\qquad (7.12)$$

Figure 7.15 shows this cubic cost function. It implies U-shaped marginal as well as average cost curves.

Cost functions can be difficult to measure. First, output data often represent an aggregate of different types of products. Total automobiles produced by General Motors, for example, involves different models of cars. Second, cost data are often obtained directly from accounting information that fails to re-

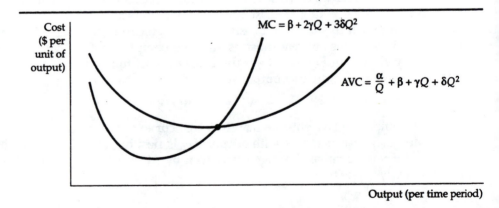

FIGURE 7.15   Cubic Cost Function.   A cubic cost function implies that the average and the marginal cost curves are U-shaped.

flect opportunity costs. Third, allocating maintenance and other plant costs to a particular product is difficult when the firm is a conglomerate that produces more than one product line.

Cost Functions and the Measurement of Scale Economies

Recall that the cost-output elasticity E_c is less than one when there are economies of scale and greater than one when there are diseconomies of scale. An alternative index, the *scale economies index* (SCI), is defined as follows:

$$SCI = 1 - E_c \qquad (7.13)$$

When $E_c = 1$, SCI $= 0$, and there are no economies or diseconomies of scale. When E_c is greater than one, SCI is negative, and there are diseconomies of scale. Finally, when E_c is less than 1, SCI is positive, and there are economies of scale.

EXAMPLE 7.6   COST FUNCTIONS FOR ELECTRIC POWER

In 1955, consumers bought 369 billion kilowatt-hours (kwh) of electricity; in 1970 they bought 1083 billion. Because there were fewer electric utilities in 1970, the output per firm had increased substantially. Was this increase due to economies of scale or other reasons? If it was the result of economies of scale, it would be economically inefficient for regulators to "break up" electric utility monopolies.

An interesting study of scale economies was based on the years 1955 and 1970 for investor-owned utilities with more than $1 million in revenues.[21] The cost of electric power was estimated by using a cost function that is somewhat more sophisticated than the quadratic and cubic functions discussed earlier.[22] Table 7.4 shows the resulting estimates of the Scale Economies Index (SCI). The results are based on a classification of all utilities into 5 size categories, with the median output (measured in kilowatt-hours) in each category listed.

The positive values of SCI tell us that all sizes of firms had some economies of scale in 1955. However, the magnitude of the economies of scale diminishes as firm size increases. The average cost curve associated with the 1955 study

TABLE 7.4   Scale Economies in the Electric Power Industry

Output (million kwh)	43	338	1109	2226	5819
Value of SCI, 1955	.41	.26	.16	.10	.04

---

[21] This example is based on Laurits Christensen and William H. Greene, "Economies of Scale in U.S. Electric Power Generation," *Journal of Political Economy* 84 (1976): 655–676.

[22] The translog cost function that was used provides a more general functional relationship than any of those we have discussed.

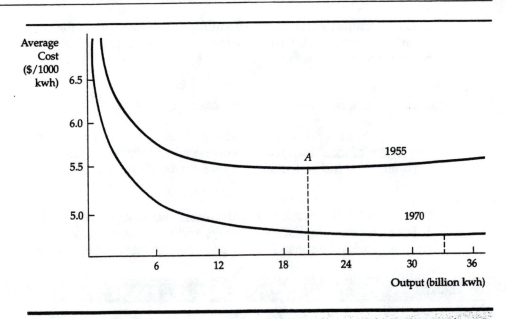

FIGURE 7.16   Average Cost of Production in the Electric Power Industry.   The average cost of electric power in 1955 achieved a minimum at approximately 20 billion kilowatt-hours. By 1970 the average cost of production had fallen sharply and achieved a minimum at an output of greater than 32 billion kilowatt-hours.

is drawn in Figure 7.16 and labeled 1955. The point of minimum average cost occurs at point A at an output of approximately 20 billion kilowatts. Because there were no firms of this size in 1955, no firm had exhausted the opportunity for returns to scale in production. Note, however, that the average cost curve is relatively flat from an output of 9 billion kilowatts and higher, a range in which 7 of 124 firms produced.

When the same cost functions were estimated with 1970 data, the cost curve, labeled 1970 in Figure 7.16, was the result. The graph shows clearly that the average costs of production fell from 1955 to 1970. (The data are in real 1970 dollars.) But the flat part of the curve now begins at about 15 billion kwh. By 1970, 24 of 80 firms were producing in this range. Thus, many more firms were operating in the flat portion of the average cost curve in which economies of scale are not an important phenomenon. More important, most of the firms were producing in a portion of the 1970 cost curve that was flatter than their point of operation on the 1955 curve. (Five firms were at a point of diseconomies of scale: Consolidated Edison [SCI = −0.003], Detroit Edison [SCI = −0.004], Duke Power [SCI = −0.012], Commonwealth Edison [SCI = −0.014], and Southern [SCI = −0.028].) Thus, unexploited scale economies were much smaller in 1970 than in 1955.

This cost function analysis makes it clear that the decline in the cost of producing electric power cannot be explained by the ability of larger firms to take advantage of economies of scale. Rather, improvements in technology unrelated to the scale of the firms' operation and the decline in the real cost of energy inputs, such as coal and oil, are important reasons for the lower costs. The tendency toward lower average cost caused by a movement to the right along an average cost curve is minimal compared with the effect of technological improvement.

EXAMPLE 7.7 A COST FUNCTION FOR THE SAVINGS AND LOAN INDUSTRY

Understanding returns to scale in the savings and loan industry is important for regulators who must decide how savings and loans should be restructured in light of the failure of numerous institutions. In this regard, the empirical estimation of a long-run cost function can be useful.[23]

Data were collected for 86 savings and loan associations for 1975 and 1976 in a region that includes Idaho, Montana, Oregon, Utah, Washington, and Wyoming. Output is difficult to measure in this case because a savings and loan association provides a service to its customers, rather than a physical product. The output Q measure reported here (and used in other studies) is the total assets of each savings and loan association. In general, the larger the asset base of an association, the higher its profitability. Long-run average cost LAC is measured by average operating expense. Output and total operating costs are measured in hundreds of millions of dollars. Average operating costs are measured as a percentage of total assets.

A quadratic long-run average cost function was estimated for the year 1975, yielding the following relationship:

$$LAC = 2.38 - 0.6153Q + 0.0536Q^2$$

The estimated long-run average cost function is U-shaped and reaches its point of minimum average cost when the total assets of the savings and loan reach $574 million.[24] (At this point the average operating expenses of the savings and loan are 0.61 percent of its total assets.) Because almost all savings and loans in the region being studied had substantially less than $574 million in assets, the cost function analysis suggests that an expansion of savings and loans through either growth or mergers would be valuable.

How appropriate such a policy is cannot be fully evaluated here, however. To do so, we would need to take into account the possible social costs associated with the lessening of competition from growth or mergers, and we would

---

[23] This example builds on J. Holton Wilson, "A Note on Scale Economies in the Savings and Loan Industry," *Business Economics* (Jan. 1981): 45–49.

[24] This can be seen by graphing the curve, or by differentiating the average cost function with respect to Q, setting it equal to 0, and solving for Q.

need to assure ourselves that this particular cost function analysis accurately estimated the point of minimum average cost.

Summary

1. Managers, investors, and economists must take into account the opportunity cost associated with the use of the firm's resources—the cost associated with the opportunities foregone when the firm uses its resources in its next best alternative.

2. In the short run, one or more of the inputs of the firm are fixed. Total cost can be divided into fixed cost and variable cost. A firm's *marginal cost* is the additional variable cost associated with each additional unit of output. The *average variable cost* is the total variable cost divided by the number of units of output.

3. When there is a single variable input, as in the short run, the presence of diminishing returns determines the shape of the cost curves. In particular, there is an inverse relationship between the marginal product of the variable input and the marginal cost of production. The average variable cost and average total cost curves are U-shaped. The short-run marginal cost curve increases beyond a certain point, and cuts both average cost curves from below at their minimum points.

4. In the long run, all inputs to the production process are variable. As a result, the choice of inputs depends both on the relative costs of the factors of production and on the extent to which the firm can substitute among inputs in its production process. The cost-minimizing input choice is made by finding the point of tangency between the isoquant representing the level of desired output and an isocost line.

5. The firm's expansion path describes how its cost-minimizing input choices vary as the scale or output of its operation increases. As a result, the expansion path provides useful information relevant for long-run planning decisions.

6. The long-run average cost curve is the envelope of the firm's short-run average cost curves, and it reflects the presence or absence of returns to scale. When there are constant returns to scale and many plant sizes are possible, the long-run cost curve is horizontal, and the envelope consists of the points of minimum short-run average cost. However, when there are increasing returns to scale initially and then decreasing returns to scale, the long-run average cost curve is U-shaped, and the envelope does not include all points of minimum short-run average cost.

7. A firm enjoys economies of scale when it can double its output at less than twice the cost. Correspondingly, there are diseconomies of scale when a doubling of output requires more than twice the cost. Scale economies and diseconomies apply even when input proportions are variable; returns to scale applies only when input proportions are fixed.

8. When a firm produces two (or more) outputs, it is important to note whether there are economies of scope in production. Economies of scope arise when the firm can produce any combination of the two outputs more cheaply than could two independent firms that each produced a single product. The degree of economies of scope is measured by the per-

centage in reduction in cost when one firm produces two products relative to the cost of producing them individually.

9. A firm's average cost of production can fall over time if the firm "learns" how to produce more effectively. The *learning curve* describes how much the input needed to produce a given output falls as the cumulative output of the firm increases.

10. Cost functions relate the cost of production to the level of output of the firm. The functions can be measured in both the short run and the long run by using either data for firms in an industry at a given time or data for an industry over time. A number of functional relationships including linear, quadratic, and cubic can be used to represent cost functions.

Questions for Review

1. A firm pays its accountant an annual retainer of $10,000. Is this an explicit or an implicit cost?

2. The owner of a small retail store does her own accounting work. How would you measure the opportunity cost of her work?

3. Suppose a chair manufacturer finds that the marginal rate of technical substitution of capital for labor in his production process is substantially greater than the ratio of the rental rate on machinery to the wage rate for assembly-line labor. How should he alter his use of capital and labor to minimize the cost of production?

4. Why are isocost lines straight lines?

5. If the marginal cost of production is increasing, does this tell you whether the average variable cost is increasing or decreasing? Explain.

6. If the marginal cost of production is greater than the average variable cost, does this tell you whether the average variable cost is increasing or decreasing? Explain.

7. If the firm's average cost curves are U-shaped, why does its average variable cost curve achieve its minimum at a lower level of output than the average total cost curve?

8. If a firm enjoys increasing returns to scale up to a certain output level, and then constant returns to scale, what can you say about the shape of the firm's long-run average cost curve?

9. How does a change in the price of one input change the firm's long-run expansion path?

10. Distinguish between economies of scale and economies of scope. Why can one be present without the other?

Exercises

1. Assume a computer firm's marginal costs of production are constant at $1000 per computer. However, the fixed costs of production are equal to $10,000.

a. Calculate the firm's average variable cost and average total cost curves.

b. If the firm wanted to minimize the average total cost of production, would it choose to be very large or very small? Explain.

2. If a firm hires a currently unemployed worker, the opportunity cost of utilizing the worker's service is zero. Is this true? Discuss.

3. a. Suppose a firm must pay an annual franchise fee, which is a fixed sum, independent of whether it produces any output. How does this tax affect the firm's fixed, marginal, and average costs?

b. Now suppose the firm is charged a tax that is proportional to the number of items it produces. Again, how does this tax affect the firm's fixed, marginal, and average costs?

4. A chair manufacturer hires its assembly-line labor for $22 an hour and calculates that the rental cost of its machinery is $110 per hour. Suppose that a chair can be produced using 4 hours of labor or machinery in any combination. If the firm is currently using 3 hours of labor for each hour of machine time, is it minimizing its costs of production? If so, why? If not, how can it improve the situation?

5. Suppose the economy takes a downturn, and labor costs fall by 50 percent and are expected to stay at that level for a long time. Show graphically how this change in the relative price of labor and capital affects the firm's expansion path.

6. You are in charge of cost control in a large metropolitan transit district. A consultant you have hired comes to you with the following report:

Our research has shown that the cost of running a bus for each trip down its line is $30 regardless of the number of passengers it carries. Each bus can carry 50 people. At rush hour, when the buses are full, the average cost per passenger is 60 cents. However, during off-peak hours, average ridership falls to 18 people, and average cost soars to $1.67 per passenger. As a result, we should encourage more rush-hour business when costs are cheaper and discourage off-peak business when costs are higher.

Do you follow the consultant's advice? Discuss.

7. An oil refinery consists of different pieces of processing equipment, each of which differs in its ability to break down heavy sulfurized crude oil into final products. The refinery process is such that the marginal cost of producing gasoline is constant up to a point as crude oil is put through a basic distilling unit. However, as the unit fills up, the firm finds that in the short run the amount of crude oil that can be processed is limited. The marginal cost of producing gasoline is also constant up to a capacity limit when crude oil is put through a more sophisticated hydrocracking unit. Graph the marginal cost of gasoline production when a basic distilling unit and a hydrocracker are used.

* 8. A computer company's cost function, which relates its average cost of production AC to its cumulative output in thousands of computers CQ and its plant size in terms of thousands of computers produced per year Q, within the production range of 10,000 to 50,000 computers, is given by

$$AC = 10 - 0.1CQ + 0.3Q$$

a. Is there a learning curve effect?
b. Are there increasing or decreasing returns to scale?
c. During its existence, the firm has produced a total of 40,000 computers and is producing 10,000 computers this year. Next year it plans to increase its production to 12,000 computers. Will its average cost of production increase or decrease? Explain.

9. The total short-run cost function of a company is given by the equation $C = 190 + 53Q$, where C is the total cost and Q is the total quantity of output, both measured in tens of thousands.

a. What is the company's fixed cost?
b. If the company produced 100,000 units of goods, what is its average variable cost?
c. What is its marginal cost per unit produced?
d. What is its average fixed cost?
e. Suppose the company borrows money and expands its factory. Its fixed cost rises by $50,000, but its variable cost falls to $45,000 per 10,000 units. The cost of interest (I) also enters into the equation. Each one-point increase in the interest rate raises costs by $30,000. Write the new cost equation.

*10. Suppose the long-run total cost function for an industry is given by the cubic equation $TC = a + bQ + cQ^2 + dQ^3$. Show (using calculus) that this total cost function is consistent with a U-shaped average cost curve for at least some values of the parameters a, b, c, d.

*11. A computer company produces hardware and software using the same plant and labor. The total cost of producing computer processing units H and software programs S is given by

$$TC = aH + bS - cHS$$

where $a, b,$ and c are positive. Is this total cost function consistent with the presence of economies or diseconomies of scale? With economies or diseconomies of scope?

CHAPTER 8

Profit Maximization and Competitive Supply

A cost curve describes the minimum cost at which a firm can produce various amounts of output. With this knowledge, we can now turn to a fundamental problem faced by every firm: How much should be produced? In this chapter, we will see how a perfectly competitive firm chooses the level of output that maximizes its profit. We will also see how the output choice of individual firms leads to a supply curve for the entire industry.

Our discussion of production and cost in Chapters 6 and 7 applies to firms in all kinds of markets, but in this chapter we discuss only firms in perfectly competitive markets. In a perfectly competitive market all firms produce the identical product, and each firm is so small in relation to the industry that its production decisions have no effect on market price. New firms can easily enter the industry if they perceive a potential for profit, and existing firms can exit the industry if they start losing money.

We begin by explaining why it makes sense to assume that firms maximize profit. We provide a rule for choosing the profit-maximizing output for firms in all markets—competitive or otherwise. Then we show how a competitive firm chooses its output in the short and long run. We see how this output choice changes as the cost of production or the prices of inputs change. In this way, we show how to derive the firm's *supply curve*. We then aggregate the supply curves of individual firms to obtain the *industry* supply curve. In the short run, firms in an industry choose which level of output to produce to maximize profit. In the long run, firms not only make output choices, but also decide whether to be in a market at all. We will see that the prospect of high profits encourages firms to enter an industry, while losses encourage them to leave.

8.1 *Profit Maximization*

In this section we analyze profit maximization by firms. First, we ask whether firms do indeed seek to maximize profit. Then, we describe a rule that any firm—whether in a competitive market or not—can use to find its profit-maximizing output level. Next, we consider the special case of a firm in a competitive market. We distinguish the demand curve facing a competitive firm from the market demand curve, and then use this information to describe the competitive firm's profit-maximization rule.

Do Firms Maximize Profit?

The assumption of profit maximization is frequently used in microeconomics because it predicts business behavior reasonably accurately and avoids unnecessary analytical complications. But whether firms do maximize profit has been controversial.

For smaller firms managed by their owners, profit is likely to dominate almost all the firm's decisions. In larger firms, however, managers who make day-to-day decisions usually have little contact with the owners (i.e., the stockholders). As a result, the owners of the firm cannot monitor the managers' behavior on a regular basis. Managers then have some leeway in how they run the firm and can deviate from profit-maximizing behavior to some extent.

Managers may be more concerned with goals such as revenue maximization to achieve growth or the payment of dividends to satisfy shareholders than with profit maximization. Managers might also be overly concerned with the firm's short-run profit (perhaps to earn a promotion or a large bonus) at the expense of its longer-run profit, even though long-run profit maximization better serves the interests of the stockholders.[1] (We discuss the implications of differences between the incentives of managers and owners of firms in greater detail in Chapter 17.)

Even so, managers' freedom to pursue goals other than long-run profit maximization is limited. If they do pursue such goals, shareholders or the boards of directors can replace them, or the firm can be taken over by new management. In any case, firms that do not come close to maximizing profit are not likely to survive. Firms that do survive in competitive industries make long-run profit maximization one of their highest priorities.

Thus, our working assumption of profit maximization is reasonable. Firms that have been in business for a long time are likely to care a lot about profit,

---

[1] To be more exact, maximizing the market value of the firm is a more appropriate goal than profit maximization because market value includes the stream of profits that the firm earns over time. It is the stream of profits that is of direct interest to the stockholders.

whatever else their managers may appear to be doing. For example, a firm that subsidizes public television may seem public-spirited and altruistic. Yet this beneficence is likely to be in the long-run financial interest of the firm because it generates goodwill for the firm and its products.

8.2 *Marginal Revenue, Marginal Cost, and Profit Maximization*

Let's begin by looking at the profit-maximizing output decision for *any* firm, whether the firm operates in a perfectly competitive market or is one that can influence price. Since profit is the difference between (total) revenue and (total) cost, to find the firm's profit-maximizing output level, we must analyze its revenue. Suppose that the firm's output is q, and that it obtains revenue R. This revenue is equal to the price of the product P times the number of units sold: $R = Pq$. The cost of production C also depends on the level of output. The firm's profit is the difference between revenue and cost:

$$\pi(q) = R(q) - C(q)$$

(Here we show explicitly that π, R, and C depend on output. Usually we will omit this reminder.)

To maximize profit, the firm selects the output for which the difference between revenue and cost is the greatest. This is shown in Figure 8.1. Revenue $R(q)$ is a curved line, which accounts for the possibility that an increased output may be accomplished only with a lower price. The slope of the line, which shows how much revenue increases when output increases by one unit, is *marginal revenue*. Because there are fixed and variable costs, $C(q)$ is not a straight line; its slope, which measures the additional cost associated with an additional unit of output, is *marginal cost*. $C(q)$ is positive when output is zero because there is a fixed cost in the short run.

For low levels of output, profit is negative—revenue is insufficient to cover fixed and variable costs. (Profit is negative when $q = 0$ because of fixed cost.) Here marginal revenue is greater than marginal cost, which tells us that increases in output will increase profit. As output increases, profit eventually becomes positive (for q greater than q_0) and increases until output reaches q^* units. Here the marginal revenue and marginal cost are equal, and q^* is the profit-maximizing output. Note that the vertical distance between revenue and cost, AB, is greatest at this point; equivalently $\pi(q)$ reaches its peak. Beyond q^* units of production, marginal revenue is less than marginal cost, and profit falls, reflecting the rapid increase in the total cost of production.

To see why q^* maximizes profit another way, suppose output is less than q^*. Then, if the firm increases output slightly, it will generate more revenues than costs. In other words, the marginal revenue (the additional revenue from pro-

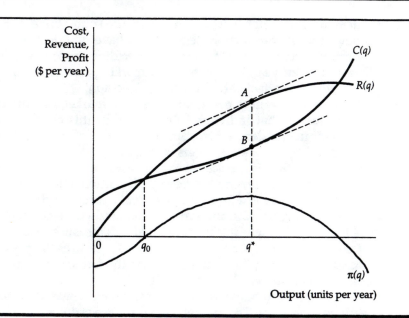

FIGURE 8.1   Profit Maximization in the Short Run.   A firm chooses output q^*, so that profit, the difference AB between revenue R and cost C, is maximized. At that output marginal revenue (the slope of the revenue curve) is equal to marginal cost (the slope of the cost curve).

ducing one more unit of output) is greater than marginal cost. Similarly, when output is greater than q^*, marginal revenue is less than the marginal cost. Only when marginal revenue and marginal cost are equal has profit been maximized.

The rule that profit is maximized when marginal revenue is equal to marginal cost holds for all firms, whether competitive or not. This important rule can also be derived algebraically. Profit, $\pi = R - C$, is maximized at the point at which an additional increment to output just leaves profit unchanged (i.e., $\Delta\pi/\Delta q = 0$):

$$\Delta\pi/\Delta q = \Delta R/\Delta q - \Delta C/\Delta q = 0$$

$\Delta R/\Delta q$ is marginal revenue MR and $\Delta C/\Delta q$ is marginal cost MC. Thus, we conclude that profit is maximized when $MR - MC = 0$, so that

$$\boxed{MR(q) = MC(q)}$$

Demand and Marginal Revenue for a Competitive Firm

Because each firm in a competitive industry sells only a small fraction of the entire industry sales, *how much output the firm decides to sell will have no effect on the market price of the product*. The market price is determined by the industry demand and supply curves. Therefore, the competitive firm is a *price taker*: It knows that its production decision will have no effect on the price of the product. For example, when a farmer is deciding how many acres of wheat to plant in a given year, he can take the market price of wheat as given. That price will not be affected by his acreage decision.

Often we will want to distinguish between market demand curves and the demand curves that individual firms face. In this chapter we will denote market output and demand by capital letters (Q and D), and the firm's output and demand by lower-case letters (q and d).

Because the firm is a price taker, the revenue curve $R(q)$ is a straight line, since for a given P, revenue increases proportionately with output. In addition, *the demand curve d facing an individual competitive firm is given by a horizontal line*. In Figure 8.2a, the farmer's demand curve corresponds to a price of $4 per bushel of wheat. The horizontal axis measures the amount of wheat that the farmer can sell, and the vertical axis measures the price. Compare the demand curve facing the firm (in this case the farmer) in Figure 8.2a, with the market demand curve D in Figure 8.2b.

The market demand curve shows how much wheat *all consumers* will buy at each possible price. The market demand curve is downward sloping because consumers buy more wheat at a lower price. The demand curve facing the

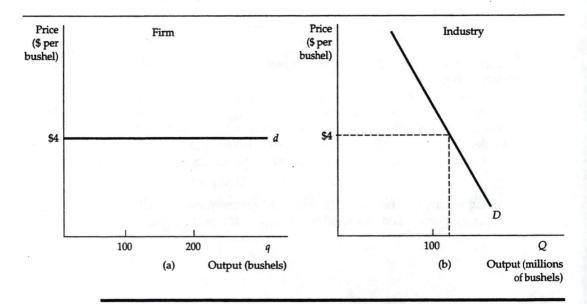

FIGURE 8.2   **Demand Curve Faced by a Competitive Firm.** A competitive firm supplies only a small portion of the total output of all the firms in an industry. Therefore, the firm takes the market price of the product as given, choosing its output on the assumption that the price will be unaffected by the output choice. In (a) the demand curve facing the firm is perfectly elastic, even though the market demand curve in (b) is downward sloping.

firm, however, is horizontal because the firm's sales will have no effect on the price. Suppose the firm increased its sales from 100 to 200 bushels of wheat. This would have almost no effect on the market because the industry output of wheat is 100 million bushels at $4 per bushel. Price is determined by the interaction of all firms and consumers in the market, not by the output decision of a single firm.

When an individual firm faces a horizontal demand curve, it can sell an additional unit of output without lowering price. As a result, the total revenue increases by an amount equal to the price (one bushel of wheat sold for $4 yields additional revenue of $4). At the same time, the average revenue received by the firm is also $4 because each bushel of wheat produced will be sold at $4. Therefore, *the demand curve d facing an individual firm in a competitive market is both its average revenue curve and its marginal revenue curve. Along this demand curve, marginal revenue and price are equal.*

Profit Maximization by a Competitive Firm

Because MR = P, and the demand curve facing a competitive firm is horizontal, the general profit-maximizing rule that applies to any firm can be simplified. A perfectly competitive firm should choose its output so that *marginal cost equals price*:

$$MC(q) = MR = P$$

Note that this is a rule for setting output, not price, since competitive firms take price as fixed. However, we show in Chapter 10 that the rule is a useful benchmark when we compare a noncompetitive firm's price with what the price would be if the market were competitive. The rule can help regulators decide what prices to set when they are regulating noncompetitive firms.

Because the choice of the profit-maximizing output by a competitive firm is so important, we will devote most of the rest of the chapter to analyzing it. We begin with the short-run output decision, and then move to the long run.

8.3 *Choosing Output in the Short Run*

How should the manager of a profit-maximizing firm choose a level of output over the short run, when the firm's plant size is fixed? In this section we show how a firm can use information about revenue and cost to make a profit-maximizing output decision.

Short-Run Profit Maximization by a Competitive Firm

In the short run, a firm operates with a fixed amount of capital and must choose the levels of its variable inputs (labor and materials) to maximize profit. Figure 8.3 shows the firm's short-run decision. The average and marginal revenue

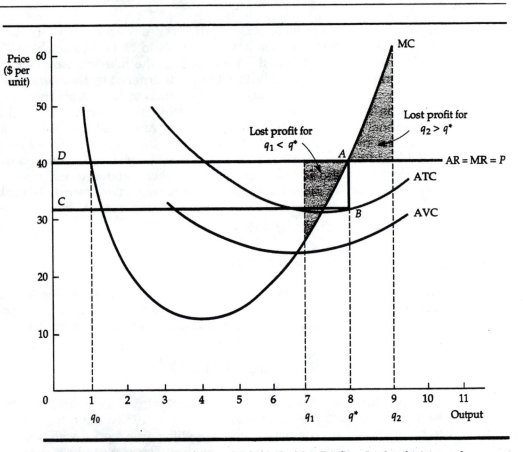

FIGURE 8.3   A Competitive Firm Making Positive Profit. In the short run, the competitive firm maximizes its profit by choosing an output q^* at which its marginal cost MC is equal to the price P (or marginal revenue MR) of its product. The profit of the firm is measured by the rectangle $ABCD$. Any lower output q_1, or higher output q_2, will lead to lower profit.

curves are drawn as horizontal lines at a price equal to $40. In this figure, we have drawn the average total cost curve ATC, the average variable cost curve AVC, and the marginal cost curve MC, so that we can see the firm's profit more easily.

Profit is maximized at point A, associated with an output $q^* = 8$ and a price of $40, because marginal revenue is equal to marginal cost at this point. At a lower output, say $q_1 = 7$, marginal revenue is greater than marginal cost, so profit could be increased by increasing output. The shaded area between $q_1 = 7$ and q^* shows the lost profit associated with producing at q_1. At a higher output, say q_2, marginal cost is greater than marginal revenue; thus, reducing output saves a cost that exceeds the reduction in revenue. The shaded area between q^* and $q_2 = 9$ shows the lost profit associated with producing at q_2.

The MR and MC curves cross at an output of q_0 as well as q^*. At q_0, however, profit is clearly not maximized. An increase in output beyond q_0 increases profit because marginal cost is well below marginal revenue. So the condition for profit maximization is that *marginal revenue equals marginal cost at a point at which the marginal cost curve is rising.*

The Short-Run Profitability of a Competitive Firm

Figure 8.3 also shows the competitive firm's short-run profit. The distance AB is the difference between price and average cost at the output level q^*, which is the average profit per unit of output. Segment BC measures the total number of units produced. Therefore, rectangle $ABCD$ is the firm's total profit.

A firm need not always earn a profit in the short run, as Figure 8.4 shows. The major difference from Figure 8.3 is the higher fixed cost of production. This raises average total cost but does not change the average variable cost and

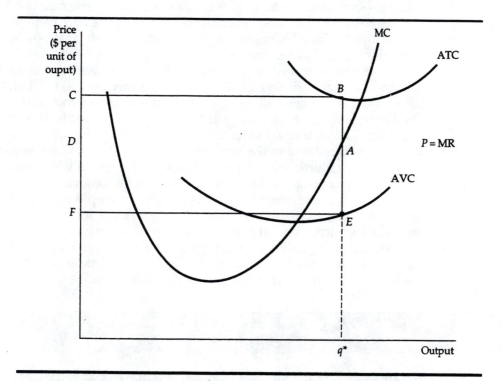

FIGURE 8.4   **A Competitive Firm Incurring Losses.**   In the short run, a competitive firm may produce at a loss (because its fixed cost is high), if it can still generate revenues that more than cover its variable cost. The firm minimizes its losses by producing at q^*, with losses $ABCD$. If the firm were to shut down, it would incur even greater losses equal to the fixed cost of production $CBEF$.

marginal cost curves. At the profit-maximizing output q^*, the price P is less than average cost, so that line segment AB measures the average *loss* from production. Likewise, the shaded rectangle $ABCD$ now measures the firm's total loss.

Why doesn't a firm that earns a loss leave the industry entirely? A firm might operate at a loss *in the short run* because it expects to earn a profit in the future as the price of its product increases or the cost of production falls. In fact, a firm has two choices in the short run: It can produce some output, or it can shut down its production temporarily. It will choose the more profitable (or the less unprofitable) of the two alternatives. In particular, *a firm will find it profitable to shut down (produce no output) when the price of its product is less than the minimum average variable cost*. In this situation, revenues from production will not cover variable costs, and losses will increase.

Figure 8.4 illustrates the case in which some production is appropriate. The output q^* is at the point where short-run losses are minimized. It is cheaper in this case to operate at q^* rather than to produce no output because price exceeds average variable cost at q^*. Each unit produced yields more revenue than cost, thereby generating higher profit than if the firm were to produce nothing. (Total profit is still negative, however, because the *fixed cost* is high.) Line segment AE measures the difference between price and average variable cost, and rectangle $AEFD$ measures the additional profit that can be earned by producing at q^* rather than at 0.

To see this another way, recall that the difference between average total cost ATC and average variable cost AVC is average fixed cost AFC. Therefore, in Figure 8.4, line segment BE represents the average fixed cost, and rectangle $CBEF$ represents the total fixed cost of production. When the firm produces no output, its loss is equal to its total fixed cost $CBEF$. But when it produces at q^*, its loss is reduced to the rectangle $ABCD$. Fixed cost, which is irrelevant to the firm's production decision in the short run, is crucial when determining whether the firm ought to leave the industry in the long run.

To summarize: The competitive firm produces no output if price is less than minimum average variable cost. When it does produce, it maximizes profit by choosing the output level at which price is equal to marginal cost. At this output level, profit is positive if price is greater than average total cost. The firm may operate at a loss in the short run. However, if it expects to continue to lose money over the long run, it will go out of business.

EXAMPLE 8.1   SOME COST CONSIDERATIONS FOR MANAGERS

The application of the rule that marginal revenue should equal marginal cost depends on the manager's ability to estimate marginal cost.[2] To obtain useful measures of cost, managers should keep three guidelines in mind.

[2] This example draws on the discussion of costs and managerial decision making in Thomas Nagle, *The Strategy and Tactics of Pricing* (Englewood Cliffs, N.J.: Prentice-Hall, 1987), Chapter 2.

First, when possible, *average variable cost should not be used as a substitute for marginal cost*. When marginal and average cost are nearly constant, there is little difference between them. However, when marginal and average cost are increasing sharply, the use of average variable cost can be misleading when deciding how much to produce. Suppose, for example, that a company has the following cost information:

Current output: 100 units per day, of which 25 units are produced
                  during overtime
Materials cost: $500 per day
Labor cost: $2000 per day (regular) plus $1000 per day (overtime)

Average variable cost is easily calculated—it is the labor and materials cost ($3500) divided by 100 units per day, or $35 per unit. But the appropriate cost is marginal cost, which could be calculated as follows: Materials cost per unit is likely to be constant whatever the output level, so that marginal materials cost is $500/100 = $5 per unit. Since the marginal cost of labor is likely to involve overtime work only, it is obtained by noting that 25 of the 100 units were produced during the overtime period. The average overtime pay per unit of production, $1000/25 = $40 per unit, provides a good estimate of the marginal cost of labor. Therefore, the marginal cost of producing an additional unit of output is $45 per unit (the marginal materials cost plus the marginal labor cost); this is much larger than the average variable cost of $35. If the manager relied on average variable cost, too much output would be produced.

Second, *a single item on a firm's accounting ledger may have two components, only one of which involves marginal cost*. Suppose, for example, that a manager is trying to cut back production. She reduces the number of hours that some employees work and lays off others. But the salary of an employee who is laid off may not be an accurate measure of the marginal cost of production when cuts are made because union contracts often require the firm to pay laid-off employees part of their salary. In this case, the marginal cost of increasing production is not the same as the savings in marginal cost when production is decreased. The savings is the labor cost after the required layoff salary has been subtracted.

Third, *all opportunity costs should be included in determining marginal cost*. Suppose a department store wants to sell children's furniture. Instead of building a new selling area, the manager decides to use part of the third floor, which had been used for appliances, for the furniture. The marginal cost of this space is the profit that would have been earned had the store continued to sell appliances there, per unit of furniture sold. This opportunity cost measure may be much greater than what the store actually paid for that part of the building.

These three guidelines can help a manager to measure marginal cost correctly. Failure to do so can cause production to be too high or too low, and thereby reduce profit.

8.4 *The Competitive Firm's Short-Run Supply Curve*

A *supply curve* for a firm tells us how much output it will produce at every possible price. We have seen that competitive firms will increase output to the point at which price is equal to marginal cost, but they will shut down if price is below average variable cost. Therefore, for positive output the firm's supply curve is the portion of the marginal cost curve that lies above the average variable cost curve. Since the marginal cost curve cuts the average variable cost curve at its minimum point (recall our discussion in Chapter 7 of marginal and average cost), *the firm's supply curve is its marginal cost curve above the point of minimum average variable cost*. For any P greater than minimum AVC, the profit-maximizing output can be read directly from the graph. At a price P_1 in Figure 8.5, for example, the quantity supplied will be q_1, and at P_2 it will be q_2. For P less than (or equal to) minimum AVC, the profit-maximizing out-

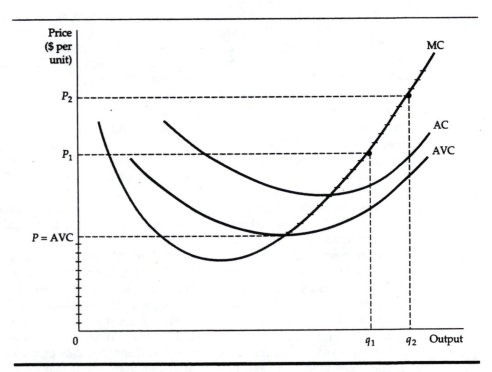

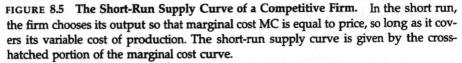

FIGURE 8.5   **The Short-Run Supply Curve of a Competitive Firm.**   In the short run, the firm chooses its output so that marginal cost MC is equal to price, so long as it covers its variable cost of production. The short-run supply curve is given by the crosshatched portion of the marginal cost curve.

put is equal to zero. In Figure 8.5 the entire supply curve is the cross-hatched portion of the vertical axis and the marginal cost curve.

Short-run supply curves for competitive firms slope upward for the same reason that marginal cost increases—the presence of diminishing returns to one or more factors of production. As a result, an increase in the market price will induce those firms already in the market to increase the quantities they produce. The higher price makes the additional production profitable and also increases the firm's *total* profit because it applies to all units that the firm produces.

The Firm's Response to an Input Price Change

When the price of its product changes, the firm changes its output level, so that the marginal cost of production remains equal to the price. Often, however, the product price changes at the same time that the prices of *inputs* change. In this section we show how the firm's output decision changes in response to a change in the prices of one of the firm's inputs.

Figure 8.6 shows a firm's marginal cost curve that is initially given by MC_1 when the firm faces a price of $5 for its product. The firm maximizes its profit by producing an output of q_1. Now suppose the price of one of the firm's inputs increases. This causes the marginal cost curve to shift upward from MC_1 to MC_2 because it now costs more to produce each unit of output. The new profit-maximizing output is q_2, at which $P = MC_2$. Thus, the higher input price causes the firm to reduce its output.

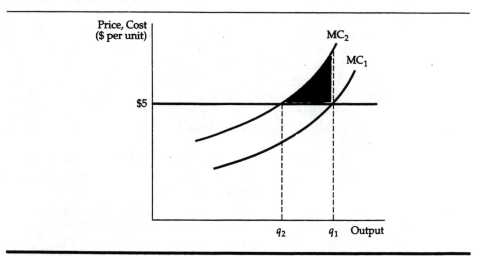

FIGURE 8.6 The Response of a Firm to a Change in Input Price. When the marginal cost of production for a firm increases (from MC_1 to MC_2), the level of output that maximizes profit falls (from q_1 to q_2).

If the firm had continued to produce q_1, it would have incurred a loss on the last unit of production. In fact, all production beyond q_2 reduces profit. The shaded area in the figure gives the total savings to the firm (or equivalently, the reduction in lost profit) associated with the reduction in output from q_1 to q_2.

EXAMPLE 8.2 THE SHORT-RUN PRODUCTION OF PETROLEUM PRODUCTS

Suppose you are managing an oil refinery and you decide to produce a particular combination of refinery products, including gasoline, jet fuel, and residual fuel oil for home heating. A lot of crude oil is available, but the amount that you refine depends on the capacity of the refinery and the cost of production. How much of the product mix should you produce each day?[3]

Information about the refinery's marginal cost of production is essential for this decision. Figure 8.7 shows the short-run marginal cost curve (SMC). Marginal cost increases with output, but in a series of uneven segments rather than as a smooth curve. The increase is in segments because the refinery uses different processing units to turn crude oil into finished products. When a particular processing unit reaches capacity, output can be increased only by substituting a more expensive process. For example, gasoline can be produced from light crude oils rather inexpensively in a processing unit called a "thermal cracker." When this unit becomes full, additional gasoline can still be produced (from heavy as well as light crude oil) but at a higher cost. In Figure 8.7 the first capacity constraint comes into effect when production reaches about 9700 barrels a day. A second capacity constraint becomes important when production increases beyond 10,700 barrels a day.

Deciding how much output to produce now becomes relatively easy. Suppose the mix of refined products can be sold for $23 per barrel. Since the marginal cost of production is close to $24 for the first unit of output, at a price of $23 no crude oil should be run through the refinery. If, however, the price of the product mix is between $24 and $25, you should produce 9700 barrels a day (filling the thermal cracker). Finally, if the price is above $25, you should use the more expensive refining unit and expand production toward 10,700 barrels a day.

Because the cost function rises in steps, you know that your production decisions need not change much in response to small changes in the price of the product. You will typically utilize sufficient crude oil to fill the appropriate processing unit until price increases (or decreases) substantially. Then you need simply calculate whether the increased price warrants using an additional, more expensive processing unit.

[3] This example is based on James M. Griffin, "The Process Analysis Alternative to Statistical Cost Functions: An Application to Petroleum Refining," *American Economic Review* 62 (1972): 46–56. The numbers have been updated and applied to a particular refinery.

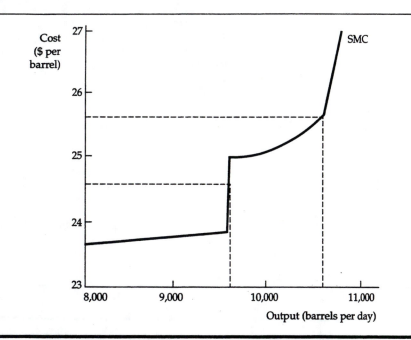

FIGURE 8.7   The Short-Run Production of Petroleum Products.   The marginal cost of producing a mix of petroleum products from crude oil increases sharply at several levels of output as the refinery shifts from one processing unit to another. As a result, the output level can be insensitive to some changes in price and very sensitive to others.

8.5 *The Short-Run Market Supply Curve*

The *short-run market supply curve* shows the amount of output that the industry will produce in the short run for every possible price. The industry's output is the sum of the quantities supplied by all the individual firms. Therefore, the market supply curve can be obtained by adding their supply curves. Figure 8.8 shows how this is done when there are only three firms, all of which have different short-run production costs. Each firm's marginal cost curve is drawn only for the portion that lies above its average variable cost curve. (We have shown only three firms to keep the graph simple, but the same analysis applies when there are many firms.)

At any price below P_1, the industry will produce no output because P_1 is the minimum average variable cost of the lowest-cost firm. Between P_1 and P_2, only firm 3 will produce, so the industry supply curve will be identical to that

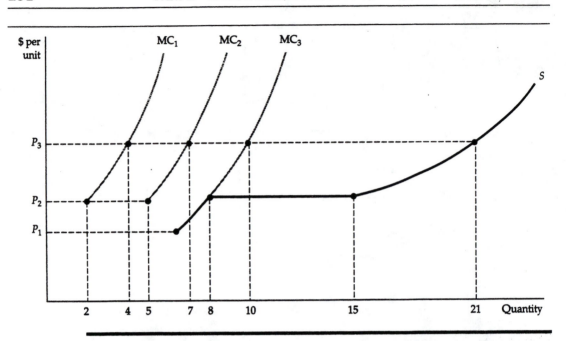

FIGURE 8.8   Industry Supply in the Short Run.   The short-run industry supply curve is the horizontal summation of the supply curves of the individual firms. Because the third firm has a lower average variable cost curve than the first two firms, the market supply curve S begins at price P_1 and follows the marginal cost curve of the third firm MC_3 until price equals P_2, where there is a kink. For all prices above P_2, the industry quantity supplied is the sum of the quantities supplied by each of the three firms.

portion of firm 3's marginal cost curve MC_3. At price P_2, the industry supply will be the sum of the quantity supplied by all three firms. Firm 1 supplies 2 units, firm 2 supplies 5 units, and firm 3 supplies 8 units; thus, industry supply is 15 units. At price P_3, firm 1 supplies 4 units, firm 2 supplies 7 units, and firm 3 supplies 10 units; in total the industry supplies 21 units. Note that the industry supply curve is upward sloping but has a kink at price P_2. With many firms in the market, however, the kink becomes unimportant, so we usually draw industry supply as a smooth, upward-sloping curve.

Finding the industry supply curve is not always as simple as adding up a set of firm supply curves. As price rises, all firms in the industry expand their output. This additional output increases the demand for inputs to production and may lead to higher input prices. As we saw in Figure 8.6, increasing input prices shifts the firms' marginal cost curves upward. For example, an increased demand for beef could also increase demand for corn and soybeans (which are used to feed cattle), and thereby cause the prices of these crops to rise. In turn, the higher input prices would cause beef firms' marginal cost curves to shift upward. This lowers each firm's output choice (for any given market price) and causes the industry supply curve to be less responsive to changes in output price than it would otherwise be.

Elasticity of Market Supply

The price elasticity of market supply measures the sensitivity of industry output to market price. Recall from Chapter 2 that the elasticity of supply E_S is the percentage change in quantity supplied Q in response to a 1 percent change in price P:

$$E_S = (\Delta Q/Q)/(\Delta P/P)$$

Because marginal cost curves are upward sloping, the short-run elasticity of supply is always positive. When marginal costs increase rapidly in response to increases in output, the elasticity of supply is low. Firms are then capacity-constrained and find it costly to increase output. But, when marginal costs increase slowly in response to increases in output, supply is relatively elastic, and a small price increase induces firms to produce much more.

   At one extreme is the case of *perfectly inelastic supply*, which arises when the industry's plant and equipment are so fully utilized that new plants must be built (as they will be in the long run) to achieve greater output. At the other extreme is the case of *perfectly elastic supply*, which arises when marginal costs are constant.

EXAMPLE 8.3   THE SHORT-RUN WORLD SUPPLY OF COPPER

In the short run, the shape of the market supply curve for a mineral such as copper depends on how the cost of mining varies within and among the world's major producers. Costs of mining, smelting, and refining copper differ because of differences in labor and transportation costs and differences in the copper content of the ore. Table 8.1 summarizes some of the relevant cost and production data for the largest copper-producing nations.[4]

   These data can be used to plot the world supply curve for copper. The supply curve is a short-run curve because it takes the existing mines as fixed. Figure 8.9 shows how this curve is constructed for the six countries listed in the table. The complete world supply curve would, of course, incorporate data for all copper-producing countries. Also, note that the curve in Figure 8.9 is an approximation. The marginal cost number for each country is an average for all copper producers in that country. In the United States, for example, some producers had a marginal cost greater than 84 cents, and some less than 84 cents.

---

[4] The former Soviet Union is excluded because of data limitations. The source is the U.S. Department of the Interior, Bureau of Mines, *Minerals Yearbook*, 1985, Tables 4 and 31.

Country	Annual Production (thousand metric tons)	Marginal Cost (dollars per pound)
Canada	760	1.10
Chile	1550	.72
Peru	373	.98
United States	1550	.84
Zaire	390	.61
Zambia	430	.67

The lowest-cost copper is mined in Zaire, where the marginal cost of refined copper was about 61 cents per pound.[5] Curve MC_Z describes this marginal cost curve. The curve is horizontal until Zaire's capacity to mine copper is reached. Curve MC_{Zm} describes Zambia's supply curve (marginal cost is 67 cents per

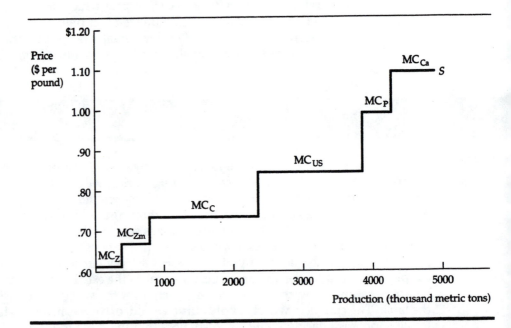

FIGURE 8.9   The Short-Run World Supply of Copper.   The supply curve for world copper is obtained by summing the marginal cost curves for each of the major copper-producing countries. The supply curve slopes upward because the marginal cost of production ranges from a low of 61 cents per pound in Zaire to a high of $1.10 per pound in Canada.

[5] We are presuming that marginal and average costs of production are approximately the same.

pound). Likewise, curves MC_C, MC_{US}, MC_P, and MC_{Ca} represent the marginal cost curves for Chile, the United States, Peru, and Canada, respectively.

The world supply curve, denoted S, is obtained by summing each nation's supply curve horizontally. The slope and the elasticity of the supply curve depend on the price of copper. At relatively low prices, such as 70 to 85 cents per pound, the supply curve is quite elastic because small price increases lead to substantial increases in refined copper. But for higher prices, say above $1.10 per pound, the supply curve becomes quite inelastic because at such prices all producers would be operating at capacity.

Producer Surplus in the Short Run

In Chapter 4 we measured consumer surplus as the difference between the maximum that a person would pay for an item and its market price. An analogous concept applies to firms. If marginal cost is rising, the price of the product is greater than marginal cost for every unit produced except the last one. As a result, firms earn a surplus on all but the last unit of output. The *producer surplus* of a firm is the sum over all units produced of the difference between the market price of the good and the marginal cost of production. Just as consumer surplus measures the area below an individual's demand curve and above the market price of the product, producer surplus measures the area above a producer's supply curve and below the market price.

Figure 8.10 illustrates short-run producer surplus for a firm. The profit-maximizing output is q^*, where $P = MC$. Producer surplus is given by the shaded area under the firm's horizontal demand curve and above its marginal cost curve, from zero output to the profit-maximizing output q^*.

When we add the marginal costs of producing each level of output from 0 to q^*, we find that the sum is the total variable cost of producing q^*. Marginal cost reflects increments to cost associated with increases in output; since fixed cost does not vary with output, the sum of all marginal costs must equal the sum of the firm's variable costs. Thus, producer surplus can alternatively be defined as the difference between the firm's revenue and its total variable cost. In Figure 8.10 producer surplus is also therefore given by the rectangle $ABCD$, which equals revenue ($0ABq^*$) minus variable cost ($0DCq^*$).

Producer surplus is closely related to profit, but is not equal to it. Producer surplus is equal to revenue net of variable cost, while profit is equal to revenue net of *all* costs, both variable and fixed:

$$\text{Producer Surplus} = PS = R - VC$$

$$\text{Profit} = \pi = R - VC - FC$$

It follows that in the short run when the fixed cost is positive, producer surplus is greater than profit.

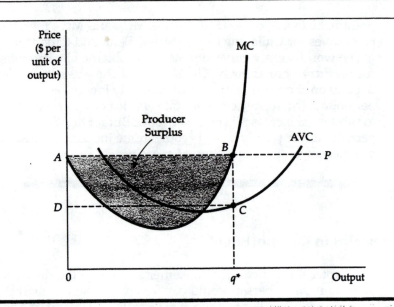

FIGURE 8.10 Producer Surplus for a Firm. The producer surplus for a firm is measured by the shaded area below the market price and above the marginal cost curve, between outputs 0 and q^*, the profit-maximizing output. Alternatively, it is equal to rectangle $ABCD$ because the sum of all marginal costs up to q^* is equal to the variable costs of producing q^*.

The extent to which firms enjoy producer surplus depends on their costs of production. Higher-cost firms have less producer surplus, and lower-cost firms have more. By adding up all of the individual firms' producer surpluses, we can determine the producer surplus for a market. This can be seen in Figure 8.11. In the figure the market supply curve begins at the vertical axis at a point that represents the average variable cost of the lowest-cost firm in the market. Producer surplus is the area that lies below the market price of the product and above the supply curve between the output levels 0 and Q^*.

8.6 *Choosing Output in the Long Run*

In the long run, a firm can alter all its inputs, including the size of the plant. It can decide to shut down (i.e., to *exit* the industry) or to begin to produce a product for the first time (i.e., to *enter* an industry). Because we are concerned here with competitive markets, we allow for *free entry* and *free exit*. In other words, we are assuming that firms may enter or exit without any legal restriction or any special costs associated with entry.[6]

---

[6] In Chapter 10 we discuss examples of barriers to entry in an industry.

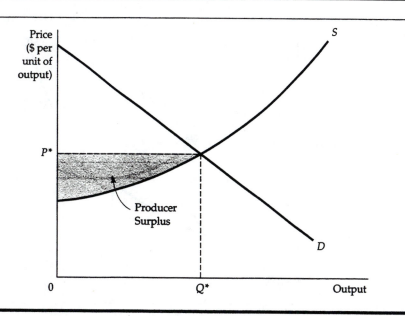

FIGURE 8.11   Producer Surplus for a Market. The producer surplus for a market is the area below the market price and above the market supply curve, between 0 and output Q^*.

Figure 8.12 shows how a competitive firm makes its long-run, profit-maximizing output decision. As in the short run, it faces a horizontal demand curve. (In Figure 8.12 the firm takes the market price of $40 as given.) Its short-run average (total) cost curve SAC and short-run marginal cost curve SMC are low enough for the firm to make a positive profit, given by rectangle ABCD, by producing an output of q_1, where SMC $= P =$ MR. The long-run average cost curve LAC reflects the presence of economies of scale up to output level q_2 and diseconomies of scale at higher output levels. The long-run marginal cost curve LMC cuts the long-run average cost from below at q_2, the point of minimum long-run average cost.

If the firm believes the market price will remain at $40, it will want to increase the size of its plant to produce an output q_3 at which its *long-run* marginal cost is equal to the $40 price. When this expansion is complete, the firm's profit margin will increase from AB to EF, and its total profit will increase from ABCD to EFGD. Output q_3 is profit-maximizing for the firm because at any lower output, say q_2, the marginal revenue from additional production is greater than the marginal cost, so expansion is desirable. But at any output greater than q_3, marginal cost is greater than marginal revenue, so additional production would reduce profit. In summary, *the long-run output of a profit-maximizing competitive firm is where long-run marginal cost is equal to price.*

Note that the higher the market price, the higher the profit that the firm can earn. Correspondingly, as the price of the product falls from $40 to $30, so does the profit of the firm. At a price of $30, the firm's profit-maximizing

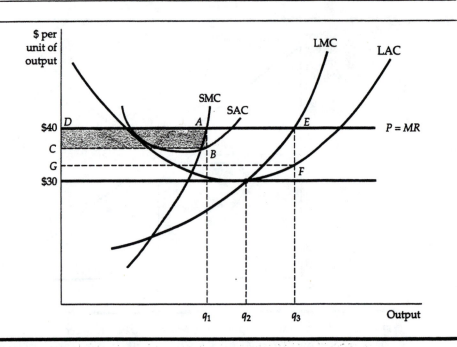

FIGURE 8.12   Output Choice in the Long Run.   The firm maximizes its profit by choosing the output at which price is equal to long-run marginal cost LMC. In the diagram, the firm increases its profit from *ABCD* to *EFGD* by increasing its output in the long run.

output is q_2, the point of long-run minimum average cost. In this case, since $P = $ ATC, the firm earns zero economic profit. As we show below, this means that investors in the firm earn a competitive return on their investment.

Zero Profit

As we saw in Chapter 7, it is important to distinguish between accounting profit and economic profit. Accounting profit is measured by the difference between the firm's revenues and costs, including actual outlays and depreciation expenses. Economic profit takes account of opportunity costs. One such opportunity cost is the return that the owners of the firm could make if their capital were used elsewhere. Suppose, for example, that the firm uses labor and capital inputs; its capital equipment has been purchased (and has been depreciated). The firm's accounting profit will equal its revenues R minus its labor costs wL, which is positive. However, its economic profit π equals its revenues R minus its labor costs wL and minus its opportunity cost of capital rK, measured by what it could rent the capital for in the market. Thus,

$$\pi = R - wL - rK = 0$$

A firm earning a negative economic profit should consider going out of business if it does not expect to improve its financial picture. However, a firm that earns zero economic profit need not go out of business because zero profit means the firm is earning a reasonable return on its investment. Of course, investors would like to earn a positive economic profit—that is what encourages entrepreneurs to develop and commercialize new ideas. But in competitive markets, as we will see, economic profits become zero in the long run. Zero economic profits signify not that the firms in the industry are performing poorly, but rather, that the industry is competitive.

Long-Run Competitive Equilibrium

Figure 8.12 shows how a $40 price induces a firm to increase its output and gives the firm a positive profit. Because profit is calculated net of the opportunity cost of investment, a positive profit means an unusually high return on investment. This high return causes investors to direct resources away from other industries and into this one—there will be *entry* into the market. Eventually the increased production associated with new entry causes the market supply curve to shift to the right, so that market output increases and the market price of the product falls.[7] Figure 8.13 illustrates this. In part (b) of the figure, the supply curve has shifted from S_1 to S_2, causing the price to fall from P_1 ($40) to P_2 ($30). In part (a), which applies to a single firm, the long-run average cost curve is tangent to the horizontal price line at output q_2.

When a firm earns zero economic profit, it has no incentive to exit the industry, and other firms have no special incentive to enter. A *long-run competitive equilibrium* occurs when three conditions hold. First, all firms in the industry are maximizing profit. Second, no firm has an incentive either to enter or exit the industry because all firms in the industry are earning zero economic profit. Third, the price of the product is such that the quantity supplied by the industry is equal to the quantity demanded by consumers.

The dynamic process that leads to long-run equilibrium creates a puzzle. Firms enter the market because of the opportunity to earn positive profit, and they exit because of losses. Yet, in long-run equilibrium, firms earn zero economic profit. Why do firms exit or enter if they know that eventually they will be no better or worse off than if they do nothing? The answer is that it can take a long time to reach a long-run equilibrium, and a substantial profit (or loss) can be made in the short run. The first firm to enter a profitable industry can earn much more short-run profit for its investors than can firms that enter later. Similarly, the first firm to exit an unprofitable industry can save its investors lots of money. Thus, the concept of long-run equilibrium tells us the *direction* that firms' behavior is likely to take. The idea of an eventual zero-profit, long-run equilibrium should not discourage a manager whose reward depends on the short-run profit that the firm earns.

---

[7] We discuss why the long-run supply curve might be upward sloping in the next section.

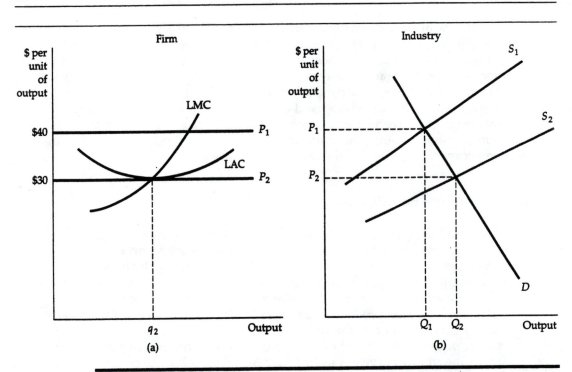

FIGURE 8.13   Long-Run Competitive Equilibrium.   Initially the long-run equilibrium price of a product is $40 per unit, as shown in (b) as the intersection of demand curve D and supply curve S_1. In (a) it is shown that firms earn a positive profit because their long-run average cost reaches a minimum of $30 (at q_2). This positive profit encourages entry of new firms and causes a shift to the right in the supply curve to S_2. The long-run equilibrium occurs at a price of $30 because each firm earns zero profit, and there is no incentive to enter or exit the industry.

To see why all the conditions for long-run equilibrium must hold, assume that all firms have identical costs, and consider what happens if too many firms enter the industry in response to an opportunity for profit. Then the supply curve in Figure 8.13b will shift further to the right, and price will fall below $30, say to $25. At that price, however, firms will lose money. As a result, some firms will exit the industry. Firms will continue to exit until the market supply curve shifts back to S_2. Only when there is no incentive to exit or enter the industry can a market be in long-run equilibrium.

Now suppose that all firms in the industry do not have identical cost curves. One firm has a patent or new idea that lets it produce at a lower average cost than all other firms. Then, it is consistent with long-run equilibrium for that firm to be earning a positive *accounting* profit (and to enjoy a higher producer surplus than other firms). As long as other investors and firms cannot acquire the patent or idea that lowers costs, they have no incentive to enter the industry. And as long as the process is particular to this product and this industry, the fortunate firm has no incentive to exit the industry. The distinction between accounting profit and economic profit is important here. If the new idea or invention is profitable, other firms in the industry will pay to use it. (Or they might attempt to buy the entire firm to acquire the patent.) The increased value of the patent thus represents an opportunity cost to the firm—it could sell the rights to the patent rather than use it. If all firms are equally efficient otherwise, once this opportunity cost is accounted for, the *economic* profit of the firm falls to zero.[8]

There are other instances in which firms earning positive accounting profit may be earning zero economic profit. Suppose, for example, that a clothing store happens to be located near a large shopping center. The additional flow of customers may substantially increase the store's accounting profit because the cost of the land is based on its historical cost. However, as far as economic profit is concerned, the cost of the land should reflect its opportunity cost, which in this case is its current market value. When the opportunity cost of land is included, the profitability of the clothing store is no higher than that of its competitors.

Thus, the condition that economic profit be zero is essential for the market to be in a long-run equilibrium. Positive economic profit, by definition, represents an opportunity for investors and an incentive to enter the industry. Positive accounting profit, however, may signal that firms already in the industry possess valuable assets, skills, or ideas, and this will not necessarily encourage entry by other firms.

Economic Rent

We have seen that some firms earn higher accounting profit than others because they have access to factors of production that are in limited supply; these might include land and natural resources, entrepreneurial skill, or other creative talent. What makes economic profit zero in the long run in these situations is the willingness of other firms to use the factors of production that are in limited supply. The positive accounting profits are therefore translated into *economic rent* that is earned by the scarce factors. *Economic rent* is defined as the difference between what firms are willing to pay for an input to production less the minimum amount necessary to buy that input. In competitive markets, in both the short and the long run, economic rent is often positive, even though profit is zero.

For example, suppose that two firms in an industry own their land outright; the minimum cost of obtaining the land is zero. One firm is located on a river and can ship its products for $10,000 a year less than the other firm, which is

---

[8] If the firm with the patent is more efficient than other firms, then it will be earning a positive profit. But if the patent holder is less efficient, it should sell off the patent and go out of business.

inland. Then, the $10,000 higher profit of the first firm is due to the $10,000 per year economic rent associated with its river location. The rent is created because the land along the river is valuable, and other firms would be willing to pay for it. Eventually, the competition for this specialized factor of production will increase its value to $10,000. Land rent—the difference between $10,000 and the zero cost of obtaining the land—is also $10,000. Note that while the economic rent has increased, the economic profit of the firm on the river has become zero.

The zero economic profit tells the firm on the river that it should remain in the industry only if it is at least as efficient in production as other firms. It also tells possible entrants to the industry that entry will be profitable only if they can produce more efficiently than firms already producing.

Producer Surplus in the Long Run

When a firm is earning a positive accounting profit, but there is no incentive for other firms to enter or exit the industry, this profit must reflect economic rent. How then does rent relate to producer surplus? Recall that producer surplus measures the difference between the market price a producer receives and the marginal cost of production. Thus, in the long run, in a competitive market, *the producer surplus that a firm earns consists of the economic rent that it enjoys from all its scarce inputs.*[9]

Suppose, for example, that a baseball team has a franchise that makes it the only team in a particular city. The team will earn a substantial accounting profit. This profit will include some economic rent because the team is more valuable with the franchise than it would be if entry into the local baseball market were unrestricted. The producer surplus earned by the baseball team would include its economic profit and the rent that reflects the difference between the current value of the team and what its value would be if an unlimited number of franchises were available.

Figure 8.14 shows that firms that earn economic rent earn the same economic profit as firms that do not earn rent. Part (a) shows the economic profit of a baseball team located in a city with several competing teams. The average price of a ticket is $7, and costs are such that the team earns zero economic profit. Part (b) shows the profit of a team with the same costs, but in a city with no competing teams. Because it is the only team in town, it can sell tickets for $10 apiece, and thereby earn an accounting profit of close to $3 on each ticket. However, the rent associated with the desirable location represents a cost to the firm—an opportunity cost—because it could sell its franchise to another team. As a result, the economic profit in the city without competition is also zero.

---

[9] In a noncompetitive market producer surplus will reflect economic profit as well as economic rent.

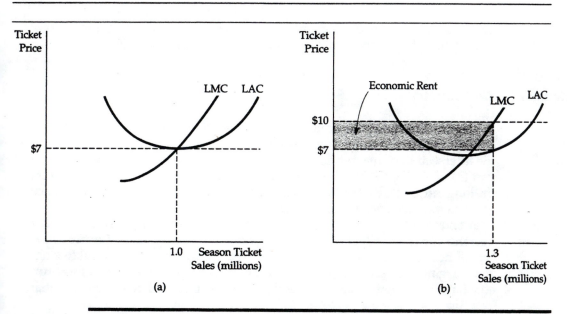

FIGURE 8.14 **Firms Earn Zero Profit in Long-Run Equilibrium.** In long-run equilibrium, all firms earn zero economic profit. In (a) a baseball team in a city with other competitive sports teams sells enough tickets so that price ($7) is equal to marginal and average cost. In (b) there are no other competitors, so a $10 price can be charged. The team increases its sales to the point at which the average cost of production plus the average economic rent is equal to the ticket price. When the opportunity cost associated with owning the franchise is taken into account, the team earns zero economic profit.

8.7 *The Industry's Long-Run Supply Curve*

In our analysis of short-run supply, we first derived the firm's supply curve and then showed how the horizontal summation of individual firms' supply curves generated a market supply curve. We cannot analyze long-run supply in the same way, however, because in the long run firms enter and exit the market as the market price changes. This makes it impossible to sum up supply curves—we don't know which firms' supplies to add.

To determine long-run supply, we assume all firms have access to the available production technology. Output is increased by using more inputs, not by invention. We also assume that the conditions underlying the market for inputs to production do not change when the industry expands or contracts. For example, an increased demand for labor does not increase a union's ability to negotiate a better wage contract for its workers.

The shape of the long-run supply curve depends on the extent to which increases and decreases in industry output affect the prices that the firms must pay for inputs into the production process. It is thus useful to distinguish among three types of industries: constant-cost, increasing-cost, and decreasing-cost.

Constant-Cost Industry

Figure 8.15 shows the derivation of the long-run supply curve for a constant-cost industry. Assume that the industry is initially in long-run equilibrium at the intersection of market demand curve D_1 and market supply curve S_1, in part (b) of the figure. Point A at the intersection of demand and supply is on the long-run supply curve S_L because it tells us that the industry will produce Q_1 units of output when the long-run equilibrium price is P_1.

To obtain other points on the long-run supply curve, suppose the market demand for the product unexpectedly increases, say because of a tax cut. A typical firm is initially producing at an output of q_1, where P_1 is equal to long-run marginal cost and long-run average cost. But the firm is also in short-run equilibrium, so that price also equals short-run marginal cost. Suppose that

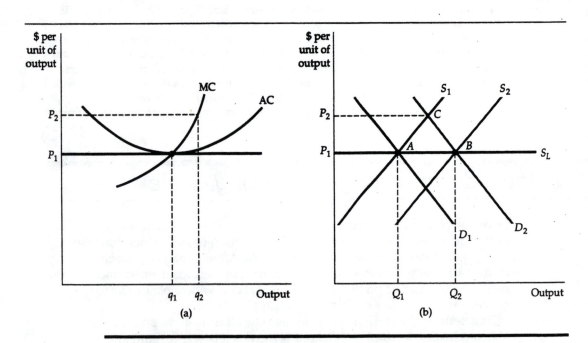

(a)   (b)

FIGURE 8.15   **Long-Run Supply in a Constant-Cost Industry.**   In (b) the long-run supply curve in a constant-cost industry is a horizontal line S_L. When demand increases, initially causing a price rise, the firm initially increases its output from q_1 to q_2 in (a). But the entry of new firms causes a shift to the right in supply. Because input prices are unaffected by the increased output of the industry, entry occurs until the original price is obtained.

the tax cut shifts the market demand curve from D_1 to D_2. Demand curve D_2 intersects supply curve S_1 at C. As a result, the price increases from P_1 to P_2.

Part (a) shows how this price increase affects a typical firm in the industry. When the price increases to P_2, the firm follows its short-run marginal cost curve and increases its output to q_2. This output choice maximizes profit because it satisfies the condition that price equal short-run marginal cost. If every firm responds this way, each firm will be earning a positive profit in short-run equilibrium. This profit will be attractive to investors and will cause existing firms to expand their operations and new firms to enter the market.

As a result, in Figure 8.15b the short-run supply curve shifts to the right, from S_1 to S_2. This shift causes the market to move to a new long-run equilibrium at the intersection of D_2 and S_2. For this intersection to be a long-run equilibrium, output must expand just enough so that firms are earning zero profit and the incentive to enter or exit the industry disappears.

In a constant-cost industry, the additional inputs necessary to produce the higher output can be purchased without an increase in the per-unit price. This might happen, for example, if unskilled labor is a major input in production, and the market wage of unskilled labor is unaffected by the increase in the demand for labor. Since the prices of inputs have not changed, the firms' cost curves are also unchanged; the new equilibrium must be at a point such as B in Figure 8.15b, at which price is equal to P_1, the original price before the unexpected increase in demand occurred.

The long-run supply curve for a constant-cost industry is, therefore, a horizontal line at a price that is equal to the long-run minimum average cost of production. At any higher price, there would be positive profit, increased entry, increased short-run supply, and thus downward pressure on price. Remember that in a constant-cost industry, input prices do not change when conditions change in the output market. Constant-cost industries can have horizontal long-run average cost curves.

Increasing-Cost Industry

In an increasing-cost industry, the prices of some or all inputs to production increase as the industry expands and the demand for the inputs grows. This might arise, for example, if the industry uses skilled labor, which becomes in short supply as the demand for it increases. Or the firm might require mineral resources that are available only on certain types of land, so that the cost of land as an input increases with output. Figure 8.16 shows the derivation of long-run supply, which is similar to the previous constant-cost derivation. The industry is initially in long-run equilibrium at A in part (b). When the demand curve unexpectedly shifts from D_1 to D_2, the short-run price of the product increases to P_2, and industry output increases from Q_1 to Q_2. A typical firm shown in part (a) increases its output from q_1 to q_2 in response to the higher price by moving along its short-run marginal cost curve. The higher profit that this and other firms earn induces new firms to enter the industry.

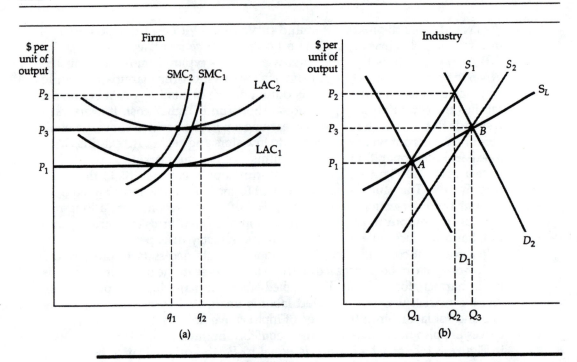

FIGURE 8.16 **Long-Run Supply in an Increasing-Cost Industry.** In (b), the long-run supply curve in an increasing-cost industry is an upward-sloping curve S_L. When demand increases, initially causing a price rise, the firms increase their output from q_1 to q_2 in (a). Then, the entry of new firms causes a shift to the right in supply. Because input prices increase as a result, the new long-run equilibrium occurs at a higher price than the initial equilibrium.

As new firms enter and output expands, the increased demand for inputs causes some or all input prices to increase. The short-run market supply curve shifts to the right as before, but not as much, and the new equilibrium at B results in a price P_3 that is higher than the initial price P_1. The higher market price is needed to ensure that firms earn zero profit in long-run equilibrium because the higher input prices raise the firms' short-run and long-run cost curves. Figure 8.16a illustrates this. The long-run average cost curve shifts up from LAC_1 to LAC_2, while the short-run marginal cost curve shifts to the left from SMC_1 to SMC_2. The new long-run equilibrium price P_3 is equal to the new long-run minimum average cost. As in the constant-cost case, the higher short-run profit caused by the initial increase in demand disappears in the long run as firms increase their output and input costs rise.

The new long-run equilibrium at B in Figure 8.16b is, therefore, on the long-run supply curve for the industry. *In an increasing-cost industry, the long-run industry supply curve is upward sloping*. The industry produces more output, but only at the higher price needed to compensate for the increase in input costs. The term "increasing cost" refers to the upward shift in the firms' long-run average cost curves, not to the positive slope of the cost curve itself.

Decreasing-Cost Industry

The industry supply curve can also be downward sloping. In this case, the unexpected increase in demand causes industry output to expand as before. But as the industry grows larger, it can take advantage of its size to obtain some of its inputs more cheaply. For example, a larger industry may allow for an improved transportation system or for a better, less expensive financial network. In this case firms' average cost curves shift downward (even though firms do not enjoy economies of scale), and the market price of the product falls. The lower market price and the lower average cost of production induce a new long-run equilibrium with more firms, more output, and a lower price. Therefore, *in a decreasing-cost industry, the long-run supply curve for the industry is downward sloping.*

It is tempting to use the decreasing-cost argument to explain why computers have fallen in price over time. But other explanations are usually more persuasive. For example, lower computer prices can be explained by improvements in technology that lower production costs, or by a learning curve. The long-run, downward-sloping supply curve arises only when expansion itself lowers input prices, or when firms can use scale or scope economies to produce at lower cost.

The Short-Run and Long-Run Effects of a Tax

In Chapter 6 we saw that a tax on a firm's input (in the form of an effluent fee) creates an incentive for the firm to change the way it uses inputs in its production process. Now we consider how a firm responds to a tax on its output. To simplify the analysis, assume that the firm uses a fixed-proportions production technology. If the firm is a polluter, the output tax can encourage the firm to reduce its output, and therefore its effluent, or the tax might be imposed just to raise revenue.

First, suppose the output tax is imposed only on this firm, and thus does not affect the market price of the product. We will see that the tax on output encourages the firm to reduce its output. Figure 8.17 shows the relevant short-run cost curves for a firm enjoying positive economic profit by producing an output of q_1 and selling its product at the market price P_1. Because the tax is assessed for every unit of output, it raises the firm's marginal cost curve from MC_1 to $MC_2 = MC_1 + t$, where t is the tax per unit of the firm's output. The tax also raises the average variable cost curve by the amount t.

A close look at Figure 8.17 shows us that the output tax can have two possible effects. First, if the tax is less than the firm's profit margin, the firm will maximize its profit by choosing an output at which its marginal cost plus the

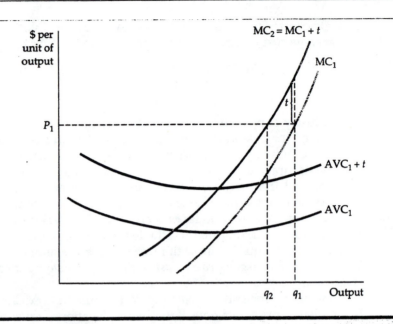

FIGURE 8.17   Effect of an Output Tax on a Competitive Firm's Output.   An output tax raises the firm's marginal cost curve by the amount of the tax. The firm will reduce its output to the point at which the marginal cost plus the tax is equal to the price of the product.

tax is equal to the price of the product. The firm's output falls from q_1 to q_2, and the implicit effect of the tax is to shift the firm's short-run supply curve upward (by the amount of the tax). Second, if the tax is greater than the firm's profit margin, then the average variable cost curve will rise, and the minimum average variable cost will be greater than the market price of the product. The firm will then choose not to produce.

Now suppose all firms in the industry are taxed and have increasing marginal costs. Since each firm reduces its output at the current market price, the total output supplied by the industry will also fall, causing the price of the product to increase. Figure 8.18 illustrates this, where an upward shift in the supply curve, from S_1 to $S_2 = S_1 + t$, causes the market price of the product to increase (by less than the amount of the tax) from P_1 to P_2. This increase in the price of the product diminishes some of the effects that we described previously. Firms will reduce their output less than they would without a price increase.

Output taxes may also encourage some firms (those whose costs are somewhat higher than others) to exit the industry. Figure 8.19 shows the long-run effects of the tax. Part (a) shows that the fee raises the long-run average cost curve for each firm. This makes production unprofitable for some firms, which choose to exit the industry in search of greater profit elsewhere. This results

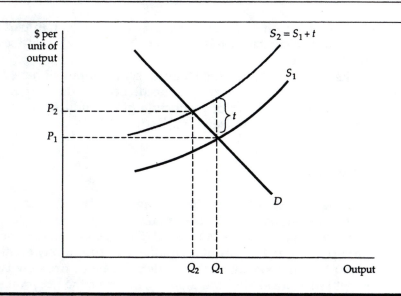

FIGURE 8.18   **Effect of an Output Tax on Industry Output.**   An output tax placed on all firms in a competitive market shifts the short-run supply curve for the industry upward by the amount of the tax. This raises the market price of the product and lowers the total output of the industry.

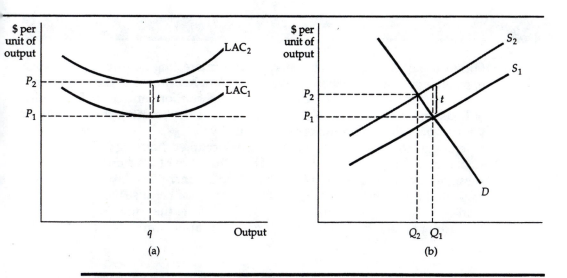

FIGURE 8.19   **The Long-Run Effects of an Output Tax.**   In the long run, the output tax will raise the average cost curve in (a) from LAC_1 to LAC_2. As firms exit the industry because of lower profits, the aggregate supply curve in (b) shifts upward and to the left. In the long-run equilibrium, quantity demanded and quantity supplied are equated at a higher price and a lower output.

in a shift to the left in the market supply curve, shown in part (b). The market price of the product increases from P_1 to P_2, and the quantity sold in the market falls from Q_1 to Q_2.

When the dust settles, the long-run equilibrium will have fewer firms and less output (and less effluent produced), because the output tax has reduced the relative profitability of production in the industry and has encouraged some investors to look elsewhere.[10]

Long-Run Elasticity of Supply

The long-run elasticity of industry supply is defined in the same way as the short-run elasticity. It is the percentage change in output ($\Delta Q/Q$) that results from a percentage change in price ($\Delta P/P$). In a constant-cost industry, the long-run supply curve is horizontal, and the long-run supply elasticity is infinitely large. (A small increase in price will induce an extremely large increase in output.) In an increasing-cost industry, however, the long-run supply elasticity will be positive. Because industries can adjust and expand in the long run, we would generally expect long-run elasticities of supply to be larger than short-run elasticities.[11] The magnitude of the elasticity will depend on the extent to which input costs increase as the market expands. For example, an industry that depends on inputs that are widely available will have a more elastic long-run supply than will an industry that uses inputs in short supply.

EXAMPLE 8.4   THE LONG-RUN SUPPLY OF HOUSING

Owner-occupied and rental housing provide interesting examples of the range of possible supply elasticities. People buy or rent housing to obtain the services that a house provides—a place to eat and sleep, comfort, and so on. If the price of housing services were to rise in one area of the country, the quantity of services provided could increase substantially.

To begin, consider the supply of owner-occupied housing in suburban or rural areas where land is not scarce. Here, the price of land does not increase substantially as the quantity of housing supplied increases. Likewise, the costs associated with construction are not likely to increase because there is a national market for lumber and other materials. Therefore, the long-run elasticity of the supply of housing is likely to be very large, approximating a constant-cost

[10] Although total market output will decline, each firm that remains in the market could produce more output and generate more effluent if the increase in the price is greater than the upward shift in the long-run average cost curve. But if policy is directed toward total industrial pollution, the response of the market, not of individual firms, is important.

[11] In some cases the opposite is true. Consider the elasticity of supply of scrap metal from a durable good like copper. Recall from Chapter 2 that because there is an existing stock of scrap, the long-run elasticity of supply will be *smaller* than the short-run elasticity.

industry. In fact, one recent study found the long-run supply curve to be nearly horizontal.[12]

Even when the elasticity of supply is measured within urban areas, where land costs rise as the demand for housing services increases, the long-run elasticity of supply is still likely to be large because land costs make up only about one-quarter of total housing costs. In one study of urban housing supply, the price elasticity was found to be 5.3.[13]

The market for rental housing is different, however. The construction of rental housing is often restricted by local zoning laws. Many communities outlaw it entirely, while others limit it to certain areas. Because urban land on which most rental housing is located is restricted and valuable, the long-run elasticity of supply of rental housing is much lower than the elasticity of supply of owner-occupied housing. As the price of rental housing services rises, new high-rise rental units are built, and older units are renovated, which increases the quantity of rental services. With urban land becoming more valuable as housing density increases, and with the cost of construction soaring with the height of buildings, the increased demand causes the input costs of rental housing to rise. In this increasing-cost case, the elasticity of supply can be much less than one; in one study the authors found the supply elasticity to be between 0.3 and 0.7.[14]

8.8 *When Is a Market Perfectly Competitive?*

Apart from agriculture, few real-world markets are perfectly competitive in the sense that each firm faces a perfectly horizontal demand curve for a homogeneous product, and that firms can freely enter or exit the industry. Nevertheless, the analysis that we have just completed is useful because many markets are *almost* perfectly competitive: Firms in these markets face highly elastic demand curves, and entry and exit are relatively easy. As a result, it is profitable to set output so that the marginal cost of production is approximately equal to price.

A simple rule of thumb to describe whether a market is close to being perfectly competitive would be appealing. Unfortunately, we have no such rule, and it is important to understand why. Consider the most obvious candidate:

---

[12] See James R. Follain, Jr., "The Price Elasticity of the Long-Run Supply of New Housing Construction," *Land Economics* (May 1979): 190–199.

[13] See Barton A. Smith, "The Supply of Urban Housing," *Journal of Political Economy* 40, No. 3 (Aug. 1976): 389–405.

[14] See Frank deLeeuw and Nkanta Ekanem, "The Supply of Rental Housing," *American Economic Review* 61 (Dec. 1971): 806–817, Table 5.2.

an industry with many firms (say at least 10 to 20). Unfortunately, the presence of many firms is neither necessary nor sufficient for an industry to approximate perfect competition because firms can implicitly or explicitly collude in setting prices.

The presence of only a few firms in a market also does not rule out competitive behavior. Suppose that five firms are in the market, but market demand for the product is very elastic. Then, the demand curve facing each firm is likely to be nearly horizontal, and the firms will behave *as if* they were operating in a perfectly competitive market. Or even if market demand is not very elastic, these five firms might compete aggressively (as we discuss in Chapter 13).

Contestable Markets

Even when only one firm is in a market, that firm may find it profit-maximizing to act as if it were competitive. The reason is that if it tries to raise price above the competitive level, other firms will enter the market, compete for customers, and force the price back down. Hence, competition among firms *within* a market can be less important than the competition *for a market*. In a *contestable market*, new firms may enter the market under essentially the same cost conditions as a firm that is already in the market. A firm can also exit the market without losing any investment in capital that is specific to that market and valueless elsewhere.[15]

Consider, for example, a neighborhood market for retail gasoline stations. It may be economical for there to be only two stations in the neighborhood, since the presence of three or more would cause all stations to lose profits. Yet this market might be contestable, since the cost of opening a gas station is not *sunk*, i.e., it is not specific to that location. As a result, it is easy for firms to enter or exit the market as economic conditions change.

Most monopolistic or oligopolistic markets are not contestable, because the incumbent firms have sunk costs. These incumbents have a competitive advantage over prospective newcomers, and can charge a price higher than marginal cost. Suppose, for example, that a firm has a local monopoly over cable television. Economies of scale make it economical for one firm to provide cable service. But, the market is not fully contestable because some of the cost incurred by the cable company is sunk, and cannot be transferred if the company were to move its business elsewhere. The cable itself can be reutilized, but much of the labor involved in moving it would be wasted, and some of the cable and other materials associated with the hookups in each house would be valueless if the company had to exit the business. Because some of the investment is sunk, a new firm competing for the business would have to bid high enough to cover all its costs, whereas the incumbent firm could set a

---

[15] The theory is developed in William J. Baumol, John C. Panzar, and Robert D. Willig, *Contestable Markets and the Theory of Industry Structure* (New York: Harcourt, Brace, Jovanovich, 1982), and criticized in William G. Shepherd, "Contestability vs. Competition," *American Economic Review* 74 (Sept. 1984): 572–587.

slightly lower price and make a substantial profit above and beyond its variable costs.

The point is that firms may behave competitively in many situations. Unfortunately, no simple indicator signifies when a market approximates perfect competition. Often it is necessary to analyze the number and size of firms and their strategic interactions, as we do in Chapters 12 and 13.

Summary

1. The managers of firms can operate in accordance with a complex set of objectives and under various constraints. However, we can assume that firms act as if they are maximizing their long-run profit.

2. Because a firm in a competitive market has a small share of total industry output, it makes its output choice under the assumption that the demand for its own output is horizontal, in which case the demand curve and the marginal revenue curve are identical.

3. In the short run, a competitive firm maximizes its profit by choosing an output at which price is equal to (short-run) marginal cost, so long as price is greater than or equal to the firm's minimum average variable cost of production.

4. The short-run market supply curve is the horizontal summation of the supply curves of the firms in an industry. It can be characterized by the elasticity of supply—the percentage change in quantity supplied in response to a percentage change in price.

5. The producer surplus for a firm is the difference between revenue of a firm and the minimum cost that would be necessary to produce the profit-maximizing output. In both the short run and the long run, producer surplus is the area under the horizontal price line and above the marginal cost of production for the firm.

6. Economic rent is the payment for a scarce factor of production less the minimum amount necessary to hire that factor. In the long run in a competitive market, producer surplus is equal to the economic rent generated by all scarce factors of production.

7. In the long run, profit-maximizing competitive firms choose the output at which price is equal to long-run marginal cost.

8. A long-run competitive equilibrium occurs when (i) firms maximize profit; (ii) all firms earn zero economic profit, so that there is no incentive to enter or exit the industry; and (iii) the quantity of the product demanded is equal to the quantity supplied.

9. The long-run supply curve for a firm is horizontal when the industry is a constant-cost industry in which the increased demand for inputs to production (associated with an increased demand for the product) has no effect on the market price of the inputs. But the long-run supply curve for a firm is upward sloping in an increasing-cost industry, where the increased demand for inputs causes the market price of some or all inputs to production to rise.

10. Many markets may approximate perfect competition in that one or more firms act as if they face a nearly horizontal demand curve. However, the number of firms in an industry is not always a good indicator of the extent to which that industry is competitive.

Questions for Review

1. Why would a firm that incurs losses choose to produce rather than shut down?

2. The supply curve for a firm in the short run is the short-run marginal cost curve (above the point of minimum average variable cost). Why is the supply curve in the long run *not* the long-run marginal cost curve (above the point of minimum average total cost)?

3. In long-run equilibrium, all firms in the industry earn zero economic profit. Why is this true?

4. What is the difference between economic profit and producer surplus?

5. Why do firms enter an industry when they know that in the long run economic profit will be zero?

6. At the beginning of the twentieth century, there were many small American automobile manufacturers. At the end of the century, there are only three large ones. Suppose that this situation is not the result of lax federal enforcement of antimonopoly laws. How do you explain the decrease in the number of manufacturers? (Hint: What is the inherent cost structure of the automobile industry?)

7. Industry X is characterized by perfect competition, so that every firm in the industry is earning zero economic profit. If the product price fell, no firms could survive. Do you agree or disagree? Discuss.

8. An increase in the demand for video films also increases the salaries of actors and actresses. Is the long-run supply curve for films likely to be horizontal or upward sloping? Explain.

9. True or false: A firm should always produce at an output at which long-run average cost is minimized. Explain.

10. Can there be constant returns to scale in an industry with an upward-sloping supply curve? Explain.

11. What assumptions are necessary for a market to be perfectly competitive? In light of what you have learned in this chapter, why is each of these assumptions important?

12. Suppose a competitive industry faces an increase in demand (i.e., the curve shifts upward). What are the steps by which a competitive market insures increased output? Does your answer change if the government imposes a price ceiling?

13. The government passes a law that allows a substantial subsidy for every acre of land used to grow tobacco. How does this program affect the long-run supply curve for tobacco?

Exercises

1. From the data in Table 8.2, show what happens to the firm's output choice and profit if the price of the product falls from $40 to $35.

2. Again, from the data in Table 8.2, show what happens to the firm's output choice and profit if the fixed cost of production increases from $50 to $100, and then to $150. What general conclusion can you reach about the effects of fixed costs on the firm's output choice?

3. Suppose you are the manager of a watchmaking firm operating in a competitive market. Your cost of production is given by $C = 100 + Q^2$, where Q is the level of output and C is total cost. (The marginal cost of production is $2Q$. The fixed cost of production is $100.)

    a. If the price of watches is $60, how many watches should you produce to maximize profit?

    b. What will the profit level be?

    c. At what minimum price will the firm produce a positive output?

4. Use the same information as in Exercise 1 to answer the following.

Output (Units)	Price ($/Unit)	Revenue ($)	Total Cost ($)	Profit ($)	Marginal Cost ($)	Marginal Revenue ($)
0	40	0	50	−50	—	—
1	40	40	100	−60	50	40
2	40	80	128	−48	28	40
3	40	120	148	−28	20	40
4	40	160	162	−2	14	40
5	40	200	180	20	18	40
6	40	240	200	40	20	40
7	40	280	222	58	22	40
8	40	320	260	60	38	40
9	40	360	305	55	45	40
10	40	400	360	40	55	40
11	40	440	425	15	65	40

a. Derive the firm's short-run supply curve. (Hint: You may want to plot the appropriate cost curves.)

b. If 100 identical firms are in the market, what is the industry supply curve?

5. A sales tax of $1 per unit of output is placed on one firm whose product sells for $5 in a competitive industry.

a. How will this tax affect the cost curves for the firm?

b. What will happen to the firm's price, output, and profit in the short run?

c. What will happen in the long run?

6. Suppose that a competitive firm's marginal cost of producing output q is given by $MC(q) = 3 + 2q$. If the market price of the firm's product is $9:

a. What level of output will the firm produce?

b. What is the firm's producer surplus?

7. Suppose that the average variable cost of the firm in problem 6 is given by $AVC(q) = 3 + q$. Suppose that the firm's fixed costs are known to be $3. Will the firm be earning a positive, negative, or zero profit in the short run?

8. A competitive industry is in long-run equilibrium. A sales tax is then placed on all firms in the industry. What do you expect to happen to the price of the product, the number of firms in the industry, and the output of each firm in the long run?

*9. A sales tax of 10 percent is placed on half the firms (the polluters) in a competitive industry. The revenue is paid to the remaining firms (the non-polluters) as a 10 percent subsidy on the value of output sold.

a. Assuming that all firms have identical constant long-run average costs before the sales tax-subsidy policy, what do you expect to happen to the price of the product, the output of each of the firms, and industry output, in the short run and the long run? (Hint: How does price relate to industry input?)

b. Can such a policy *always* be achieved with a balanced budget in which tax revenues are equal to subsidy payments? Why? Explain.

CHAPTER 10

Market Power: Monopoly and Monopsony

*I*n a perfectly competitive market, there are enough sellers and buyers of a good so that no single seller or buyer can affect its price. Price is determined by the market forces of supply and demand. Individual firms take the market price as a given in deciding how much to produce and sell, and consumers take it as a given in deciding how much to buy.

Monopoly and *monopsony*, the subjects of this chapter, are the polar opposites of perfect competition. A *monopoly* is a market that has only one seller, but many buyers. A *monopsony* is just the opposite—a market with many sellers, but only one buyer. Monopoly and monopsony are closely related, which is why we cover them in the same chapter.

We first discuss the behavior of a monopolist. Because a monopolist is the sole producer of a product, the market demand curve relates the price that the monopolist receives to the quantity it offers for sale. We will see how a monopolist can take advantage of its control over price and how the profit-maximizing price and quantity differ from what would prevail in a competitive market. In general, the monopolist's quantity will be lower and its price higher than the competitive quantity and price. This imposes a cost on society because fewer consumers buy the product, and those who do pay more for it. This is why the antitrust laws forbid firms from monopolizing most markets. When economies of scale make monopoly desirable—for example, with local electric power companies—we will see how the government can then increase efficiency by regulating the monopolist's price.

Pure monopoly is rare, but in many markets only a few firms compete with each other. The interactions of firms in such markets can be complicated and often involve aspects of strategic gaming, a topic covered in Chapters 12 and 13. In any case, the firms may be able to affect price and may find it profitable to charge a price higher than marginal cost. These firms have *monopoly power*.

319

We will discuss the determinants of monopoly power, its measurement, and its implications for pricing.

Next we will turn to *monopsony*. Unlike a competitive buyer, the price that a monopsonist pays depends on the quantity that it purchases. The monopsonist's problem is to choose the quantity that maximizes its net benefit from the purchase—the value derived from the good less the money paid for it. By showing how the choice is made, we will demonstrate the close parallel between monopsony and monopoly.

Pure monopsony is also unusual. But many markets have only a few buyers, who can purchase the good for less than they would pay in a competitive market. These buyers have *monopsony power*. Typically this occurs in markets for inputs to production. For example, the three large U.S. car manufacturers have monopsony power in the markets for tires, car batteries, and other parts. We will discuss the determinants of monopsony power, its measurement, and its implications for pricing.

Monopoly and monopsony power are two forms of *market power*. Market power refers to the ability—by a seller or a buyer—to affect the price of a good.[1] Since sellers or buyers have at least some market power (in most real-world markets), we need to understand how market power works and its implications for firms and consumers.

10.1 *Monopoly*

As the sole producer of a product, a monopolist is in a unique position. If the monopolist decides to raise the price of the product, it need not worry about competitors who, by charging a lower price, would capture a larger share of the market at the monopolist's expense. The monopolist *is* the market and has complete control over the amount of output offered for sale.

But this does not mean that the monopolist can charge as high a price as it wants—at least not if its objective is to maximize profit. This textbook is a case in point. Prentice Hall, Inc. owns the copyright and is therefore a monopoly producer of this book. Then why doesn't it sell the book for $350 a copy? Because few people would buy it, and Prentice Hall would earn a much lower profit.

To maximize profit, the monopolist must first determine the characteristics of market demand, as well as its costs. Knowledge of demand and cost is crucial for a firm's economic decision making. Given this knowledge, the

---

[1] The courts often use the term "monopoly power" to mean a substantial amount of market power, and in particular enough to warrant scrutiny under the antitrust laws. In this book, however, we use "monopoly power" to mean market power on the part of sellers, whether substantial or not.

monopolist must then decide how much to produce and sell. The price per unit the monopolist receives then follows directly from the market demand curve. (Equivalently, the monopolist can determine price, and the quantity it will sell at that price follows from the market demand curve.)

Average Revenue and Marginal Revenue

The monopolist's average revenue—the price it receives per unit sold—is just the market demand curve. To choose its profit-maximizing output level, the monopolist also needs to know its *marginal revenue*, that is, the change in revenue that results from a unit change in output. To see the relationship among total, average, and marginal revenue, consider a firm facing the following demand curve: $P = 6 - Q$.

Table 10.1 shows the behavior of total, average, and marginal revenue for this demand curve. Note that revenue is zero when the price is $6 because at that price nothing is sold. However, at a price of $5 one unit is sold, and then total (and marginal) revenue is $5. An increase in quantity sold from 1 to 2 increases revenue from $5 to $8, so that marginal revenue is $3. As quantity sold increases from 2 to 3, marginal revenue falls to $1, and when it increases from 3 to 4, marginal revenue becomes negative. When marginal revenue is positive, revenue is increasing with quantity, but when marginal revenue is negative, revenue is decreasing.

When the demand curve is downward sloping, the price (average revenue) is greater than marginal revenue because all units are sold at the same price. To increase sales by 1 unit, the price must fall, so that all units sold, not just the additional unit, earn less revenue. Note what happens in Table 10.1 when output is increased from 1 to 2 units, and price is reduced to $4. Marginal revenue is $3: $4 (the revenue from the sale of the additional unit of output) less $1 (the loss of revenue from selling the first unit for $4 instead of $5). Thus, marginal revenue ($3) is less than price ($4).

Price P	Quantity Q	Total Revenue R	Marginal Revenue MR	Average Revenue AR
$6	0	$0	—	—
5	1	5	$5	$5
4	2	8	3	4
3	3	9	1	3
2	4	8	−1	2
1	5	5	−3	1

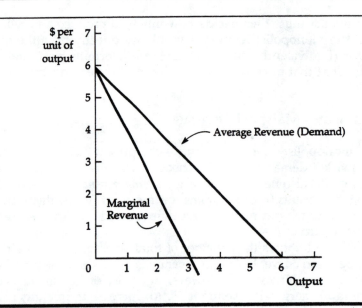

FIGURE 10.1 Average and Marginal Revenue. Average and marginal revenue are shown for the demand curve $P = 6 - Q$.

Figure 10.1 plots average and marginal revenue for the data in Table 10.1. Our demand curve is a straight line, and in this case the marginal revenue curve has twice the slope of the demand curve (and the same intercept).[2]

The Monopolist's Output Decision

What quantity should the monopolist produce? In Chapter 8 we saw that to maximize profit, a firm must set output so that marginal revenue is equal to marginal cost. This is the solution to the monopolist's problem. In Figure 10.2, the market demand curve D is the monopolist's average revenue curve. It specifies the price per unit that the monopolist receives as a function of its output level. Also shown are the corresponding marginal revenue curve MR and the average and marginal cost curves, AC and MC. Marginal revenue and marginal cost are equal at quantity Q^*. Then from the demand curve, we find the price P^* that corresponds to this quantity Q^*.

How can we be sure that Q^* is the profit-maximizing quantity? Suppose the monopolist produces a smaller quantity Q_1 and receives the corresponding

---

[2] If the demand curve is written so that price is a function of quantity, $P = a - bQ$, total revenue is given by $PQ = aQ - bQ^2$. Marginal revenue (using calculus) is $d(PQ)/dQ = a - 2bQ$. In this example, demand is $P = 6 - Q$ and marginal revenue is $MR = 6 - 2Q$. (This holds only for small changes in Q, and therefore does not exactly match the data in Table 10.1.)

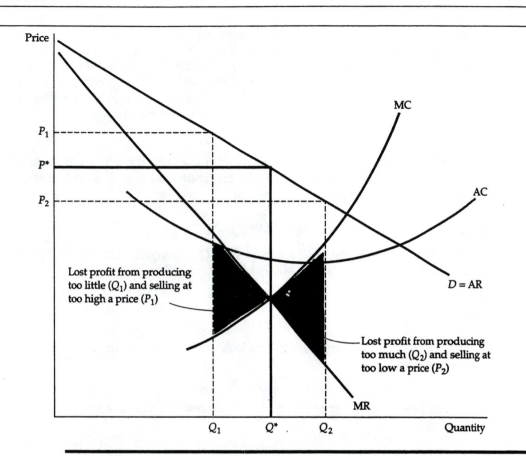

FIGURE 10.2   Profit Is Maximized When Marginal Revenue Equals Marginal Cost.
Q^* is the output level at which MR = MC. If the firm produces a smaller output, say Q_1,
it sacrifices some profit because the extra revenue that could be earned from producing
and selling the units between Q_1 and Q^* exceeds the cost of producing them. Similarly,
expanding output from Q^* to Q_2 would reduce profit, because the additional cost would
exceed the additional revenue.

higher price P_1. As Figure 10.2 shows, marginal revenue would then exceed
marginal cost, so if the monopolist produced a little more than Q_1, it would
receive extra profit (MR − MC) and thereby increase its total profit. In fact, the
monopolist could keep increasing output, adding more to its total profit until
output Q^*, at which point the incremental profit earned from producing one more
unit is zero. So the smaller quantity Q_1 is not profit maximizing, even though
it allows the monopolist to charge a higher price. By producing Q_1 instead of
Q^*, the monopolist's total profit would be smaller by an amount equal to the
shaded area below the MR curve and above the MC curve, between Q_1 and Q^*.

In Figure 10.2, the larger quantity Q_2 is likewise not profit maximizing. At
this quantity marginal cost exceeds marginal revenue, so if the monopolist pro-

duced a little less than Q_2, it would increase its total profit (by MC − MR). The monopolist could increase its profit even more by reducing output all the way to Q^*. The increased profit achieved by producing Q^* instead of Q_2 is given by the area below the MC curve and above the MR curve, between Q^* and Q_2.

We can also see algebraically that Q^* maximizes profit. Profit π is the difference between revenue and cost, both of which depend on Q:

$$\pi(Q) = R(Q) - C(Q)$$

As Q is increased from zero, profit will increase until it reaches a maximum, and then begin to decrease. Thus, the profit-maximizing Q is such that the incremental profit resulting from a small increase in Q is just zero (i.e., $\Delta\pi/\Delta Q = 0$). Then

$$\Delta\pi/\Delta Q = \Delta R/\Delta Q - \Delta C/\Delta Q = 0$$

But $\Delta R/\Delta Q$ is marginal revenue, and $\Delta C/\Delta Q$ is marginal cost, so the profit-maximizing condition is that MR − MC = 0, or MR = MC.

An Example

To grasp this result more clearly, let's look at an example. Suppose the cost of production is

$$C(Q) = 50 + Q^2$$

(i.e., there is a fixed cost of $50, and variable cost is Q^2). And suppose demand is given by

$$P(Q) = 40 - Q$$

By setting marginal revenue equal to marginal cost, you can verify that profit is maximized when $Q = 10$, which corresponds to a price of $30.[3]

Cost, revenue, and profit are plotted in Figure 10.3a. When the firm produces little or no output, profit is negative because of the fixed cost. Profit increases as Q increases, until it reaches a maximum of $150 at $Q^* = 10$, and then decreases as Q is increased further. And at the point of maximum profit, the slopes of the revenue and cost curves are the same. (Note that the tangent lines rr′ and cc′ are parallel.) The slope of the revenue curve is $\Delta R/\Delta Q$, or marginal revenue, and the slope of the cost curve is $\Delta C/\Delta Q$, or marginal cost. Profit is maximized when marginal revenue equals marginal cost, so the slopes are equal.

Figure 10.3b shows the corresponding average and marginal revenue curves, and average and marginal cost curves. Marginal revenue and marginal cost intersect at $Q^* = 10$. At this quantity, average cost is $15 per unit, and price is $30 per unit, so average profit is $30 − $15 = $15 per unit. Since 10 units are sold, profit is (10)($15) = $150, the area of the shaded rectangle.

---

[3] Note that average cost is $C(Q)/Q = 50/Q + Q$, and marginal cost is $\Delta C/\Delta Q = 2Q$. Revenue is $R(Q) = P(Q)Q = 40Q - Q^2$, so marginal revenue is MR = $\Delta R/\Delta Q = 40 - 2Q$. Setting marginal revenue equal to marginal cost gives $40 - 2Q = 2Q$, or $Q = 10$.

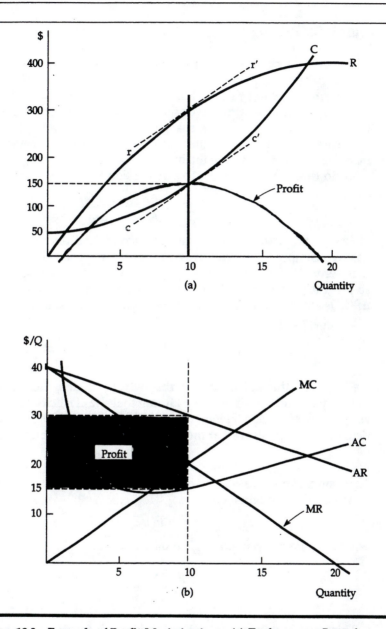

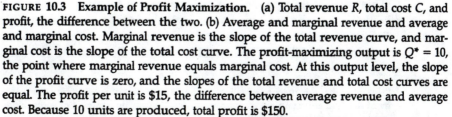

FIGURE 10.3   **Example of Profit Maximization.**   (a) Total revenue R, total cost C, and profit, the difference between the two. (b) Average and marginal revenue and average and marginal cost. Marginal revenue is the slope of the total revenue curve, and marginal cost is the slope of the total cost curve. The profit-maximizing output is $Q^* = 10$, the point where marginal revenue equals marginal cost. At this output level, the slope of the profit curve is zero, and the slopes of the total revenue and total cost curves are equal. The profit per unit is $15, the difference between average revenue and average cost. Because 10 units are produced, total profit is $150.

A Rule of Thumb for Pricing

We know that price and output should be chosen so that marginal revenue equals marginal cost, but how can the manager of a firm find the correct price and output level in practice? Most managers have only limited knowledge of the average and marginal revenue curves that their firms face. Similarly, they might know only the firm's marginal cost over a limited output range. We therefore want to translate the condition that marginal revenue should equal marginal cost into a rule of thumb that can be more easily applied in practice.

To do this, we first rewrite the expression for marginal revenue:

$$MR = \frac{\Delta R}{\Delta Q} = \frac{\Delta(PQ)}{\Delta Q}$$

Note that the extra revenue from an incremental unit of quantity, $\Delta(PQ)/\Delta Q$, has two components. Producing one extra unit and selling it at price P brings in revenue $(1)(P) = P$. But the firm faces a downward-sloping demand curve, so producing and selling this extra unit also results in a small drop in price $\Delta P/\Delta Q$, which reduces the revenue from *all* units sold (i.e., a change in revenue $Q[\Delta P/\Delta Q]$). Thus,

$$MR = P + Q\frac{\Delta P}{\Delta Q} = P + P\left(\frac{Q}{P}\right)\left(\frac{\Delta P}{\Delta Q}\right)$$

We obtained the expression on the right by taking the term $Q(\Delta P/\Delta Q)$ and multiplying and dividing it by P. Recall that the elasticity of demand is defined as $E_d = (P/Q)(\Delta Q/\Delta P)$. Hence, $(Q/P)(\Delta P/\Delta Q)$ is the reciprocal of the elasticity of demand, $1/E_d$, measured at the profit-maximizing output, and

$$MR = P + P(1/E_d)$$

Now, since the firm's objective is to maximize profit, we can set marginal revenue equal to marginal cost:

$$P + P(1/E_d) = MC$$

which can be rearranged to give us

$$\boxed{\frac{P - MC}{P} = -\frac{1}{E_d}} \qquad (10.1)$$

This relationship provides a rule of thumb for pricing. The left-hand side, $(P - MC)/P$, is the markup over marginal cost as a percentage of price. The relationship says that this markup should equal minus the inverse of the elasticity of demand.[4] (This will be a positive number because the elasticity of demand

----

[4] Remember that this markup equation applies at the point of a profit maximum. If both the elasticity of demand and marginal cost vary considerably over the range of outputs under consideration, you may have to know the entire demand and marginal cost curves to determine the optimum output level. On the other hand, this equation can be used to check whether a particular output level and price are optimal.

is negative.) Equivalently, we can rearrange this equation to express price directly as a markup over marginal cost:

$$P = \frac{MC}{1 + (1/E_d)}$$
(10.2)

For example, if the elasticity of demand is -4 and marginal cost is \$9 per unit, price should be $\$9/(1 - \frac{1}{4}) = \$9/.75 = \$12$ per unit.

How does the price set by a monopolist compare with the price under competition? In Chapter 8 we saw that in a perfectly competitive market price equals marginal cost. A monopolist charges a price that exceeds marginal cost, but by an amount that depends inversely on the elasticity of demand. As the markup equation (10.1) shows, if demand is extremely elastic, E_d is a large negative number, and price will be very close to marginal cost, so that a monopolized market will look much like a competitive one. In fact, when demand is very elastic, there is little benefit to being a monopolist.

Shifts in Demand

In a competitive market, there is a clear relationship between price and the quantity supplied. That relationship is the supply curve, which, as we saw in Chapter 8, represents the marginal cost of production for the industry as a whole. The supply curve tells us how much will be produced at every price.

A monopolistic market has no supply curve. In other words, there is no one-to-one relationship between price and the quantity produced. The reason is that the monopolist's output decision depends not only on marginal cost, but also on the shape of the demand curve. As a result, shifts in demand do not trace out a series of prices and quantities as happens with a competitive supply curve. Instead, shifts in demand can lead to changes in price with no change in output, changes in output with no change in price, or changes in both.

This is illustrated in Figures 10.4a and 10.4b. In both parts of the figure, the demand curve is initially D_1, the corresponding marginal revenue curve is MR_1, and the monopolist's initial price and quantity are P_1 and Q_1. In Figure 10.4a the demand curve is shifted down and rotated; the new demand and marginal revenue curves are shown as D_2 and MR_2. Note that MR_2 intersects the marginal cost curve at the same point that MR_1 does. As a result, the quantity produced stays the same. Price, however, falls to P_2.

In Figure 10.4b the demand curve is shifted up and rotated. The new marginal revenue curve MR_2 intersects the marginal cost curve at a larger quantity, Q_2 instead of Q_1. But the shift in the demand curve is such that the price charged is exactly the same.

Shifts in demand usually cause changes in both price and quantity. But the special cases shown in Figure 10.4 illustrate an important distinction between monopoly and competitive supply. A competitive industry supplies a specific quantity at every price. No such relationship exists for a monopolist, which,

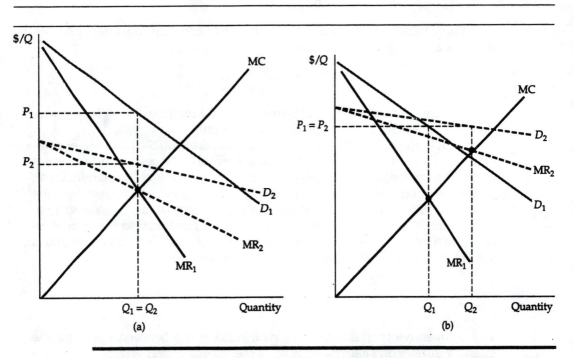

FIGURE 10.4a   **Shift in Demand Leads to Change in Price but Same Output.**   The demand curve D_1 shifts to new demand curve D_2. But the new marginal revenue curve MR_2 intersects marginal cost at the same point that the old marginal revenue curve MR_1 did. The profit-maximizing output therefore remains the same, although price falls from P_1 to P_2.

FIGURE 10.4b   **Shift in Demand Leads to Change in Output but Same Price.**   The new marginal revenue curve MR_2 intersects marginal cost at a higher output level Q_2. But because demand is now more elastic, price remains the same.

depending on how demand shifts, might supply several different quantities at the same price, or the same quantity at different prices.

The Effect of a Tax

A tax on output can also have a different effect on a monopolist than on a competitive industry. In Chapter 9 we saw that when a specific (i.e., per unit) tax is imposed on a competitive industry, the market price rises by an amount that is less than the tax, and that the burden of the tax is shared by producers and consumers. Under monopoly, however, price can sometimes rise by *more* than the amount of the tax.

Analyzing the effect of a tax on a monopolist is straightforward. Suppose a specific tax of t dollars per unit is levied, so that the monopolist must remit t dollars to the government for every unit it sells. Therefore, the firm's marginal (and average) cost is increased by the amount of the tax t. If MC was the firm's original marginal cost, its optimal production decision is now given by

$$MR = MC + t$$

Graphically, we shift the marginal cost curve upwards by an amount t, and find the new intersection with marginal revenue. Figure 10.5 shows this. Here Q_0 and P_0 are the quantity and price before the tax is imposed, and Q_1 and P_1 are the quantity and price after the tax.

Shifting the marginal cost curve upwards results in a smaller quantity and higher price. Sometimes price increases by less than the tax, but not always—in Figure 10.5, price increases by *more* than the tax. This would be impossible in a competitive market, but it can happen with a monopolist because the relationship between price and marginal cost depends on the elasticity of demand. Suppose, for example, that a monopolist faces a constant elasticity demand curve, with elasticity -2. Equation (10.2) then tells us that price will equal twice marginal cost. With a tax t, marginal cost increases to $MC + t$, so price increases to $2(MC + t) = 2MC + 2t$; that is, it rises by twice the amount of the tax. (However, the monopolist's profit nonetheless falls with the tax.)

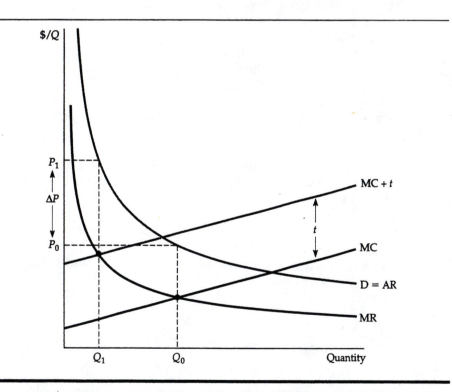

FIGURE 10.5   Effect of Excise Tax on Monopolist.   With a tax t per unit, the firm's effective marginal cost is increased by the amount t to $MC + t$. In this example, the increase in price ΔP is larger than the tax t.

*The Multiplant Firm

We have seen that a firm maximizes profit by setting output where marginal revenue equals marginal cost. For many firms, production takes place in two or more different plants whose operating costs can differ. However, the logic used in choosing output levels is very similar to that for the single-plant firm.

Suppose a firm has two plants. What should its total output be, and how much of that output should each plant produce? We can find the answer intuitively in two steps.

First, whatever the total output, it should be divided between the two plants so that *marginal cost is the same in each plant*. Otherwise the firm could reduce its costs and increase its profit by reallocating production. For example, if marginal cost at plant 1 were higher than at plant 2, the firm could produce the same output at a lower total cost by producing less at plant 1 and more at plant 2.

Second, we know that total output must be such that *marginal revenue equals marginal cost*. Otherwise, the firm could increase its profit by raising or lowering total output. For example, suppose marginal costs were the same at each plant, but marginal revenue exceeded marginal cost. Then the firm would do better by producing more at both plants because the revenue earned from the additional units would exceed the cost. Since marginal costs must be the same at each plant, and marginal revenue must equal marginal cost, we see that profit is maximized when *marginal revenue equals marginal cost at each plant*.

We can also derive this result algebraically. Let Q_1 and C_1 be the output and cost of production for plant 1, Q_2 and C_2 be the output and cost of production for plant 2, and $Q_T = Q_1 + Q_2$ be total output. Then profit is

$$\pi = PQ_T - C_1(Q_1) - C_2(Q_2)$$

The firm should increase output from each plant until the incremental profit from the last unit produced is zero. Setting incremental profit from output at plant 1 to zero:

$$\frac{\Delta\pi}{\Delta Q_1} = \frac{\Delta(PQ_T)}{\Delta Q_1} - \frac{\Delta C_1}{\Delta Q_1} = 0$$

Here $\Delta(PQ_T)/\Delta Q_1$ is the revenue from producing and selling one more unit, i.e., marginal revenue, MR, for all of the firm's output. The next term, $\Delta C_1/\Delta Q_1$, is marginal cost at plant 1, MC_1. We thus have $MR - MC_1 = 0$, or

$$MR = MC_1$$

Similarly, setting incremental profit from output at plant 2 to zero,

$$MR = MC_2$$

Putting these relations together, we see that the firm should produce so that

$$\boxed{MR = MC_1 = MC_2} \qquad (10.3)$$

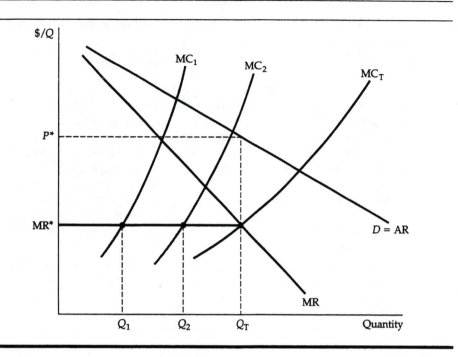

FIGURE 10.6   Production with Two Plants.   A firm with two plants maximizes profits by choosing output levels Q_1 and Q_2 so that marginal revenue MR (which depends on *total* output) equals marginal costs for each plant, MC_1 and MC_2.

Figure 10.6 illustrates this for a firm with two plants. MC_1 and MC_2 are the marginal cost curves for the two plants. (Note that plant 1 has higher marginal costs than plant 2.) Also shown is a curve labelled MC_T. This is the firm's total marginal cost and is obtained by horizontally summing MC_1 and MC_2.[5] Now we can find the profit-maximizing output levels Q_1, Q_2, and Q_T. First, find the intersection of MC_T with MR; that determines total output Q_T. Next, draw a horizontal line from that point on the marginal revenue curve to the vertical axis; point MR* determines the firm's marginal revenue. The intersections of the marginal revenue line with MC_1 and MC_2 give the outputs Q_1 and Q_2 for the two plants, as shown in Equation (10.3).

Note that total output Q_T determines the firm's marginal revenue (and hence its price P^*), but Q_1 and Q_2 determine marginal costs at each of the two plants. Since MC_T was found by horizontally summing MC_1 and MC_2, we know that $Q_1 + Q_2 = Q_T$. Hence these output levels satisfy the condition that $MR = MC_1 = MC_2$.

---

[5] Note the similarity to the way we obtained a competitive industry's supply curve in Chapter 8 by horizontally summing the marginal cost curves of the individual firms.

10.2 *Monopoly Power*

Pure monopoly is rare. Markets in which several firms compete with one another are much more common. We say more about the forms this competition can take in Chapters 12 and 13. But we should explain here why in a market with several firms, each firm is likely to face a downward-sloping demand curve, and therefore will produce so that price exceeds marginal cost.

Suppose, for example, that four firms produce toothbrushes, which have the market demand curve shown in Figure 10.7a. Let's assume that these four firms are producing an aggregate of 20,000 toothbrushes per day (5000 per day each), and selling them at $1.50 each. Note that market demand is relatively inelastic; you can verify that at this $1.50 price, the elasticity of demand is −1.5.

Now suppose that Firm *A* is deciding whether to lower its price to increase sales. To make this decision, it needs to know how its sales would respond to

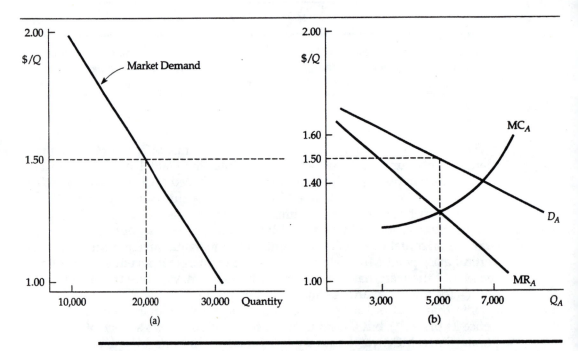

FIGURE 10.7a   **Market Demand for Toothbrushes.**
FIGURE 10.7b   **Demand for Toothbrushes as Seen by Firm A.**   At a market price of $1.50, elasticity of market demand is −1.5. Firm A, however, sees a much more elastic demand curve D_A because of competition from other firms. At a price of $1.50, Firm A's demand elasticity is −6. Still, Firm A has some monopoly power. Its profit-maximizing price is $1.50, which exceeds marginal cost.

a change in its price. In other words, it needs some idea of the demand curve *it* faces, as opposed to the *market* demand curve. A reasonable possibility is shown in Figure 10.7b, where the firm's demand curve D_A is much more elastic than the market demand curve. (At the $1.50 price the elasticity is −6.0.) The firm might anticipate that by raising price from $1.50 to $1.60, its sales will drop, say, from 5000 units to 3000, as consumers buy more toothbrushes from the other firms. (If *all* firms raised their prices to $1.60, sales for Firm A would fall only to 4500.) But for several reasons, sales won't drop to zero, as they would in a perfectly competitive market. First, Firm A's toothbrushes might be a little different from its competitors, so some consumers will pay a bit more for them. Second, the other firms might also raise their prices. Similarly, Firm A might anticipate that by lowering its price from $1.50 to $1.40, it can sell more, perhaps 7000 toothbrushes instead of 5000. But it will not capture the entire market. Some consumers might still prefer the competitors' toothbrushes, and the competitors might also lower their prices.

So Firm A's demand curve depends on how much its product differs from its competitors' products and on how the four firms compete with one another. We will discuss product differentiation and interfirm competition in Chapters 12 and 13. But one important point should be clear: *Firm A is likely to face a demand curve that is more elastic than the market demand curve, but not infinitely elastic like the demand curve facing a perfectly competitive firm.*

Given knowledge of its demand curve, how much should Firm A produce? The same principle applies: The profit-maximizing quantity equates marginal revenue and marginal cost. In Figure 10.7b that quantity is 5000 units, and the corresponding price is $1.50, which exceeds marginal cost. So although Firm A is not a pure monopolist, *it does have monopoly power*—it can profitably charge a price greater than marginal cost. Of course, its monopoly power is less than it would be if it had driven away the competition and monopolized the market, but it might still be substantial.

This raises two questions. First, how can we *measure* monopoly power, so that we can compare one firm with another? (So far we have been talking about monopoly power only in *qualitative* terms.) Second, what are the *sources* of monopoly power, and why do some firms have more monopoly power than others? We address both these questions below, although a more complete answer to the second question will be provided in Chapters 12 and 13.

Measuring Monopoly Power

Remember the important distinction between a perfectly competitive firm and a firm with monopoly power: For the competitive firm, price equals marginal cost; for the firm with monopoly power, price exceeds marginal cost. Therefore, a natural way to measure monopoly power is to examine the extent to which the profit-maximizing price exceeds marginal cost. In particular, we can use the markup ratio of price minus marginal cost to price that we introduced earlier as part of a rule of thumb for pricing. This measure of monopoly power was introduced by economist Abba Lerner in 1934 and is called *Lerner's Degree of Monopoly Power*:

$$L = (P - MC)/P$$

This Lerner index always has a value between zero and one. For a perfectly competitive firm, $P = MC$ so that $L = 0$. The larger L is, the greater the degree of monopoly power.

This index of monopoly power can also be expressed in terms of the elasticity of demand facing the firm. Using equation (10.1), we know that

$$L = (P - MC)/P = -1/E_d \qquad (10.4)$$

Remember, however, that E_d is now the elasticity of the *firm's* demand curve, and not the market demand curve. In the toothbrush example discussed above, the elasticity of demand for Firm A is −6.0, and the degree of monopoly power is $\frac{1}{6} = 0.167$.[6]

Note that considerable monopoly power does not necessarily imply high profits. Profit depends on *average* cost relative to price. Firm A might have more monopoly power than Firm B, but might earn a lower profit because it has much higher average costs.

The Rule of Thumb for Pricing

In the previous section, we used equation (10.2) to compute price as a simple markup over marginal cost:

$$P = \frac{MC}{1 + (1/E_d)}$$

This relationship provides a rule of thumb for *any* firm with monopoly power, if we remember that E_d is the elasticity of demand for the *firm*, and not the elasticity of *market* demand.

It is harder to determine the elasticity of demand for the firm than for the market because the firm must consider how its competitors will react to price changes. Essentially, the manager must estimate the percentage change in the firm's unit sales that is likely to result from a 1 percent change in the price the firm charges. This estimate might be based on a formal model or on the manager's intuition and experience.

Given an estimate of the firm's elasticity of demand, the manager can calculate the proper markup. If the firm's elasticity of demand is large, this markup

---

[6] There are three problems with applying the Lerner index to the analysis of public policy toward firms. First, because marginal cost is difficult to measure, average variable cost is often used in Lerner index calculations. Second, if the firm prices below its optimal price (possibly to avoid legal scrutiny), its potential monopoly power will not be noted by the index. Third, the index ignores dynamic aspects of pricing such as effects of the learning curve, shifts in demand, etc. See Robert S. Pindyck, "The Measurement of Monopoly Power in Dynamic Markets," *Journal of Law and Economics* 28 (April 1985): 193–222.

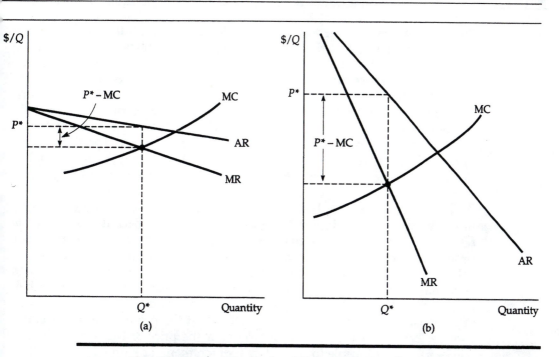

FIGURE 10.8   Elasticity of Demand and Price Markup.   The markup $(P - MC)/P$ is equal to minus the inverse of the elasticity of demand. If demand is elastic as in (a), the markup is small, and the firm has little monopoly power. The opposite is true if demand is inelastic, as in (b).

will be small (and we can say that the firm has very little monopoly power). If the firm's elasticity of demand is small, this markup will be large (and the firm will have considerable monopoly power). Figures 10.8a and 10.8b illustrate these two extremes.

EXAMPLE 10.1   MARKUP PRICING: SUPERMARKETS TO DESIGNER JEANS

Three examples should help clarify the use of markup pricing. Consider a retail supermarket chain. Although the elasticity of market demand for food is small (about −1), several supermarkets usually serve most areas, so no single supermarket can raise its prices very much without losing many customers to other stores. As a result, the elasticity of demand for any one supermarket is often as large as −10. Substituting this number for E_d in equation (10.2), we find $P = MC/(1 - 0.1) = MC/(0.9) = (1.11)MC$. In other words, the manager of a typical supermarket should set prices about 11 percent above marginal cost. For a reasonably wide range of output levels (over which the size of the store and the number of its employees will remain fixed), marginal cost includes the cost of purchasing the food at wholesale, together with the costs of storing the food, arranging it on the shelves, etc. For most supermarkets the markup is indeed about 10 or 11 percent.

Small convenience stores, which are often open on Sundays or even 24 hours a day, typically charge higher prices than supermarkets. Why? Because a convenience store faces a less elastic demand curve. Its customers are generally less price sensitive. They might need a quart of milk or a loaf of bread late at night, or find it inconvenient to drive to the supermarket. The elasticity of demand for a convenience store is about −5, so the markup equation implies that its prices should be about 25 percent above marginal cost, as indeed they typically are.

The Lerner index, $(P − MC)/P$, tells us that the convenience store has more monopoly power, but does it make larger profits? No. Because its volume is far smaller and its average fixed costs are larger, it usually earns a much smaller profit than a large supermarket, despite its higher markup.

Finally, consider a producer of designer jeans. Many companies produce jeans, but some consumers will pay much more for jeans with a designer label. Just how much more they will pay—or more exactly, how much sales will drop in response to higher prices—is a question that the producer must carefully consider because it is critical in determining the price at which the clothing will be sold (at wholesale to retail stores, which then mark up the price further for sale to their customers). With designer jeans, demand elasticities in the range of −3 to −4 are typical for the major labels. This means that price should be 33 to 50 percent higher than marginal cost. Marginal cost is typically $12 to $18 per pair, and the wholesale price is in the $18 to $27 range.

EXAMPLE 10.2   THE PRICING OF PRERECORDED VIDEOCASSETTES

During the mid-1980s, the number of households owning videocassette recorders (VCRs) grew rapidly, as did the markets for rentals and sales of prerecorded cassettes. Although many more videocassettes are rented through small retail outlets than are sold outright, the market for sales is large and growing. Producers, however, found it difficult to decide what price to charge for their cassettes. As a result, in 1985 popular movies were selling for vastly different prices as the data for that year show in Table 10.2.

Note that *The Empire Strikes Back* was selling for nearly $80, while *Star Trek*, a film that appealed to the same audience and was about as popular, sold for only about $25. These price differences reflected uncertainty and a wide divergence of views on pricing by producers. The issue was whether lower prices would induce consumers to buy the videocassettes rather than rent them. Because producers do not share in the retailers' revenues from rentals, they should charge a low price for cassettes only if that will induce enough con-

TABLE 10.2 The Prices of Videos in 1985 and 1993			
1985		**1993**	
Title	Retail Price ($)	Title	Retail Price ($)
Purple Rain	$29.98	*Batman Returns*	$19.95
Raiders of the Lost Ark	24.95	*Lethal Weapon 3*	17.95
Jane Fonda Workout	59.95	*Terminator 2*	17.95
The Empire Strikes Back	79.98	*Beauty and the Beast*	19.95
An Officer and A Gentleman	24.95	*Teenage Mutant Ninja Turtle Movie*	14.95
Star Trek: The Motion Picture	24.95	*Home Alone 2*	17.95
Star Wars	39.98	*Aladdin*	17.95

sumers to buy them. Because the market was young, producers had no good estimates of the elasticity of demand, so they based prices on hunches or trial and error.[7]

As the market matured, however, sales data and market research studies put pricing decisions on firmer ground. They strongly indicated that demand was elastic and that the profit-maximizing price was in the range of $15 to $30. As one industry analyst said, "People are becoming collectors. . . . As you lower the price you attract households that would not have considered buying at a higher price point."[8] And, indeed, as Table 10.2 shows, by 1993 most producers had lowered prices across the board. As a result, sales and profits increased.

10.3 *Sources of Monopoly Power*

Why do some firms have considerable monopoly power, and other firms have little or none? Remember that monopoly power is the ability to set price above marginal cost, and the amount by which price exceeds marginal cost depends inversely on the firm's elasticity of demand. As equation (10.3) shows, the less elastic its demand curve, the more monopoly power a firm has. The ultimate determinant of monopoly power is therefore the firm's elasticity of demand. The question is, why do some firms (e.g., a supermarket chain) face a demand

---

[7] "Video Producers Debate the Value of Price Cuts," *New York Times*, Feb. 19, 1985.

[8] "Studios Now Stressing Video Sales Over Rentals," *New York Times*, Oct. 17, 1989. For a detailed study of videocassette pricing, see Carl E. Enomoto and Soumendra N. Ghosh, "Pricing in the Home-Video Market," New Mexico State University working paper, 1992.

curve that is more elastic, while others (e.g., a producer of designer clothing) face one that is less elastic?

Three factors determine a firm's elasticity of demand. First is the *elasticity of market demand*. The firm's own demand will be at least as elastic as market demand, so the elasticity of market demand limits the potential for monopoly power. Second is the *number of firms* in the market. If there are many firms, it is unlikely that any one firm will be able to affect price significantly. Third is the *interaction among firms*. Even if only two or three firms are·in the market, each firm will be unable to profitably raise price very much if the rivalry among them is aggressive, with each firm trying to capture as much of the market as it can. Let's examine each of these three determinants of monopoly power.

The Elasticity of Market Demand

If there is only one firm—a pure monopolist—its demand curve is the market demand curve. Then the firm's degree of monopoly power depends completely on the elasticity of market demand. More often, however, several firms compete with one another; then the elasticity of market demand sets a lower limit on the magnitude of the elasticity of demand for each firm. Recall our example of the toothbrush producers that was illustrated in Figure 10.7. The market demand for toothbrushes might not be very elastic, but each firm's demand will be more elastic. How much more depends on how the firms compete with one another. (In Figure 10.7, the elasticity of market demand is -1.5, and the elasticity of demand for each firm is -6.) But no matter how the firms compete, the elasticity of demand for each firm could never become smaller in magnitude than -1.5.

The demand for oil is fairly inelastic (at least in the short run), which is why OPEC could raise oil prices far above marginal production cost during the 1970s and early 1980s. The demands for such commodities as coffee, cocoa, tin, and copper are much more elastic, which is why attempts by producers to cartelize those markets and raise prices have largely failed. In each case, the elasticity of market demand limits the potential monopoly power of individual producers.

The Number of Firms

The second determinant of a firm's demand curve, and hence its monopoly power, is the number of firms in the market. Other things being equal, the monopoly power of each firm will fall as the number of firms increases. As more and more firms compete, each firm will find it harder to raise prices and avoid losing sales to other firms.

What matters, of course, is not just the total number of firms, but the number of "major players" (i.e., firms that have a significant share of the market). For example, if only two large firms account for 90 percent of sales in a market, with another 20 firms accounting for the remaining 10 percent, the two large firms might have considerable monopoly power. When only a few firms account for most of the sales in a market, the market is highly *concentrated*.[9]

It is sometimes said (not always jokingly) that the greatest fear of American business is competition. That may or may not be true. But we would certainly expect that when only a few firms are in a market, their managers would prefer that no new firms enter the market. An increase in the number of firms can only reduce the monopoly power of each incumbent firm. An important aspect of competitive strategy (discussed in detail in Chapter 13) is finding ways to create *barriers to entry*—conditions that deter entry by new competitors.

Sometimes there are natural barriers to entry. For example, one firm may have a *patent* on the technology needed to produce a particular product. This makes it impossible for other firms to enter the market, at least until the patent expires.[10] Other legally created rights work in the same way—a *copyright* can limit the sale of a book, music, or a computer software program to a single company, and the need for a government *license* can prevent new firms from entering the market for telephone service, television broadcasting, or interstate trucking. Finally, *economies of scale* may make it too costly for more than a few firms to supply the entire market. In some cases the economies of scale may be so large that it is most efficient for a single firm—*a natural monopoly*—to supply the entire market. We will discuss scale economies and natural monopoly in more detail shortly.

The Interaction Among Firms

How competing firms interact is also an important—and sometimes the most important—determinant of monopoly power. Suppose there are four firms in a market. They might compete aggressively, undercutting one another's prices to capture more market share. This would probably drive prices down to nearly competitive levels. Each firm will be afraid to raise its price for fear of being undercut and losing its market share, and thus it will have little or no monopoly power.

On the other hand, the firms might not compete much. They might even collude (in violation of the antitrust laws), agreeing to limit output and raise prices. Raising prices in concert rather than individually is more likely to be profitable, so collusion can generate substantial monopoly power.

We will discuss the interaction among firms in detail in Chapters 12 and 13. Now we simply want to point out that other things equal, monopoly power is smaller when firms compete aggressively and is larger when they cooperate.

---

[9] A statistic called the *concentration ratio*, which measures the fraction of sales accounted for by, say, the four largest firms, is often used to describe the concentration of a market. Concentration is one, but not the only, determinant of market power.

[10] In the United States, patents last for 17 years.

Remember that a firm's monopoly power often changes over time, as its operating conditions (market demand and cost), its behavior, and the behavior of its competitors change. Monopoly power must therefore be thought of in a dynamic context. For example, the market demand curve might be very inelastic in the short run but much more elastic in the long run. (This is the case with oil, which is why OPEC had considerable short-run but less long-run monopoly power.) Furthermore, real or potential monopoly power in the short run can make an industry more competitive in the long run. Large short-run profits can induce new firms to enter an industry, thereby reducing monopoly power over the longer term.

10.4 *The Social Costs of Monopoly Power*

In a competitive market, price equals marginal cost, while monopoly power implies that price exceeds marginal cost. Because monopoly power results in higher prices and lower quantities produced, we would expect it to make consumers worse off and the firm better off. But suppose we value the welfare of consumers the same as that of producers. Does monopoly power make consumers and producers in the aggregate better or worse off?

We can answer this question by comparing the consumer and producer surplus that results when a competitive industry produces a good with the surplus that results when a monopolist supplies the entire market.[11] (We assume that the competitive market and the monopolist have the same cost curves.) Figure 10.9 shows the average and marginal revenue curves and marginal cost curve for the monopolist. To maximize profit, the firm produces at the point where marginal revenue equals marginal cost, so that the price and quantity are P_m and Q_m. In a competitive market, price must equal marginal cost, so the competitive price and quantity, P_c and Q_c, are found at the intersection of the average revenue (demand) curve and the marginal cost curve. Now let's examine how surplus changes if we move from the competitive price and quantity, P_c and Q_c, to the monopoly price and quantity, P_m and Q_m.

Under monopoly the price is higher, and consumers buy less. Because of the higher price, those consumers who buy the good lose surplus of an amount given by rectangle A. Those consumers who do not buy the good at price P_m but will buy at price P_c also lose surplus, of an amount given by triangle B. The total loss of consumer surplus is therefore $A + B$. The producer, however, gains rectangle A by selling at the higher price but loses triangle C, the additional profit it would have earned by selling $Q_c - Q_m$ at price P_c. The total gain in producer surplus is therefore $A - C$. Subtracting the loss of consumer surplus from the gain in producer surplus, we see a net loss of surplus given by $B + C$. This is the *deadweight loss from monopoly power*. Even if the monopolist's

---

[11] If there were two or more firms, each with some monopoly power, the analysis would be more complex. However, the basic results would be the same.

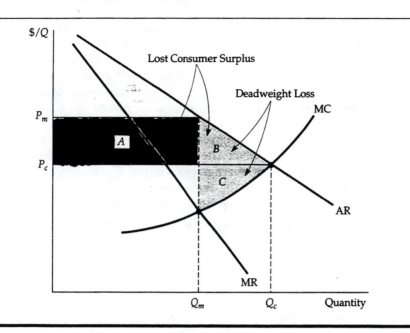

FIGURE 10.9   **Deadweight Loss from Monopoly Power.**   The shaded rectangle and triangles show changes in consumer and producer surplus when moving from competitive price and quantity, P_c and Q_c, to a monopolist's price and quantity, P_m and Q_m. Because of the higher price, consumers lose $A + B$ and producer gains $A - C$. The deadweight loss is $-B - C$.

profits were taxed away and redistributed to the consumers of its products, there would be an inefficiency because output would be lower than under competition. The deadweight loss is the social cost of this inefficiency.

There may be an additional social cost of monopoly power that goes beyond the deadweight loss in triangles B and C. The firm may spend large amounts of money in a socially unproductive way to acquire, maintain, or exercise its monopoly power. This might involve advertising, lobbying, and legal efforts to avoid government regulation or antitrust scrutiny. Or it might mean installing but not utilizing extra productive capacity to convince potential competitors that they will be unable to sell enough to make entry worthwhile. Roughly speaking, the economic incentive to incur these costs should bear a direct relation to the gains to the firm from having monopoly power (i.e., rectangle A minus triangle C). Therefore, the larger the transfer from consumers to the firm (rectangle A), the larger the social cost of monopoly.

Price Regulation

Because of its social cost, antitrust laws prevent firms from accumulating excessive amounts of monopoly power. We will say more about the antitrust laws at the end of the chapter. Here, we examine another means by which society can limit monopoly power—price regulation.

We saw in Chapter 9 that in a competitive market, price regulation always results in a deadweight loss. This need not be the case, however, when a firm has monopoly power. On the contrary, price regulation can eliminate the deadweight loss that results from monopoly power.

Figure 10.10 illustrates price regulation. P_m and Q_m are the price and quantity that result without regulation. Now suppose the price is regulated to be no higher than P_1. Since the firm can charge no more than P_1 for output levels up to Q_1, its new average revenue curve is a horizontal line at P_1. For output levels greater than Q_1, the new average revenue curve is identical to the old average revenue curve because at these output levels the firm will charge less than P_1, and so it would be unaffected by the regulation.

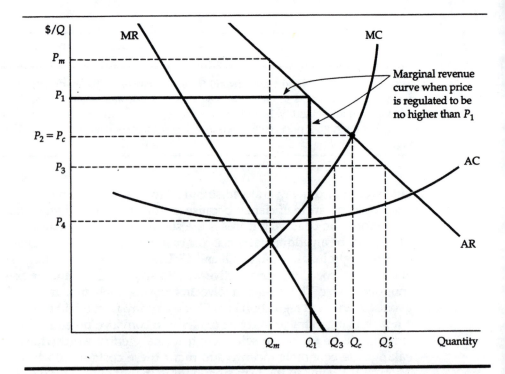

FIGURE 10.10 **Price Regulation.** If left alone, a monopolist produces Q_m and charges P_m. When the government imposes a price ceiling of P_1 the firm's average and marginal revenue are constant and equal to P_1 for output levels up to Q_1. For larger output levels, the original average and marginal revenue curves apply. The new marginal revenue curve is therefore the gray-shaded line, which intersects the marginal cost curve at Q_1. When price is lowered to P_c, at the point where marginal cost intersects average revenue, output increases to its maximum Q_c. This is the output that would be produced by a competitive industry. Lowering price further, to P_3, reduces output to Q_3 and causes a shortage, $Q_3' - Q_3$.

The firm's new marginal revenue curve corresponds to its new average revenue curve, and is shown by the gray-shaded line in the figure. For output levels up to Q_1, marginal revenue equals average revenue. For output levels greater than Q_1, the new marginal revenue curve is identical to the original curve. The firm will produce quantity Q_1 because that is where its marginal revenue curve intersects its marginal cost curve. You can verify that at price P_1 and quantity Q_1 the deadweight loss from monopoly power is reduced.

As the price is lowered further, the quantity produced continues to increase and the deadweight loss to decline. At price P_c, where average revenue and marginal cost intersect, the quantity produced has increased to the competitive level, and the deadweight loss from monopoly power has been eliminated. Reducing the price even more, say to P_3, results in a *reduction* in quantity. This is equivalent to imposing a price ceiling on a competitive industry. A shortage develops, $(Q'_3 - Q_3)$, as well as a deadweight loss from regulation. As the price is lowered further, the quantity produced continues to fall, and the shortage grows. Finally, if the price is lowered below P_4, the minimum average cost, the firm loses money and goes out of business.

Price regulation is most often practiced for *natural monopolies,* such as local utility companies. Figure 10.11 illustrates natural monopoly. Note that average

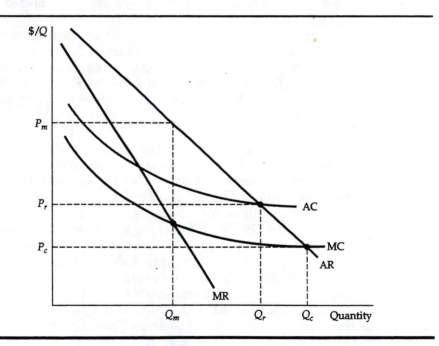

FIGURE 10.11 **Regulating the Price of a Natural Monopoly.** A firm is a natural monopoly because it has economies of scale (declining average and marginal costs) over its entire output range. If price were regulated to be P_c, the firm would lose money and go out of business. Setting the price at P_r yields the largest possible output consistent with the firm's remaining in business; excess profit is zero.

cost is declining everywhere, so marginal cost is always below average cost. Unregulated, the firm would produce Q_m at P_m. Ideally, the regulatory agency would like to push the firm's price down to the competitive level P_c, but then the firm could not meet its average cost and would go out of business. The best alternative is therefore to set the price at P_r, where average cost and average revenue intersect. Then the firm earns no monopoly profit, and output is as large as it can be without driving the firm out of business.

Regulation in Practice

Recall that the competitive price (P_c in Figure 10.10) is found where the firm's marginal cost and average revenue (demand) curves intersect. Likewise, for a natural monopoly, the minimum feasible price (P_r in Figure 10.11) is found where average cost and demand intersect. Unfortunately, it is often difficult to determine these prices accurately in practice because the firm's demand and cost curves may shift as market conditions evolve.

As a result, the regulation of a monopoly is usually based on the rate of return that it earns on its capital. The regulatory agency determines an allowed price, so that this rate of return is in some sense "competitive" or "fair." This is called *rate-of-return regulation*: The maximum price allowed is based on the (expected) rate of return that the firm will earn.[12]

Unfortunately, difficult problems arise when implementing rate-of-return regulation. First, although it is a key element in determining the firm's rate of return, the firm's undepreciated capital stock is difficult to value. Second, a "fair" rate of return must be based on the firm's actual cost of capital, but that cost in turn depends on the behavior of the regulatory agency (and on investors' perceptions of what future allowed rates of return will be).

The difficulty of agreeing on a set of numbers to be used in rate-of-return calculations often leads to delays in the regulatory response to changes in cost and other market conditions, as well as long and expensive regulatory hearings. The major beneficiaries are usually lawyers, accountants, and, occasionally, economic consultants. The net result is *regulatory lag*—the delays of a year or more that are usually required to change the regulated price.

In the 1950s and 1960s, regulatory lag worked to the advantage of regulated firms. During those decades costs were typically falling (usually as a result of scale economies achieved as firms grew), so regulatory lag allowed these firms, at least for a while, to enjoy actual rates of return greater than those ultimately deemed "fair" at the end of regulatory proceedings. Beginning in the 1970s, however, the situation changed, and regulatory lag worked to the detriment of regulated firms. For example, when oil prices rose sharply, electric utilities

---

[12] Regulatory agencies typically use a formula like the following to determine price:

$$P = \text{AVC} + (D + T + sK)/Q,$$

where AVC is average variable cost, Q is output, s is the allowed "fair" rate of return, D is depreciation, T is taxes, and K is the firm's current capital stock.

needed to raise their prices. Regulatory lag caused many of them to earn rates of return well below the "fair" rates they had been earning earlier.

10.7 *Limiting Market Power: The Antitrust Laws*

We have seen that market power—whether of sellers or buyers—harms potential purchasers who could have bought at competitive prices, and this leads to a deadweight loss. Excessive market power also raises problems of equity and fairness; if a firm has significant monopoly power, it will profit at the expense of consumers. In theory, the firm's excess profits could be taxed away

---

[17] For a detailed discussion of the market for automobile components, see Michael E. Porter, "Note on Supplying the Automobile Industry," Harvard Business School Case No. 9–378–219, July 1981.

and redistributed to the buyers of its products, but such a redistribution is often impractical. It is difficult to determine what portion of a firm's profit is attributable to monopoly power, and it is even more difficult to locate all the buyers and reimburse them in proportion to their purchases. So in addition to the deadweight loss, excessive market power can lead to a socially objectionable transfer of money.

How, then, can society prevent market power from becoming excessive? For a natural monopoly, such as an electric utility company, direct price regulation is the answer. But more generally, the answer is to prevent firms from acquiring excessive market power in the first place. In the United States, this is done via the antitrust laws.

The primary objective of the antitrust laws is to promote a competitive economy by prohibiting actions that restrain, or are likely to restrain, competition, and by restricting the forms of market structure that are allowable.

Monopoly power can arise in a number of ways, each of which is covered by the antitrust laws. Section 1 of the Sherman Act (which was passed in 1890) prohibits contracts, combinations, or conspiracies in restraint of trade. One obvious example of an illegal combination is an explicit agreement among producers to restrict their outputs and "fix" price above the competitive level. But *implicit* collusion in the form of *parallel pricing* can also be construed as violating the law. Firm *A* and Firm *B* need not meet or talk on the telephone to violate the Sherman Act; the publication of pricing information that leads to an implicit understanding can suffice.[18]

Section 2 of the Sherman Act makes it illegal to monopolize or to attempt to monopolize a market and prohibits conspiracies that result in monopolization. The Clayton Act (1914) did much to pinpoint the kinds of practices that are likely to be anticompetitive. For example, the Clayton Act makes it unlawful to require the buyer or lessor of a good not to buy from a competitor. And it makes it illegal to engage in *predatory pricing*—pricing designed to drive current competitors out of business and to discourage new entrants (so that the predatory firm can enjoy higher prices in the future).

Monopoly power can also be achieved by a merger of firms into a larger and more dominant firm, or by one firm acquiring or taking control of another firm by purchasing its stock. The Clayton Act prohibits mergers and acquisitions if they "substantially lessen competition" or "tend to create a monopoly."

The antitrust laws also limit the activities of firms that have legally obtained monopoly power. For example, the Clayton Act, as amended by the Robinson-

---

[18] The Sherman Act applies to all firms that do business in the United States (to the extent that a conspiracy to restrain trade could affect U.S. markets). However, foreign governments (or firms operating under their government's control) are not subject to the act, so OPEC need not fear the wrath of the Justice Department. Also, firms *can* collude with respect to *exports*. The *Webb-Pomerene Act* (1918) allows price fixing and related collusion with respect to export markets, *as long as domestic markets are unaffected by such collusion*. Firms operating in this manner must form a "Webb-Pomerene Association" and register it with the government.

Patman Act (1936), makes it illegal to discriminate by charging buyers of essentially the same product different prices. (As we will see in the next chapter, price discrimination is a common practice. It becomes the target of antitrust action when monopoly power is substantial.)

Another important component of the antitrust laws is the *Federal Trade Commission Act* (1914, amended in 1938, 1973, 1975), which created the Federal Trade Commission (FTC). This act supplements the Sherman and Clayton acts by fostering competition through a whole set of prohibitions against unfair and anticompetitive practices, such as deceptive advertising and labeling, agreements with retailers to exclude competing brands, and so on. Because these prohibitions are interpreted and enforced in administrative proceedings before the FTC, the act provides powers that are very broad and reach further than other antitrust laws.

The antitrust laws are actually phrased vaguely in terms of what is and what is not allowed. The laws are intended to provide a general statutory framework to give the Justice Department, the FTC, and the courts wide discretion in interpreting and applying them. This is important because it is difficult to know in advance what might be an impediment to competition, and this ambiguity creates a need for common law (i.e., courts interpreting statutes) and supplemental provisions and rulings (e.g., by the FTC and the Justice Department).

Enforcement of the Antitrust Laws

The antitrust laws are enforced in three ways. The first is through the Antitrust Division of the Department of Justice. As an arm of the executive branch, its enforcement policies closely reflect the view of whatever administration is in power. As the result of an external complaint or an internal study, the department can decide to institute a criminal proceeding, bring a civil suit, or both. The result of a criminal action can be fines for the corporation and fines or jail sentences for individuals. For example, individuals who conspire to fix prices or rig bids can be charged with a *felony*, and if found guilty may be sentenced to jail—something to remember if you are planning to parlay your knowledge of microeconomics into a successful business career! Losing a civil action forces a corporation to cease its anticompetitive practices.

The second means of enforcement is through the administrative procedures of the Federal Trade Commission. Again, action can result from an external complaint or from the FTC's own initiative. Should the FTC decide that action is required, it can either request a voluntary understanding to comply with the law, or it can decide to seek a formal commission order, requiring compliance.

The last and the most common means of enforcement is via *private proceedings*. Individuals or companies can sue for *treble (threefold) damages* inflicted on their business or property. The possibility of having to pay treble damages can be a strong deterrent to would-be violators of the laws. Individuals or companies can also ask the courts for an injunction to force a wrongdoer to cease anticompetitive actions.

The U.S. antitrust laws are more stringent and far-reaching than those of most other countries. Some people have argued that the laws have prevented American industry from competing effectively in international markets. The laws certainly constrain American business, and they may at times have put American firms at a disadvantage in world markets. But this must be weighed against their benefits. The laws have been crucial for maintaining competition, and competition is essential for economic efficiency, innovation, and growth.

EXAMPLE 10.4   A PHONE CALL ABOUT PRICES

In 1981 and early 1982, American Airlines and Braniff Airways were competing fiercely with each other for passengers. A fare war broke out as the firms undercut each other's prices to capture market share. On February 21, 1982, Robert Crandall, president and chief executive officer of American Airlines, made a phone call to Howard Putnam, president and chief executive of Braniff Airways. To Mr. Crandall's later surprise, the call had been taped. It went like this:[19]

Mr. Crandall: I think it's dumb as hell for Christ's sake, all right, to sit here and pound the @!#$%&! out of each other and neither one of us making a @!#$%&! dime.

Mr. Putnam: Well . . .

Mr. Crandall: I mean, you know, @!#$%&!, what the hell is the point of it?

Mr. Putnam: But if you're going to overlay every route of American's on top of every route that Braniff has—I just can't sit here and allow you to bury us without giving our best effort.

Mr. Crandall: Oh sure, but Eastern and Delta do the same thing in Atlanta and have for years.

Mr. Putnam: Do you have a suggestion for me?

Mr. Crandall: Yes, I have a suggestion for you. Raise your @!#$%&! fares 20 percent. I'll raise mine the next morning.

Mr. Putnam: Robert, we . . .

Mr. Crandall: You'll make more money and I will, too.

Mr. Putnam: We can't talk about pricing!

Mr. Crandall: Oh @!#$%&!, Howard. We can talk about any @!#$%&! thing we want to talk about.

Mr. Crandall was wrong. Corporate executives cannot talk about anything they want. Talking about prices and agreeing to fix them is a clear violation of Section 1 of the Sherman Act. Mr. Putnam must have known this because he

[19] According to the *New York Times*, Feb. 24, 1983.

promptly rejected Mr. Crandall's suggestion. After learning about the call, the Justice Department filed a suit accusing Mr. Crandall of violating the antitrust laws by proposing to fix prices.

Proposing to fix prices is not enough to violate Section 1 of the Sherman Act. The two parties must *agree* to collude for the law to be violated. Therefore, because Mr. Putnam had rejected Mr. Crandall's proposal, Section 1 had not been violated. The court later ruled, however, that a proposal to fix prices could be an attempt to monopolize part of the airline industry, and if so would violate Section 2 of the Sherman Act. American Airlines promised the Justice Department never again to engage in such activity.

Summary

1. Market power is the ability of sellers or buyers to affect the price of a good.

2. Market power comes in two forms. When sellers charge a price that is above marginal cost, we say that they have monopoly power, and we measure the amount of monopoly power by the extent to which price exceeds marginal cost. When buyers can obtain a price that is below their marginal value of the good, we say they have monopsony power, and we measure the amount of monopsony power by the extent to which marginal value exceeds price.

3. Monopoly power is determined in part by the number of firms competing in the market. If there is only one firm—a pure monopoly—monopoly power depends entirely on the elasticity of market demand. The less elastic demand is, the more monopoly power the firm will have. When there are several firms, monopoly power also depends on how the firms interact. The more aggressively they compete, the less monopoly power each firm will have.

4. Monopsony power is determined in part by the number of buyers in the market. If there is only one buyer—a pure monopsony—monopsony power depends on the elasticity of market supply. The less elastic supply is, the more monopsony power the buyer will have. When there are several buyers, monopsony power also depends on how aggressively the buyers compete for supplies.

5. Market power can impose costs on society. Monopoly and monopsony power both cause production to be below the competitive level, so that there is a deadweight loss of consumer and producer surplus.

6. Sometimes, scale economies make pure monopoly desirable. But the government will still want to regulate price to maximize social welfare.

7. More generally, we rely on the antitrust laws to prevent firms from obtaining excessive market power.

Questions for Review

1. Suppose a monopolist was producing at a point where its marginal cost exceeded its marginal revenue. How should it adjust its output level to increase its profit?

2. We write the percentage markup of prices over marginal cost as $(P - MC)/P$. For a profit-maximizing monopolist, how does this markup depend on the elasticity of demand? Why can this markup be viewed as a measure of monopoly power?

3. Why is there no market supply curve under monopoly?

4. Why might a firm have monopoly power even if it is not the only producer in the market?

5. What are some of the sources of monopoly power? Give an example of each.

6. What factors determine how much monopoly power an individual firm is likely to have? Explain each one briefly.

7. Why is there a social cost to monopoly power? If the gains to producers from monopoly power could be redistributed to consumers, would the social cost of monopoly power be eliminated? Explain briefly.

8. Why will a monopolist's output increase if the government forces it to lower its price? If the government wants to set a price ceiling that maximizes the monopolist's output, what price should it set?

9. How should a monopsonist decide how much of a product to buy? Will it buy more or less than a competitive buyer? Explain briefly.

10. What is meant by the term "monopsony power"? Why might a firm have monopsony power even if it is not the only buyer in the market?

11. What are some sources of monopsony power? What determines how much monopsony power an individual firm is likely to have?

12. Why is there a social cost to monopsony power? If the gains to buyers from monopsony power could be redistributed to sellers, would the social cost of monopsony power be eliminated? Explain briefly.

13. How do the antitrust laws limit market power in the United States? Give examples of the major provisions of the laws.

14. Explain briefly how the U.S. antitrust laws are actually enforced.

Exercises

1. Will an increase in the demand for a monopolist's product always result in a higher price? Explain. Will an increase in the supply facing a monopsonist buyer always result in a lower price? Explain.

2. Caterpillar Tractor is one of the largest producers of farm tractors in the world. They hire you to advise them on their pricing policy. One of the things the company would like to know is how much a 5 percent increase in price is likely to reduce sales. What would you need to know to help the company with their problem? Explain why these facts are important.

3. A firm faces the following average revenue (demand) curve:

$$P = 100 - 0.01Q$$

where Q is weekly production and P is price, measured in cents per unit. The firm's cost function is given by $C = 50Q + 30,000$. Assuming the firm maximizes profits,

    a. What is the level of production, price, and total profit per week?

    b. The government decides to levy a tax of 10 cents per unit on this product. What will the new level of production, price, and profit be as a result?

4. The table below shows the demand curve facing a monopolist who produces at a constant marginal cost of $10:

Price	Quantity
27	0
24	2
21	4
18	6
15	8
12	10
9	12
6	14
3	16
0	18

a. Calculate the firm's marginal revenue curve.

b. What are the firm's profit-maximizing output and price? What is the firm's profit?

c. What would the equilibrium price and quantity be in a competitive industry?

d. What would the social gain be if this monopolist were forced to produce and price at the competitive equilibrium? Who would gain and lose as a result?

5. A firm has two factories, for which costs are given by:

$$\text{Factory \#1: } C_1(Q_1) = 10Q_1^2$$

$$\text{Factory \#2: } C_2(Q_2) = 20Q_2^2$$

The firm faces the following demand curve:

$$P = 700 - 5Q$$

where Q is total output, i.e., $Q = Q_1 + Q_2$.

a. On a diagram, draw the marginal cost curves for the two factories, the average and marginal revenue curves, and the total marginal cost curve (i.e., the marginal cost of producing $Q = Q_1 + Q_2$). Indicate the profit-maximizing output for each factory, total output, and price.

b. Calculate the values of Q_1, Q_2, Q, and P that maximize profit.

c. Suppose labor costs increase in Factory #1 but not in Factory #2. How should the firm adjust (i.e., raise, lower, or leave unchanged): Output in Factory #1? Output in Factory #2? Total output? Price?

6. A drug company has a monopoly on a new patented medicine. The product can be made in either of two plants. The costs of production for the two plants are $MC_1 = 20 + 2Q_1$, and $MC_2 = 10 + 5Q_2$. The firm's estimate of the demand for the prod-

uct is $P = 20 - 3(Q_1 + Q_2)$. How much should the firm plan to produce in each plant, and at what price should it plan to sell the product?

7. One of the more important antitrust cases of this century involved the Aluminum Company of America (Alcoa) in 1945. At that time, Alcoa controlled about 90 percent of primary aluminum production in the United States, and the company had been accused of monopolizing the aluminum market. In its defense, Alcoa argued that although it indeed controlled a large fraction of the primary market, secondary aluminum (i.e., aluminum produced from the recycling of scrap) accounted for roughly 30 percent of the total supply of aluminum, and many competitive firms were engaged in recycling. Therefore, Alcoa argued, it did not have much monopoly power.

a. Provide a clear argument *in favor* of Alcoa's position.

b. Provide a clear argument *against* Alcoa's position.

c. The 1945 decision by Judge Learned Hand has been called "one of the most celebrated judicial opinions of our time." Do you know what Judge Hand's ruling was?

8. A monopolist faces the demand curve $P = 11 - Q$, where P is measured in dollars per unit and Q in thousands of units. The monopolist has a constant average cost of $6 per unit.

a. Draw the average and marginal revenue curves, and the average and marginal cost curves. What are the monopolist's profit-maximizing price and quantity, and what is the resulting profit? Calculate the firm's degree of monopoly power using the Lerner index.

b. A government regulatory agency sets a price ceiling of $7 per unit. What quantity will be produced, and what will the firm's profit be? What happens to the degree of monopoly power?

c. What price ceiling yields the largest level of output? What is that level of output? What is the firm's degree of monopoly power at this price?

9. Michelle's Monopoly Mutant Turtles (MMMT) has the exclusive right to sell Mutant Turtle t-shirts in the United States. The demand for these t-shirts is $Q = 10,000/P^2$. The firm's short-run cost is SRTC = $2000 + 5Q$, and its long-run cost is LRTC = $6Q$.

a. What price should MMMT charge to maximize profit in the short run? What quantity does it sell, and how much profit does it make? Would it be better off shutting down in the short run?

b. What price should MMMT charge in the long run? What quantity does it sell and how much profit does it make? Would it be better off shutting down in the long run?

c. Can we expect MMMT to have lower marginal cost in the short run than in the long run? Explain why.

10. The employment of teaching assistants (TAs) by major universities can be characterized as a monopsony. Suppose the demand for TAs is $W = 30,000 - 125n$, where W is the wage (as an annual salary), and n is the number of TAs hired. The supply of TAs is given by $W = 1000 + 75n$.

a. If the university takes advantage of its monopsonist position, how many TAs will it hire? What wage will it pay?

b. If, instead, the university faced an infinite supply of TAs at the annual wage level of $10,000, how many TAs would it hire?

*11. Dayna's Doorstops, Inc. (DD), is a monopolist in the doorstop industry. Its cost is $C = 100 - 5Q + Q^2$, and demand is $P = 55 - 2Q$.

a. What price should DD set to maximize profit, and what output does the firm produce? How much profit and consumer surplus does DD generate?

b. What would output be if DD acted like a perfect competitor and set MC = P? What profit and consumer surplus would then be generated?

c. What is the deadweight loss from monopoly power in part (a)?

d. Suppose the government, concerned about the high price of doorstops, sets a maximum price for doorstops at $27. How does this affect price, quantity, consumer surplus, and DD's profit? What is the resulting deadweight loss?

e. Now suppose the government sets the maximum price at $23. How does this affect price, quantity, consumer surplus, DD's profit, and deadweight loss?

f. Finally, consider a maximum price of $12. What will this do to quantity, consumer surplus, profit, and deadweight loss?

*12. There are 10 households in Lake Wobegon, Minnesota, each with a demand for electricity of $Q = 50 - P$. Lake Wobegon Electric's (LWE) cost of producing electricity is TC = $500 + Q$.

a. If the regulators of LWE want to make sure that there is no deadweight loss in this market, what price will they force LWE to charge? What will output be in that case? Calculate consumer surplus and LWE's profit with that price.

b. If the regulators want to make sure that LWE doesn't lose money, what is the lowest price they can impose? Calculate output, consumer surplus, and profit in that case. Is there any deadweight loss?

c. Kristina knows that deadweight loss is something that this small town can do without. She suggests that each household be required to pay a fixed amount just to receive any electricity at all, and then a per-unit charge for electricity. Then LWE can break even while charging the price you calculated in part (a). What fixed amount would each household have to pay for Kristina's plan to work? Why are you sure that no household will choose instead to refuse the payment and go without electricity?

*13. A monopolist faces the following demand curve:
$$Q = 144/P^2$$
where Q is the quantity demanded and P is price. Its *average variable* cost is
$$AVC = Q^{1/2}$$
and its *fixed cost* is 5.

a. What are its profit-maximizing price and quantity? What is the resulting profit?

b. Suppose the government regulates the price to be no greater than $4 per unit. How much will the monopolist produce, and what will its profit be?

c. Suppose the government wants to set a ceiling price that induces the monopolist to produce the largest possible output. What price will do this?

CHAPTER *11*

Pricing with Market Power

As we explained in Chapter 10, market power is quite common. Many industries have only a few producers, so that each producer has some monopoly power. And many firms, as buyers of raw materials, labor, or specialized capital goods, have some monopsony power in the markets for these factor inputs. The problem the managers of these firms face is how to use their market power most effectively. They must decide how to set prices, choose quantities of factor inputs, and determine output in both the short and long run to maximize the firm's profit.

Managers of firms with market power have a harder job than those who manage perfectly competitive firms. A firm that is perfectly competitive in output markets has no influence over market price. As a result, its managers need only worry about the cost side of the firm's operations, choosing output so that price is equal to marginal cost. But the managers of a firm with monopoly power must also worry about the characteristics of demand. Even if they set a single price for the firm's output, they must obtain at least a rough estimate of the elasticity of demand to determine what that price (and corresponding output level) should be. Furthermore, one can often do much better by using a more complicated pricing strategy, for example, charging different prices to different customers. To design such pricing strategies, managers need ingenuity and even more information about demand.

This chapter explains how firms with market power set prices. We begin with the basic objective of every pricing strategy—capturing consumer surplus and converting it into additional profit for the firm. Then we discuss how this can be done using *price discrimination*. Here different prices are charged to different customers, sometimes for the same product, and sometimes for small variations in the product. Because price discrimination is widely practiced in one form or another, it is important to understand how it works.

Next, we discuss the *two-part tariff*. Here customers must pay in advance for the right to purchase units of the good at a later time (and at additional cost). The classic example of this is an amusement park, where customers pay a fee to enter, and then an additional fee for each ride they go on. Although amusement park may seem like a rather specialized market, there are many other examples of two-part tariffs: the price of a Gillette razor, which gives the owner the opportunity to purchase Gillette razor blades; the price of a Polaroid camera, which gives the owner the opportunity to purchase Polaroid film; or the monthly subscription cost of a mobile telephone, which gives users the opportunity to make phone calls from their automobiles, paying by the message unit as they do so.

We will also discuss *bundling*. This pricing strategy simply involves tying products together and selling them as a package. For example: a personal computer that comes bundled with several software packages; a one-week vacation in Hawaii in which the airfare, rental car, and hotel are bundled and sold at a single package price; or a luxury car, in which the air conditioning, power windows, and stereo are "standard" features.

Finally, we will examine the use of *advertising* by firms with market power. As we will see, deciding how much money to spend on advertising requires information about demand, and is closely related to the firm's pricing decision. We will derive a simple rule of thumb for determining the profit-maximizing advertising-to-sales ratio.

11.1 *Capturing Consumer Surplus*

All the pricing strategies that we will examine have one thing in common—they are ways of capturing consumer surplus and transferring it to the producer. You can see this more clearly in Figure 11.1. Suppose the firm sold all its output at a single price. To maximize profit, it would pick a price P^* and corresponding output Q^* at the intersection of its marginal cost and marginal revenue curves. The firm would then be profitable, but its managers might wonder if they could make it even more profitable.

They know that some customers (in region A of the demand curve) would pay more than P^*. But raising price would mean losing some customers, selling less, and earning smaller profits. Similarly, other potential customers are not buying the firm's product because they will not pay a price as high as P^*. Many of them, however, would pay prices higher than the firm's marginal cost. (These customers are in region B of the demand curve.) By lowering its price, the firm could sell to some of these customers, but it would then earn less revenue from its existing customers, and again profits would shrink.

How can the firm capture the consumer surplus (or at least part of it) from its customers in region A, and perhaps also sell profitably to some of its potential customers in region B? Charging a single price clearly will not do the

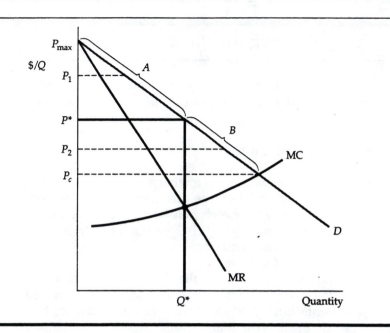

FIGURE 11.1 Capturing Consumer Surplus. If a firm can charge only one price for all its customers, that price will be P^* and the quantity produced will be Q^*. Ideally, the firm would like to charge a higher price to consumers willing to pay more than P^*, thereby capturing some of the consumer surplus under region A of the demand curve. The firm would also like to sell to consumers willing to pay prices lower than P^* but only if that does not entail lowering the price to other consumers. In that way the firm could also capture some of the surplus under region B of the demand curve.

trick. However, the firm might charge different prices to different customers, according to where the customers are along the demand curve. For example, some customers in the upper end of region A would be charged the higher price P_1, some in region B would be charged the lower price P_2, and some in between would be charged P^*. This is the basis of *price discrimination*—charging different prices to different customers. The problem, of course, is to identify the different customers, and to get them to pay different prices. We will see how this can be done in the next section.

The other pricing techniques that we will discuss in this chapter—two-part tariffs and bundling—also expand the range of the firm's market to include more customers and to capture more consumer surplus. In each case we will examine the amount by which the firm's profit can be increased, as well as the effect on consumer welfare. (As we will see, when there is a high degree of monopoly power these pricing techniques can sometimes make both consumers and the producer better off.) We turn first to price discrimination.

11.2 *Price Discrimination*

Price discrimination can take three broad forms, which we call first-, second-, and third-degree price discrimination. We will examine them in turn.

First-Degree Price Discrimination

Ideally, a firm would like to charge a different price to each of its customers. If it could, it would charge each customer the maximum price that customer is willing to pay for each unit bought. We call this maximum price the customer's *reservation price*. The practice of charging each customer his or her reservation price is called perfect *first-degree price discrimination*.[1] Let's see how it affects the firm's profit.

First, we need to know the profit the firm earns when it charges only the single price P^* in Figure 11.2. To find out, we can add the profit on each incremental unit produced and sold, up to the total quantity Q^*. This incremental profit is the marginal revenue less the marginal cost for each unit. In Figure 11.2, this marginal revenue is highest and marginal cost lowest for the first unit. For each additional unit, marginal revenue falls and marginal cost rises, so the firm produces the total output Q^*, where marginal revenue and marginal cost are equal. Total variable profit is simply the sum of the profits on each incremental unit produced, and therefore, it is given by the tan shaded area in Figure 11.2, between the marginal revenue and marginal cost curves.[2] Consumer surplus, which is the area between the average revenue curve and the price P^* that customers pay, is outlined as a dark triangle.

Now, what happens if the firm can perfectly price discriminate? Since each consumer is charged exactly what he or she is willing to pay, the marginal revenue curve is no longer relevant to the firm's output decision. Instead, the incremental revenue earned from each additional unit sold is simply the price paid for that unit, and is therefore given by the demand curve.

Since price discrimination does not affect the firm's cost structure, the cost of each additional unit is again given by the firm's marginal cost curve. Therefore, *the profit from producing and selling each incremental unit is now the difference between demand and marginal cost*. As long as demand exceeds marginal cost, the firm can increase its profit by expanding production, and it will do so until it produces a total output Q^{**}. At Q^{**} demand is equal to marginal cost, and producing more reduces profit.

---

[1] We are assuming that each customer buys one unit of the good. If a customer bought more than one unit, the firm would have to charge different prices for each of the units.

[2] Recall that total profit π is the difference between total revenue R and total cost C, so incremental profit is just $\Delta\pi = \Delta R - \Delta C = MR - MC$. Total variable profit is found by summing all the $\Delta\pi$s, and thus it is the area between the MR and MC curves. This ignores fixed costs, which are independent of the firm's output and pricing decisions.

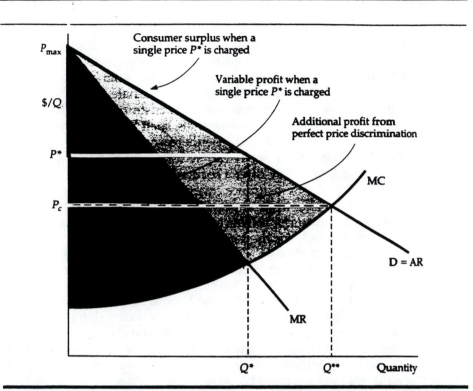

FIGURE 11.2   Additional Profit from Perfect First-Degree Price Discrimination.   The firm charges each consumer his or her reservation price, so it is profitable to expand output to Q^{**}. When only a single price, P^* is charged, the firm's variable profit is the area between the marginal revenue and marginal cost curves. With perfect price discrimination, this profit expands to the area between the demand curve and the marginal cost curve.

Total profit is now given by the area between the demand and marginal cost curves.[3] Note from Figure 11.2 that total profit is now much larger. (The additional profit resulting from price discrimination is shown by the red shaded area.) Note also that since every customer is being charged the maximum amount that he or she is willing to pay, all consumer surplus has been captured by the firm.

In practice, perfect first-degree price discrimination is almost never possible. First, it is usually impractical to charge each and every customer a different price (unless there are only a few customers).[4] Second, a firm usually does

---

[3] Incremental profit is again $\Delta\pi = \Delta R - \Delta C$, but ΔR is given by the price to each customer (i.e., the average revenue curve), so $\Delta\pi = AR - MC$. Total profit is the sum of these $\Delta\pi$s and is given by the area between the AR and MC curves.

[4] And recall that even if it could be done, it might violate the antitrust laws if it is deemed to be anticompetitive.

not know the reservation price of each customer. Even if the firm could ask how much each customer would be willing to pay, it probably would not receive honest answers. After all, it is in the customers' interest to claim that they would pay very little (because then they would be charged a low price).

Sometimes, however, firms can discriminate imperfectly by charging a few different prices based on estimates of customers' reservation prices. This happens frequently when professionals, such as doctors, lawyers, accountants, or architects, who know their clients reasonably well, are the "firms." Then the client's willingness to pay can be assessed, and fees set accordingly. For example, a doctor may offer a reduced fee to a low-income patient whose willingness to pay or insurance coverage is low, but charge higher fees to upper-income or better-insured patients. And an accountant, having just completed a client's tax returns, is in an excellent position to estimate how much the client is willing to pay for the service.

Another example is a car salesperson, who typically works with a 15 percent profit margin. The salesperson can give part of this away to the customer by making a "deal," or can insist that the customer pay the sticker price for the car. A good salesperson knows how to size up customers and determine whether they will look elsewhere for a car if they don't receive a sizable discount. The customer who is likely to leave and shop around receives a big discount (from the salesperson's point of view, a small profit is better than no sale and no profit), but the customer in a hurry is offered little or no discount. In other words, a successful car salesperson knows how to price discriminate!

Still another example is how colleges and universities charge tuition. Colleges don't charge different tuition rates to different students in the same degree program. Instead, they offer financial aid, in the form of a scholarship or subsidized loan, which reduces the *net* tuition that the student must pay. By requiring those who seek aid to disclose information about family income and wealth, colleges can link the amount of aid to the student's ability (and hence willingness) to pay. Thus, students who are financially well off pay more for their education, but students who are less well off pay less.

Figure 11.3 illustrates this kind of imperfect first-degree price discrimination. Here, if only a single price were charged, it would be P_4. Instead, six different prices are charged, the lowest of which, P_6, is just above the point where marginal cost intersects the demand curve. Note that those customers who would not have been willing to pay a price of P_4 or greater are actually better off in this situation—they are now in the market and may be enjoying at least some consumer surplus. In fact, if price discrimination brings enough new customers into the market, consumer welfare can increase, so that both the producer and consumers are better off.

Second-Degree Price Discrimination

In some markets, each consumer purchases many units of the good over any given period, and the consumer's demand declines with the number of units

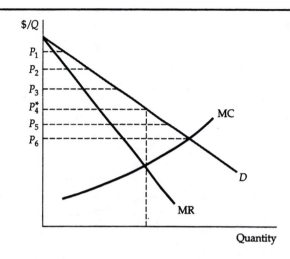

FIGURE 11.3   First-Degree Price Discrimination in Practice. Firms usually don't know the reservation price of every consumer. But sometimes reservation prices can be roughly identified. Here, six different prices are charged. The firm earns higher profits, but some consumers may also benefit. With a single price P_4^*, there are fewer consumers. The consumers who now pay P_5 or P_6 may have a surplus.

purchased. Examples include water, heating fuel, and electricity. Consumers may each purchase a few hundred kilowatt-hours of electricity a month, but their willingness to pay declines with increasing consumption. (The first hundred kilowatt-hours may be worth a lot to the consumer—operating a refrigerator and providing for minimal lighting. Conservation becomes easier with the additional units, and may be worthwhile if the price is high.) In this situation, a firm can discriminate according to the quantity consumed. This is called *second-degree price discrimination,* and it works by charging different prices for different quantities or "blocks" of the same good or service.

An example of second-degree price discrimination is block pricing by electric power companies. If there are scale economies so that average and marginal costs are declining, the state agency that controls the company's rates may encourage block pricing. By expanding output and achieving greater scale economies, consumer welfare can be increased, even allowing for greater profit to the company. The reason is that prices are reduced overall, while the savings from the lower unit costs still permit the power company to make a reasonable profit.

Figure 11.4 illustrates second-degree price discrimination for a firm with declining average and marginal costs. If a single price were charged, it would be P_0, and the quantity produced would be Q_0. Instead, three different prices are charged, based on the quantities purchased. The first block of sales is priced at P_1, the second at P_2, and the third at P_3.

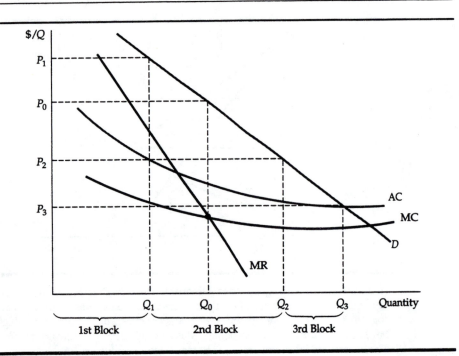

FIGURE 11.4   **Second-Degree Price Discrimination.**   Different prices are charged for different quantities, or "blocks," of the same good. Here, there are three blocks, with corresponding prices P_1, P_2, and P_3. There are also economies of scale, and average and marginal costs are declining. Second-degree price discrimination can then make consumers better off by expanding output and lowering cost.

Third-Degree Price Discrimination

A well-known liquor company has what seems to be a strange pricing practice. The company produces a vodka that it advertises as one of the smoothest and best-tasting available. This vodka is called "Three Star Golden Crown," and it is sold for about $16 a bottle.[5] However, the company also takes some of this same vodka and bottles it under the name "Old Sloshbucket," which is sold for about $8 a bottle. Why does it do this? Has the president of the company been spending too much time near the vats?

Perhaps, but this liquor company is also practicing *third-degree price discrimination*, and it does it because the practice is profitable. This form of price discrimination divides consumers into two or more groups with separate demand

---

[5] We have changed the names to protect the innocent.

curves for each group. This is the most prevalent form of price discrimination, and examples abound: regular versus "special" airline fares; the premium versus nonpremium brand of liquor, canned food or frozen vegetables; discounts to students and senior citizens; and so on.

In each case, some characteristic is used to divide consumers into distinct groups. For example, for many goods, students and senior citizens are usually willing to pay less on average than the rest of the population (because their incomes are lower), and identity can be readily established (via college ID or a driver's license). Likewise, to separate vacationers from business travelers (whose companies are usually willing to pay much higher fares), airlines can put restrictions on special low-fare tickets, such as requiring advance purchase. With the liquor company, or the premium versus nonpremium (e.g., supermarket label) brand of food, the label itself divides consumers; many consumers are willing to pay more for a name brand, even though the nonpremium brand is identical or nearly identical (and in fact is sometimes manufactured by the same company that produced the premium brand).

If third-degree price discrimination is feasible, how should the firm decide what price to charge each group of consumers? Let's think about this in two steps. First, we know that however much is produced, total output should be divided between the groups of customers, so that the marginal revenues for each group are equal. Otherwise, the firm would not be maximizing profit. For example, if there are two groups of customers and the marginal revenue for the first group, MR_1, exceeds the marginal revenue for the second group, MR_2, the firm could clearly do better by shifting output from the second group to the first. It would do this by lowering the price to the first group and raising the price to the second group. So whatever the two prices are, they must be such that the marginal revenues for the different groups are equal.

Second, we know that *total* output must be such that the marginal revenue for each group of consumers is equal to the marginal cost of production. Again, if this were not the case, the firm could increase its profit by raising or lowering total output (and lowering or raising its prices to both groups). For example, suppose the marginal revenues were the same for each group of consumers, but marginal revenue exceeded the marginal cost of production. The firm could then make a greater profit by increasing its total output. It would lower its prices to both groups of consumers, so that the marginal revenues for each group fell (but were still equal to each other), and approached marginal cost (which would increase as total output increased).

Let's look at this algebraically. Let P_1 be the price charged to the first group of consumers, P_2 the price charged to the second group, and $C(Q_T)$ the total cost of producing output $Q_T = Q_1 + Q_2$. Then total profit is given by

$$\pi = P_1 Q_1 + P_2 Q_2 - C(Q_T)$$

The firm should increase its sales to each group of consumers, Q_1 and Q_2, until the incremental profit from the last unit sold is zero. First, we set incremental profit for sales to the first group of consumers equal to zero:

$$\frac{\Delta\pi}{\Delta Q_1} = \frac{\Delta(P_1 Q_1)}{\Delta Q_1} - \frac{\Delta C}{\Delta Q_1} = 0$$

Here $\Delta(P_1 Q_1)/\Delta Q_1$ is the incremental revenue from an extra unit of sales to the first group of consumers (i.e., MR_1). The next term, $\Delta C/\Delta Q_1$, is the incremental cost of producing this extra unit, i.e., marginal cost, MC. We thus have

$$MR_1 = MC$$

Similarly, for the second group of consumers, we must have

$$MR_2 = MC$$

Putting these relations together, we see that prices and output must be set so that

$$\boxed{MR_1 = MR_2 = MC} \qquad (11.1)$$

Again, marginal revenue must be equal across groups of consumers and must equal marginal cost.

Managers may find it easier to think in terms of the relative prices that should be charged to each group of consumers, and to relate these prices to the elasticities of demand. Recall that we can write marginal revenue in terms of the elasticity of demand:

$$MR = P(1 + 1/E_d)$$

Then $MR_1 = P_1(1 + 1/E_1)$ and $MR_2 = P_2(1 + 1/E_2)$, where E_1 and E_2 are the elasticities of demand for the firm's sales in the first and second markets, respectively. Now equating MR_1 and MR_2 gives the following relationship that must hold for the prices:

$$\boxed{\frac{P_1}{P_2} = \frac{(1 + 1/E_2)}{(1 + 1/E_1)}} \qquad (11.2)$$

As you would expect, the higher price will be charged to consumers with the lower demand elasticity. For example, if the elasticity of demand for consumers in group 1 is -2, and the elasticity for consumers in group 2 is -4, we will have $P_1/P_2 = (1 - \frac{1}{4})/(1 - \frac{1}{2}) = (\frac{3}{4})/(\frac{1}{2}) = 1.5$. In other words, the price charged to the first group of consumers should be 1.5 times as high as the price charged to the second group.

Figure 11.5 illustrates third-degree price discrimination. Note that the demand curve D_1 for the first group of consumers is less elastic than the curve

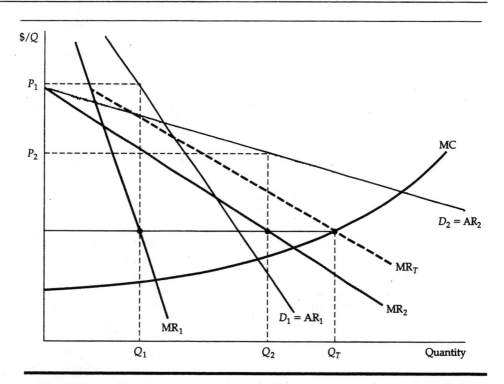

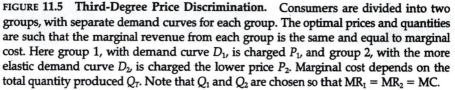

FIGURE 11.5   **Third-Degree Price Discrimination.**   Consumers are divided into two groups, with separate demand curves for each group. The optimal prices and quantities are such that the marginal revenue from each group is the same and equal to marginal cost. Here group 1, with demand curve D_1, is charged P_1, and group 2, with the more elastic demand curve D_2, is charged the lower price P_2. Marginal cost depends on the total quantity produced Q_T. Note that Q_1 and Q_2 are chosen so that $MR_1 = MR_2 = MC$.

for the second group, and the price charged to the first group is likewise higher. The total quantity produced, $Q_T = Q_1 + Q_2$, is found by summing the marginal revenue curves MR_1 and MR_2 horizontally, which yields the dashed curve MR_T, and finding its intersection with the marginal cost curve. Since MC must equal MR_1 and MR_2, we can draw a horizontal line leftwards from this intersection to find the quantities Q_1 and Q_2.

It may not always be worthwhile for the firm to try to sell to more than one group of consumers. In particular, if demand is small for the other group of consumers and marginal cost is rising steeply, the increased cost of producing and selling to this other group may outweigh the increase in revenue. Thus, in Figure 11.6, the firm is better off charging a single price P^* and selling only to the larger group of consumers because the additional cost of serving the smaller market would outweigh the additional revenue.

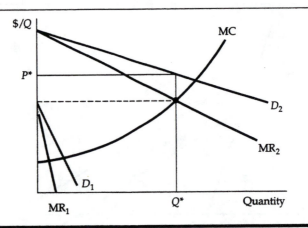

FIGURE 11.6   No Sales to Smaller Market.   Even if third-degree price discrimination is feasible, it doesn't always pay to sell to both groups of consumers if marginal cost is rising. Here, the first group of consumers, with demand D_1, are not willing to pay much for the good. It is unprofitable to sell to them because the price would have to be too low to compensate for the resulting increase in marginal cost.

The producers of processed foods and related consumer goods often issue coupons that let one buy the product at a discount. These coupons are usually distributed as part of an advertisement for the product, and they may appear in a newspaper or magazine, or as part of a promotional mailing. For example, a coupon for a particular breakfast cereal might be worth 25 cents toward the purchase of a box of the cereal. Why do firms issue these coupons? Why not just lower the price of the product, and thereby save the costs of printing and collecting the coupons?

Coupons provide a means of price discrimination. Studies show that only about 20 to 30 percent of all consumers regularly bother to clip, save, and use coupons when they go shopping. These consumers tend to be more sensitive to price than those who ignore coupons. They generally have more price-elastic demands and lower reservation prices. So by issuing coupons, a cereal company can separate its customers into two groups, and in effect charge the more price-sensitive customers a lower price than the other customers.

Rebate programs work the same way. For example, Kodak ran a program in which a consumer could mail in a form together with the proof of purchase of three rolls of film, and receive a rebate of $1.50. Why not just lower the price of film by 50 cents a roll? Because only those consumers with relatively price-sensitive demands bother to send in the material and request a rebate. Again, the program is a means of price discrimination.

| | Price Elasticity | |
Product	Nonusers	Users
Toilet tissue	−0.60	−0.66
Stuffing/dressing	−0.71	−0.96
Shampoo	−0.84	−1.04
Cooking/salad oil	−1.22	−1.32
Dry mix dinners	−0.88	−1.09
Cake mix	−0.21	−0.43
Cat food	−0.49	−1.13
Frozen entrees	−0.60	−0.95
Gelatin	−0.97	−1.25
Spaghetti sauces	−1.65	−1.81
Creme rinse/conditioner	−0.82	−1.12
Soups	−1.05	−1.22
Hot dogs	−0.59	−0.77

Can consumers really be divided into distinct groups in this way? Table 11.1 shows the results of a statistical study in which, for a variety of products, price elasticities of demand were estimated for users and nonusers of coupons.[6] This study confirms that users of coupons tend to have more price-sensitive demands. It also shows the extent to which the elasticities differ for the two groups of consumers, and how the difference varies from one product to another.

These elasticity estimates by themselves do not tell a firm what price to set and how large a discount to offer through its coupons because they pertain to *market demand*, not the demand for the firm's particular brand. For example, Table 11.1 indicates that the elasticity of demand for cake mix is −0.21 for nonusers of coupons and −0.43 for users. But the elasticity of demand for any of the eight or ten major brands of cake mix on the market will be far larger than either of these numbers—about eight or ten times as large, as a rule of thumb.[7] So for any one brand of cake mix, say, Pillsbury, the elasticity of demand for users of coupons might be about −4, versus about −2 for nonusers. From equation (11.2) we can therefore determine that the price to nonusers of coupons should be about 1.5 times the price to users. In other words, if a box of cake mix sells for $1.50, the company should offer coupons that give a 50 cent discount.

---

[6] The study is by Chakravarthi Narasimhan, "A Price Discrimination Theory of Coupons," *Marketing Science* (Spring 1984).

[7] This rule of thumb follows if interfirm competition can be described by the Cournot model, which we discuss in Chapter 12.

Travelers are often amazed at the variety of fares available for a round-trip flight from New York to Los Angeles. For example, the first-class fare was recently almost $2,000; the regular (unrestricted) economy fare was about $1,200; and special discount fares (often requiring the purchase of a ticket two weeks in advance and/or a Saturday night stayover) could be bought for as little as $500. Although first-class service is not the same as economy service with a minimum stay requirement, the difference would not seem to warrant a price that is four times as high. Why, then, do airlines set fares this way?

The reason is that these fares provide a profitable form of price discrimination for airlines. The gains from discriminating are large, because different types of customers, with very different elasticities of demand, purchase these different types of tickets. Table 11.2 shows price (and income) elasticities of demand for three categories of service within the United States: first-class, unrestricted coach, and discount tickets. (A discounted ticket often has restrictions and may be partly nonrefundable.)

Note that the demand for discounted fares is about two or three times as price elastic as first-class or unrestricted coach service. The reason is that discounted tickets are usually used by families and other leisure travelers, while first-class and unrestricted coach tickets are more often bought by business travelers, who have little choice about when they travel, and whose companies pick up the tab. Of course, these elasticities pertain to market demand, and with several airlines competing for customers, the elasticities of demand for each airline will be larger. But the *relative* sizes of elasticities across the three categories of service should be about the same. When elasticities of demand differ so widely, it should not be surprising that airlines set such different fares for different categories of service.

Price discrimination has become increasingly sophisticated in the United States. A wide variety of fares is available, depending on how far in advance the ticket is bought, the percentage of the fare that is refundable if the trip is

| | Fare Category | | |
Elasticity	First-Class	Unrestricted Coach	Discount
Price	−0.3	−0.4	−0.9
Income	1.2	1.2	1.8

changed or cancelled, and whether the trip includes a weekend stay.[8] The objective of the airlines has been to discriminate more finely among travelers with different reservation prices. As American Airlines' vice-president of pricing and product planning explained it, "You don't want to sell a seat to a guy for $69 when he is willing to pay $400."[9] At the same time, an airline would rather sell a seat for $69 than leave it empty.

11.3 *Intertemporal Price Discrimination and Peak-Load Pricing*

Intertemporal price discrimination is an important and widely practiced pricing strategy closely related to third-degree price discrimination. Here consumers are separated into different groups with different demand functions by being charged different prices at different points in time.

To see how intertemporal price discrimination works, think about how an electronics company might price new, technologically advanced equipment, such as videocassette recorders during the 1970s, compact disc players in the early 1980s, and most recently, digital tape players. In Figure 11.7, D_1 is the (inelastic) demand curve for a small group of consumers who value the product highly and do not want to wait to buy it (e.g., stereo buffs who value high-quality sound and want the latest equipment). D_2 is the demand curve for the broader group of consumers who are more willing to forgo the product if the price is too high. The strategy, then, is to initially offer the product at the high price P_1, selling mostly to consumers on demand curve D_1. Later, after this first group of consumers has bought the product, the price is lowered to P_2, and sales are made to the larger group of consumers on demand curve D_2.[10]

There are other examples of intertemporal price discrimination. One involves charging a high price for a first-run movie, then lowering the price after the movie has been out a year. Another, practiced almost universally by publishers, is to charge a high price for the hardcover edition of a book, and then to release the paperback version at a much lower price about a year later.

---

[8] Airlines also allocate the number of seats on each flight that will be available for each fare category. This is based on the total demand and mix of passengers expected for each flight. Methods for doing this are discussed in Peter P. Belobaba, "Airline Yield Management: An Overview of Seat Inventory Control," *Transportation Science* 21 (May 1987): 63–73.

[9] "The Art of Devising Air Fares," *New York Times*, March 4, 1987.

[10] The prices of new electronic products also come down over time because costs fall as producers start to achieve greater scale economies and move down the learning curve. But even if costs did not fall, producers can make more money by first setting a high price and then reducing it over time, thereby discriminating and capturing consumer surplus.

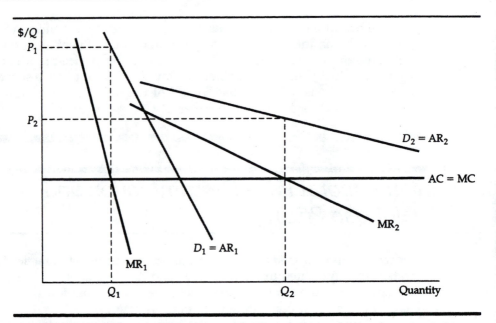

FIGURE 11.7   Intertemporal Price Discrimination. Here, consumers are divided into groups by changing the price over time. Initially, the price is high, and the firm captures surplus from consumers who have a high demand for the good and are unwilling to wait to buy it. Later, the price is reduced to appeal to the mass market.

Many people think that the lower price of the paperback is due to a much lower cost of production, but this is not true. Once a book has been edited and typeset, the marginal cost of printing an additional copy, whether hardcover or paperback, is quite low, perhaps a dollar or so. The paperback version is sold for much less not because it is much cheaper to print, but because high-demand consumers have already purchased the hardbound edition, and the remaining consumers generally have more elastic demands.

Peak-load pricing is another form of intertemporal price discrimination. For some goods and services, demand peaks at particular times—for roads and tunnels during commuter rush hours, for electricity during late summer afternoons, and for ski resorts and amusement parks on weekends. Marginal cost is also high during these peak periods because of capacity constraints. Prices should thus be higher during peak periods.

This is illustrated in Figure 11.8, where D_1 is the demand curve for the peak period, and D_2 is the demand curve for the nonpeak period. The firm sets marginal revenue equal to marginal cost for each period, obtaining the high price P_1 for the peak period, and the lower price P_2 for the nonpeak period, with corresponding quantities Q_1 and Q_2. This increases the firm's profit above what it would be if it charged one price for all periods. It is also more efficient—the

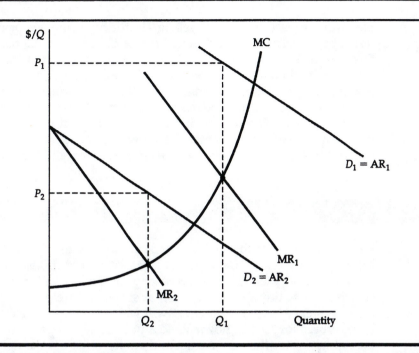

FIGURE 11.8   Peak-Load Pricing.   Demands for some goods and services increase sharply during particular times of the day or year. Charging a higher price P_1 during the peak periods is more profitable for the firm than charging a single price at all times. It is also more efficient because marginal cost is higher during peak periods.

sum of producer and consumer surplus is greater because prices are closer to marginal cost.[11]

Note that peak-load pricing is different from third-degree price discrimination. With third-degree price discrimination, marginal revenue has to be equal for each group of consumers and equal to marginal cost. The reason is that the costs of serving the different groups are not independent. For example, with unrestricted versus discounted air fares, increasing the number of seats sold at discounted fares affects the cost of selling unrestricted tickets—marginal cost rises rapidly as the airplane fills up. But this is not so with peak-load pricing (and for that matter, with most instances of intertemporal price discrimination). Selling more tickets for the ski lifts or amusement park on a weekday does not significantly raise the cost of selling tickets on the weekend. Similarly, selling more electricity during the off-peak period will not sig-

---

[11] The efficiency gain from peak-load pricing is important. If the firm were a regulated monopolist (e.g., an electric utility), the regulatory agency should set the prices P_1 and P_2 at the points where the *demand* curves, D_1 and D_2, intersect the marginal cost curve, rather than where the marginal revenue curves intersect marginal cost. Consumers then realize the entire efficiency gain.

nificantly increase the cost of selling electricity during the peak period. As a result, price and sales in each period can be determined independently by setting marginal cost equal to marginal revenue for each period.

Movie theaters, which charge more for the evening show than for the matinee, are another example of this. For most movie theaters the marginal cost of serving customers during the matinee is independent of the marginal cost during the evening. The owner of a movie theater can determine the optimal prices for the evening and matinee shows independently, using estimates of demand in each period along with estimates of marginal cost.

Publishing both hardbound and paperback editions of a book allows publishers to price discriminate. As they do with most goods, consumers differ considerably in their willingness to pay for books. For example, some consumers want to buy a new best seller as soon as it is released, even if the price is $25. Other consumers, however, will wait a year until the book is available in paperback for $6. But how should a publishing company decide that $25 is the right price for the new hardbound edition and $6 is the right price for the paperback edition? And how long should it wait before bringing out the paperback edition?

The key is to divide consumers into two groups, so that those who are willing to pay a high price do so, and only those unwilling to pay a high price wait and buy the paperback. This means that significant time must be allowed to pass before the paperback is released. If consumers know that the paperback will be available within a few months, they will have little incentive to buy the hardbound edition.[12] On the other hand, the publisher cannot wait too long to bring out the paperback edition, or else interest in the book will wane, and the market will dry up. As a result, publishers typically wait twelve to eighteen months before releasing the paperback edition.

What about price? Setting the price of the hardbound edition is difficult because, except for a few authors whose books always seem to sell, a publisher has little data with which to estimate demand for a book that is about to be published, other than the sales of similar books in the past. But usually only aggregate data are available for each category of book. So most new novels, for example, are released at similar prices. It is clear, however, that those consumers willing to wait for the paperback edition have demands that are far

---

[12] Some consumers will buy the hardbound edition even if the paperback is already available because it is more durable and more attractive on a bookshelf. This must be taken into account when setting prices, but it is of secondary importance compared with intertemporal price discrimination.

more elastic than those of bibliophiles. It is not surprising, then, that paperback editions sell for so much less than hardbound ones.[13]

11.4 *The Two-Part Tariff*

The two-part tariff is related to price discrimination and provides another means of extracting consumer surplus. It requires consumers to pay a fee up front for the right to buy a product. Consumers then pay an additional fee for each unit of the product they wish to consume. The classic example of this is an amusement park.[14] You pay an admission fee to enter, and you also pay a certain amount for each ride you go on. The owner of the park has to decide whether to charge a high entrance fee and a low price for the rides, or alternatively, to admit people for free but charge high prices for the rides.

The two-part tariff has been applied in many settings: tennis and golf clubs (you pay an annual membership fee, plus a fee for each use of a court or round of golf); the rental of large mainframe computers (you pay a flat monthly fee plus a fee for each unit of processing time consumed); telephone service (you pay a monthly hook-up fee plus a fee for message units); a Polaroid camera (you pay for the camera, which lets you productively consume the film, which you pay for by the package); and safety razors (you pay for the razor, which lets you consume the blades that fit only that brand of razor).

The problem for the firm is how to set the entry fee (which we denote by T) versus the usage fee (which we denote by P). Assuming that the firm has some market power, should it set a high entry fee and low usage fee, or vice versa? To see how a firm can solve this problem, we need to understand the basic principles involved.

Let us begin with an artificial but simple case. Suppose only one consumer is in the market (or many consumers with identical demand curves). Suppose also that the firm knows this consumer's demand curve. Now, remember that the firm wants to capture as much consumer surplus as possible. In this case, the solution is straightforward: Set the usage fee P equal to marginal cost, and the entry fee T equal to the total consumer surplus for each consumer. Thus, in Figure 11.9, the consumer pays T^* (or a bit less) to use the product, and

---

[13] The hardbound and paperback editions are often published by different companies. The author's agent auctions the rights to the two editions, but the contract for the paperback specifies a delay to protect the sales of the hardbound edition. The principle still applies, however. The length of the delay and the prices of the two editions are chosen to intertemporally price discriminate.

[14] See Walter Oi, "A Disneyland Dilemma: Two-Part Tariffs for a Mickey Mouse Monopoly," *Quarterly Journal of Economics* (Feb. 1971): 77–96.

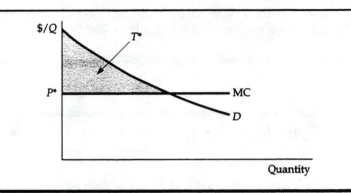

FIGURE 11.9   Two-Part Tariff with a Single Consumer.   The consumer has demand curve D. The firm maximizes profit by setting usage fee P equal to marginal cost and entry fee T equal to the entire surplus of the consumer.

P^* = MC per unit consumed. With the fees set this way, the firm captures *all* the consumer surplus as its profit.

Now, suppose there are two different consumers (or two groups of identical consumers). The firm, however, can set only *one* entry fee and one usage fee. The firm would thus no longer want to set the usage fee equal to marginal cost. If it did, it could make the entry fee no larger than the consumer surplus of the consumer with the smaller demand (or else it would lose that consumer), and this would not give a maximum profit. Instead, the firm should set the usage fee *above* marginal cost, and then set the entry fee equal to the remaining consumer surplus of the consumer with the smaller demand.

Figure 11.10 illustrates this. With the optimal usage fee at P^* greater than MC, the firm's profit is $2T^* + (P^* - MC)(Q_1 + Q_2)$. (There are two consumers, and each pays T^*.) You can verify that this profit is more than twice the area of triangle ABC, the consumer surplus of the consumer with the smaller demand when P = MC. To determine the exact values of P^* and T^*, the firm would need to know (in addition to its marginal cost) the demand curves D_1 and D_2. It would then write down its profit as a function of P and T, and choose the two prices that maximize this function. (See Exercise 10 for an example of how to do this.)

Most firms, however, face a variety of consumers with different demands. Unfortunately, there is no simple formula to calculate the optimal two-part tariff in this case, and some trial and error might be required. But there is always a trade-off: A lower entry fee means more entrants and thus more profit from sales of the item. However, as the entry fee becomes smaller and the number of entrants larger, the profit derived from the entry fee will fall. The problem, then, is to pick an entry fee that results in the optimum number of entrants, that is, the fee that allows for maximum profit. In principle, one can do this by starting with a price for sales of the item P, finding the optimum

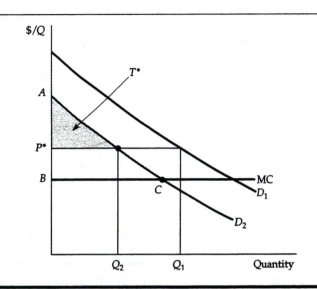

FIGURE 11.10   Two-Part Tariff with Two Consumers.   The profit-maximizing usage fee P^* will exceed marginal cost. The entry fee T^* is equal to the surplus of the consumer with the smaller demand. The resulting profit is $2T^* + (P^* - MC) \times (Q_1 + Q_2)$. Note that this profit is larger than twice the area of triangle ABC.

entry fee T, and then estimating the resulting profit. The price P is then changed, and the corresponding entry fee calculated, along with the new profit level. By iterating this way, one can approach the optimal two-part tariff.

Figure 11.11 illustrates this. Here, the firm's profit π is divided into two components, each of which is plotted as a function of the entry fee T, assuming a fixed sales price P. The first component π_a is the profit from the entry fee, and is equal to the revenue $n(T)T$, where $n(T)$ is the number of entrants. (Note that a high T implies a small n.) Initially, as T is increased from zero, the revenue $n(T)T$ rises. Eventually, however, further increases in T will make n so small that $n(T)T$ falls. The second component, π_s, is the profit from sales of the item itself at price P, and is equal to $(P - MC)Q$, where Q is the rate at which entrants purchase the item. Q will be larger the larger the number of entrants n. Thus π_s falls when T is increased because a higher T reduces n.

Starting with a number for P, we determine the optimal (profit-maximizing) T^*. We then change P, find a new T^*, and determine whether profit is now higher or lower. This is repeated until profit has been maximized.

Obviously, more data are needed to design an optimal two-part tariff than to choose a single price. Knowing marginal cost and the aggregate demand curve is not enough. It is impossible (in most cases) to determine the demand curve of every consumer, but one would at least like to know by how much

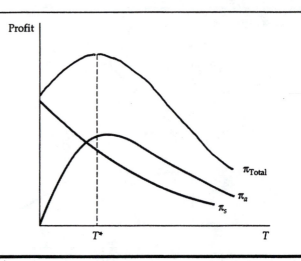

FIGURE 11.11   Two-Part Tariff with Many Different Consumers.   Total profit π is the sum of the profit from the entry fee π_a and the profit from sales π_s. Both π_a and π_s depend on T, the entry fee:

$$\pi = \pi_a + \pi_s = n(T)T + (P - MC)Q(n)$$

where n is the number of entrants, which depends on the entry fee T, and Q is the rate of sales, which is greater the larger is n. Here T^* is the profit-maximizing entry fee, given P. To calculate optimum values for P and T one can start with a number for P, find the optimum T, and then estimate the resulting profit. P is then charged and the corresponding T is recalculated, along with the new profit level.

individual demands differ from one another. If consumers' demands for your product are fairly similar, you would want to charge a price P that is close to marginal cost, and make the entry fee T large. This is the ideal situation from the firm's point of view because most of the consumer surplus could then be captured. On the other hand, if consumers have different demands for your product, you would probably want to set P substantially above marginal cost, and charge a lower entry fee T. But then the two-part tariff is a much less effective means of capturing consumer surplus; setting a single price may do almost as well.

Firms are perpetually searching for innovative pricing strategies, and a few have devised and introduced a two-part tariff with a "twist"—the entry fee T entitles the customer to a certain number of free units. For example, if you buy a Gillette razor, several blades are usually included in the package. And the monthly lease fee for a large mainframe computer usually includes some free usage before usage is charged. This twist lets the firm set a higher entry fee T without losing as many small consumers. These small consumers might pay little or nothing for usage under this scheme, so the higher entry fee will capture their surplus without driving them out of the market, while also capturing more of the surplus of the large consumers.

EXAMPLE 11.4   POLAROID CAMERAS

In 1971 Polaroid introduced its new SX-70 camera. This camera was sold, not leased, to individual consumers. Nevertheless, because it sold its film separately, Polaroid could apply a two-part tariff to the pricing of the SX-70. Let us examine how this pricing device gave Polaroid greater profits than would have been possible if its camera had used ordinary roll film, and how Polaroid might have determined the optimal prices for each part of its two-part tariff. Some time later, Kodak entered the market with a competing self-developing film and camera.[15] We will also consider the effect of Kodak's entry into the market on Polaroid's prices and profits.

First, let's make it clear why the pricing of the SX-70 (and Polaroid's other cameras and film as well) involved a two-part tariff. Polaroid had a monopoly on both its camera and the film. (Only Polaroid film could be used in the camera.) Consumers bought the camera and film to take instant pictures: The camera was the "entry fee" that provided access to the consumption of instant pictures, which was what consumers ultimately demanded.[16] In this sense, the price of the camera was like the entry fee at an amusement park. However, while the marginal cost of allowing someone entry into the park is close to zero, the marginal cost of producing a camera was significantly above zero, and thus had to be taken into account when designing the two-part tariff.

It was important that Polaroid have a monopoly on the film as well as the camera. If the camera had used ordinary roll film, competitive forces would have pushed the price of film close to its marginal cost. If all consumers had identical demands, Polaroid could still have captured all the consumer surplus by setting a high price for the camera (equal to the surplus of each consumer). But in practice, consumers were heterogeneous, and the optimal two-part tariff required a price for the film well above marginal cost. (In fact Polaroid got—and still gets—most of its profits from film rather than cameras.) Polaroid needed its monopoly on the film to maintain this high price.

How should Polaroid have selected its prices for the camera and film? It could have begun with some analytical spadework. Its profit is given by

$$\pi = PQ + nT - C_1(Q) - C_2(n)$$

where P is the price of the film, T is the price of the camera, Q is the quantity of film sold, n is the number of cameras sold, and $C_1(Q)$ and $C_2(n)$ are the costs of producing film and cameras, respectively.

Polaroid wanted to maximize its profit π, taking into account that Q and n depend on P and T. Given a heterogeneous base of potential consumers, this

---

[15] In 1984 the courts ruled that Kodak's camera and film involved a patent infringement, and Kodak was forced to withdraw from the instant picture market in 1985. However, it played an important role in this market for nearly a decade.

[16] We are simplifying here. In fact some consumers obtain utility just from owning the camera, even if they take few or no pictures. Adults, like children, enjoy new toys, and can obtain pleasure from the mere possession of a technologically innovative good.

dependence on P and T might only have been guessed at initially, drawing on knowledge of related products. Later, a better understanding of demand and of how Q and n depend on P and T might have been possible as the firm accumulated data from its sales experience. Knowledge of C_1 and C_2 may have been easier to come by, perhaps from engineering and statistical studies (as discussed in Chapter 7).

Given some initial guesses or estimates for $Q(P)$, $n(T)$, $C_1(Q)$, and $C_2(n)$, Polaroid could have calculated the profit-maximizing prices P and T. It could also have determined how sensitive these prices were to uncertainty over demand and cost. This could have provided a guideline for trial-and-error pricing experiments. Over time these experiments would also have told Polaroid more about demand and cost, so that it could refine its two-part tariff.[17]

Did the entry of Kodak with a competing instant camera and film mean that Polaroid lost its ability to use a two-part tariff to extract consumer surplus? No—only Polaroid film could be used in Polaroid cameras, and Polaroid still had some monopoly power to exploit. However, its monopoly power was reduced, the amount of consumer surplus that could potentially be extracted was smaller, and prices had to be changed. With demand now more elastic, Polaroid would have wanted to reduce the price of its cameras significantly (and indeed it did). Assuming that consumers remained as heterogeneous as before, Polaroid might also have wanted to reduce the price of its film.

*11.5 Bundling

You have probably seen the 1939 film, *Gone with the Wind*. It is a classic that is nearly as popular now as it was then. Yet we would guess that you have not seen *Getting Gertie's Garter*, a flop that the same film company (Loews) also produced in 1939. And we would also guess that you didn't know that these two films were priced in what was then an unusual and innovative way.[18]

Movie theaters that leased *Gone with the Wind* also had to lease *Getting Gertie's Garter*. (Movie theaters pay the film companies or their distributors a daily or weekly fee for the films they lease.) In other words, these two films were *bundled*, i.e., sold as a package. Why would the film company do this?

You might think that the answer is obvious: *Gone with the Wind* was a great film and *Gertie* was a lousy film, so bundling the two forced movie theaters to lease *Gertie*. But this answer doesn't make economic sense. Suppose a theater's

---

[17] Setting prices for a product such as a Polaroid camera is clearly not a simple matter. We have ignored the *dynamic* behavior of cost and demand: how production costs fall as the firm moves down its learning curve, and how demand changes over time as the market begins to saturate.

[18] For those readers who claim to know all this, our final trivia question is: Who played the role of Gertie in *Getting Gertie's Garter*?

reservation price (the maximum price it will pay) for *Gone with the Wind* is $12,000 per week, and its reservation price for *Gertie* is $3000 per week. Then the most it would pay for *both* films is $15,000, whether it takes the films individually or as a package.

Bundling makes sense when *customers have heterogeneous demands,* and when the firm cannot price discriminate. With films, different movie theaters serve different groups of patrons and therefore may well have different demands for films. For example, the theater might appeal to different age groups, who have different relative film preferences.

To see how a film company can use this heterogeneity to its advantage, suppose there are *two* movie theaters, and their reservation prices for our two films are as follows:

	Gone with the Wind	Getting Gertie's Garter
Theater A	$12,000	$3,000
Theater B	$10,000	$4,000

If the films are rented separately, the maximum price that could be charged for *Wind* is $10,000 because charging more than this would exclude Theater B. Similarly, the maximum price that could be charged for *Gertie* is $3000. Charging these two prices would yield $13,000 from each theater, for a total of $26,000 in revenue. But suppose the films are *bundled.* Theater A values the *pair* of films at $15,000 ($12,000 + $3000), and Theater B values the pair at $14,000 ($10,000 + $4000). So we can charge each theater $14,000 for the pair of films, and earn a total revenue of $28,000. Clearly, we can earn more revenue ($2000 more) by bundling the films.

Why is bundling more profitable than selling the films separately? Because (in this example) the *relative* valuations of the two films are reversed. In other words, although both theaters would pay much more for *Wind* than for *Gertie,* Theater A would pay more than Theater B for *Wind* ($12,000 vs. $10,000), while Theater B would pay more than Theater A for *Gertie* ($4000 vs. $3000). In technical terms, we say that the demands are *negatively correlated*—the customer willing to pay the most for *Wind* is willing to pay the least for *Gertie.* To see why this is critical, suppose demands were *positively correlated,* that is, Theater A would pay more for *both* films:

	Gone with the Wind	Getting Gertie's Garter
Theater A	$12,000	$4,000
Theater B	$10,000	$3,000

The most that Theater A would pay for the pair of films is now $16,000, but the most that Theater B would pay for the pair is only $13,000. So if the films were bundled, the maximum price that could be charged for the package is $13,000, yielding a total revenue of $26,000, the same as by selling the films separately.

Now, suppose a firm is selling two different goods to many consumers. To analyze the possible advantages of bundling, we will use a simple diagram to describe the preferences of the consumers in terms of their reservation prices and their consumption decisions given the prices charged. In Figure 11.12 the horizontal axis is r_1, which is the reservation price of a consumer for good 1, and the vertical axis is r_2, which is the reservation price for good 2. The figure shows the reservation prices for three consumers. Consumer A is willing to pay up to $3.25 for good 1 and up to $6 for good 2; consumer B is willing to pay $8.25 for good 1 and up to $3.25 for good 2; and consumer C is willing to pay up to $10 for each of the goods. In general, the reservation prices for any number of consumers can be plotted this way.

Suppose there are many consumers, and the products are sold separately, at prices P_1 and P_2, respectively. Figure 11.13 shows how consumers can be divided into groups. Consumers in region I of the graph have reservation prices that are above the prices being charged for each of the goods, and so will buy both goods. Consumers in region II have a reservation price for good 2 that is above P_2, but a reservation price for good 1 that is below P_1; they will buy only good 2. Similarly, consumers in region IV will buy only good 1. Finally, consumers in region III have reservation prices below the prices charged for each of the goods, and so will buy neither good.

Now suppose the goods are sold as a bundle, for a total price of P_B. We can then divide the graph into two regions, as in Figure 11.14. Any given consumer will buy the bundle only if its price is less than or equal to the sum of that consumer's reservation prices for the two goods. The dividing line is therefore the equation $P_B = r_1 + r_2$, or equivalently, $r_2 = P_B - r_1$. Consumers in region I have reservation prices that add up to more than P_B, so they will buy

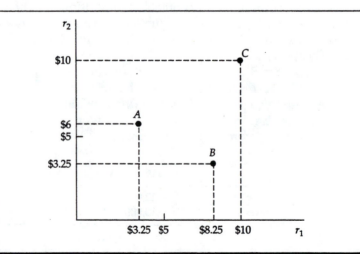

FIGURE 11.12   Reservation Prices.   Reservation prices r_1 and r_2 for two goods are shown for three consumers, labeled A, B, and C. Consumer A is willing to pay up to $3.25 for good 1 and up to $6 for good 2.
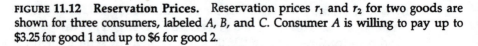

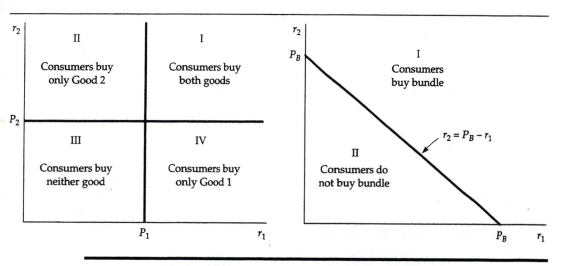

FIGURE 11.13 (left)   Consumption Decisions When Products Are Sold Separately. The reservation prices of consumers in region I exceed the prices P_1 and P_2 for the two goods, so these consumers buy both goods. Consumers in regions II and IV buy only one of the goods, and consumers in region III buy neither good.

FIGURE 11.14 (right)   Consumption Decisions When Products Are Bundled. Consumers compare the *sum* of their reservation prices, $r_1 + r_2$, with the price of the bundle P_B. They buy the bundle only if $r_1 + r_2$ is at least as large as P_B.

the bundle. Consumers in region II have reservation prices that add up to less than P_B, so they will not buy the bundle.

Depending on the prices charged, some of the consumers in region II of Figure 11.14 might have bought one of the goods if they had been sold separately. These consumers are lost to the firm, however, when it sells the goods as a bundle. The firm, then, has to determine whether it can do better by bundling.

In general, the effectiveness of bundling depends on how negatively correlated demands are. In other words, it works best when consumers who have a high reservation price for good 1 have a low reservation price for good 2, and vice versa. Figures 11.15a and b show two extremes. In Figure 11.15a each point represents the two reservation prices of a consumer. Note that the demands for the two goods are perfectly positively correlated—consumers with a high reservation price for good 1 also have a high reservation price for good 2. If the firm bundles and charges a price $P_B = P_1 + P_2$, it will make the same profit it would if it sold the goods separately at prices P_1 and P_2. In Figure 11.15b, on the other hand, demands are perfectly negatively correlated—a higher reservation price for good 2 implies a proportionately lower one for good 1. In this case, bundling is the ideal strategy. By charging the price P_B shown in the figure, the firm can capture *all* the consumer surplus.

Figure 11.16, which shows the movie example that we introduced at the beginning of this section, illustrates how the demands of the two movie theaters are negatively correlated. (Theater A will pay relatively more for *Gone with the*

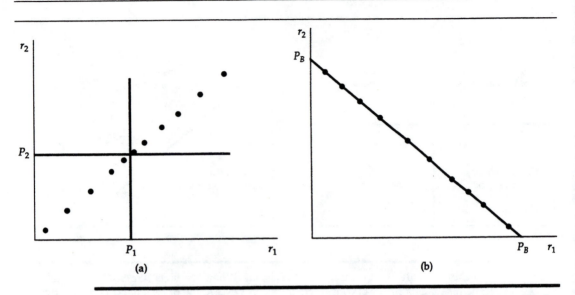

FIGURE 11.15   Reservation Prices.   In (a), demands are perfectly positively correlated, so the firm does not gain by bundling. It would earn the same profit as by selling the goods separately. In (b), demands are perfectly negatively correlated. Bundling is the ideal strategy—all the consumer surplus can be extracted.

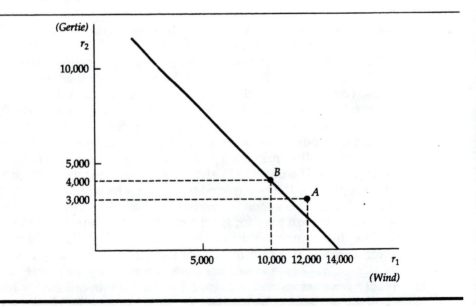

FIGURE 11.16   Movie Example.   Consumers A and B are two movie theaters. The diagram shows their reservation prices for the films *Gone with the Wind* and *Getting Gertie's Garter*. Since the demands are negatively correlated, bundling pays.

Wind, but Theater *B* will pay relatively more for *Getting Gertie's Garter.*) This makes it more profitable to rent the films as a bundle, priced at $14,000.

Mixed Bundling

So far, we have assumed that the firm has two options—either to sell the goods separately or as a bundle. But there is a third option, called *mixed bundling.* As the name suggests, the firm offers its products both separately and as a bundle, with a package price below the sum of the individual prices. Mixed bundling is often the ideal strategy when demands are only somewhat negatively correlated, and/or when marginal production costs are significant. (Thus far, we have assumed that marginal production costs are zero.)

In Figure 11.17, mixed bundling is the most profitable strategy. Here, demands are perfectly negatively correlated, but there are significant marginal

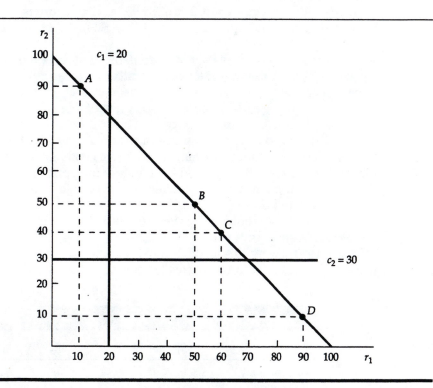

FIGURE 11.17   Mixed Versus Pure Bundling.   With positive marginal costs, mixed bundling may be more profitable than pure bundling, as in this example. Consumer *A* has a reservation price for good 1 that is below marginal cost c_1, and consumer *D* has a reservation price for good 2 that is below marginal cost c_2. With mixed bundling, consumer *A* is induced to buy only good 2, and consumer *D* is induced to buy only good 1, reducing the firm's cost.

costs. (The marginal cost of producing good 1 is $20, and the marginal cost of producing good 2 is $30.) Four consumers are shown, labeled A through D. Now, let's compare three strategies—selling the goods separately at prices $P_1 =$ $50 and $P_2 = $90; selling the goods only as a bundle (a strategy that we will refer to as "pure bundling") at a price of $100; or mixed bundling, where the goods are sold separately at prices $P_1 = P_2 = $89.95, or as a bundle at a price of $100.

Table 11.3 shows these three strategies and the resulting profits. (You can try other prices for P_1, P_2, and P_B to verify that those given in the table maximize profit for each strategy.) When the goods are sold separately, only consumers B, C, and D buy good 1, and only consumer A buys good 2, so that the total profit is $3($50 - $20) + 1($90 - $30) = 150. With pure bundling, all four consumers buy the bundle for $100, so that total profit is $4($100 - $20 - $30) = 200. As we should expect, pure bundling is better than selling the goods separately because consumers' demands are negatively correlated. But what about mixed bundling? Now consumer D buys only good 1 for $89.95, consumer A buys only good 2 for $89.95, and consumers B and C buy the bundle for $100. Total profit is now $($89.95 - $20) + ($89.95 - $30) + 2($100 - $20 - $30) = 229.90.

Here, mixed bundling is the most profitable strategy, even though demands are perfectly negatively correlated (i.e., all four consumers have reservation prices on the line $r_2 = 100 - r_1$). The reason is that for each good, marginal production cost exceeds the reservation price of one consumer. For example, consumer A has a reservation price of $90 for good 2, but a reservation price of only $10 for good 1. Since the cost of producing a unit of good 1 is $20, the firm would prefer that consumer A buy only good 2, and not the bundle. It can achieve this by offering good 2 separately for a price just below consumer A's reservation price, while also offering the bundle at a price acceptable to consumers B and C.

Mixed bundling would *not* be the preferred strategy in this example if marginal costs were zero, because then there would be no benefit in excluding consumer A from buying good 1 and consumer D from buying good 2. We leave it to you to demonstrate this (see Exercise 12).[19]

	P_1	P_2	P_B	Profit
Sell separately	$50	$90	—	$150
Pure bundling	—	—	$100	$200
Mixed bundling	$89.95	$89.95	$100	$229.90

TABLE 11.3

[19] For further discussion of bundling, see William J. Adams and Janet L. Yellin, "Commodity Bundling and the Burden of Monopoly," *Quarterly Journal of Economics* 90 (Aug. 1976): 475–498. Sometimes a firm with monopoly power will find it profitable to bundle its product with the product of another

EXAMPLE 11.5   THE COMPLETE DINNER VS. À LA CARTE: A RESTAURANT'S PRICING PROBLEM

Many restaurants offer complete dinners as well as an à la carte menu. Why? Most customers go out to eat knowing roughly how much they are willing to spend for dinner (and choose the restaurant accordingly). However, the customers that enter a restaurant have different preferences. For example, some value an appetizer highly, but could happily skip the dessert. Other customers have just the opposite preferences—they attach little value to the appetizer, but dessert is essential. And finally, some customers attach moderate values to both the appetizer and dessert. What pricing strategy lets the restaurant capture as much consumer surplus as possible from these heterogeneous customers? The answer, of course, is mixed bundling.

For a restaurant, mixed bundling means offering both complete dinners (the appetizer, main course, and dessert come as a package) and an à la carte menu (the customer buys the appetizer, main course, and dessert separately). This allows the à la carte menu to be priced to capture consumer surplus from customers who value some dishes much more highly than other dishes. (Such customers would correspond to consumers A and D in Figure 11.17.) At the same time, the complete dinner retains those customers who have lower variations in their reservation prices for different dishes (e.g., customers who attach a moderate value to both the appetizer and dessert).

For example, if the restaurant expects to attract customers willing to spend about $20 for dinner, it might charge about $5 for the appetizers, about $14 for a typical main dish, and about $4 for dessert. It could also offer a complete dinner, which includes an appetizer, main course, and dessert, for $20. Then, the customer who loves dessert but couldn't care less about an appetizer will order only the main dish and dessert, and spend $18 (and the restaurant will save the cost of preparing an appetizer). At the same time, another customer who attaches a moderate value (say, $3 or $3.50) to both the appetizer and dessert will buy the complete dinner.

Unfortunately for consumers, perhaps, creative pricing can be more important than creative cooking for the financial success of a restaurant. Successful restaurateurs know their customers' demand characteristics and use that knowledge to design a pricing strategy that extracts as much consumer surplus as possible.

---

firm; see Richard L. Schmalensee, "Commodity Bundling by Single-Product Monopolies," *Journal of Law and Economics* 25 (April 1982): 67–71. Bundling can also be profitable when the products are substitutes or complements. See Arthur Lewbel, "Bundling of Substitutes or Complements," *International Journal of Industrial Organization* 3 (1985): 101–107.

Tying

Tying is a general term that refers to any requirement that products be bought or sold in some combination. Bundling is a common form of tying, but tying can also take other forms. For example, suppose a firm sells a product (such as a copying machine), the use of which requires the consumption of a secondary product (such as paper). The consumer who buys the first product is also required to buy the secondary product from the same company. This requirement is usually imposed through a contract. Note that this is different from the examples of bundling discussed earlier. In those examples, the consumer might have been happy to buy just one of the products. In this case, however, the first product is useless without access to the secondary product.

Why might firms use this kind of pricing practice? One of the main benefits of tying is that it often allows a firm to *meter demand*, and thus to practice price discrimination more effectively. For example, during the 1950s, when Xerox had a monopoly on copying machines but not on paper, customers who leased a Xerox copier also had to buy Xerox paper. This allowed Xerox to meter consumption (customers who used a machine intensively bought more paper), and thereby apply a two-part tariff to the pricing of its machines. Also during the 1950s, IBM required customers who leased its mainframe computers to use paper computer cards made only by IBM. By pricing these cards well above marginal cost, IBM was effectively charging higher prices for computer usage to customers with larger demands.[20]

Tying can also have other uses. An important one is to protect customer goodwill connected with a brand name. This is why franchises are often required to purchase inputs from the franchiser. For example, Mobil Oil requires its service stations to sell only Mobil motor oil, Mobil batteries, and so on. Similarly, until recently, a McDonald's franchisee had to purchase all materials and supplies—from the hamburgers to the paper cups—from McDonald's, thus ensuring product uniformity and protecting the brand name.[21]

---

*11.6 *Advertising*

We have seen how firms can utilize their market power when making pricing decisions. Pricing is important for a firm, but most firms with market power have another important decision to make: how much to advertise. In this sec-

---

[20] However, antitrust actions forced IBM to discontinue this pricing practice.

[21] In some cases, the courts ruled that tying is not necessary to protect customer goodwill and is anticompetitive, so now a McDonald's franchisee can buy supplies from any McDonald's approved source. For a discussion of some of the antitrust issues involved in franchise tying, see Benjamin Klein and Lester F. Saft, "The Law and Economics of Franchise Tying Contracts," *Journal of Law and Economics* 28 (May 1985): 345–361.

tion we will see how firms with market power can make profit-maximizing advertising decisions, and how those decisions depend on the characteristics of demand for the firm's product.[22]

For simplicity, we will assume that the firm sets only one price for its product. We will also assume that having done sufficient market research, it knows how its quantity demanded depends on both its price P *and* its advertising expenditures in dollars A; that is, it knows $Q(P,A)$. Figure 11.18 shows the firm's demand and cost curves with and without advertising. AR and MR are the firm's

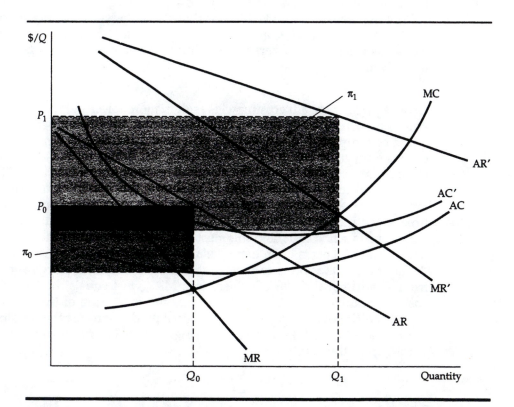

FIGURE 11.18 **Effects of Advertising.**   AR and MR are average and marginal revenue when the firm doesn't advertise, and AC and MC are average and marginal cost. The firm produces Q_0 and receives a price P_0. Its total profit π_0 is given by the gray-shaded rectangle. If the firm advertises, its average and marginal revenue curves shift to the right. Average cost rises (to AC'), but marginal cost remains the same. The firm now produces Q_1 (where MR' = MC), and receives a price P_1. Its total profit, π_1, is now larger.

[22] A perfectly competitive firm has little reason to advertise, since by definition it can sell as much as it produces at a market price that it takes as given. That is why it would be unusual to see a producer of corn or soybeans advertise.

average and marginal revenue curves when it doesn't advertise, and AC and MC are its average and marginal cost curves. It produces a quantity Q_0, where MR = MC, and receives a price P_0. Its profit per unit is the difference between P_0 and average cost, so its total profit π_0 is given by the gray-shaded rectangle.

Now suppose the firm advertises. This causes its demand curve to shift out and to the right; the new average and marginal revenue curves are given by AR' and MR'. Advertising is a fixed cost, so the firm's average cost curve rises (to AC'). Marginal cost, however, remains the same. With advertising, the firm produces Q_1 (where MR' = MC), and receives a price P_1. Its total profit π_1, given by the red-shaded rectangle, is now much larger.

While the firm in Figure 11.18 is clearly better off advertising, the figure does not help us determine *how much* advertising the firm should do. Our firm must choose its price P and advertising expenditure A to maximize profit, which is now given by:

$$\pi = PQ(P,A) - C(Q) - A$$

Given a price, more advertising will result in more sales, and hence more revenue. But what is the firm's profit-maximizing advertising expenditure? You might be tempted to say that the firm should increase its advertising expenditures until the last dollar of advertising just brings forth an additional dollar of revenue, that is, until the marginal revenue from advertising, $\Delta(PQ)/\Delta A$, is just equal to 1. But as Figure 11.18 shows, this reasoning omits an important element. Remember that advertising leads to increased output (in the figure, output increased from Q_0 to Q_1). But increased output in turn means increased production costs, and this must be taken into account when comparing the costs and benefits of an extra dollar of advertising.

The correct decision is to increase advertising until the marginal revenue from an additional dollar of advertising, MR_{Ads}, just equals the *full* marginal cost of that advertising. That full marginal cost is the sum of the dollar spent directly on the advertising and the marginal production cost that results from the increased sales that advertising brings about. Thus the firm should advertise up to the point that[23]

$$MR_{Ads} = P\frac{\Delta Q}{\Delta A} = 1 + MC\frac{\Delta Q}{\Delta A}$$

(11.3)

$$= \textit{full marginal cost of advertising}$$

This rule is often ignored by managers, who justify advertising budgets by comparing the expected benefits (i.e., added sales) only with the cost of the advertising. But additional sales mean increased production costs, which must also be taken into account.

---

[23] To derive this using calculus, differentiate $\pi(Q,A)$ with respect to A, and set the derivative equal to zero:

$$\partial\pi/\partial A = P(\partial Q/\partial A) - MC(\partial Q/\partial A) - 1 = 0$$

Rearranging gives equation (11.3).

A Rule of Thumb for Advertising

Like the rule MR = MC, equation (11.3) is sometimes difficult to apply in practice. In Chapter 10 we saw that MR = MC implies the following rule of thumb for pricing: $(P - MC)/P = -1/E_P$, where E_P is the firm's price elasticity of demand. We can combine this rule of thumb for pricing with equation (11.3) to obtain a rule of thumb for advertising.

First, rewrite equation (11.3) as follows:

$$(P - MC)\frac{\Delta Q}{\Delta A} = 1$$

Now multiply both sides of this equation by A/PQ, the *advertising-to-sales ratio*:

$$\frac{P - MC}{P}\left[\frac{A}{Q}\frac{\Delta Q}{\Delta A}\right] = \frac{A}{PQ}$$

The term in brackets, $(A/Q)(\Delta Q/\Delta A)$, is the *advertising elasticity of demand*, i.e., the percentage change in the quantity demanded that results from a 1 percent increase in advertising expenditures. We will denote this elasticity by E_A. Since $(P - MC)/P$ must equal $-1/E_P$, we can rewrite this equation as follows:

$$\boxed{A/PQ = -(E_A/E_P)} \qquad (11.4)$$

Equation (11.4) is a rule of thumb for advertising. It says that to maximize profit, the firm's advertising-to-sales ratio should be equal to minus the ratio of the advertising and price elasticities of demand. Given information (from, say, market research studies) on these two elasticities, the firm can use this rule to check that its advertising budget is not too small or too large.

To put this rule into perspective, assume that a firm is generating sales revenue of $1,000,000 per year while allocating only $10,000 (1% of its revenues) to advertising. The firm knows that its advertising elasticity of demand is .2, so that a doubling of its advertising budget from $10,000 to $20,000 should increase sales by 20%. The firm also knows that the price elasticity of demand for its product is −4. Should the firm increase its advertising budget, knowing that with a price elasticity of demand of −4, its markup of price over marginal cost is substantial? The answer is yes; equation (11.4) tells us that the firm's advertising-to-sales ratio should be −(.2/−4) = 5%, so the firm should increase its advertising budget from $10,000 to $50,000.

This rule makes intuitive sense. It says firms should advertise a lot if (i) demand is very sensitive to advertising (E_A is large), or (ii) demand is not very price elastic (E_P is small). While (i) is obvious, why should firms advertise more when the price elasticity of demand is small? The reason is that a small elasticity of demand implies a large markup of price over marginal cost, so that the marginal profit from each extra unit sold is high. In this case, if advertising can help sell a few more units, it will be worth its cost.[24]

EXAMPLE 11.6   ADVERTISING: SUPERMARKETS TO DESIGNER JEANS

In Example 10.1 we looked at the use of markup pricing by supermarkets, convenience stores, and makers of designer jeans, and saw how in each case the markup of price over marginal cost depended on the firm's price elasticity of demand. Now let's see why these firms, and also producers of laundry detergent, advertise as much (or as little) as they do.

First, supermarkets. We said that the price elasticity of demand for a typical supermarket is around -10. To determine the advertising-to-sales ratio, we also need to know the advertising elasticity of demand. This number can vary considerably depending on what part of the country the supermarket is in, and whether it is in a city, suburb, or rural area, but 0.1 to 0.3 would be a reasonable range. Substituting these numbers into equation (11.4), we find that the manager of a typical supermarket should have an advertising budget that is around 1 to 3 percent of sales—which is indeed what many supermarkets spend on advertising.

Convenience stores have lower price elasticities of demand (around -5), but their advertising-to-sales ratios are usually less than those for supermarkets (and are often zero). Why? Because convenience stores mostly serve customers who live nearby, and might need a few items late at night, or don't want to drive to the supermarket. These customers already know about the convenience store and are unlikely to change their buying habits if the store advertises. Hence E_A is very small, and advertising is not worthwhile.

Advertising is quite important for makers of designer jeans, who will have advertising-to-sales ratios as high as 10 or 20 percent. We said that price elasticities of demand in the range of -3 to -4 are typical for the major labels, and advertising elasticities of demand can range from .3 to as high as 1. (Advertising is important in making consumers aware of the label and giving it an aura and image.) So, these levels of advertising would seem to make sense.

Laundry detergents have among the very highest advertising-to-sales ratios, sometimes exceeding 30 percent, even though demand for any one brand is at least as price elastic as it is for designer jeans. What justifies all the advertising? The answer is a very large advertising elasticity. The demand for

[24] Advertising often affects the price elasticity of demand, and this must be taken into account by the firm. For some products, advertising broadens the market by attracting a large range of customers, or creating a bandwagon effect. This is likely to make demand more price elastic than it would have been otherwise. (But E_A is likely to be large, so that advertising will still be worthwhile.) Sometimes advertising is used to differentiate a product from others (by creating an image, allure, or brand identification), so that its demand is less price elastic than it would otherwise be.

any one brand of laundry detergent depends crucially on advertising; without it, consumers would have little basis for selecting any one brand.[25]

Summary

1. Firms with market power are in an enviable position because they have the potential to earn large profits, but realizing that potential may depend critically on the firm's pricing strategy. Even if the firm sets a single price, it needs an estimate of the elasticity of demand for its output. More complicated strategies, which can involve setting several different prices, require even more information about demand.

2. A pricing strategy aims to enlarge the customer base that the firm can sell to, and capture as much consumer surplus as possible. There are a number of ways to do this, and they usually involve setting more than a single price.

3. Ideally, the firm would like to perfectly price discriminate, i.e., charge each customer his or her reservation price. In practice this is almost always impossible. On the other hand, various forms of imperfect price discrimination are often used to increase profits.

4. The two-part tariff is another means of capturing consumer surplus. Customers must pay an "entry" fee, which allows them to buy the good at a per-unit price. The two-part tariff is most effective when customer demands are relatively homogeneous.

5. When demands are heterogeneous and negatively correlated, bundling can increase profits. With pure bundling, two or more different goods are sold only as a package. With mixed bundling, the customer can buy the goods individually or as a package.

6. Bundling is a special case of tying, a requirement that products be bought or sold in some combination. Tying can be used to meter demand or to protect customer goodwill associated with a brand name.

7. Advertising can further increase profits. The profit-maximizing advertising-to-sales ratio is equal in magnitude to the ratio of the advertising and price elasticities of demand.

Questions for Review

1. Suppose a firm can practice perfect, first-degree price discrimination. What is the lowest price it will charge, and what will its total output be?

2. How does a car salesperson practice price discrimination? How does the ability to discriminate correctly affect his or her earnings?

---

[25] For an overview of statistical approaches to estimating the advertising elasticity of demand, see Ernst R. Berndt, *The Practice of Econometrics* (Reading, Mass: Addison-Wesley, 1990), Chapter 8.

3. Electric utilities often practice second-degree price discrimination. Why might this improve consumer welfare?

4. Give some examples of third-degree price discrimination. Can third-degree price discrimination be effective if the different groups of consumers have different levels of demand but the same price elasticities?

5. Show why optimal, third-degree price discrimination requires that marginal revenue for each group of consumers equals marginal cost. Use this condition to explain how a firm should change its prices and total output if the demand curve for one group of consumers shifted outward, so that marginal revenue for that group increased.

6. How is peak-load pricing a form of price discrimination? Can it make consumers better off? Give an example.

7. How can a firm determine an optimal two-part tariff if it has two customers with different demand curves? (Assume that it knows the demand curves.)

8. Why is the pricing of a Gillette safety razor a form of a two-part tariff? Must Gillette be a mo-

nopoly producer of its blades as well as its razors? Suppose you were advising Gillette on how to determine the two parts of the tariff. What procedure would you suggest?

9. Why did Loews bundle *Gone with the Wind* and *Getting Gertie's Garter*? What characteristic of demands is needed for bundling to increase profits?

10. How does mixed bundling differ from pure bundling? Under what conditions is mixed bundling preferred to pure bundling? Why do many restaurants practice mixed bundling (by offering a complete dinner as well as an à la carte menu) instead of pure bundling?

11. How does tying differ from bundling? Why might a firm want to practice tying?

12. Why is it incorrect to advertise up to the point that the last dollar of advertising expenditures generates another dollar of sales? What is the correct rule for the marginal advertising dollar?

13. How can a firm check that its advertising-to-sales ratio is not too high or too low? What information would it need?

Exercises

1. Price discrimination requires the ability to sort customers and the ability to prevent arbitrage. Explain how the following can function as price discrimination schemes and discuss both sorting and arbitrage:

    a. requiring airline travelers to spend at least one Saturday night away from home to qualify for a low fare.

    b. insisting on delivering cement to buyers, and basing prices on buyers' locations.

    c. selling food processors along with coupons that can be sent to the manufacturer to obtain a $10 rebate.

    d. offering temporary price cuts on bathroom tissue.

    e. charging high-income patients more than low-income patients for plastic surgery.

2. If the demand for drive-in movies is more elastic for couples than for single individuals, it will be optimal for theaters to charge one admission fee for the driver of the car and an extra fee for passengers. True or False? Explain.

3. When pricing automobiles for wholesale delivery to dealers, American car companies typically charge a much higher percentage markup over cost for "luxury option" items (such as vinyl roof, carpeting, decorative trim, etc.) than for the car itself or for more "basic" options such as power steering and automatic transmission. Explain why.

4. Suppose that BMW can produce any quantity of cars at a constant marginal cost equal to $15,000 and a fixed cost of $20 million. You are asked to advise the CEO as to what prices and quantities BMW should set for sales in Europe and in the U.S. The demand for BMWs in each market is given by:

$$Q_E = 18,000 - 400P_E \text{ and } Q_U = 5500 - 100P_U$$

where the subscript E denotes Europe, the subscript U denotes the United States, and all prices and costs are in thousands of dollars. Assume that BMW can restrict U.S. sales to authorized BMW dealers only.

a. What quantity of BMWs should the firm sell in each market and what will the price be in each market? What is the total profit?

b. If BMW were forced to charge the same price in each market, what would be the quantity sold in each market, the equilibrium price, and the company's profit?

5. A monopolist is deciding how to allocate output between two markets. The two markets are separated geographically (East Coast and Midwest). Demand and marginal revenue for the two markets are:

$$P_1 = 15 - Q_1 \qquad MR_1 = 15 - 2Q_1$$
$$P_2 = 25 - 2Q_2 \qquad MR_2 = 25 - 4Q_2$$

The monopolist's total cost is $C = 5 + 3(Q_1 + Q_2)$. What are price, output, profits, marginal revenues, and deadweight loss (i) if the monopolist can price discriminate? (ii) if the law prohibits charging different prices in the two regions?

6. Elizabeth Airlines (EA) flies only one route: Chicago–Honolulu. The demand for each flight on this route is $Q = 500 - P$. Elizabeth's cost of running each flight is $30,000 plus $100 per passenger.

a. What is the profit-maximizing price EA will charge? How many people will be on each flight? What is EA's profit for each flight?

b. Elizabeth learns that the fixed costs per flight are in fact $41,000 instead of $30,000. Will she stay in this business long? Illustrate your answer using a graph of the demand curve that EA faces, EA's average cost curve when fixed costs are $30,000, and EA's average cost curve when fixed costs are $41,000.

c. Wait! Elizabeth finds out that two different types of people fly to Honolulu. Type A is business people with a demand of $Q_A = 260 - 0.4P$. Type B is students whose total demand is $Q_B = 240 - 0.6P$. The students are easy to spot, so Elizabeth decides to charge them different prices. Graph each of these demand curves and the hor-

izontal sum of them. What price does Elizabeth charge the students? What price does she charge the other customers? How many of each type are on each flight?

d. What would EA's profit be for each flight? Would she stay in business? Calculate the consumer surplus of each consumer group. What is the total consumer surplus?

e. Before EA started price discriminating, how much consumer surplus was the Type A demand getting from air travel to Honolulu? Type B? Why did the total surplus decline with price discrimination, even though the total quantity sold was unchanged?

7. Many retail video stores offer two alternative plans for renting films:

a. A two-part tariff: Pay an annual membership fee (e.g., $40), and then pay a small fee for the daily rental of each film (e.g., $2 per film per day).

b. A straight rental fee: Pay no membership fee, but pay a higher daily rental fee (e.g., $4 per film per day).

What is the logic behind the two-part tariff in this case? Why offer the customer a choice of two plans, rather than simply a two-part tariff?

8. Sal's satellite company broadcasts TV to subscribers in Los Angeles and New York. The demand functions for each of these two groups are

$$Q_{NY} = 50 - (\tfrac{1}{3})P_{NY}$$
$$Q_{LA} = 80 - (\tfrac{2}{3})P_{LA}$$

where Q is in thousands of subscriptions per year, and P is the subscription price per year. The cost of providing Q units of service is given by

$$C = 1000 + 30Q$$

where $Q = Q_{NY} + Q_{LA}$.

a. What are the profit-maximizing prices and quantities for the N.Y. and L.A. markets?

b. As a consequence of a new satellite that the Pentagon recently deployed, people in Los Angeles receive Sal's New York broadcasts, and people in New York receive Sal's Los Angeles broadcasts. As a result, anyone in New York or Los Angeles can receive Sal's broadcasts by subscribing in either city. Hence Sal can only charge a single price. What price should he charge, and what quantities will he sell in N.Y. and L.A.?

c. In which of the above situations, (a) or (b), is Sal better off? In terms of consumer surplus, which situation do people in New York prefer and which do people in Los Angeles prefer? Why?

* 9. You are an executive for Super Computer, Inc. (SC), which rents out super computers. SC receives a fixed rental payment per time period in exchange for the right to unlimited computing at a rate of P cents per second. SC has two types of potential customers of equal number—ten businesses and ten academic institutions. Each business customer has the demand function $Q = 10 - P$, where Q is in millions of seconds per month; each academic institution has the demand $Q = 8 - P$. The marginal cost to SC of additional computing is two cents per second, no matter what the volume.

a. Suppose that you could separate business and academic customers. What rental fee and usage fee would you charge each group? What are your profits?

b. Suppose you were unable to keep the two types of customers separate, and you charged a zero rental fee. What usage fee maximizes your profits? What are your profits?

c. Suppose you set up one two-part tariff; that is, you set one rental and one usage fee that both business and academic customers face. What usage and rental fees will you set? What are your profits? Explain why price is not equal to marginal cost.

10. As the owner of the only tennis club in an isolated wealthy community, you must decide on membership dues and fees for court time. There are two types of tennis players. "Serious" players have demand

$$Q_1 = 6 - P$$

where Q_1 is court hours per week and P is the fee per hour for each individual player. There are also "occasional" players with demand

$$Q_2 = 3 - (1/2)P$$

Assume that there are 1000 players of each type. You have plenty of courts, so that the marginal cost of court time is zero. You have fixed costs of $5000 per week. Serious and occasional players look alike, so you must charge them the same prices.

a. Suppose that to maintain a "professional" atmosphere, you want to limit membership to serious players. How should you set the *annual* membership dues and court fees (assume 52 weeks per

year) to maximize profits, keeping in mind the constraint that only serious players choose to join? What are profits (per week)?

b. A friend tells you that you could make greater profits by encouraging both types of players to join. Is the friend right? What annual dues and court fees would maximize weekly profits? What would these profits be?

c. Suppose that over the years young, upwardly mobile professionals move to your community, all of whom are serious players. You believe there are now 3000 serious players and 1000 occasional players. Is it still profitable to cater to the occasional player? What are the profit-maximizing annual dues and court fees? What are profits per week?

11. Figure 11.12 shows the reservation prices of three consumers for two goods. Assuming that marginal production cost is zero for both goods, can the producer make the most money by selling the goods separately, by bundling, or by "mixed" bundling (i.e., offering the goods separately or as a bundle)? What prices should be charged?

12. Go back to the example in Figure 11.17. Suppose the marginal costs c_1 and c_2 were zero. Show that in this case pure bundling is the most profitable pricing strategy, and not mixed bundling. What price should be charged for the bundle, and what will the firm's profit be?

13. On October 22, 1982, an article appeared in the *New York Times* about IBM's pricing policy. The previous day IBM had announced major price cuts on most of its small and medium-sized computers. The article said:

"IBM probably has no choice but to cut prices periodically to get its customers to purchase more and lease less. If they succeed, this could make life more difficult for IBM's major competitors. Outright purchases of computers are needed for ever larger IBM revenues and profits, says Morgan Stanley's Ulric Weil in his new book, *Information Systems in the '80's*. Mr. Weil declares that IBM cannot revert to an emphasis on leasing."

a. Provide a brief but clear argument *in support* of the claim that IBM should try "to get its customers to purchase more and lease less."

b. Provide a brief but clear argument *against* this claim.

c. What factors determine whether leasing or selling is preferable for a company like IBM? Explain briefly.

14. You are selling two goods, 1 and 2, to a market consisting of three consumers with reservation prices as follows:

Consumer	for 1	for 2
A	10	70
B	40	40
C	70	10

The unit cost of each product is $20.

a. Compute the optimal prices and profits for (i) selling the goods separately, (ii) pure bundling, and (iii) mixed bundling.

b. Which strategy is most profitable? Why?

15. Your firm produces two products, the demands for which are independent. Both products are produced at zero marginal cost. You face four consumers (or groups of consumers) with the following reservation prices:

Consumer	Good 1 ($)	Good 2 ($)
A	30	90
B	40	60
C	60	40
D	90	30

a. Consider three alternative pricing strategies: (i) selling the goods separately; (ii) pure bundling; (iii) mixed bundling. For *each strategy*, determine the optimal prices to be charged and the resulting profits. Which strategy is best?

b. Now suppose the production of each good entails a marginal cost of $35. How does this change your answers to (a)? Why is the optimal strategy now different?

*16. Consider a firm with monopoly power that faces the demand curve

$$P = 100 - 3Q + 4A^{1/2}$$

and has the total cost function

$$C = 4Q^2 + 10Q + A$$

where A is the level of advertising expenditures, and P and Q are price and output.

a. Find the values of A, Q, and P that maximize this firm's profit.

b. Calculate the Lerner index of monopoly power, $L = (P - MC)/P$, for this firm at its profit-maximizing levels of A, Q, and P.

Transfer Pricing in the Integrated Firm

So far we have studied the firm's pricing decision assuming that it sells its output in an *outside market*, i.e., to consumers or to other firms. Many firms, however, are *vertically integrated*—they contain several divisions, with some divisions producing parts and components that other divisions use to produce the finished product.[1] For example, each of the major U.S. automobile companies has "upstream" divisions that produce engines, brakes, radiators, and other components that the "downstream" divisions use to produce the finished products. *Transfer pricing* refers to the valuation of these parts and components within the firm. *Transfer prices* are internal prices at which the parts and components from upstream divisions are "sold" to downstream divisions. Transfer prices must be chosen correctly because they are the signals that divisional managers use to determine output levels.

This appendix shows how a profit-maximizing firm chooses its transfer prices and divisional output levels. We will also examine other issues raised by vertical integration. For example, suppose a computer firm's upstream division produces memory chips that are used by a downstream division to produce the final product. If other firms also produce these chips, should our firm obtain all its chips from the upstream division, or should it also buy some on the outside market? Should the upstream division produce more chips than are needed by the downstream division, selling the excess in the market? And how should the firm coordinate the upstream and downstream divisions? In particular, can we design incentives for the divisions, so that the firm's profit is maximized?

We begin with the simplest case—there is no outside market for the output of the upstream division, i.e., the upstream division produces a good that is neither produced nor used by any other firm. Next we consider what happens when there is an outside market for the upstream division's output.

Transfer Pricing When There Is No Outside Market

Consider a firm that has three divisions: Two upstream divisions produce inputs to a downstream processing division. The two upstream divisions pro-

---

[1] A firm is *horizontally integrated* when it has several divisions that produce the same product or closely related products. Many firms are both vertically and horizontally integrated.

duce quantities Q_1 and Q_2, and have total costs $C_1(Q_1)$ and $C_2(Q_2)$. The down-stream division produces a quantity Q using the production function

$$Q = f(K, L, Q_1, Q_2)$$

where K and L are capital and labor inputs, and Q_1 and Q_2 are the intermediate inputs from the upstream divisions. Excluding the costs of the inputs Q_1 and Q_2, the downstream division has a total production cost $C_d(Q)$. The total revenue from sales of the final product is $R(Q)$.

We assume there are *no outside markets* for the intermediate inputs Q_1 and Q_2. (They can be used only by the downstream division.) Then the firm has two problems. First, what quantities Q_1, Q_2, and Q maximize its profit? Second, is there an incentive scheme that will decentralize the firm's management? In particular, is there a set of transfer prices P_1 and P_2, so that *if each division maximizes its own divisional profit, the profit of the overall firm will also be maximized*?

To solve these problems, note that the firm's total profit is

$$\pi(Q) = R(Q) - C_d(Q) - C_1(Q_1) - C_2(Q_2) \tag{A11.1}$$

Now, what is the level of Q_1 that maximizes this profit? It is the level at which *the cost of the last unit of Q_1 is just equal to the additional revenue it brings to the firm.* The cost of producing one extra unit of Q_1 is the marginal cost $\Delta C_1/\Delta Q_1 = MC_1$. How much extra revenue results from the unit? An extra unit of Q_1 allows the firm to produce more final output Q of an amount $\Delta Q/\Delta Q_1 = MP_1$, the marginal product of Q_1. An extra unit of final output results in additional revenue $\Delta R/\Delta Q = MR$, but it also results in additional cost to the downstream division, of an amount $\Delta C_d/\Delta Q = MC_d$. Thus, the *net marginal revenue* NMR_1 that the firm earns from an extra unit of Q_1 is $(MR - MC_d)MP_1$. Setting this equal to the marginal cost of the unit, we obtain the following rule for profit maximization:[2]

$$\boxed{NMR_1 = (MR - MC_d)MP_1 = MC_1} \tag{A11.2}$$

Going through the same steps for the second intermediate input gives

$$\boxed{NMR_2 = (MR - MC_d)MP_2 = MC_2} \tag{A11.3}$$

Note from equations (A11.2) and (A11.3) that it is *incorrect* to determine the firm's final output level Q by setting marginal revenue equal to marginal cost for the downstream division, i.e., by setting $MR = MC_d$. Doing so ignores the cost of producing the intermediate input. (MR exceeds MC_d because this cost

[2] Using calculus, we can obtain this by differentiating equation (A11.1) with respect to Q_1:
$$d\pi/dQ_1 = (dR/dQ)(\partial Q/\partial Q_1) - (dC_d/dQ)(\partial Q/\partial Q_1) - dC_1/dQ_1$$
$$= (MR - MC_d)MP_1 - MC_1$$
Setting $d\pi/dQ = 0$ to maximize profit gives equation (A11.2).

is positive.) Also, note that equations (A11.2) and (A11.3) are standard conditions of marginal analysis—the output of each upstream division should be such that its marginal cost is equal to its marginal contribution to the profit of the overall firm.

Now, what transfer prices P_1 and P_2 should be "charged" to the downstream division for its use of the intermediate inputs? Remember that if each of the three divisions uses these transfer prices to maximize its own divisional profit, the profit of the overall firm should be maximized. The two upstream divisions will maximize their divisional profits, π_1 and π_2, which are given by

$$\pi_1 = P_1 Q_1 - C_1(Q_1)$$

and

$$\pi_2 = P_2 Q_2 - C_2(Q_2)$$

Since the upstream divisions take P_1 and P_2 as given, they will choose Q_1 and Q_2 so that $P_1 = MC_1$ and $P_2 = MC_2$. Similarly, the downstream division will maximize

$$\pi(Q) = R(Q) - C_d(Q) - P_1 Q_1 - P_2 Q_2$$

Since the downstream division also takes P_1 and P_2 as given, it will choose Q_1 and Q_2 so that

$$(MR - MC_d)MP_1 = NMR_1 = P_1 \qquad\qquad (A11.4)$$

and

$$(MR - MC_d)MP_2 = NMR_2 = P_2 \qquad\qquad (A11.5)$$

Note that by setting the transfer prices equal to the respective marginal costs ($P_1 = MC_1$ and $P_2 = MC_2$), the profit-maximizing conditions given by equations (A11.2) and (A11.3) will be satisfied. We therefore have a simple solution to the transfer pricing problem: *Set each transfer price equal to the marginal cost of the respective upstream division.* Then when each division is told to maximize its own profit, the quantities Q_1 and Q_2 that the upstream divisions will want to produce will be the same quantities that the downstream division will want to "buy," and they will maximize the total profit of the firm.

We can illustrate this graphically with the following example. Race Car Motors, Inc., has two divisions. The upstream Engine Division produces engines, and the downstream Assembly Division puts together automobiles, using one engine (and a few other parts) in each car. In Figure A11.1, the average revenue curve AR is Race Car Motors' demand curve for cars. (Note that the firm has monopoly power in the automobile market.) MC_A is the marginal cost of assembling automobiles, *given the engines* (i.e., it does not include the cost of the engines). Since the car requires one engine, the marginal product of the engines is one, so that the curve labeled $MR - MC_A$ is also the net marginal revenue curve for engines: $NMR_E = (MR - MC_A)MP_E = MR - MC_A$.

The profit-maximizing number of engines (and number of cars) is given by the intersection of the net marginal revenue curve NMR_E with the marginal

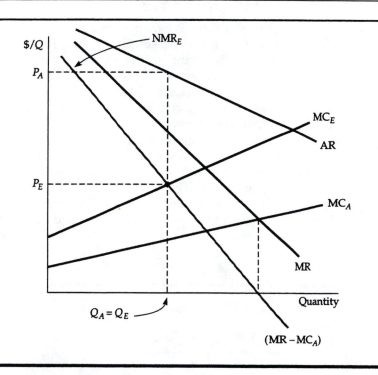

FIGURE A11.1   Race Car Motors, Inc.   The firm's upstream division should produce a quantity of engines Q_E that equates its marginal cost of engine production MC_E with the downstream division's net marginal revenue of engines NMR_E. Since the firm uses one engine in every car, NMR_E is the difference between the marginal revenue from selling cars and the marginal cost of assembling them, i.e., $MR - MC_A$. The optimal transfer price for engines P_E equals the marginal cost of producing them. Finished cars are sold at price P_A.

cost curve for engines MC_E. Having determined the number of cars it will produce, and knowing its divisional cost functions, the management of Race Car Motors can now set the transfer price P_E that correctly values the engines used to produce its cars. It is this transfer price that should be used to calculate divisional profit (and year-end bonuses for the divisional managers).

Transfer Pricing with a Competitive Outside Market

Now suppose there is a *competitive* outside market for the intermediate good produced by an upstream division. Since the outside market is competitive, there is a single market price at which one can buy or sell the good. Therefore, *the marginal cost of the intermediate good is simply the market price.* Since the optimal transfer price must equal marginal cost, it must also equal the competitive market price.

To see this, suppose there is a competitive market for the engines that Race Car Motors produces. If the market price is low, Race Car Motors may want to buy some or all of its engines in the market; if it is high, it may want to sell engines in the market. Figure A11.2 illustrates the first case. For quantities below $Q_{E,1}$, the upstream division's marginal cost of producing engines MC_E is below the market price $P_{E,M}$, and for quantities above $Q_{E,1}$ it is above the market price. The firm should obtain engines at least cost, so the marginal cost of engines MC_E^* is the upstream division's marginal cost for quantities up to $Q_{E,1}$ and the market price for quantities above $Q_{E,1}$. Note that Race Car Motors uses more engines and produces more cars than it would have had there not been an outside engine market. The downstream division now buys $Q_{E,2}$ engines and produces an equal number of automobiles. However, it "buys" only $Q_{E,1}$ of these engines from the upstream division, and buys the rest on the open market.

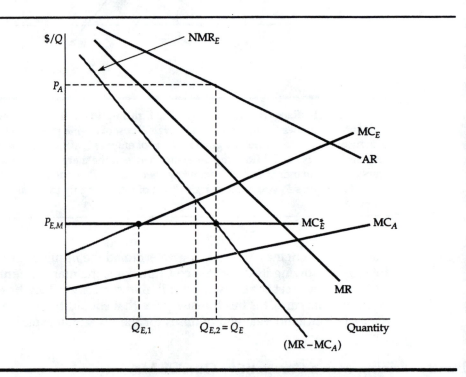

FIGURE A11.2   **Race Car Motors Buys Engines in a Competitive Outside Market.** The firm's marginal cost of engines MC_E^* is the upstream division's marginal cost for quantities up to $Q_{E,1}$ and the market price $P_{E,M}$ for quantities above $Q_{E,1}$. The downstream division should use a total of $Q_{E,2}$ engines to produce an equal number of cars; then the marginal cost of engines equals net marginal revenue. $Q_{E,2} - Q_{E,1}$ of these engines are bought in the outside market. The upstream division "pays" the downstream division the transfer price $P_{E,M}$ for the remaining $Q_{E,1}$ engines.

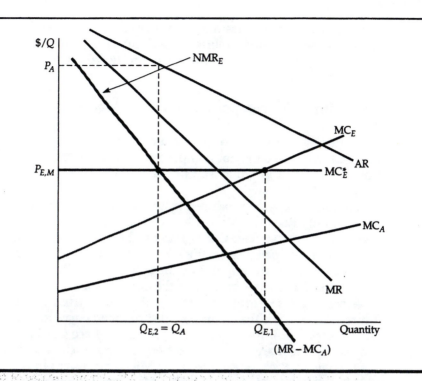

FIGURE A11.3   Race Car Motors Sells Engines in a Competitive Outside Market.   The optimal transfer price is again the market price $P_{E,M}$. This price is above the point at which MC_E intersects NMR_E, so the upstream division sells some of its engines in the outside market. The upstream division produces $Q_{E,1}$ engines, the quantity at which MC_E equals $P_{E,M}$. The downstream division uses only $Q_{E,2}$ of these, the quantity at which NMR_E equals $P_{E,M}$. Compared with Figure A11.1, in which there is no outside market, more engines but fewer cars are produced.

It might appear strange that Race Car Motors should have to go into the open market to buy engines, when it can make those engines itself. If it made all its own engines, however, its marginal cost of producing engines would exceed the competitive market price, and although the profit of the upstream division would be higher, *the total profit of the firm would be lower.*

Figure A11.3 shows the case where Race Car Motors *sells* engines in the outside market. Now the competitive market price $P_{E,M}$ is above the transfer price that the firm would have set had there not been an outside market. In this case the upstream Engine Division produces $Q_{E,1}$ engines, but only $Q_{E,2}$ engines are used by the downstream division to produce automobiles. The rest are sold in the outside market at the price $P_{E,M}$.

Note that compared with a situation in which there is no outside engine market, Race Car Motors is producing more engines but fewer cars. Why not produce this larger number of engines, but use all of them to produce more cars? Because the engines are too valuable. On the margin, the net revenue that can be earned from selling them in the outside market is higher than the net revenue from using them to build additional cars.

Transfer Pricing with a Noncompetitive Outside Market

Now suppose there is an outside market for the output of the upstream division, but that market is not competitive—the firm has monopoly power. The same principles apply, but we must be careful when measuring net marginal revenue.

Suppose the engine produced by the upstream Engine Division is a special one that only Race Car Motors can make. There is an outside market for this engine, however, so Race Car Motors can be a monopoly supplier to that market and can also produce engines for its own use. What is the optimal transfer price for use of the engines by the downstream division, and at what price (if any) should engines be sold in the outside market?

We must find the firm's net marginal revenue from the sale of engines. In Figure A11.4, $D_{E,M}$ is the outside market demand curve for engines, and $MR_{E,M}$ is the corresponding marginal revenue curve. Race Car Motors therefore has two sources of marginal revenue from the production and sale of an additional engine—the marginal revenue $MR_{E,M}$ from sales in the outside market and the net marginal revenue $(MR - MC_A)$ from the use of the engines by the downstream division. By summing these two curves horizontally, we obtain the *total net marginal revenue curve for engines*; it is the gray line labeled NMR_E.

The intersection of the marginal cost and total net marginal revenue curves gives the quantity of engines $Q_{E,1}$ that the upstream division should produce and the optimal transfer price P_E^*. (Again, the optimal transfer price is equal to marginal cost.) But note that only $Q_{E,2}$ of these engines are used by the downstream division to make cars. (This is the quantity at which the downstream division's net marginal revenue, $MR - MC_A$, is equal to the transfer price P_E^*.) The remaining engines $Q_{E,3}$ are sold in the outside market. However, they are not sold at the transfer price P_E^*. Instead the firm exercises its monopoly power and sells them at the higher price $P_{E,M}$.

Why pay the upstream division only P_E^* per engine when the firm is selling engines in the outside market at the higher price $P_{E,M}$? Because if the upstream division is paid more than P_E^* (and thereby encouraged to produce more engines), the marginal cost of engines will rise and exceed the net marginal revenue from their use by the downstream division. And if the price charged in the outside market were lowered, the marginal revenue from sales in that market would fall below marginal cost. At the prices P_E^* and $P_{E,M}$, marginal revenues and marginal cost are equal: $MR_{E,M} = (MR - MC_A) = MC_E$.

A Numerical Example

Suppose Race Car Motors has the following demand for its automobiles:

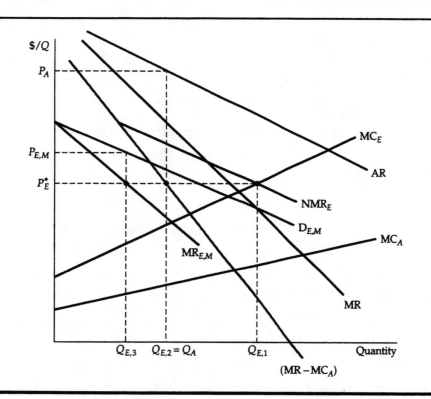

FIGURE A11.4 Race Car Motors Is a Monopoly Supplier of Engines to an Outside Market. $D_{E,M}$ is the outside market demand curve for engines, $MR_{E,M}$ is the corresponding marginal revenue curve, and $(MR - MC_A)$ is the net marginal revenue from the use of engines by the downstream division. The *total net marginal revenue curve for engines* NMR_E is the horizontal sum of these two marginal revenues. The optimal transfer price P_E^* and the quantity of engines that the upstream division produces $Q_{E,1}$ are found where $MC_E = NMR_E$. $Q_{E,2}$ of these engines are used by the downstream division, the quantity at which the downstream division's net marginal revenue, $MR - MC_A$, is equal to the transfer price P_E^*. The remaining engines $Q_{E,3}$ are sold in the outside market at the price $P_{E,M}$.

$$P = 20,000 - Q$$

so that its marginal revenue is

$$MR = 20,000 - 2Q$$

The downstream division's cost of assembling cars is

$$C_A(Q) = 8,000Q$$

so that the division's marginal cost is $MC_A = 8,000$. The upstream division's cost of producing engines is

$$C_E(Q_E) = 2Q_E^2$$

so that the division's marginal cost is $MC_E(Q_E) = 4Q_E$.

(a) First, suppose there is *no outside market* for the engines. How many engines and cars should the firm produce, and what should the transfer price for engines be? To solve this problem, we set the net marginal revenue for engines equal to the marginal cost of producing engines. Since each car has one engine, $Q_E = Q$, and the net marginal revenue of engines is

$$NMR_E = MR - MC_A = 12{,}000 - 2Q_E$$

Now set NMR_E equal to MC_E:

$$12{,}000 - 2Q_E = 4Q_E$$

so that $6Q_E = 12{,}000$, and $Q_E = 2{,}000$. The firm should therefore produce 2,000 engines and 2,000 cars. The optimal transfer price is the marginal cost of these 2,000 engines: $P_E = 4Q_E = \$8{,}000$.

(b) Now suppose that engines can be bought or sold for \$6,000 in an *outside competitive market*. This is below the \$8,000 transfer price that is optimal when there is no outside market, so the firm should buy some engines outside. Its marginal cost of engines, and the optimal transfer price, is now \$6,000. Set this \$6,000 marginal cost equal to the net marginal revenue of engines:

$$6{,}000 = NMR_E = 12{,}000 - 2Q_E$$

Thus the total quantity of engines and cars is now 3,000. The company now produces more cars (and sells them at a lower price) because its cost of engines is lower. Also, since the transfer price for the engines is now \$6,000, the upstream Engine Division supplies only 1,500 engines (because $MC_E(1{,}500) = \$6{,}000$). The remaining 1,500 engines are bought in the outside market.

(c) Now suppose Race Car Motors is the only producer of these engines, but can sell them in an outside market. Demand in the outside market is:

$$P_{E,M} = 10{,}000 - Q_E$$

so that the marginal revenue from sales in the market is:

$$MR_{E,M} = 10{,}000 - 2Q_E$$

To determine the optimal transfer price, we find the *total* net marginal revenue by horizontally summing $MR_{E,M}$ with the net marginal revenue from "sales" to the downstream division, $12{,}000 - 2Q_E$, as in Figure 11A.4. For outputs Q_E greater than 1,000, this is:

$$NMR_{E,Total} = 11{,}000 - Q_E$$

Now set this equal to the marginal cost of producing engines:

$$11{,}000 - Q_E = 4Q_E$$

Therefore, the total quantity of engines produced should be $Q_E = 2{,}200$.

How many of these engines should go to the downstream division, and how many to the outside market? Note that the marginal cost of producing these 2,200 engines, and therefore the optimal transfer price, is $4Q_E = \$8,800$. Set this equal to the marginal revenue from sales in the outside market:

$$8,800 = 10,000 - 2Q_E$$

or $Q_E = 600$. Therefore 600 engines should be sold in the outside market. Finally, set this $8,800 transfer price equal to the net marginal revenue from "sales" to the downstream division:

$$8,800 = 12,000 - 2Q_E$$

or $Q_E = 1,600$. So 1,600 engines should be supplied to the downstream division for use in the production of 1,600 cars.

Exercises

1. Review the numerical example about Race Car Motors. Calculate the profit earned by the upstream division, the downstream division, and the firm as a whole in each of the three cases examined: (a) no outside market for engines; (b) a competitive market for engines in which the market price is $6000; and (c) the firm is a monopoly supplier of engines to an outside market. In which case does Race Car Motors earn the most profit? In which case does the upstream division earn the most? the downstream division?

2. Ajax Computer makes a computer for climate control in office buildings. The company uses a microprocessor produced by its upstream division, along with other parts bought in outside competitive markets. The microprocessor is produced at a constant marginal cost of $500, and the marginal cost of assembling the computer (including the cost of the other parts) by the downstream division is a constant $700. The firm has been selling the computer for $2000, and until now there has been no outside market for the microprocessor.

a. Suppose an outside market for the microprocessor develops and Ajax has monopoly power in that market, selling microprocessors for $1000 each. Assuming that demand for the microprocessor is unrelated to the demand for the Ajax computer, what transfer price should Ajax apply to the microprocessor for its use by the downstream division? Should its production of computers be increased, decreased, or left unchanged? Explain briefly.

b. How would your answer to (a) change if the demands for the computer and the microprocessors were competitive; i.e., some of the people who buy the microprocessors use them to make climate control systems of their own?

3. Reebok produces and sells running shoes. It faces a market demand schedule $P = 11 - 1.5Q_s$, where Q_s is the number of pairs of shoes sold (in thousands) and P is the price in dollars per thousand pairs of shoes. Production of each pair of shoes requires 1 square yard of leather. The leather is shaped and cut by the Form Division of Reebok. The cost function for leather is

$$TC_L = 1 + Q_L + 0.5Q_L^2$$

where Q_L is the quantity of leather (in thousands of square yards) produced. The cost function for running shoes is (excluding the leather)

$$TC_s = 2Q_s$$

a. What is the optimal transfer price?

b. Leather can be bought and sold in a competitive market at the price of $P_F = 1.5$. In this case, how much leather should the Form Division supply internally? How much should it supply to the outside market? Will Reebok buy any leather in the outside market? Find the optimal transfer price.

c. Now suppose the leather is unique and of extremely high quality. Therefore, the Form Division may act as a monopoly supplier to the outside market as well as a supplier to the downstream division. Suppose the outside demand for leather is given by $P = 32 - Q_L$. What is the optimal transfer price for the use of leather by the downstream division? At what price, if any, should leather be sold to the outside market? What quantity, if any, will be sold to the outside market?

CHAPTER *12*

Monopolistic Competition and Oligopoly

12.2 *Oligopoly*

In an oligopolistic market, the product may or may not be differentiated. What matters is that only a few firms account for most or all of total production. In some oligopolistic markets, some or all of the firms earn substantial profits over the long run because *barriers to entry* make it difficult or impossible for new firms to enter the market. Oligopoly is a prevalent form of market structure. Examples of oligopolistic industries include automobiles, steel, aluminum, petrochemicals, electrical equipment, and computers.

Why might barriers to entry arise? We discussed some of the reasons in Chapter 10. Scale economies may make it unprofitable for more than a few firms to coexist in the market; patents or access to a technology may exclude potential competitors; and the need to spend money for name recognition and market reputation may discourage entry by new firms. These are "natural" entry barriers—they are basic to the structure of the particular market. In addition, incumbent firms may take *strategic actions* to deter entry. For example, they might threaten to flood the market and drive prices down if entry occurs, and to make that threat credible, they can construct excess production capacity.

Managing an oligopolistic firm is complicated because pricing, output, advertising, and investment decisions involve important strategic considerations. Because only a few firms are competing, each firm must carefully consider how its actions will affect its rivals, and how its rivals are likely to react.

Suppose that because of sluggish car sales, Ford is considering a 10 percent price cut to stimulate demand. It must think carefully about how GM and Chrysler will react. They might not react at all, or they might cut their prices only slightly, in which case Ford could enjoy a substantial increase in sales, largely at the expense of its competitors. Or they might match Ford's price cut, in which case all three automakers will sell more cars but might make much lower profits because of the lower prices. Another possibility is that GM and Chrysler will cut their prices by even more than Ford did. They might cut price by 15 percent to punish Ford for rocking the boat, and this in turn might lead to a price war and to a drastic fall in profits for all three firms. Ford must carefully weigh all these possibilities. In fact, for almost any major economic decision a firm makes—setting price, determining production levels, undertaking a major promotion campaign, or investing in new production capacity—it must try to determine the most likely response of its competitors.

These strategic considerations can be complex. When making decisions, each firm must weigh its competitors' reactions, knowing that these competitors will also weigh *its* reactions to *their* decisions. Furthermore, decisions, reactions, reactions to reactions, and so forth are dynamic, evolving over time. When the managers of a firm evaluate the potential consequences of their decisions, they must assume that their competitors are as rational and intelligent as they are. Then, they must put themselves in their competitors' place and consider how they would react.

Equilibrium in an Oligopolistic Market

When we study a market, we usually want to determine the price and quantity that will prevail in equilibrium. For example, we saw that in a perfectly competitive market the equilibrium price equates the quantity supplied with the quantity demanded. Then we saw that for a monopoly an equilibrium occurs when marginal revenue equals marginal cost. Finally, when we studied monopolistic competition, we saw how a long-run equilibrium results as the entry of new firms drives profits to zero.

In these markets, each firm could take price or market demand as given, and didn't have to worry much about its competitors. In an oligopolistic market, however, a firm sets price or output based partly on strategic considerations regarding the behavior of its competitors. At the same time, the competitors' decisions depend on the firm's decision. How then can we figure out what the market price and output will be in equilibrium, or whether there will even be an equilibrium? To answer these questions, we need an underlying principle to describe an equilibrium when firms make decisions that explicitly take each other's behavior into account.

Remember how we described an equilibrium in competitive and monopolistic markets: *When a market is in equilibrium, firms are doing the best they can and have no reason to change their price or output.* Hence, a competitive market is in equilibrium when the quantity supplied equals the quantity demanded, because then each firm is doing the best it can—it is selling all that it produces and is maximizing its profit. Likewise, a monopolist is in equilibrium when marginal revenue equals marginal cost, because then it is doing the best it can and is maximizing its profit.

With some modification, we can apply this same principle to an oligopolistic market. Now, however, each firm will want to do the best it can *given what its competitors are doing.* And what should the firm assume that its competitors are doing? Since the firm will do the best it can given what its competitors are doing, *it is natural to assume that these competitors will do the best they can given what the firm is doing.* Each firm, then, takes its competitors into account, and assumes that its competitors are doing likewise.

This may seem a bit abstract at first, but it is logical, and as we will see, it gives us a basis for determining an equilibrium in an oligopolistic market. The concept was first explained clearly by the mathematician John Nash in 1951, so we call the equilibrium it describes a *Nash equilibrium.* It is an important concept that we will use repeatedly:

> *Nash Equilibrium:*   Each firm is doing the best it can given what its competitors are doing.

We discuss this equilibrium concept in more detail in Chapter 13, where we show how it can be applied to a broad range of strategic problems. In this chapter we will apply the concept to the analysis of oligopolistic markets.

The Cournot Model

We will begin with a simple model of *duopoly*—two firms competing with each other—first introduced by the French economist Augustin Cournot in 1838. Suppose the firms produce a homogeneous good and know the market demand curve. *Each firm must decide how much to produce, and the two firms make their decisions at the same time.* When making its production decision, each firm takes its competitor into account. It knows that its competitor is *also* deciding how much to produce, and the price it receives will depend on the *total output* of both firms.

The essence of the Cournot model is that *each firm treats the output level of its competitor as fixed, and then decides how much to produce.* To see how this works, let's consider the output decision of Firm 1. Suppose Firm 1 thinks that Firm 2 will produce nothing. Then Firm 1's demand curve is the market demand curve. In Figure 12.3 this is shown as $D_1(0)$, which means the demand curve for Firm 1, assuming Firm 2 produces zero. Figure 12.3 also shows the corresponding marginal revenue curve $MR_1(0)$. We have assumed that Firm 1's marginal cost MC_1 is constant. As shown in the figure, Firm 1's profit-maximizing output is 50 units, the point where $MR_1(0)$ intersects MC_1. So if Firm 2 produces zero, Firm 1 should produce 50.

Suppose, instead, that Firm 1 thinks Firm 2 will produce 50 units. Then Firm 1's demand curve is the market demand curve shifted to the left by 50. In Figure 12.3 this is labeled $D_1(50)$, and the corresponding marginal revenue curve is labeled $MR_1(50)$. Firm 1's profit-maximizing output is now 25 units,

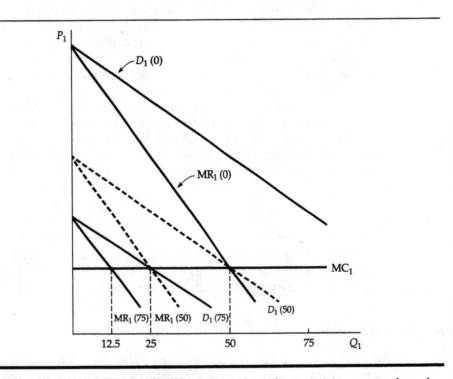

FIGURE 12.3   Firm 1's Output Decision. Firm 1's profit-maximizing output depends on how much it thinks Firm 2 will produce. If it thinks Firm 2 will produce nothing, its demand curve, labeled $D_1(0)$, is the market demand curve. The corresponding marginal revenue curve, labeled $MR_1(0)$, intersects Firm 1's marginal cost curve MC_1 at an output of 50 units. If Firm 1 thinks Firm 2 will produce 50 units, its demand curve, $D_1(50)$, is shifted to the left by this amount. Profit maximization now implies an output of 25 units. Finally, if Firm 1 thinks Firm 2 will produce 75 units, Firm 1 will produce only 12.5 units.

the point where $MR_1(50) = MC_1$. Now, suppose Firm 1 thinks Firm 2 will produce 75 units. Then Firm 1's demand curve is the market demand curve shifted to the left by 75. It is labeled $D_1(75)$ in Figure 12.3, and the corresponding marginal revenue curve is labeled $MR_1(75)$. Firm 1's profit-maximizing output is now 12.5 units, the point where $MR_1(75) = MC_1$. Finally, suppose Firm 1 thinks Firm 2 will produce 100 units. Then Firm 1's demand and marginal revenue curves (not shown in the figure) would intersect its marginal cost curve on the vertical axis; if Firm 1 thinks that Firm 2 will produce 100 units or more, it should produce nothing.

To summarize: If Firm 1 thinks Firm 2 will produce nothing, it will produce 50; if it thinks Firm 2 will produce 50, it will produce 25; if it thinks Firm 2 will produce 75, it will produce 12.5; and if it thinks Firm 2 will produce 100, then it will produce nothing. *Firm 1's profit-maximizing output is thus a decreasing schedule of how much it thinks Firm 2 will produce.* We call this schedule Firm 1's *reaction curve* and denote it by $Q_1^*(Q_2)$. This curve is plotted in Figure 12.4, where each of the four output combinations we found above is shown as an x.

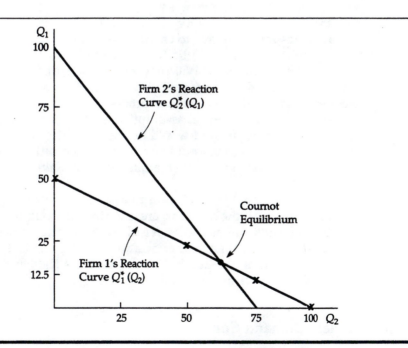

FIGURE 12.4   Reaction Curves and Cournot Equilibrium.   Firm 1's reaction curve shows how much it will produce as a function of how much it thinks Firm 2 will produce. (The xs, at $Q_2 = 0$, 50, and 75, correspond to the examples shown in Figure 12.3.) Firm 2's reaction curve shows its output as a function of how much it thinks Firm 1 will produce. In Cournot equilibrium, each firm correctly assumes how much its competitor will produce, and thereby maximizes its own profits. Therefore, neither firm will move from this equilibrium.

We can go through the same kind of analysis for Firm 2 (i.e., determine Firm 2's profit-maximizing quantity given various assumptions about how much Firm 1 will produce). The result will be a reaction curve for Firm 2, i.e., a schedule $Q_2^*(Q_1)$ that relates its output to the output it thinks Firm 1 will produce. If Firm 2's marginal cost curve is different from that of Firm 1, its reaction curve will also differ in form from that of Firm 1. For example, Firm 2's reaction curve might look like the one drawn in Figure 12.4.

How much will each firm produce? Each firm's reaction curve tells it how much to produce, given the output of its competitor. In equilibrium, each firm sets output according to its own reaction curve, so the equilibrium output levels are found at the *intersection* of the two reaction curves. We call the resulting set of output levels a *Cournot equilibrium*. In this equilibrium, each firm correctly assumes how much its competitor will produce, and it maximizes its profit accordingly.

Note that this Cournot equilibrium is an example of a Nash equilibrium.[2] Remember that in a Nash equilibrium, each firm is doing the best it can given what its competitors are doing. As a result, no firm has any incentive to change its behavior. In the Cournot equilibrium, each duopolist is producing an amount that maximizes its profit *given what its competitor is producing*, so neither duopolist has any incentive to change its output.

Suppose the firms are initially producing output levels that differ from the Cournot equilibrium. Will they adjust their outputs until the Cournot equilibrium is reached? Unfortunately, the Cournot model says nothing about the dynamics of the adjustment process. In fact, during any adjustment process, the model's central assumption that each firm can assume that its competitor's output is fixed would not hold. Neither firm's output would be fixed, because both firms would be adjusting their outputs. We need different models to understand dynamic adjustment, and we will examine some in Chapter 13.

When is it rational for each firm to assume that its competitor's output is fixed? It is rational if the two firms are choosing their outputs only once because then their outputs cannot change. It is also rational once they are in the Cournot equilibrium because then neither firm would have any incentive to change its output. When using the Cournot model, we must therefore confine ourselves to the behavior of firms in equilibrium.

Example: A Linear Demand Curve

Let's work through an example—two identical firms facing a linear market demand curve. This will help clarify the meaning of a Cournot equilibrium and let us compare it with the competitive equilibrium and the equilibrium that results if the firms collude and choose their output levels cooperatively.

---

[2] Hence it is sometimes called a *Cournot-Nash equilibrium*.

Suppose our duopolists face the following market demand curve:

$$P = 30 - Q$$

where Q is the *total* production of both firms (i.e., $Q = Q_1 + Q_2$). Also, suppose both firms have zero marginal cost:

$$MC_1 = MC_2 = 0$$

Then we can determine the reaction curve for Firm 1 as follows. To maximize profit, the firm sets marginal revenue equal to marginal cost. Firm 1's total revenue R_1 is given by

$$R_1 = PQ_1 = (30 - Q)Q_1$$
$$= 30Q_1 - (Q_1 + Q_2)Q_1$$
$$= 30Q_1 - Q_1^2 - Q_2Q_1$$

The firm's marginal revenue MR_1 is just the incremental revenue ΔR_1 resulting from an incremental change in output ΔQ_1:

$$MR_1 = \Delta R_1/\Delta Q_1 = 30 - 2Q_1 - Q_2$$

Now, setting MR_1 equal to zero (the firm's marginal cost), and solving for Q_1, we find:

$$\textit{Firm 1's Reaction Curve:} \quad Q_1 = 15 - \frac{1}{2}Q_2 \qquad (12.1)$$

The same calculation applies to Firm 2:

$$\textit{Firm 2's Reaction Curve:} \quad Q_2 = 15 - \frac{1}{2}Q_1 \qquad (12.2)$$

The equilibrium output levels are the values for Q_1 and Q_2 that are at the intersection of the two reaction curves, i.e., that are the solution to equations (12.1) and (12.2). By replacing Q_2 in equation (12.1) with the expression on the right-hand side of (12.2), you can verify that the equilibrium output levels are

$$\textit{Cournot Equilibrium:} \quad Q_1 = Q_2 = 10$$

The total quantity produced is therefore $Q = Q_1 + Q_2 = 20$, so the equilibrium market price is $P = 30 - Q = 10$.

Figure 12.5 shows the Cournot reaction curves and this Cournot equilibrium. Note that Firm 1's reaction curve shows its output Q_1 in terms of Firm 2's output Q_2. Similarly, Firm 2's reaction curve shows Q_2 in terms of Q_1. (Since the firms are identical, the two reaction curves have the same form. They look different because one gives Q_1 in terms of Q_2, and the other gives Q_2 in terms of Q_1.) The Cournot equilibrium is at the intersection of the two curves. At this point each firm is maximizing its own profit, given its competitor's output.

We have assumed that the two firms compete with each other. Suppose, instead, that the antitrust laws were relaxed and the two firms could collude. They would set their outputs to maximize *total profit*, and presumably they

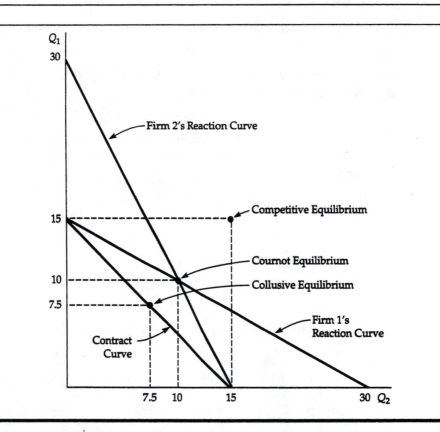

FIGURE 12.5 **Duopoly Example.** The demand curve is $P = 30 - Q$, and both firms have zero marginal cost. In Cournot equilibrium, each firm produces 10. The contract curve shows combinations of Q_1 and Q_2 that maximize *total* profits. If the firms collude and share profits equally, they will each produce 7.5. Also shown is the competitive equilibrium, in which price equals marginal cost, and profit is zero.

would split that profit evenly. Total profit is maximized by choosing total output Q so that marginal revenue equals marginal cost, which in this example is zero. Total revenue for the two firms is

$$R = PQ = (30 - Q)Q = 30Q - Q^2$$

so marginal revenue is

$$MR = \Delta R/\Delta Q = 30 - 2Q$$

Setting MR equal to zero, we see that total profit is maximized when $Q = 15$.

Any combination of outputs Q_1 and Q_2 that add up to 15 maximizes total profit. The curve $Q_1 + Q_2 = 15$, called the *contract curve*, is therefore all pairs of outputs Q_1 and Q_2 that maximize total profit. This curve is also shown in Figure 12.5. If the firms agree to share the profits equally, they will each produce half of the total output:

$$Q_1 = Q_2 = 7.5$$

As you would expect, both firms now produce less—and earn higher profits—than in the Cournot equilibrium. Figure 12.5 shows this collusive equilibrium and the *competitive* output levels found by setting price equal to marginal cost. (You can verify that they are $Q_1 = Q_2 = 15$, which implies that each firm makes zero profit.) Note that the Cournot outcome is much better (for the firms) than perfect competition, but not as good as the outcome from collusion.

12.3 *First Mover Advantage—*
The Stackelberg Model

We have assumed that our two duopolists make their output decisions at the same time. Now let's see what happens if one of the firms can set its output first. There are two questions of interest. First, is it advantageous to go first? Second, how much will each firm now produce?

Continuing with our example, we assume both firms have zero marginal cost, and that the market demand curve is given by $P = 30 - Q$, where Q is the total output. *Suppose Firm 1 sets its output first, and then Firm 2, after observing Firm 1's output, makes its output decision.* In setting output, *Firm 1 must therefore consider how Firm 2 will react.* This is different from the Cournot model, in which neither firm has any opportunity to react.

Let's begin with Firm 2. Because it makes its output decision *after* Firm 1, it takes Firm 1's output as fixed. Therefore, Firm 2's profit-maximizing output is given by its Cournot reaction curve, which we found to be

$$\text{Firm 2's Reaction Curve:} \quad Q_2 = 15 - \frac{1}{2}Q_1 \qquad (12.2)$$

What about Firm 1? To maximize profit, it chooses Q_1, so that its marginal revenue equals its marginal cost of zero. Recall that Firm 1's revenue is

$$R_1 = PQ_1 = 30Q_1 - Q_1^2 - Q_2Q_1 \qquad (12.3)$$

Because R_1 depends on Q_2, Firm 1 must anticipate how much Firm 2 will produce. Firm 1 knows, however, that Firm 2 will choose Q_2 according to the reaction curve (12.2). Substituting equation (12.2) for Q_2 into equation (12.3), we find that Firm 1's revenue is

$$R_1 = 30Q_1 - Q_1^2 - Q_1\left(15 - \frac{1}{2}Q_1\right)$$

$$= 15Q_1 - \frac{1}{2}Q_1^2$$

so its marginal revenue is

$$MR_1 = \Delta R_1/\Delta Q_1 = 15 - Q_1 \qquad (12.4)$$

Setting $MR_1 = 0$ gives $Q_1 = 15$. And from Firm 2's reaction curve (12.2), we find that $Q_2 = 7.5$. Firm 1 produces twice as much as Firm 2 and makes twice as much profit. *Going first gives Firm 1 an advantage.* This may appear counter-intuitive: It seems disadvantageous to announce your output first. Why, then, is going first a strategic advantage?

The reason is that announcing first creates a fait accompli—no matter what your competitor does, your output will be large. To maximize profit, your competitor must take your large output level as given and set a low level of output for itself. (If your competitor produced a large level of output, this would drive price down, and you would both lose money. So unless your competitor views "getting even" as more important than making money, it would be irrational for it to produce a large amount.) This kind of "first mover advantage" occurs in many strategic situations, as we will see in Chapter 13.

The Cournot and Stackelberg models are alternative representations of oligopolistic behavior. Which model is the more appropriate depends on the industry. For an industry composed of roughly similar firms, none of which has a strong operating advantage or leadership position, the Cournot model is probably the more appropriate. On the other hand, some industries are dominated by a large firm that usually takes the lead in introducing new products or setting price; the mainframe computer market is an example, with IBM the leader. Then the Stackelberg model may be more realistic.

12.5 *Competition versus Collusion: The Prisoners' Dilemma*

A Nash equilibrium is a *noncooperative* equilibrium—each firm makes the decisions that give it the highest possible profit, given the actions of its competitors. As we have seen, the resulting profit earned by each firm is higher than it would be under perfect competition, but lower than if the firms colluded.

Collusion is, however, illegal, and most managers prefer to stay out of jail and not pay stiff fines. But if cooperation can lead to higher profits, why don't firms cooperate *without* explicitly colluding? In particular, if you and your competitor can both figure out the profit-maximizing price you would agree to charge *if* you were to collude, *why not just set that price and hope your competitor*

---

[7] This Nash equilibrium can also be derived algebraically from the demand curve and cost data above. We leave this to you as an exercise.

will do the same? If your competitor *does* do the same, you will both make more money.

The problem is that your competitor *probably won't* choose to set price at the collusive level. Why not? *Because your competitor would do better by choosing a lower price, even if it knew that you were going to set price at the collusive level.*

To understand this, let's go back to our example of price competition from the last section. The firms in that example each have a fixed cost of $20, have zero variable cost, and face the following demand curves:

$$\text{Firm 1's Demand:} \qquad Q_1 = 12 - 2P_1 + P_2 \qquad \text{(12.6a)}$$

$$\text{Firm 2's Demand:} \qquad Q_2 = 12 - 2P_2 + P_1 \qquad \text{(12.6b)}$$

We found that in the Nash equilibrium each firm will charge a price of $4 and earn a profit of $12, whereas if the firms collude they will charge a price of $6 and earn a profit of $16. Now suppose the firms do not collude, but that Firm 1 charges the $6 collusive price, hoping that Firm 2 will do the same. If Firm 2 *does* do the same, it will earn a profit of $16. But what if it charges the $4 price instead? Then, Firm 2 would earn a profit of

$$\pi_2 = P_2 Q_2 - 20 = (4)[12 - (2)(4) + 6] - 20 = \$20$$

Firm 1, on the other hand, will earn a profit of

$$\pi_1 = P_1 Q_1 - 20 = (6)[12 - (2)(6) + 4] - 20 = \$4$$

So if Firm 1 charges $6 but Firm 2 charges only $4, Firm 2's profit will increase to $20. And it will do so at the expense of Firm 1's profit, which will fall to $4. Clearly, Firm 2 does best by charging only $4. And similarly, Firm 1 does best by charging only $4. If Firm 2 charges $6 and Firm 1 charges $4, Firm 1 will earn a $20 profit, and Firm 2 will earn only $4.

Table 12.3 summarizes the results of these different pricing possibilities. In deciding what price to set, the two firms are playing a *noncooperative game*— each firm independently does the best it can, taking its competitor into account. Table 12.3 is called the *payoff matrix* for this game because it shows the profit (or payoff) to each firm given its decision and the decision of its competitor. For example, the upper left-hand corner of the payoff matrix tells us that if both firms charge $4, each firm will make a $12 profit. The upper right-hand

		Firm 2	
		Charge $4	Charge $6
Firm 1	Charge $4	$12, $12	$20, $4
	Charge $6˘	$4, $20	$16, $16

corner tells us that if Firm 1 charges $4 and Firm 2 charges $6, Firm 1 will make $20, and Firm 2 will make $4.

This payoff matrix can clarify the answer to our original question: Why don't firms behave cooperatively, and thereby earn higher profits, even if they can't collude? In this case, cooperating means *both* firms charging $6 instead of $4, and thereby earning $16 instead of $12. The problem is that each firm always makes more money by charging $4, *no matter what its competitor does*. As the payoff matrix shows, if Firm 2 charges $4, Firm 1 does best by charging $4. And if Firm 2 charges $6, Firm 1 still does best by charging $4. Similarly, Firm 2 always does best by charging $4, no matter what Firm 1 does. As a result, unless the two firms can sign an enforceable agreement to charge $6, neither firm can expect its competitor to charge $6, and both will charge $4.

A classic example in game theory, called the *Prisoners' Dilemma*, illustrates the problem oligopolistic firms face. It goes as follows: Two prisoners have been accused of collaborating in a crime. They are in separate jail cells and cannot communicate with each other. Each has been asked to confess to the crime. If both prisoners confess, each will receive a prison term of five years. If neither confesses, the prosecution's case will be difficult to make, so the prisoners can expect to plea bargain and receive a term of two years. On the other hand, if one prisoner confesses and the other does not, the one who confesses will receive a term of only one year, while the other will go to prison for ten years. If you were one of these prisoners, what would you do—confess or not confess?

The payoff matrix in Table 12.4 summarizes the possible outcomes. (Note that the "payoffs" are negative; the entry in the lower right-hand corner of the payoff matrix means a two-year sentence for each prisoner.) As the table shows, these prisoners face a dilemma. If they could only both agree not to confess (in a way that would be binding), then each would go to jail for only two years. But they can't talk to each other, and even if they could, can they trust each other? If Prisoner A does not confess, he risks being taken advantage of by his former accomplice. After all, *no matter what Prisoner A does, Prisoner B comes out ahead by confessing*. Similarly, Prisoner A always comes out ahead by confessing, so Prisoner B must worry that by not confessing, she will be taken advantage of. Therefore, both prisoners will probably confess and go to jail for five years.

| | | Prisoner B | |
		Confess	Don't Confess
Prisoner A	Confess	−5, −5	−1, −10
	Don't Confess	−10, −1	−2, −2

Oligopolistic firms often find themselves in a Prisoners' Dilemma. They must decide whether to compete aggressively, attempting to capture a larger share of the market at their competitor's expense, or to "cooperate" and compete more passively, coexisting with their competitors and settling for the market share they currently hold, and perhaps even implicitly colluding. If the firms compete passively, setting high prices and limiting output, they will make higher profits than if they compete aggressively.

Like our prisoners, however, each firm has an incentive to "fink" and undercut its competitors, and each knows that its competitors have the same incentive. As desirable as cooperation is, each firm worries—with good reason—that if it competes passively, its competitor might compete aggressively, taking the lion's share of the market. In the pricing problem illustrated in Table 12.3, both firms do better by "cooperating" and charging a high price. But the firms are in a Prisoners' Dilemma, where neither firm can trust or expect its competitor to set a high price.

In Example 12.2, we examined the problem that arose when P&G, Unilever, and Kao Soap were all planning to enter the Japanese market for Gypsy Moth Tape at the same time. They all faced the same cost and demand conditions, and each firm had to decide on a price that took its competitors into account. In Table 12.2, we tabulated the profits to P&G corresponding to alternative prices that it and its competitors might charge. We argued that P&G should expect its competitors to charge a price of $1.40, and should do the same.

P&G would be better off if it *and its competitors* all charged a price of $1.50. This is clear from the payoff matrix in Table 12.5. (This payoff matrix is the portion of Table 12.2 corresponding to prices of $1.40 and $1.50, with the payoffs to P&G's competitors also tabulated.) If all the firms charge $1.50, they will

TABLE 12.5 Payoff Matrix for Pricing Problem

		Unilever and Kao[9]	
		Charge $1.40	Charge $1.50
P&G	Charge $1.40	$12, $12	$29, $11
	Charge $1.50	$3, $21	$20, $20

[8] As in Example 12.2, some of the facts about the product and the market have been altered to protect P&G's proprietary interests.

[9] Assumes that Unilever and Kao both charge the same price. Entries represent profits in thousands of dollars per month.

each make a profit of $20,000 per month, instead of the $12,000 per month they make by charging $1.40. Then why don't they charge $1.50?

Because these firms are in a Prisoners' Dilemma. No matter what Unilever and Kao do, P&G makes more money by charging $1.40. For example, if Unilever and Kao charge $1.50, P&G can make $29,000 per month by charging $1.40, versus $20,000 by charging $1.50. This is also true for Unilever and for Kao. For example, if P&G charges $1.50 and Unilever and Kao both charge $1.40, they will each make $21,000, instead of $20,000.[10] As a result, P&G knows that if it sets a price of $1.50, its competitors will have a strong incentive to undercut and charge $1.40. P&G will then have only a small share of the market and will make only $3000 per month profit. Should P&G make a leap of faith and charge $1.50? If you were faced with this dilemma, what would you do?

12.6 *Implications of the Prisoners' Dilemma for Oligopolistic Pricing*

Does the Prisoners' Dilemma doom oligopolistic firms to aggressive competition and low profits? Not necessarily. Although our imaginary prisoners have only one opportunity to confess, most firms set output and price over and over again, continually observing their competitors' behavior and adjusting their own accordingly. This allows firms to develop reputations from which trust can arise. As a result, oligopolistic coordination and cooperation can sometimes prevail.

Take, for example, an industry made up of three or four firms that have co-existed for a long time. Over the years, the managers of those firms might grow tired of losing money because of price wars, and an implicit understanding might arise in which all the firms maintain high prices, and no firm attempts to take market share from its competitors. Although each firm might be tempted to undercut its competitors, the managers know that the gains from this will be short lived. They know their competitors will retaliate, and the result will be renewed warfare and lower profits over the long run.

This resolution of the Prisoners' Dilemma occurs in some industries, but not in others. Sometimes managers are not content with the moderately high profits resulting from implicit collusion and prefer to compete aggressively to try and capture most of the market. Sometimes implicit understandings are difficult to reach. For example, firms with different costs and different assess-

---

[10] If P&G and Kao both charged $1.50 and *only* Unilever undercut and charged $1.40, Unilever would make $29,000 per month. It is especially profitable to be the only firm charging the low price.

ments of market demand might disagree about what the "correct" collusive price is. Firm *A* might think the "correct" price is $10, while Firm *B* thinks it is $9. When it sets a $9 price, Firm *A* might view this as an attempt to undercut, and might retaliate by lowering its price to $8, so a price war begins.

As a result, in many industries implicit collusion is short lived. There is often a fundamental layer of mistrust, so warfare erupts as soon as one firm is perceived by its competitors to be "rocking the boat" by changing its price or doing too much advertising.

Price Rigidity

Because implicit collusion tends to be fragile, oligopolistic firms often have a strong desire for stability, particularly with respect to price. This is why *price rigidity* can be a characteristic of oligopolistic industries. Even if costs or demand change, firms are reluctant to change price. If costs fall or market demand declines, firms are reluctant to lower price because that might send the wrong message to their competitors, and thereby set off a round of price warfare. And if costs or demand rises, firms are reluctant to raise price because they are afraid that their competitors might not also raise their prices.

This price rigidity is the basis of the well-known "kinked demand curve" model of oligopoly. According to this model, each firm faces a demand curve kinked at the currently prevailing price *P**. (See Figure 12.7.) At prices above *P**, the demand curve is very elastic. The reason is that the firm believes that if it raises its price above *P**, other firms will not follow suit, and it will therefore lose sales and much of its market share. On the other hand, the firm believes that if it lowers its price below *P**, other firms will follow suit because they will not want to lose *their* shares of the market, so that sales will expand only to the extent that a lower market price increases total market demand.

Because the firm's demand curve is kinked, its marginal revenue curve is discontinuous. (The bottom part of the marginal revenue curve corresponds to the less elastic part of the demand curve, as shown by the solid portions of each curve.) As a result, the firm's costs can change without resulting in a change in price. As shown in the figure, marginal cost could increase, but it would still equal marginal revenue at the same output level, so that price stays the same.

The kinked demand curve model is attractively simple, but it does not really explain oligopolistic pricing. It says nothing about how firms arrived at price *P** in the first place, and why they didn't arrive at some different price. It is useful mainly as a description of price rigidity, rather than an explanation of it.[11] The explanation for price rigidity comes from the Prisoners' Dilemma and from firms' desires to avoid mutually destructive price competition.

---

[11] Also, the model has not stood up well to empirical tests; there is evidence that rival firms do match price increases as well as decreases.

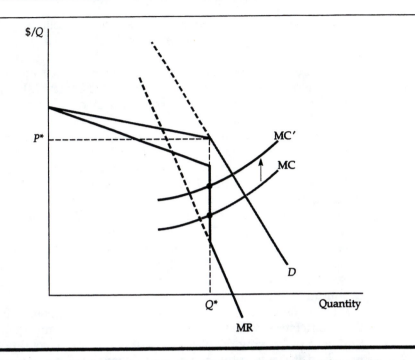

FIGURE 12.7 The Kinked Demand Curve. Each firm believes that if it raises its price above the current price P*, none of its competitors will follow suit, so it will lose most of its sales. Each firm also believes that if it lowers price, everyone will follow suit, and its sales will increase only to the extent that market demand increases. As a result, the firm's demand curve D is kinked at price P*, and its marginal revenue curve MR is discontinuous at that point. If marginal cost increases from MC to MC', the firm will still produce the same output level Q* and charge the same price P*.

Price Signaling and Price Leadership

One of the main impediments to implicitly collusive pricing is that it is difficult for firms to agree (without talking to each other) on what the price should be. Agreement becomes particularly problematic when cost and demand conditions are changing, and thus the "correct" price is also changing. *Price signaling* is a form of implicit collusion that sometimes gets around this problem. For example, a firm might announce that it has raised its price (perhaps through a press release) and hope that its competitors will take this as a signal that they should also raise their prices. If the competitors go along with this, a pattern of *price leadership* might be established. Here the first firm sets the price, and the other firms, the "price followers," follow suit. This solves the problem of agreeing on price—just charge what the leader is charging.

For example, suppose that three oligopolistic firms are currently charging $10 for their product. (If they all know the market demand curve, this might be the Nash equilibrium price.) Suppose that by colluding, they could all set a price of $20 and greatly increase their profits. Meeting and agreeing to set a price of $20 is illegal. But suppose instead that Firm A raises its price to $15, and announces to the business press that it is doing so because higher prices are needed to restore economic vitality to the industry. Firms B and C might view this as a clear message—Firm A is seeking their cooperation in raising prices. They might then raise their own prices to $15. Firm A might then increase price further, say to $18, and Firms B and C might go along and raise their prices as well. Whether or not the profit-maximizing price of $20 is reached (or surpassed), a pattern of coordination and implicit collusion has now been established that from the firms' point of view may be nearly as effective as meeting and formally agreeing on a price.[12]

This example of signaling and price leadership is extreme, and might lead to an antitrust lawsuit. But in some industries, a large firm might naturally emerge as a leader, with the other firms deciding that they are best off just matching the leader's prices, rather than trying to undercut the leader or each other. An example is the U.S. automobile industry, where General Motors has traditionally been the price leader.

Price leadership can also serve as a way for oligopolistic firms to deal with their reluctance to change prices, a reluctance that arises out of fear of being undercut or "rocking the boat." As cost and demand conditions change, firms may find it increasingly necessary to change prices that for some time had remained rigid. Then the firms might look to a price leader to signal when and by how much the price should change. Sometimes a large firm will naturally act as leader, and sometimes different firms will be the leader from time to time. The example of commercial banking that follows illustrates this.

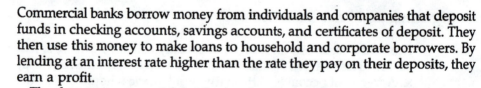

Commercial banks borrow money from individuals and companies that deposit funds in checking accounts, savings accounts, and certificates of deposit. They then use this money to make loans to household and corporate borrowers. By lending at an interest rate higher than the rate they pay on their deposits, they earn a profit.

The largest commercial banks in the United States—Bank of America, Bankers Trust Co., Chase Manhattan Bank, Chemical Bank, Citibank, Morgan Guaranty Trust Co., and Wells Fargo, among others—compete with each other to make loans to large corporate clients. The main form of competition is over price, in this case the interest rate they charge corporate clients for loans. If competition becomes aggressive, the interest rates they charge fall, and so do their profits. To avoid aggressive competition, a form of price leadership has evolved.

---

[12] For a formal model of how price leadership of this sort can facilitate collusion, see Julio J. Rotemberg and Garth Saloner, "Collusive Price Leadership," *Journal of Industrial Economics*, 1990.

TABLE 12.6   The Prime Rate

Date	Bank	Rate Change
December 18, 1984	Manufacturers Hanover	$11\frac{1}{4} \rightarrow 10\frac{3}{4}$
December 19, 1984	Bankers Trust	$11\frac{1}{4} \rightarrow 10\frac{3}{4}$
December 20, 1984	All others	$11\frac{1}{4} \rightarrow 10\frac{3}{4}$
January 15, 1985	Manufacturers Hanover	$10\frac{3}{4} \rightarrow 10\frac{1}{2}$
January 16, 1985	All others	$10\frac{3}{4} \rightarrow 10\frac{1}{2}$
May 16, 1985	Bankers Trust	$10\frac{1}{2} \rightarrow 10$
May 17, 1985	Citibank, Chase	$10\frac{1}{2} \rightarrow 10$
May 18, 1985	All others	$10\frac{1}{2} \rightarrow 10$
June 19, 1985, A.M.	Morgan Guaranty	$10 \rightarrow 9\frac{1}{2}$
June 19, 1985, P.M.	All others	$10 \rightarrow 9\frac{1}{2}$
March 7, 1986, A.M.	Chase Manhattan	$9\frac{1}{2} \rightarrow 9$
March 7, 1986, P.M.	All others	$9\frac{1}{2} \rightarrow 9$
April 22, 1986, A.M.	Chase Manhattan	$9 \rightarrow 8\frac{1}{2}$
April 22, 1986, P.M.	All others	$9 \rightarrow 8\frac{1}{2}$
July 14, 1986, A.M.	Chemical Bank	$8\frac{1}{2} \rightarrow 8$
July 14, 1986, P.M.	All others	$8\frac{1}{2} \rightarrow 8$
August 26, 1986	Wells Fargo	$8 \rightarrow 7\frac{1}{2}$
August 27, 1986	All others	$8 \rightarrow 7\frac{1}{2}$

The interest rate that banks charge large corporate clients is called the *prime rate*. This rate is widely cited in newspapers, and so is a convenient focal point for price leadership. Most large banks charge the same or nearly the same prime rate, and they avoid making frequent changes in the rate that might be destabilizing and lead to competitive warfare. The prime rate changes only when money market conditions have changed enough so that other interest rates have risen or fallen substantially. When that happens, one of the major banks announces a change in its rate, and the other banks quickly follow suit. Different banks act as leader from time to time, but when one bank announces a change, the other banks follow within two or three days.

Table 12.6 shows the evolution of the prime rate from late 1984 through the middle of 1986, which was a period of falling interest rates. Note that on December 18, 1984, for example, Manufacturers Hanover lowered its prime rate from $11\frac{1}{4}$ percent to $10\frac{3}{4}$ percent, and all the other major banks followed suit within two days. On May 16, 1985, Bankers Trust was the first to lower its rate, this time from $10\frac{1}{2}$ to 10 percent, and again all the other banks followed suit within two days. On several occasions, all banks changed their rates within the same day.

Table 12.6 also shows that changes in the prime rate were relatively infrequent. Other market interest rates were fluctuating considerably during this period, but the prime rate changed only after the other rates had changed sub-

---

[13] Source: *Wall Street Journal*, various issues. Manufacturers Hanover Trust Co. has since merged with Chemical Bank.

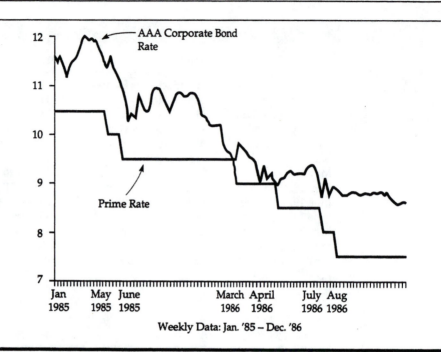

FIGURE 12.8 **Prime Rate versus Corporate Bond Rate.** The prime rate is the rate that major banks charge large corporate customers for short-term loans. It changes only infrequently because banks are reluctant to undercut one another. When a change does occur, it begins with one bank, and other banks quickly follow suit. The corporate bond rate is the return on long-term corporate bonds. Because these bonds are widely traded, this rate fluctuates with market conditions.

stantially. Figure 12.8 shows this by comparing the prime rate with the rate on high-grade (AAA), long-term corporate bonds during 1985 and 1986. Note the long periods during which the prime rate did not change.

The Dominant Firm Model

In some oligopolistic markets, one large firm has a major share of total sales, and a group of smaller firms supplies the remainder of the market. The large firm might then act as a *dominant firm*, setting a price that maximizes its own profits. The other firms, which individually could have little influence over price anyway, would then act as perfect competitors; they take the price set by the dominant firm as given and produce accordingly. But what price should the dominant firm set? To maximize profit, it must take into account how the output of the other firms depends on the price it sets.

Figure 12.9 shows how a dominant firm sets its price. Here, D is the market demand curve, and S_F is the supply curve (i.e., the aggregate marginal cost curve of the smaller fringe firms). The dominant firm must determine *its* demand curve D_D. As the figure shows, this is just the difference between market demand and the supply of fringe firms. For example, at price P_1 the supply of fringe firms is just equal to market demand, so the dominant firm can sell nothing at this price. At a price P_2 or less, fringe firms will not supply any of the good, so the dominant firm faces the market demand curve. At prices between P_1 and P_2, the dominant firm faces the demand curve D_D.

Corresponding to D_D is the dominant firm's marginal revenue curve MR_D. MC_D is the dominant firm's marginal cost curve. To maximize its profit, the dominant firm produces quantity Q_D at the intersection of MR_D and MC_D. From the demand curve D_D, we find price P^*. At this price, fringe firms sell a quantity Q_F, so that the total quantity sold is $Q_T = Q_D + Q_F$.

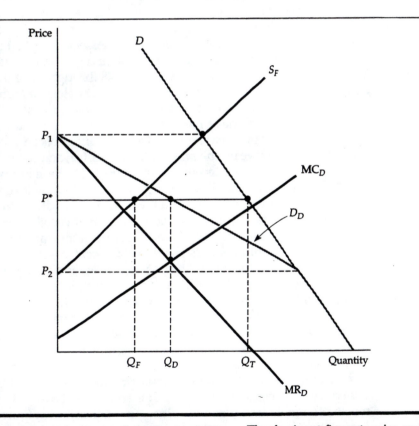

FIGURE 12.9 **Price Setting by a Dominant Firm.** The dominant firm sets price, and the other firms sell as much as they want at that price. The dominant firm's demand curve, D_D, is the difference between market demand D and the supply of fringe firms S_F. The dominant firm produces a quantity Q_D at the point where its marginal revenue MR_D is equal to its marginal cost MC_D. The corresponding price is P^*. At this price, fringe firms sell Q_F, so that total sales is Q_T.

12.7 Cartels

Producers in a cartel explicitly agree to cooperate in setting prices and output levels. Not all the producers in an industry need to join the cartel, and most cartels involve only a subset of producers. But if enough producers adhere to the cartel's agreements, and if market demand is sufficiently inelastic, the cartel may drive prices well above competitive levels.

Cartels are often international. The U.S. antitrust laws prohibit American companies from colluding, but the antitrust laws of other countries are much weaker and are sometimes poorly enforced. Furthermore, nothing prevents countries, or companies owned or controlled by foreign governments, from forming a cartel. For example, the OPEC cartel is an international agreement among oil-producing countries, which for over a decade succeeded in raising world oil prices far above what they would have been otherwise.

Other international cartels have also succeeded in raising prices. For example, during the mid-1970s, the International Bauxite Association (IBA) quadrupled bauxite prices, and a secretive international uranium cartel pushed up uranium prices. Some cartels had longer successes: From 1928 through the early 1970s, a cartel called Mercurio Europeo kept the price of mercury close to monopoly levels, and an international cartel monopolized the iodine market from 1878 through 1939. However, most cartels have failed to raise prices. An international copper cartel operates to this day, but it has never had a significant impact on copper prices. And cartel attempts to drive up the prices of tin, coffee, tea, and cocoa have also failed.[14]

Why do some cartels succeed while others fail? There are two requisites for cartel success. First, a stable cartel organization must be formed whose members agree on price and production levels and then adhere to that agreement. Unlike our prisoners in the Prisoners' Dilemma, cartel members can talk to each other to formalize an agreement. This does not mean, however, that agreeing is easy. Different members may have different costs, different assessments of market demand, and even different objectives, and they may therefore want to set price at different levels. Furthermore, each member of the cartel will be tempted to "cheat" by lowering its price slightly to capture a larger market share than it was allotted. Most often, only the threat of a long-term return to competitive prices deters cheating of this sort. But if the profits from cartelization are large enough, that threat may be sufficient.

The second requisite for success is the potential for monopoly power. Even if a cartel can solve its organizational problems, there will be little room to raise price if it faces a highly elastic demand curve. Potential monopoly power may be the most important condition for success; if the potential gains from cooperation are large, cartel members will have more incentive to solve their organizational problems.

---

[14] See Robert S. Pindyck, "The Cartelization of World Commodity Markets," *American Economic Review* 69 (May 1979): 154–158; and Jeffrey K. MacKie-Mason and Robert S. Pindyck, "Cartel Theory and Cartel Experience in International Minerals Markets," in *Energy: Markets and Regulation* (Cambridge, Mass.: MIT Press, 1986).

The Analysis of Cartel Pricing

Only rarely do *all* the producers of a good combine to form a cartel. A cartel usually accounts for only a portion of total production and must take the supply response of competitive (noncartel) producers into account when setting price. Cartel pricing can thus be analyzed by using the dominant firm model discussed earlier. We will apply this model to two cartels, the OPEC oil cartel and the CIPEC copper cartel.[15] This will help us understand why OPEC was so successful in raising price, while CIPEC was not.

Figure 12.10 illustrates the case of OPEC. Total Demand TD is the total world demand curve for crude oil, and S_c is the competitive (non-OPEC) supply curve. The demand for OPEC oil D_{OPEC} is the difference between total demand and competitive supply, and MR_{OPEC} is the corresponding marginal revenue curve. MC_{OPEC} is OPEC's marginal cost curve; OPEC has much lower pro-

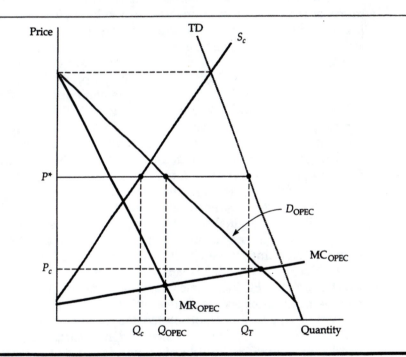

FIGURE 12.10   The OPEC Oil Cartel.   TD is the total world demand curve for oil, and S_c is the competitive (non-OPEC) supply curve. OPEC's demand D_{OPEC} is the difference between the two. Because both total demand and competitive supply are inelastic, OPEC's demand is inelastic. OPEC's profit-maximizing quantity Q_{OPEC} is found at the intersection of its marginal revenue and marginal cost curves; at this quantity, OPEC charges price P^*. If OPEC producers had not cartelized, price would be P_c, where OPEC's demand and marginal cost curves intersect.

---

[15] CIPEC is the French acronym for International Council of Copper Exporting Countries.

duction costs than do non-OPEC producers. OPEC's marginal revenue and marginal cost are equal at quantity Q_{OPEC}, which is the quantity that OPEC will produce. We see from OPEC's demand curve that the price will be P^* at which competitive supply is Q_c.

Suppose petroleum-exporting countries had not formed a cartel and instead had produced competitively. Price would then have equaled marginal cost. We can therefore determine the competitive price from the point where OPEC's demand curve intersects its marginal cost curve. That price, labeled P_c, is much lower than the cartel price P^*. Because both total demand and non-OPEC supply are inelastic, the demand for OPEC oil is also fairly inelastic; thus the cartel has substantial monopoly power. It used that power to drive prices well above competitive levels.

In Chapter 2 we stressed the importance of distinguishing between short-run and long-run supply and demand, and that distinction is important here. The total demand and non-OPEC supply curves in Figure 12.10 apply to a short- or intermediate-run analysis. In the long run, both demand and supply will be much more elastic, which means that OPEC's demand curve will also be much more elastic. As a result, we would expect that in the long run OPEC would be unable to maintain a price that is so much above the competitive level. Indeed, during 1982–1989, oil prices fell in real terms, largely because of the long-run adjustment of demand and non-OPEC supply.

Figure 12.11 provides a similar analysis of CIPEC. CIPEC consists of four copper-producing countries: Chile, Peru, Zambia, and Zaire, which collectively account for about a third of world copper production. In these countries production costs are lower than those of non-CIPEC producers, but except for Chile, not much lower. In Figure 12.11 CIPEC's marginal cost curve is therefore drawn only a little below the non-CIPEC supply curve. CIPEC's demand curve D_{CIPEC} is the difference between total demand TD and non-CIPEC supply S_c. CIPEC's marginal cost and marginal revenue curves intersect at quantity Q_{CIPEC}, with the corresponding price P^*. Again, the competitive price P_c is found at the point where CIPEC's demand curve intersects its marginal cost curve. Note that this price is very close to the cartel price P^*.

Why can't CIPEC increase copper prices much? As Figure 12.11 shows, the total demand for copper is more elastic than for oil. (Other materials, such as aluminum, can easily be substituted for copper.) Also, competitive supply is much more elastic. Even in the short run, non-CIPEC producers can easily expand supply if prices should rise (in part because of the availability of supply from scrap metal). Thus CIPEC's potential monopoly power is small.[16]

As the examples of OPEC and CIPEC illustrate, successful cartelization requires two things. First, the total demand for the good must not be very price elastic. Second, either the cartel must control nearly all the world's supply, or if it doesn't, the supply of noncartel producers must not be price elastic. Most international commodity cartels have failed because few world markets meet both these conditions.

---

[16] For a detailed analysis of OPEC and CIPEC, see R. S. Pindyck, "Gains to Producers from the Cartelization of Exhaustible Resources," *Review of Economics and Statistics* (May 1978): 238–251.

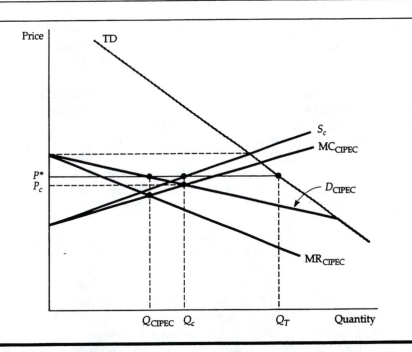

FIGURE 12.11   The CIPEC Copper Cartel.   TD is the total demand for copper, and S_c is the competitive (non-CIPEC) supply. CIPEC's demand D_{CIPEC} is the difference between the two. Both total demand and competitive supply are relatively elastic, so CIPEC's demand curve is elastic, and CIPEC has very little monopoly power. Note that CIPEC's optimal price P^* is close to the competitive price P_c.

Many people think of intercollegiate athletics as an extracurricular activity for college students and a diversion for fans. They assume that universities support athletics avidly because it gives amateur athletes a chance to develop their skills and play football or basketball before a large audience, and also provides entertainment and promotes school spirit and alumni support. Although it does these things, intercollegiate athletics is also a big—and an extremely profitable—industry.

Like any industry, intercollegiate athletics has firms and consumers. The "firms" are the universities that support and finance teams. The inputs to production are the coaches, student athletes, and capital in the form of stadiums and playing fields. The consumers, many of whom are current or former college students, are the fans who buy tickets to games, and the TV and radio networks that pay to broadcast the games. There are many firms and consumers, which suggests that the industry is competitive. But the persistently high level of profits in this industry is inconsistent with competition—a large state university can regularly earn more than $6 million a year in profits from football games alone.[17] This profitability is the result of monopoly power, obtained via cartelization.

The cartel organization is the National Collegiate Athletic Association (NCAA). The NCAA restricts competition in a number of important activities. To reduce bargaining power by student athletes, the NCAA creates and enforces rules regarding eligibility and terms of compensation. To reduce output competition by firms, it limits the number of games that can be played each season and the number of teams that can participate in each division. And to limit price competition, the NCAA has, until 1984, been the sole negotiator for all football television contracts, thereby monopolizing one of the main sources of industry revenues.[18]

Has the NCAA been a successful cartel? Like most cartels, its members have occasionally broken its rules and regulations. But until 1984, it had increased the monopoly power of this industry well above what it would have been otherwise. In 1984, however, the Supreme Court ruled that the NCAA's monopolization of football television contracts was illegal, and that individual universities could negotiate their own contracts. As a result, more college football is shown on television, and the revenues to the schools have dropped somewhat. But although the Supreme Court's ruling reduced the NCAA's monopoly power, it did not eliminate it. Intercollegiate athletics remains very profitable, thanks to the cartel.

Summary

1. In a monopolistically competitive market, firms compete by selling differentiated products, which are highly substitutable. New firms can enter or exit easily. Firms have only a small amount of monopoly power. In the long run, entry will occur until profits are driven to zero. Firms then produce with excess capacity (i.e., at output levels below those that minimize average cost).

2. In an oligopolistic market, only a few firms account for most or all of production. Barriers to entry allow some firms to earn substantial profits, even over the long run. Economic decisions involve strategic considerations—each firm must consider how its actions will affect its rivals, and how they are likely to react.

3. In the Cournot model of oligopoly, firms make their output decisions at the same time, each taking the other's output as fixed. In equilibrium, each firm is maximizing its profit,

[17] See "In Big-Time College Athletics, the Real Score Is in Dollars," *New York Times*, March 1, 1987.

[18] See James V. Koch, "The Intercollegiate Athletics Industry," in Walter Adams, *The Structure of American Industry*, 7th ed. (New York: Macmillan, 1986). Koch provides a detailed and informative discussion of the nature of this industry and the behavior of the NCAA cartel.

given the output of its competitor, so no firm has an incentive to change its output. The firms are therefore in a Nash equilibrium. Each firm's profit is higher than under perfect competition, but less than what it would earn by colluding.

4. In the Stackelberg model, one firm sets its output first. That firm has a strategic advantage and earns a higher profit. It knows it can choose a large output, and its competitors will have to choose small outputs if they want to maximize profits.

5. The Nash equilibrium concept can also be applied to markets in which firms produce substitute goods and compete by setting price. In equilibrium, each firm maximizes its profit, given the prices of its competitors, and so has no incentive to change price.

6. Firms would earn higher profits by collusively agreeing to raise prices, but the antitrust laws usually prohibit this. They might all set a high price without colluding, each hoping its competitors will do the same, but they are in a Prisoners' Dilemma, which makes this unlikely. Each firm has an incentive to cheat by lowering its price and capturing sales from its competitors.

7. The Prisoners' Dilemma creates price rigidity in oligopolistic markets. Firms are reluctant to change prices for fear of setting off a round of price warfare.

8. Price leadership is a form of implicit collusion that sometimes gets around the Prisoners' Dilemma. One firm sets price, and the other firms follow with the same price.

9. In a cartel, producers explicitly collude in setting prices and output levels. Successful cartelization requires that the total demand not be very price elastic, and that either the cartel control most supply or else the supply of noncartel producers be inelastic.

Questions for Review

1. What are the characteristics of a monopolistically competitive market? What happens to the equilibrium price and quantity in such a market if one firm introduces a new, improved product?

2. Why is the firm's demand curve flatter than the total market demand curve in monopolistic competition? Suppose a monopolistically competitive firm is making a profit in the short run. What will happen to its demand curve in the long run?

3. Some experts have argued that too many brands of breakfast cereal are on the market. Give an argument to support this view. Give an argument against it.

4. Why is the Cournot equilibrium stable (i.e., why don't firms have any incentive to change their output levels once in equilibrium)? Even if they can't collude, why don't firms set their outputs at the joint profit-maximizing levels (i.e., the levels they would have chosen had they colluded)?

5. In the Stackelberg model, the firm that sets output first has an advantage. Explain why.

6. Explain the meaning of a Nash equilibrium when firms are competing with respect to price. Why is the equilibrium stable? Why don't the firms raise their prices to the level that maximizes joint profits?

7. The kinked demand curve describes price rigidity. Explain how the model works. What are its limitations? Why does price rigidity arise in oligopolistic markets?

8. Why does price leadership sometimes evolve in oligopolistic markets? Explain how the price leader determines a profit-maximizing price.

9. Why has the OPEC oil cartel succeeded in raising prices substantially, while the CIPEC copper cartel has not? What conditions are necessary for successful cartelization? What organizational problems must a cartel overcome?

Exercises

1. Suppose all firms in a monopolistically competitive industry were merged into one large firm. Would that new firm produce as many different brands? Would it produce only a single brand? Explain.

2. Consider the following duopoly. Demand is given by $P = 10 - Q$, where $Q = Q_1 + Q_2$. The firms' cost functions are $C_1(Q_1) = 4 + 2Q_1$ and $C_2(Q_2) = 3 + 3Q_2$.

   a. Suppose both firms have entered the industry. What is the joint profit-maximizing level of output? How much will each firm produce? How would your answer change if the firms have not yet entered the industry?

   b. What is each firm's equilibrium output and profit if they behave noncooperatively? Use the Cournot model. Draw the firms' reaction curves, and show the equilibrium.

   c. How much should Firm 1 be willing to pay to purchase Firm 2 if collusion is illegal, but the takeover is not?

3. A monopolist can produce at a constant average (and marginal) cost of $AC = MC = 5$. The firm faces a market demand curve given by $Q = 53 - P$.

   a. Calculate the profit-maximizing price and quantity for this monopolist. Also calculate the monopolist's profits.

   b. Suppose a second firm enters the market. Let Q_1 be the output of the first firm and Q_2 be the output of the second. Market demand is now given by

$$Q_1 + Q_2 = 53 - P$$

   Assuming that this second firm has the same costs as the first, write the profits of each firm as functions of Q_1 and Q_2.

   c. Suppose (as in the Cournot model) each firm chooses its profit-maximizing level of output under the assumption that its competitor's output is fixed. Find each firm's "reaction curve" (i.e., the rule that gives its desired output in terms of its competitor's output).

   d. Calculate the Cournot equilibrium (i.e., the values of Q_1 and Q_2 for which both firms are doing as well as they can given their competitor's output). What are the resulting market price and profits of each firm?

*e. Suppose there are N firms in the industry, all with the same constant marginal cost, $MC = 5$. Find the Cournot equilibrium. How much will each firm produce, what will be the market price, and how much profit will each firm earn? Also, show that as N becomes large, the market price approaches the price that would prevail under perfect competition.

4. This exercise is a continuation of Exercise 3. We return to two firms with the same constant average and marginal cost, $AC = MC = 5$, facing the market demand curve $Q_1 + Q_2 = 53 - P$. Now we will use the Stackelberg model to analyze what will happen if one of the firms makes its output decision ahead of the other one.

   a. Suppose Firm 1 is the Stackelberg leader (i.e., makes its output decisions ahead of Firm 2). Find the reaction curves that tell each firm how much to produce in terms of the output of its competitor.

   b. How much will each firm produce, and what will its profit be?

5. Suppose that two identical firms produce widgets and that they are the only firms in the market. Their costs are given by $C_1 = 30Q_1$ and $C_2 = 30Q_2$, where Q_1 is the output of Firm 1, and Q_2 is the output of Firm 2. Price is determined by the following demand curve:

$$P = 150 - Q$$

   where $Q = Q_1 + Q_2$.

   a. Find the Cournot–Nash equilibrium. Calculate the profit of each firm at this equilibrium.

   b. Suppose the two firms form a cartel to maximize joint profits. How many widgets will be produced? Calculate each firm's profit.

   c. Suppose Firm 1 were the only firm in the industry. How would the market output and Firm 1's profit differ from that found in part (b) above?

   d. Returning to the duopoly of part (b), suppose Firm 1 abides by the agreement, but Firm 2 cheats by increasing production. How many widgets will Firm 2 produce? What will be each firm's profits?

6. Suppose the airline industry consisted of only two firms: American and Texas Air Corp. Let the two firms have identical cost functions, $C(q) = 40q$. Assume the demand curve for the industry is given by $P = 100 - Q$, and that each firm expects the other to behave as a Cournot competitor.
a. Calculate the (Cournot-Nash) equilibrium for each firm, assuming that each chooses the output level that maximizes its profits taking its rival's output as given. What are the profits of each firm?
b. What would be equilibrium quantity if Texas Air had constant marginal and average costs of 25, and American had constant marginal and average costs of 40?
c. Assuming that both firms have the original cost function, $C(q) = 40q$, how much should Texas Air be willing to invest to lower its marginal cost from 40 to 25, assuming that American will not follow suit? How much should American be willing to spend to reduce its marginal cost to 25, assuming that Texas Air will have marginal costs of 25 regardless of American's actions?

7. Demand for light bulbs can be characterized by $Q = 100 - P$, where Q is in millions of boxes of lights sold, and P is the price per box. There are two producers of lights, Everglow and Dimlit. They have identical cost functions:

$$C_i = 10Q_i + \tfrac{1}{2}Q_i^2 \ (i = E, D)$$

$$Q = Q_E + Q_D$$

a. Unable to recognize the potential for collusion, the two firms act as short-run perfect competitors. What are the equilibrium values of Q_E, Q_D, and P? What are each firm's profits?
b. Top management in both firms is replaced. Each new manager independently recognizes the oligopolistic nature of the light bulb industry and plays Cournot. What are the equilibrium values of Q_E, Q_D, and P? What are each firm's profits?
c. Suppose the Everglow manager guesses correctly that Dimlit has a Cournot conjectural variation, so Everglow plays Stackelberg. What are the equilibrium values of Q_E, Q_D, and P? What are each firm's profits?
d. If the managers of the two companies collude, what are the equilibrium values of Q_E, Q_D, and P? What are each firm's profits?

8. Two firms compete by choosing price. Their demand functions are

$$Q_1 = 20 - P_1 + P_2$$
and
$$Q_2 = 20 + P_1 - P_2$$

where P_1 and P_2 are the prices charged by each firm, respectively, and Q_1 and Q_2 are the resulting demands. (Note that the demand for each good depends only on the difference in prices; if the two firms colluded and set the same price, they could make that price as high as they want, and earn infinite profits.) Marginal costs are zero.
a. Suppose the two firms set their prices at the *same time*. Find the resulting Nash equilibrium. What price will each firm charge, how much will it sell, and what will its profit be? (Hint: Maximize the profit of each firm with respect to its price.)
b. Suppose Firm 1 sets its price *first*, and then Firm 2 sets its price. What price will each firm charge, how much will it sell, and what will its profit be?
c. Suppose you are one of these firms, and there are three ways you could play the game: (i) Both firms set price at the same time. (ii) You set price first. (iii) Your competitor sets price first. If you could choose among these, which would you prefer? Explain why.

* 9. The dominant firm model can help us understand the behavior of some cartels. Let us apply this model to the OPEC oil cartel. We will use isoelastic curves to describe world demand W and noncartel (competitive) supply S. Reasonable numbers for the price elasticities of world demand and noncartel supply are $-\tfrac{1}{2}$ and $\tfrac{1}{2}$, respectively. Then, expressing W and S in millions of barrels per day (mb/d), we could write

$$W = 160P^{-1/2}$$
and
$$S = (3\tfrac{1}{3})P^{1/2}$$

Note that OPEC's net demand is $D = W - S$.
a. Sketch the world demand curve W, the non-OPEC supply curve S, OPEC's net demand curve D, and OPEC's marginal revenue curve. For purposes of approximation, assume OPEC's production cost is zero. Indicate OPEC's optimal price, OPEC's optimal production, and non-OPEC production on the diagram. Now, show on the diagram how the various curves will shift, and how OPEC's optimal price will change if non-OPEC supply becomes more expensive because reserves of oil start running out.

b. Calculate OPEC's optimal (profit-maximizing) price. (Hint: Because OPEC's cost is zero, just write the expression for OPEC revenue and find the price that maximizes it.)

c. Suppose the oil-consuming countries were to unite and form a "buyers' cartel" to gain monopsony power. What can we say, and what can't we say, about the impact this would have on price?

*10. A lemon-growing cartel consists of four orchards. Their total cost functions are

$$TC_1 = 20 + 5Q_1^2$$

$$TC_2 = 25 + 3Q_2^2$$

$$TC_3 = 15 + 4Q_3^2$$

$$TC_4 = 20 + 6Q_4^2$$

(TC is in hundreds of dollars, Q is in cartons per month picked and shipped.)

a. Tabulate total, average, and marginal costs for each firm for output levels between 1 and 5 cartons per month (i.e., for 1, 2, 3, 4, and 5 cartons).

b. If the cartel decided to ship 10 cartons per month and set a price of 25 per carton, how should output be allocated among the firms?

c. At this shipping level, which firm has the most incentive to cheat? Does any firm *not* have an incentive to cheat?

CHAPTER 13

Game Theory and Competitive Strategy

*U*nlike a pure monopoly or a perfectly competitive firm, most firms must consider the likely responses of competitors when they make strategic decisions about price, advertising expenditure, investment in new capital, and other variables. Although we began to explore some of these strategic decisions in the last chapter, there are many questions about market structure and firm behavior that we have not yet addressed. For example, why do firms tend to collude in some markets and compete aggressively in others? How do some firms manage to deter entry by potential competitors? And how should firms make pricing decisions when demand or cost conditions are changing, or new competitors are entering the market?

To answer these questions, we will use game theory to extend our analysis of strategic decision making by firms. The application of game theory has been an important development in microeconomics. This chapter explains some of this theory and shows how it can be used to understand how markets evolve and operate, and how managers should think about the strategic decisions they continually face. We will see, for example, what happens when oligopolistic firms must set and adjust prices strategically over time, so that the Prisoners' Dilemma, which we discussed in Chapter 12, is repeated over and over. We will discuss how firms can make strategic moves that give them an advantage over their competitors or the edge in a bargaining situation. And we will see how firms can use threats, promises, or more concrete actions to deter entry by potential competitors.

13.1 *Gaming and Strategic Decisions*

First, we should clarify what gaming and strategic decision making are all about. In essence, we are concerned with the following question: *If I believe that my competitors are rational and act to maximize their own profits, how should I take their behavior into account when making my own profit-maximizing decisions?*

As we will see, this question can be difficult to answer, even under conditions of complete symmetry and perfect information (i.e., my competitors and I have the same cost structure and are fully informed about each others' costs, about demand, etc.). Moreover, we will be concerned with more complex situations in which firms have different costs, different types of information, and various degrees and forms of competitive "advantage" and "disadvantage."

Noncooperative versus Cooperative Games

The economic games that firms play can be either *cooperative* or *noncooperative*. A game is *cooperative* if the players can negotiate binding contracts that allow them to plan joint strategies. A game is *noncooperative* if negotiation and enforcement of a binding contract are not possible.

An example of a cooperative game is the bargaining between a buyer and a seller over the price of a rug. If the rug costs $100 to produce and the buyer values the rug at $200, a cooperative solution to the game is possible because an agreement to sell the rug at any price between $101 and $199 will maximize the sum of the buyer's consumer surplus and the seller's profit, while making both parties better off. Another cooperative game would involve two firms in an industry, which negotiate a joint investment to develop a new technology (where neither firm would have enough know-how to succeed on its own). If the firms can sign a binding contract to divide the profits from their joint investment, a cooperative outcome that makes both parties better off is possible.[1] An example of a noncooperative game is a situation in which two competing firms take each other's likely behavior into account and independently determine a pricing or advertising strategy to win market share.

Note that the fundamental difference between cooperative and noncooperative games lies in the contracting possibilities. In cooperative games binding contracts are possible; in noncooperative games they are not.

We will be concerned mostly with noncooperative games. In any game, however, the most important aspect of strategy design is *understanding your*

---

[1] Bargaining over a rug is called a *constant sum* game because no matter what the selling price, the sum of consumer surplus and profit will be the same. Negotiating over a joint venture is a *nonconstant sum* game: the total profit that results from the venture will depend on the outcome of the negotiations, e.g., the resources that each firm devotes to the venture.

opponent's point of view, and (assuming your opponent is rational) deducing how he or she is likely to respond to your actions. This may seem obvious—of course, one must understand an opponent's point of view. Yet even in simple gaming situations, people often ignore or misjudge their opponents' positions and the rational responses those positions imply.

An example of this is the following game devised by Martin Shubik.[2] A dollar bill is auctioned, but in an unusual way. The highest bidder receives the dollar in return for the amount bid. However, the second-highest bidder must also hand over the amount he or she bid—and get nothing in return. *If you were playing this game, how much would you bid for the dollar bill?*

Classroom experience shows that students often end up bidding more than a dollar for the dollar. In a typical scenario, one player bids 20 cents, and another 30 cents. The lower bidder now stands to lose 20 cents, but figures he can earn a dollar by raising his bid, and so bids 40 cents. The escalation continues until two players carry the bidding to a dollar against 90 cents. Now the 90-cent bidder has to choose between bidding $1.10 for the dollar, or paying 90 cents to get nothing. Most often, he raises his bid, and the bidding escalates further. In some experiments, the "winning" student has ended up paying more than $3 for the dollar!

How could intelligent students put themselves in this position? By failing to think through the likely response of the other players, and the sequence of events it implies. How much would you bid for the dollar? We hope nothing.

In the rest of this chapter, we will examine simple games that involve pricing, advertising, and investment decisions. The games are simple in that, *given some behavioral assumption,* we can determine the best strategy for each firm. But even for these simple games, we will find that the correct behavioral assumptions are not always easy to make, and will depend on how the game is played (e.g., how long the firms stay in business, their reputations, etc.). Therefore, when reading this chapter, you should try to understand the basic issues involved in making strategic decisions. You should also keep in mind the importance of carefully assessing your opponent's position and rational response to your actions, as Example 13.1 illustrates.

EXAMPLE 13.1   ACQUIRING A COMPANY

You represent Company A (the acquirer), which is considering acquiring Company T (the target).[3] You plan to offer cash for all of Company T's shares, but you are unsure what price to offer. The complication is this: The value of Company T, indeed, its viability, depends on the outcome of a major oil exploration project that it is currently undertaking. If the project fails, Company T under current management will be worth nothing. But if it succeeds, Company

---

[2] Martin Shubik, *Game Theory in the Social Sciences* (Cambridge, Mass.: MIT Press, 1982).

[3] This is a revised version of an example designed by Max Bazerman for a course at MIT.

T's value under current management could be as high as $100/share. All share values between $0 and $100 are considered equally likely.

It is well known, however, that Company T will be worth much more under the progressive management of Company A than under current management. In fact, whatever the ultimate value under current management, *Company T will be worth 50 percent more under the management of Company A.* If the project fails, Company T is worth $0/share under either management. If the exploration project generates a $50/share value under current management, the value under Company A will be $75/share. Similarly, a $100/share value under Company T implies a $150/share value under Company A, and so on.

You must determine what price Company A should offer for Company T's shares. This offer must be made *now, before* the outcome of the exploration project is known. From all indications, Company T would be happy to be acquired by Company A, *for the right price.* You expect Company T to delay a decision on your bid until the exploration results are in and then accept or reject your offer before news of the drilling results reaches the press.

Thus, *you (Company A) will not know the results of the exploration project when submitting your price offer, but Company T will know the results when deciding whether to accept your offer. Also, Company T will accept any offer by Company A that is greater than the (per share) value of the company under current management.* As the representative of Company A, you are considering price offers in the range $0/share (i.e., making no offer at all) to $150/share. *What price per share should you offer for Company T's stock?*

Note: The typical response—to offer between $50 and $75 per share—is wrong. The correct answer to this problem appears at the end of this chapter, but we urge you to try to answer it on your own.

13.2 *Dominant Strategies*

How can we decide on the best strategy for playing a game? How can we determine a game's likely outcome? We need something to help us determine how the rational behavior of each player will lead to an equilibrium solution. Some strategies may be successful if competitors make certain choices, but will fail if they make other choices. Other strategies, however, may be successful whatever competitors choose to do. We begin with the concept of a *dominant strategy—one that is optimal for a player no matter what an opponent does.*

The following example illustrates this in a duopoly setting. Suppose Firms *A* and *B* sell competing products and are deciding whether to undertake advertising campaigns. Each firm, however, will be affected by its competitor's decision. The possible outcomes of the game are illustrated by the payoff matrix in Table 13.1. (Recall that the payoff matrix summarizes the possible

TABLE 13.1 Payoff Matrix for Advertising Game

		Firm B	
		Advertise	Don't Advertise
Firm A	Advertise	10, 5	15, 0
	Don't Advertise	6, 8	10, 2

outcomes of the game; the first number in each cell is the payoff to *A* and the second is the payoff to *B*.) Observe from this payoff matrix that if both firms decide to advertise, Firm *A* will make a profit of 10, and Firm *B* will make a profit of 5. If Firm *A* advertises and Firm *B* doesn't, Firm *A* will earn 15, and Firm *B* will earn zero. And similarly for the other two possibilities.

What strategy should each firm choose? First, consider Firm *A*. It should clearly advertise because no matter what Firm *B* does, Firm *A* does best by advertising. (If Firm *B* advertises, *A* earns a profit of 10 if it advertises, but only 6 if it doesn't. And if *B* does not advertise, *A* earns 15 if it advertises, but only 10 if it doesn't.) Thus, advertising is a dominant strategy for Firm *A*. The same is true for Firm *B*; no matter what Firm *A* does, Firm *B* does best by advertising. Therefore, assuming that both firms are rational, we know that the outcome for this game is that *both firms will advertise*. This outcome is easy to determine because both firms have dominant strategies.

However, not every game has a dominant strategy for each player. To see this, let's change our advertising example slightly. The payoff matrix in Table 13.2 is the same as in Table 13.1, except for the bottom right-hand corner—if neither firm advertises, Firm *B* will again earn a profit of 2, but Firm *A* will earn a profit of 20 (perhaps because Firm *A*'s ads are largely defensive, designed to refute Firm *B*'s claims, and expensive; so by not advertising, Firm *A* can reduce its expenses considerably).

Now Firm *A* has no dominant strategy. *Its optimal decision depends on what Firm B does*. If Firm *B* advertises, then Firm *A* does best by advertising; but if Firm *B* does not advertise, Firm *A* also does best by not advertising. Now

TABLE 13.2 Modified Advertising Game

		Firm B	
		Advertise	Don't Advertise
Firm A	Advertise	10, 5	15, 0
	Don't Advertise	6, 8	20, 2

suppose both firms must make their decisions at the same time. What should Firm *A* do?

To answer this, Firm *A* must put itself in Firm *B*'s shoes. What decision is best from Firm *B*'s point of view, and what is Firm *B* likely to do? The answer is clear: Firm *B* has a dominant strategy—advertise, no matter what Firm *A* does. (If Firm *A* advertises, *B* earns 5 by advertising and 0 by not advertising. If *A* doesn't advertise, *B* earns 8 if it advertises and 2 if it doesn't.) Therefore, Firm *A* can conclude that Firm *B* will advertise. This means that Firm *A* should itself advertise (and thereby earn 10 instead of 6). The equilibrium is that both firms will advertise. It is the logical outcome of the game because Firm *A* is doing the best it can, given Firm *B*'s decision; and Firm *B* is doing the best it can, given Firm *A*'s decision.

13.3 *The Nash Equilibrium Revisited*

To determine the likely outcome of a game, we have been seeking "self-enforcing," or "stable," strategies. Dominant strategies are stable, but in many games, one or more players do not have a dominant strategy. We therefore need a more general equilibrium concept. In Chapter 12 we introduced the concept of a *Nash equilibrium* and saw that it is widely applicable and intuitively appealing.[4]

Recall that a Nash equilibrium is a set of strategies (or actions) such that *each player is doing the best it can given the actions of its opponents*. Since each player has no incentive to deviate from its Nash strategy, the strategies are stable. In the example shown in Table 13.2, the Nash equilibrium is that both firms advertise. It is a Nash equilibrium because, given the decision of its competitor, each firm is satisfied that it has made the best decision possible, and has no incentive to change its decision.

In Chapter 12 we used the Nash equilibrium to study output and pricing by oligopolistic firms. In the Cournot model, for example, each firm sets its own output while taking the outputs of its competitors as fixed. We saw that in a Cournot equilibrium, no firm has an incentive to change its output unilaterally because each firm is doing the best it can given the decisions of its competitors. Hence a Cournot equilibrium is a Nash equilibrium.[5] We also examined models in which firms choose price, taking the prices of their com-

---

[4] Our discussion of the Nash equilibrium, and of game theory in general, is at an introductory level. For a more in-depth discussion of game theory and its applications, see James W. Friedman, *Game Theory with Applications to Economics* (New York: Oxford University Press, 1990); David Kreps, *A Course in Microeconomic Theory* (Princeton, N.J.: Princeton University Press, 1990); and Drew Fudenberg and Jean Tirole, *Game Theory* (Cambridge, Mass.: MIT Press, 1991).

[5] A Stackelberg equilibrium is also a Nash equilibrium. In the Stackelberg model, the rules of the game are different: One firm makes its output decision before its competitor does. Under these rules, each firm is doing the best it can given the decision of its competitor.

petitors as fixed. Again, in the Nash equilibrium, each firm is earning the largest profit it can given the prices of its competitors, and thus has no incentive to change its price.

It is helpful to compare the concept of a Nash equilibrium with that of an equilibrium in dominant strategies:

Dominant Strategies:	I'm doing the best I can *no matter what you do.* You're doing the best you can *no matter what I do.*
Nash Equilibrium:	I'm doing the best I can *given what you are doing.* You're doing the best you can *given what I am doing.*

Note that a dominant strategy equilibrium is a special case of a Nash equilibrium.

In the advertising game of Table 13.2 there is a single Nash equilibrium—both firms advertise. In general, a game does not have to have a single Nash equilibrium. Sometimes there is no Nash equilibrium, and sometimes there are several (i.e., several sets of strategies are stable and self-enforcing). A few more examples will help to clarify this.[6]

Consider the following "product choice" problem. Two breakfast cereal companies face a market in which two new variations of cereal can be successfully introduced—provided each variation is introduced by only one firm. There is a market for a new "crispy" cereal and for a new "sweet" cereal, but each firm has the resources to introduce only one new product. Then the payoff matrix for the two firms might look like the one in Table 13.3.

In this game each firm is indifferent about which product it produces, so long as it does not introduce the same product as its competitor. If coordination were possible, the firms would probably agree to divide the market. But what will happen if the firms must behave *noncooperatively*? Suppose that somehow—perhaps through a news release—Firm 1 indicates it is about to introduce the sweet cereal, and Firm 2 (after hearing this) indicates it will introduce the crispy one. Now, given the action it believes its opponent is taking, neither firm has an incentive to deviate from its proposed action. If it

		Firm 2	
		Crispy	Sweet
Firm 1	Crispy	−5, −5	10, 10
	Sweet	10, 10	−5, −5

[6] Several of these examples were developed by Garth Saloner.

takes the proposed action, its payoff is 10, but if it deviates—given that its opponent's action remains unchanged—its payoff will be −5. Therefore, the strategy set given by the bottom left-hand corner of the payoff matrix is stable and constitutes a Nash equilibrium: Given the strategy of its opponent, each firm is doing the best it can and has no incentive to deviate.

Note that the upper right-hand corner of the payoff matrix is also a Nash equilibrium, which might occur if Firm 1 indicated it was about to produce the crispy cereal. Each Nash equilibrium is stable because *once the strategies are chosen*, no player will unilaterally deviate from them. However, without more information, we have no way of knowing which equilibrium (crispy/sweet vs. sweet/crispy) is likely to result—or if *either* will result. Of course, both firms have a strong incentive to reach *one* of the two Nash equilibria—if they both introduce the same type of cereal, they will both lose money. The fact that the two firms are not allowed to collude does not mean that they will not reach a Nash equilibrium. As an industry develops, understandings often evolve as firms "signal" each other about the paths the industry is to take.

Maximin Strategies

The concept of a Nash equilibrium relies heavily on individual rationality. Each player's choice of strategy depends not only on its own rationality, but also on that of its opponent. This can be a limitation, as the example in Table 13.4 shows.

In this game, playing "right" is a dominant strategy for Player 2 because by using this strategy, Player 2 will do better (earning 1 rather than 0), no matter what Player 1 does. Thus, Player 1 should expect Player 2 to play the "right" strategy. In this case Player 1 would do better by playing "bottom" (and earning 2) than by playing "top" (and earning 1). Clearly the outcome (bottom, right) is a Nash equilibrium for this game, and you can verify that it is the only Nash equilibrium. But note that Player 1 had better be sure that Player 2 understands the game and is rational. If Player 2 should happen to make a mistake and play "left," it would be extremely costly to Player 1.

If you were Player 1, what would you do? If you tend to be cautious, and you are concerned that Player 2 might not be fully informed or rational, you

TABLE 13.4   Maximin Strategy

		Player 2	
		Left	Right
Player 1	Top	1, 0	1, 1
	Bottom	−1000, 0	2, 1

		Prisoner B	
		Confess	Don't Confess
Prisoner A	Confess	−5, −5	−1, −10
	Don't Confess	−10, −1	−2, −2

TABLE 13.5 Prisoners' Dilemma

might choose to play "top," in which case you will be assured of earning 1, and you will have no chance of losing 1000. Such a strategy is called a *maximin strategy* because it *maximizes the minimum gain that can be earned.* If both players used maximin strategies, the outcome would be (top, right). A maximin strategy is conservative, but not profit maximizing (since Player 1 earns a profit of 1 rather than 2). Note that if Player 1 *knew for certain* that Player 2 was using a maximin strategy, it would prefer to play "bottom" (and earn 2), instead of following the maximin strategy of playing "top."

What is the Nash equilibrium for the Prisoners' Dilemma discussed in Chapter 12? Table 13.5 shows the payoff matrix for the Prisoners' Dilemma. For the two prisoners, the ideal outcome is one in which neither confessed, so that they both get two years in prison. However, confessing is a *dominant strategy* for each prisoner—it yields a higher payoff regardless of the strategy of the other prisoner. Dominant strategies are also maximin strategies. Therefore, the outcome in which both prisoners confess is both a Nash equilibrium and a maximin solution. Thus, in a very strong sense, it is rational for each prisoner to confess.

*Mixed Strategies

In all of the games that we examined so far, we have considered strategies in which players make a specific choice or take a specific action: advertise or don't advertise, set a price of $4 or a price of $6, and so on. Strategies of this kind are called *pure strategies.* There are games, however, in which pure strategies are not the best way to play.

An example is the game of "Matching Pennies." In this game, each player chooses heads or tails, and the two players reveal their coins at the same time. If the coins match (i.e., both are heads or both are tails), Player A wins and receives a dollar from Player B. If the coins do not match, Player B wins and receives a dollar from Player A. The payoff matrix is shown in Table 13.6.

Note that there is no Nash equilibrium in pure strategies for this game. Suppose, for example, that Player A chose the strategy of playing heads. Then Player B would want to play tails. But if Player B plays tails, Player A would also want to play tails. No combination of heads or tails leaves both players satisfied, so that neither would want to change strategies.

		Player B	
		Heads	Tails
Player A	Heads	1, −1	−1, 1
	Tails	−1, 1	1, −1

Although there is no Nash equilibrium in pure strategies, there is a Nash equilibrium in *mixed strategies*. *A mixed strategy is a strategy in which the player makes a random choice among two or more possible actions, based on a set of chosen probabilities.* In this game, for example, Player A might simply flip the coin, thereby playing heads with probability $\frac{1}{2}$ and playing tails with probability $\frac{1}{2}$. In fact, if Player A follows this strategy and Player B does the same, we will have a Nash equilibrium; both players will be doing the best they can given what the opponent is doing. Note that the outcome of the game is random, but the *expected payoff* is 0 for each player.

It may seem strange to play a game by choosing actions randomly. But put yourself in the position of Player A and think what would happen if you followed a strategy *other* than just flipping the coin. Suppose, for example, you decided to play heads. If Player B knows this, she would play tails, and you would lose. Even if Player B didn't know your strategy, if the game were played over and over again, she could eventually discern your pattern of play and choose a strategy that countered it. Of course, you would then want to change your strategy—which is why this would not be a Nash equilibrium. Only if you and your opponent both choose heads or tails randomly with probability $\frac{1}{2}$, would neither of you have any incentive to change strategies.[7]

One reason to consider mixed strategies is that some games (such as "Matching Pennies") do not have any Nash equilibria in pure strategies. It can be shown, however, that *every* game has at least one Nash equilibrium, once we allow for mixed strategies.[8] Hence, mixed strategies provide solutions to games when pure strategies fail. Of course, whether solutions involving mixed strategies are reasonable will depend on the particular game and players. Mixed strategies are likely to be very reasonable for "Matching Pennies," poker, and other such games. A firm, on the other hand, might not find it reasonable to believe that its competitor will set its price randomly.

Some games have Nash equilibria both in pure strategies and in mixed strategies. An example is "The Battle of the Sexes," a game that you might

[7] You can check that the use of different probabilities, say ¾ for heads and ¼ for tails, does not generate a Nash equilibrium.

[8] More precisely, every game with a finite number of players and a finite number of actions has at least one Nash equilibrium. For a proof, see David M. Kreps, *A Course in Microeconomic Theory* (Princeton, N.J.: Princeton University Press, 1990), p. 409.

		Joan	
		Wrestling	Opera
Jim	Wrestling	2, 1	0, 0
	Opera	0, 0	1, 2

TABLE 13.7   The Battle of the Sexes

find familiar. It goes like this. Jim and Joan would like to spend Saturday night together, but have different tastes in entertainment. Joan would like to go to the opera, but Jim prefers mud wrestling. (Feel free to reverse these preferences.) As the payoff matrix in Table 13.7 shows, Joan would most prefer to go to the opera with Jim, but prefers watching mud wrestling with Jim to going to the opera alone, and similarly for Jim.

First, note that there are two Nash equilibria in pure strategies for this game—the one in which Jim and Joan both watch mud wrestling, and the one in which they both go to the opera. Jim, of course, would prefer the first of these outcomes and Joan the second, but both outcomes are equilibria—neither Jim nor Joan would want to change his or her decision, given the decision of the other.

This game also has an equilibrium in mixed strategies: Jim chooses wrestling with probability $\frac{2}{3}$ and opera with probability $\frac{1}{3}$, and Joan chooses wrestling with probability $\frac{1}{3}$ and opera with probability $\frac{2}{3}$. You can check that if Joan uses this strategy, Jim cannot do better with any other strategy, and vice versa.[9] The outcome is random, and Jim and Joan will each have an expected payoff of $\frac{2}{3}$.

Should we expect Jim and Joan to use these mixed strategies? Unless they're very risk loving or in some other way a strange couple, probably not. By agreeing to either form of entertainment, each will have a payoff of at least 1, which exceeds the expected payoff of $\frac{2}{3}$ from randomizing. In this game as in many others, mixed strategies provide another solution, but not a very realistic one. Hence for the remainder of this chapter we will focus on pure strategies.

13.4 Repeated Games

We saw in Chapter 12 that in oligopolistic markets, firms often find themselves in a Prisoners' Dilemma when making output or pricing decisions. Can firms

---

[9] Suppose Jim randomizes, letting p be the probability of wrestling, and $(1 - p)$ the probability of opera. Since Joan is using probabilities of $\frac{1}{3}$ for wrestling and $\frac{2}{3}$ for opera, the probability that both will choose wrestling is $(\frac{1}{3})p$, and the probability that both will choose opera is $(\frac{2}{3})(1 - p)$. Hence Jim's expected payoff is $2(\frac{1}{3})p + 1(\frac{2}{3})(1 - p) = (\frac{2}{3})p + \frac{2}{3} - (\frac{2}{3})p = \frac{2}{3}$. This is independent of p, so Jim cannot do better in terms of expected payoff no matter what he chooses.

find a way out of this dilemma, so that oligopolistic coordination and cooperation (whether explicit or implicit) could prevail?

To answer this question, we must recognize that the Prisoners' Dilemma, as we have described it so far, is static and thus limited. Although some prisoners may have only one opportunity in life to confess or not, most firms set output and price over and over again. In real life, firms play a *repeated game*. With each repetition of the Prisoners' Dilemma, firms can develop reputations about their behavior, and study the behavior of their competitors.

How does repetition change the likely outcome of the game? Suppose you are Firm 1 in the Prisoners' Dilemma illustrated by the payoff matrix in Table 13.8. If you and your competitor both charge a high price, you will both make a higher profit than if you both charged a low price. However, you are afraid to charge a high price because if your competitor charges a low price, you will lose money and, to add insult to injury, your competitor will get rich. But suppose this game is repeated over and over again—for example, you and your competitor simultaneously announce your prices on the first day of every month. Should you then play the game differently, perhaps changing your price over time in response to your competitor's behavior?

In an interesting study, Robert Axelrod asked game theorists to come up with the best strategy they could think of to play this game in a repeated manner.[10] (A possible strategy might be: "I'll start off with a high price, then lower my price, but then if my competitor lowers its price, I'll raise mine for a while before lowering it again, etc.") Then, in a computer simulation, Axelrod played these strategies off against one another to see which worked best.

As you would expect, any given strategy would work better against some strategies than it would against others. The objective, however, was to find the strategy that was most robust, i.e., would work best on average against *all*, or almost all, other strategies. The result was surprising. The strategy that worked best was extremely simple—it was a *"tit-for-tat"* strategy: I start out with a high price, which I maintain so long as you continue to "cooperate" and also charge a high price. As soon as you lower your price, however, I follow suit and lower mine. If you later decide to cooperate and raise your price again, I'll immediately raise my price as well.

| | | Firm 2 | |
		Low Price	High Price
Firm 1	Low Price	10, 10	100, −50
	High Price	−50, 100	50, 50

[10] See Robert Axelrod, *The Evolution of Cooperation* (New York: Basic Books, 1984).

Why does this tit-for-tat strategy work best? In particular, can I expect that using the tit-for-tat strategy will induce my competitor to behave cooperatively (and charge a high price)?

Suppose the game is *infinitely repeated*. In other words, my competitor and I repeatedly set price month after month, *forever*. Cooperative behavior (i.e., charging a high price) is then the rational response to a tit-for-tat strategy. (This assumes that my competitor knows, or can figure out, that I am using a tit-for-tat strategy.) To see why, suppose that in one month my competitor sets a low price and undercuts me. In that month it will make a large profit. But the competitor knows that the following month I will set a low price, so that its profit will fall, and will remain low as long as we both continue to charge a low price. Since the game is infinitely repeated, the cumulative loss of profits that results must outweigh any short-term gain that accrued during the first month of undercutting. Thus, it is not rational to undercut.

In fact, with an infinitely repeated game, my competitor does not even have to be sure that I am playing tit-for-tat to make cooperation the rational strategy for it to follow. Even if the competitor believes there is only some chance that I am playing tit-for-tat, it will still be rational for it to start by charging a high price, and maintain the high price as long as I do. The reason is that with infinite repetition of the game, the *expected* gains from cooperation will outweigh those from undercutting. This will be true even if the probability that I am playing tit-for-tat (and so will continue cooperating) is small.

Now suppose the game is repeated a *finite* number of times—say *N* months. (*N* can be large as long as it is finite.) If my competitor (Firm 2) is rational, *and believes that I am rational*, it would reason as follows: "Because Firm 1 is playing tit-for-tat, I (Firm 2) cannot undercut—that is, *until the last month*. I *should* undercut in the last month because then I can make a large profit that month, and afterwards the game is over, so that Firm 1 cannot retaliate. Therefore," figures Firm 2, "I will charge a high price until the last month, and then I will charge a low price."

However, since I (Firm 1) have also figured this out, I also plan to charge a low price in the last month. Of course, Firm 2 can figure this out as well, and therefore *knows* I will charge a low price in the last month. But then what about the next-to-last month? Firm 2 figures that it should undercut and charge a low price in the next-to-last month, because there will be no cooperation anyway in the last month. But, of course, I have figured this out too, so I *also* plan to charge a low price in the next-to-last month. And because the same reasoning applies to each preceding month, the only rational outcome is for both of us to charge a low price every month.

Since most of us do not expect to live forever, the tit-for-tat strategy seems of little value; once again we are stuck in the Prisoners' Dilemma without a way out. However, there *is* a way out if my competitor *has even a slight doubt about my "rationality."*

Suppose my competitor thinks (it need not be certain) that I am playing tit-for-tat. It also thinks that *perhaps* I am playing tit-for-tat "blindly," or with limited rationality, in the sense that I have failed to work out the logical implications of a finite time horizon as discussed above. My competitor thinks, for example, that perhaps I have not figured out that it will undercut me in the last month, so that I should also charge a low price in the last month, so that it should charge a low price in the next-to-last month, and so on. *"Perhaps,"* thinks my competitor, "Firm 1 will play tit-for-tat blindly, charging a high price as long as I charge a high price." Then (if the time horizon is long enough), it *is* rational for my competitor to maintain a high price until the last month (when it will undercut me).

Note that we have stressed the word "perhaps." My competitor need not be sure that I am playing tit-for-tat "blindly," or even that I am playing tit-for-tat at all. Just the *possibility* of this can make cooperative behavior a good strategy (until near the end) if the time horizon is long enough. Although my competitor's conjecture about how I am playing the game might be wrong, cooperative behavior is profitable *in expected value terms*. With a long time horizon, the sum of current and future profits, weighted by the probability that the conjecture is correct, can exceed the sum of profits from warfare, even if the competitor is the first to undercut.[11]

Most managers don't know how long they and their firms will be competing with their rivals, and this also serves to make cooperative behavior a good strategy. Although the number of months that the firms compete is probably finite, managers are unlikely to know just what that number is. As a result, the unravelling argument that begins with a clear expectation of undercutting in the last month no longer applies. As with an infinitely repeated game, it will be rational to play tit-for-tat.

Thus, in a repeated game, the Prisoners' Dilemma can have a cooperative outcome. In most markets the game is, in fact, repeated over a long and uncertain length of time, and managers have doubts about how "perfectly rationally" they and their competitors operate. As a result, in some industries, particularly those in which only a few firms compete over a long period under stable demand and cost conditions, cooperation prevails, even though no contractual arrangements are made. (The water meter industry, discussed below, is an example of this.) In many other industries, however, there is little or no cooperative behavior.

Sometimes cooperation breaks down or never begins because there are too many firms. More often, the failure to cooperate is the result of rapidly shifting demand or cost conditions. Uncertainties about demand or costs make it difficult for the firms in the industry to reach an implicit understanding of what cooperation should entail. (Remember that an *explicit* understanding, arrived at through meetings and discussions, could lead to an antitrust conviction.) Suppose, for example, that cost differences or different beliefs about demand lead one firm to conclude that cooperation means charging $50, but lead a

---

[11] After all, if I am wrong and my competitor charges a low price, I can shift my strategy at the cost of only one period's profit, a minor cost in light of the substantial profit that I can make if we both choose to set a high price. These results on the repeated Prisoners' Dilemma were first developed by David Kreps, Paul Milgrom, John Roberts, and Robert Wilson, "Rational Cooperation in the Finitely Repeated Prisoners' Dilemma," *Journal of Economic Theory* 27 (1982): 245–252.

second firm to think it means charging $40. If the second firm charges $40, the first firm might view that as a grab for market share and respond in tit-for-tat fashion with a $35 price. A price war could then develop.

EXAMPLE 13.2 OLIGOPOLISTIC COOPERATION IN THE WATER METER INDUSTRY

For more than 30 years, almost all the water meters sold in the United States have been produced by four American companies: Rockwell International, Badger Meter, Neptune Water Meter Company, and Hersey Products. Rockwell has had about a 35 percent share of the market, and the other three firms have together had about a 50 to 55 percent share.[12]

Most buyers of water meters are municipal water utilities, who install the meters in residential and commercial establishments so that they can measure water consumption and bill consumers accordingly. Since the cost of the water meters is a small part of the total cost of providing water, the utilities are concerned mainly that the meters be accurate and reliable. The price of the meters is thus not a primary issue, and demand is very price inelastic. Demand is also very stable; every residence or commercial establishment must have a water meter, so demand grows slowly along with the population.

In addition, utilities tend to have long-standing relationships with suppliers and are reluctant to shift from one supplier to another. This creates a barrier to entry because any new entrant will find it difficult to lure customers from existing firms. Substantial economies of scale create a second barrier to entry: To capture a significant share of the market, a new entrant would have to invest in a large factory. This virtually precludes entry by new firms.

With inelastic and stable demand and little threat of entry by new firms, the existing four firms could earn substantial monopoly profits if they set prices cooperatively. If, on the other hand, they compete aggressively, with each firm cutting price to try and increase its own share of the market, profits would fall to nearly competitive levels. The firms are thus in a Prisoners' Dilemma. Can cooperation prevail?

It can and *has* prevailed since the 1960s. Remember that the same four firms have been playing a *repeated game* for decades. Demand has been stable and predictable, and over the years the firms have been able to assess their own and each other's costs. In this situation, tit-for-tat strategies work well; it pays each firm to cooperate, as long as its competitors are cooperating.

So, the firms operate as though they were members of a country club. There is rarely an attempt to undercut price, and each firm appears satisfied with its share of the market. And while the business may appear dull, it is certainly profitable. All four firms have been earning returns on their investments that far exceed those in more competitive industries.

[12] This example is based in part on Nancy Taubenslag, "Rockwell International," Harvard Business School Case No. 9–383–019, July 1983.

In March 1983, American Airlines, whose president, Robert Crandall, had become notable for his use of the telephone (see Example 10.4), proposed that all airlines adopt a uniform fare schedule based on mileage. The rate per mile would depend on the length of the trip, with the lowest rate of 15 cents per mile for trips over 2,500 miles, higher rates for shorter trips, and the highest rate, 53 cents per mile, for trips under 250 miles. For example, a one-way coach ticket from Boston to Chicago, a distance of 932 miles, would cost $233 (based on a rate of 25 cents per mile for trips between 751 and 1,000 miles).

This proposal would do away with the many different fares (some heavily discounted) then available. The cost of a ticket from one city to another would depend only on the number of miles between those cities. As a senior vice-president of American Airlines said, "The new streamlined fare structure will help reduce fare confusion." Most other major airlines reacted favorably to the plan and began to adopt it. A vice-president of TWA said, "It's a good move. It's very businesslike." United Airlines quickly announced that it would adopt the plan on routes where it competes with American, which includes most of its system, and TWA and Continental said that they would adopt it for all of their routes.[13]

Why did American Airlines propose this fare structure, and what made it so attractive to the other airlines? Was it really to "help reduce fare confusion"? No, the aim was to reduce price competition and achieve a collusive pricing arrangement. Prices had been driven down by competitive undercutting, as airlines competed for market share. And as Robert Crandall had learned less than a year earlier, fixing prices over the telephone is illegal. Instead, the companies would implicitly fix prices by agreeing to use the same formula for fares.

The plan failed, a victim of the Prisoners' Dilemma. Only two weeks after the plan was announced and adopted by most airlines, Pan Am, which was dissatisfied with its small share of the U.S. market, dropped its fares. American, United, and TWA, afraid of losing their own shares of the market, quickly dropped their fares to match Pan Am. The price-cutting continued, and fortunately for consumers, the plan was soon dead.

This episode exemplifies the problem of oligopolistic pricing. One economist summarized it accurately: "You can't blame American Airlines for trying. After all, it is the American Way to try to cartelize prices with a simple formula. But it is also in the great tradition of open competition in this country to frustrate any such establishment of cartel prices by competitive chiseling."[14]

American Airlines introduced another simplified, four-tier fare structure in April 1992, which was quickly adopted by most major carriers. But it, too, soon

[13] "American to Base Fares on Mileage," *New York Times*, March 15, 1983; "Most Big Airlines Back American's Fare Plan," *New York Times*, March 17, 1983.

[14] Paul W. MacAvoy, "A Plan That Won't Endure Competition," *New York Times*, April 3, 1983.

fell victim to competitive discounts. In May 1992, Northwest Airlines announced a "kids fly free" program, and American responded with a summer half-price sale, which other carriers matched. As a result, the airline industry lost billions of dollars in 1992.

13.5 *Sequential Games*

In most of the games we have discussed so far, both players move at the same time. For example, in the Cournot model of duopoly, both firms set output at the same time. In *sequential games*, the players move in turn. The Stackelberg model discussed in Chapter 12 is an example of a sequential game; one firm sets output before the other does. There are many other examples: an advertising decision by one firm and the response by its competitor, entry-deterring investment by an incumbent firm and the decision whether to enter the market by a potential competitor, or a new government regulatory policy and the investment and output response of the firms being regulated.

We will look at a variety of sequential games in the remainder of this chapter. As we will see, they are often easier to analyze than games in which the players move at the same time. In a sequential game, the key is to think through the possible actions and rational reactions of each player.

As a simple example, let's return to the product choice problem first discussed in Section 13.3. This involves two companies who face a market in which two new variations of breakfast cereal can be successfully introduced, as long as each firm introduces only one variation. This time, let's change the payoff matrix slightly. As Table 13.9 shows, the new sweet cereal will inevitably be a better seller than the new crispy cereal, earning a profit of 20 rather than 10 (perhaps because consumers prefer sweet things to crispy things). Both the new cereals will still be profitable, however, as long as each is introduced by only one firm. (Compare Table 13.9 with Table 13.3.)

		Firm 2 Crispy	Firm 2 Sweet
Firm 1	Crispy	−5, −5	10, 20
	Sweet	20, 10	−5, −5

Suppose that both firms, in ignorance of each other's intentions, must announce their decisions independently and simultaneously. Both will then probably introduce the sweet cereal—and both will lose money.

Now suppose that Firm 1 can introduce its new cereal first. (Perhaps it can gear up its production faster.) We now have a sequential game: Firm 1 introduces a new cereal, and then Firm 2 introduces one. What will be the outcome of this game? When making its decision, Firm 1 must consider the rational response of its competitor. It knows that whichever cereal it introduces, Firm 2 will introduce the other kind. Hence it will introduce the sweet cereal, knowing that Firm 2 will respond by introducing the crispy one.

The Extensive Form of a Game

This outcome can be deduced from the payoff matrix in Table 13.9, but sometimes sequential games are easier to visualize if we represent the possible moves in the form of a decision tree. This is called the *extensive form* of the game, and is shown in Figure 13.1. The figure shows the possible choices of Firm 1 (introduce a crispy or a sweet cereal), and then the possible responses of Firm 2 for each of those choices. The resulting payoffs are given at the end of each branch. For example, if Firm 1 produces a crispy cereal and Firm 2 responds by also producing a crispy cereal, each firm will have a payoff of −5.

To find the solution to the extensive form game, work backwards from the end. For Firm 1, the best sequence of moves is the one in which it earns 20, and Firm 2 earns 10. Thus, it can deduce that it should produce the sweet cereal, because then Firm 2's best response is to produce the crispy cereal.

The Advantage of Moving First

In this product-choice game, there is a clear advantage to moving first; by introducing the sweet cereal, Firm 1 creates a fait accompli that leaves Firm 2

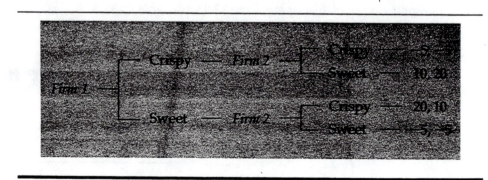

FIGURE 13.1   Product Choice Game in Extensive Form.

little choice but to introduce the crispy one. This is much like the first-mover advantage that we saw in the Stackelberg model in Chapter 12. In that model the firm that moves first can choose a large level of output, thereby giving its competitor little choice but to choose a small level of output.

To clarify the nature of this first-mover advantage, it would be useful to review the Stackelberg model and compare it to the Cournot model in which both firms choose their outputs simultaneously. As in Chapter 12, we will use the example in which two duopolists face the market demand curve:

$$P = 30 - Q$$

where Q is total production, i.e., $Q = Q_1 + Q_2$. We will also assume, as before, that both firms have zero marginal cost. Recall that the Cournot equilibrium is then $Q_1 = Q_2 = 10$, so that $P = 10$, and each firm earns a profit of 100. Recall also that if the two firms colluded, they would set $Q_1 = Q_2 = 7.5$, so that $P = 15$, and each firm earns a profit of 112.50. Finally, recall from Section 12.3 that in the Stackelberg model in which Firm 1 moves first, the outcome is $Q_1 = 15$ and $Q_2 = 7.5$, so that $P = 7.50$, and the firms' profits are 112.50 and 56.25, respectively.

These and a few other possible outcomes are summarized in the payoff matrix of Table 13.10. If both firms move simultaneously, the only solution to the game is that both firms produce 10 and earn 100. In this Cournot equilibrium each firm is doing the best it can given what its competitor is doing. If Firm 1 moves first, however, it knows its decision will constrain Firm 2's choice. Observe from the payoff matrix that if Firm 1 sets $Q_1 = 7.5$, Firm 2's best response will be to set $Q_2 = 10$, which will give Firm 1 a profit of 93.75 and Firm 2 a profit of 125. If Firm 1 sets $Q_1 = 10$. Firm 2 will set $Q_2 = 10$, and both firms will earn 100. But if Firm 1 sets $Q_1 = 15$, Firm 2 will set $Q_2 = 7.5$, so that Firm 1 earns 112.50, and Firm 2 earns 56.25. Thus, the most Firm 1 can earn is 112.50, and it does this by setting $Q_1 = 15$. Compared to the Cournot outcome, when Firm 1 moves first, it does better— and Firm 2 does much worse.

TABLE 13.10   Choosing Output

		Firm 2		
		7.5	10	15
	7.5	112.50, 112.50	93.75, 125	56.25, 112.50
Firm 1	10	125, 93.75	100, 100	50, 75
	15	112.50, 56.25	75, 50	0, 0

13.6 *Threats, Commitments, and Credibility*

The product choice problem and the Stackelberg model are two examples of how a firm that moves first can create a fait accompli that gives it an advantage over its competitor. In this section we'll take a broader look at the advantage a firm can have by moving first, and also consider what determines *which* firm goes first. We will focus on the following question: *What actions can a firm take to gain advantage in the marketplace?* For example, how might a firm deter entry by potential competitors, or induce existing competitors to raise prices, reduce output, or leave the market altogether? Or how might a firm reach an implicit agreement with its competitors that is heavily weighted in its own favor?

An action that gives a firm this kind of advantage is called a *strategic move*. A good definition of a strategic move was given by Thomas Schelling, who first explained the concept and its implications: "A strategic move is one that influences the other person's choice in a manner favorable to one's self, by affecting the other person's expectations of how one's self will behave. One constrains the partner's choice by constraining one's own behavior."[15]

The idea of constraining your own behavior to gain an advantage may seem paradoxical, but we'll soon see that it is not. Let's consider a few examples.

First, let's return once more to the product-choice problem shown in Table 13.9. The firm that introduces its new breakfast cereal first will do best. *But which firm will introduce its cereal first?* Even if both firms require the same amount of time to gear up production, each has an incentive to *commit itself first to the sweet cereal.* The key word is "commit." If Firm 1 simply announces it will produce the sweet cereal, Firm 2 will have little reason to believe it. After all, Firm 2, knowing the incentives, can make the same announcement louder and more vociferously. Firm 1 must constrain its own behavior—Firm 2 must be convinced that Firm 1 has *no choice* but to produce the sweet cereal. Such an action by Firm 1 might include an expensive advertising campaign describing the new sweet cereal well before its introduction, thereby putting Firm 1's reputation on the line. Firm 1 might also sign a contract for the forward delivery of a large quantity of sugar (and make the contract public, or at least send a copy to Firm 2). The idea is for Firm 1 to *commit itself* to produce the sweet cereal. Commitment is a strategic move that will induce Firm 2 to make the decision Firm 1 wants it to make—to produce the crispy cereal.

Why can't Firm 1 simply *threaten* Firm 2, vowing to produce the sweet cereal even if Firm 2 does the same? Because Firm 2 has little reason to believe the threat and can make the same threat itself. A threat is useful only if it is credible. The following example should help make this clear.

---

[15] Thomas C. Schelling, *The Strategy of Conflict* (New York: Oxford University Press, 1960), p. 160. (1980 edition published by Harvard University Press.) For a general discussion of strategic moves in business planning, see Michael E. Porter, *Competitive Strategy* (New York: Free Press, 1980).

		Firm 2	
		High Price	Low Price
Firm 1	High Price	100, 80	80, 100
	Low Price	20, 0	10, 20

Empty Threats

Suppose Firm 1 produces personal computers that can be used both as word processors and to do other tasks. Firm 2 produces only dedicated word processors. As the payoff matrix in Table 13.11 shows, as long as Firm 1 charges a high price for its computers, both firms can make a good deal of money. Even if Firm 2 charges a low price for its word processors, many people will still buy Firm 1's computers (because they can do so many other things), although some will be induced by the price differential to buy the dedicated word processor instead. However, if Firm 1 charges a low price for its computers, Firm 2 will also have to charge a low price (or else make zero profit), and the profit of both firms will be significantly reduced.

Firm 1 would prefer the outcome in the upper left-hand corner of the matrix. For Firm 2, however, charging a low price is clearly a dominant strategy. Thus, the outcome in the upper right-hand corner will prevail (no matter which firm sets its price first).

Firm 1 would probably be viewed as the "dominant" firm in this industry because its pricing actions will have the greatest impact on overall industry profits. Then, can't Firm 1 induce Firm 2 to charge a high price by *threatening* to charge a low price itself if Firm 2 charges a low price? No, as the payoff matrix in Table 13.11 makes clear. *Whatever* Firm 2 does, Firm 1 will be much worse off if it charges a low price. As a result, its threat is not credible.

Commitment and Credibility

Sometimes firms can make a threat credible. To see how, consider the following example. Race Car Motors, Inc., produces cars, and Far Out Engines, Ltd., produces specialty car engines. Far Out Engines sells most of its engines to Race Car Motors, and a few to a limited outside market. Nonetheless, it depends heavily on Race Car Motors, and makes its production decisions in response to the production plans of Race Car Motors.

We thus have a sequential game in which Race Car Motors is the "leader." It will decide what kind of cars to build, and Far Out Engines will then decide

TABLE 13.12a Production Choice Problem

		Race Car Motors	
		Small Cars	Big Cars
Far Out Engines	Small Engines	3, 6	3, 0
	Big Engines	1, 1	8, 3

what kind of engines to produce. The payoff matrix in Table 13.12a shows the possible outcomes of this game. (Profits are in millions of dollars.) Observe that Race Car Motors will do best by deciding to produce small cars. It knows that in response to this, Far Out Engines will produce small engines, most of which Race Car Motors will then buy for its new cars. As a result, Far Out Engines will make $3 million, and Race Car Motors will earn $6 million.

Far Out Engines, however, would much prefer the outcome in the lower right-hand corner of the payoff matrix. If it could produce big engines, *and* Race Car Motors produced big cars and therefore bought the big engines, it would make $8 million. (Race Car Motors, however, would make only $3 million.) Can Far Out Engines induce Race Car Motors to produce big cars instead of small ones?

Suppose Far Out Engines *threatens* to produce big engines no matter what Race Car Motors does, and no other engine producer can easily satisfy the needs of Race Car Motors. If Race Car Motors believed this, it would produce big cars, since it would have trouble finding engines for its small cars, and would earn only $1 million instead of $3 million. But the threat is not credible. Once Race Car Motors announced its intentions to produce small cars, Far Out Engines would have no incentive to carry out its threat.

Far Out Engines can make its threat credible by visibly and irreversibly reducing some of *its own* payoffs in the matrix, so that its choices become constrained. In particular, Far Out Engines must reduce its profits from small engines (the payoffs in the top row of the matrix). It might do this by *shutting down or destroying some of its small engine production capacity*. This would result in the payoff matrix shown in Table 13.12b. Now Race Car Motors *knows* that

TABLE 13.12b Modified Production Choice Problem

		Race Car Motors	
		Small Cars	Big Cars
Far Out Engines	Small Engines	0, 6	0, 0
	Big Engines	1, 1	8, 3

whatever kind of car it produces, Far Out Engines will produce big engines. (If Race Car Motors produces the small cars, Far Out Engines will sell the big engines as best it can to other car producers, and will make only $1 million. But this is better than making no profits by producing small engines. Race Car Motors will also have to look elsewhere for its engines, so its profit will also be lower, at $1 million.) Now it is clearly in Race Car Motors' interest to produce the large cars. By making a strategic move that *seemingly puts itself at a disadvantage*, Far Out Engines has improved the outcome of the game.

Strategic commitments of this kind can be effective, but they are risky and depend heavily on the committing firm's having accurate knowledge of the payoff matrix and the industry. Suppose, for example, that Far Out Engines commits itself to producing big engines, but is surprised to find that another firm can produce small engines at a low cost. The commitment may then lead Far Out Engines to bankruptcy rather than to continued high profits.

Developing the right kind of *reputation* can also give one a strategic advantage. Again, consider Far Out Engines' desire to produce big engines for Race Car Motors' big cars. Suppose the managers of Far Out Engines develop a reputation for being irrational—perhaps downright crazy. They threaten to produce big engines no matter what Race Car Motors does. (Refer to Table 13.12a.) Now the threat might be credible without any further action; after all, you can't be sure that an irrational manager will always make a profit-maximizing decision. In gaming situations, the party that is known (or thought) to be a little crazy can have a significant advantage. The game of "chicken" (two cars careen toward each other, and the first driver to swerve to the side is the loser) is a dramatic example of this.

Developing a reputation can be an especially important strategy in a repeated game. A firm might find it advantageous to behave irrationally for several plays of the game. This might give it a reputation that will allow it to increase its long-run profits substantially.

EXAMPLE 13.4   WAL-MART STORES' PREEMPTIVE INVESTMENT STRATEGY

Wal-Mart Stores, Inc., is an enormously successful chain of discount retail stores started by Sam Walton in 1969.[16] Its success was unusual in the industry. During the 1960s and 1970s, rapid expansion by existing firms and the entry and expansion of new firms made discount retailing increasingly competitive. During the 1970s and 1980s, industrywide profits fell, and large discount chains—including such giants as King's, Korvette's, Mammoth Mart, W. T. Grant, and Woolco—went bankrupt. Wal-Mart Stores, however, kept on growing

---

[16] This example is based in part on information in Pankaj Ghemawat, "Wal-Mart Stores' Discount Operations," Harvard Business School, 1986.

TABLE 13.13   The Discount Store Preemption Game

		Company X	
		Enter	Don't Enter
Wal-Mart	Enter	−10, −10	20, 0
	Don't Enter	0, 20	0, 0

(from 153 stores in 1976 to 1009 in 1986) and became even more profitable. By the end of 1985, Sam Walton was one of the richest people in the United States.

How did Wal-Mart Stores succeed where others failed? The key is in Wal-Mart's expansion strategy. To charge less than ordinary department stores and small retail stores, discount stores rely on size, no frills, and high inventory turnover. Through the 1960s, the conventional wisdom held that a discount store could succeed only in a city with a population of 100,000 or more. Sam Walton disagreed and decided to open his stores in small Southwestern towns; by 1970 there were 30 Wal-Mart stores in small towns in Arkansas, Missouri, and Oklahoma. The stores succeeded because Wal-Mart had created 30 "local monopolies." Discount stores that had opened in larger towns and cities were competing with other discount stores, which drove prices and profit margins down. These small towns, however, had room for only one discount operation. Wal-Mart could undercut the nondiscount retailers but never had to worry that another discount store would open and compete with it.

By the mid-1970s, other discount chains realized that Wal-Mart had a profitable strategy: Open a store in a small town that could support only one discount store and enjoy a local monopoly. There are a lot of small towns in the United States, so the issue became who would get to each town first. Wal-Mart now found itself in a *preemption game* of the sort illustrated by the payoff matrix in Table 13.13. As the matrix shows, if Wal-Mart enters a town, but Company X doesn't, Wal-Mart would make 20, and Company X would make 0. Similarly, if Wal-Mart doesn't enter, but Company X does, Wal-Mart makes 0, and Company X makes 20. But if Wal-Mart and Company X *both* enter, *they will both lose 10.*

This game has two Nash equilibria—the lower left-hand corner and the upper right-hand corner. Which equilibrium results depends on *who moves first*. If Wal-Mart moves first, it can enter, knowing that the rational response of Company X will be not to enter, so that Wal-Mart will be assured of earning 20. *The trick is therefore to preempt*—to set up stores in other small towns quickly, before Company X (or Company Y or Z) can do so. That is exactly what Wal-Mart did. By 1986 it had 1009 stores in operation and was earning an annual profit of $450 million. And while other discount chains were going under, Wal-Mart continued to grow; by 1993 it had over 1800 stores and was earning an annual profit of over $1.5 billion.

13.7 *Entry Deterrence*

Barriers to entry, which are an important source of monopoly power and profits, sometimes arise naturally. For example, economies of scale, patents and licenses, or access to critical inputs can create entry barriers. However, firms themselves can sometimes deter entry by potential competitors.

To deter entry, *the incumbent firm must convince any potential competitor that entry will be unprofitable.* To see how this might be done, put yourself in the position of an incumbent monopolist facing a prospective entrant, Firm X. Suppose that to enter the industry, Firm X will have to pay a (sunk) cost of $40 million to build a plant. You, of course, would like to induce Firm X to stay out of the industry. If X stays out, you can continue to charge a high price and enjoy monopoly profits. As shown in the upper right-hand corner of the payoff matrix in Table 13.14a, you would then earn $100 million in profits.

If Firm X does enter the market, you must make a decision. You can be "accommodating," maintaining a high price in the hope that X will do the same. You will then earn only $50 million in profit because you will have to share the market. The new entrant X will earn a *net* profit of $10 million: $50 million less the $40 million cost of constructing a plant. (This outcome is shown in the upper left-hand corner of the payoff matrix.) Alternatively, you can increase your production capacity, produce more, and force price down. Increasing production capacity is costly, however, and lower prices will mean lower revenues. Warfare will therefore mean lower profits for both you and Firm X. As Table 13.14a shows, your profit will fall to $30 million, and Firm X will have a net loss of $10 million: the $30 million that it earns from sales less the $40 million for the cost of its plant.

If Firm X thinks you will be accommodating and maintain a high price after entry, it will find it profitable to enter and will do so. Suppose you threaten to expand output and fight a price war to keep X out. If X believed the threat, it would not enter the market because it would expect to lose $10 million. However, the threat is not credible. As Table 13.14a shows (and as the potential competitor knows), *once entry has occurred, it will be in your best interest to accommodate and maintain a high price.* Firm X's rational move is to enter the market; the outcome will be the upper left-hand corner of the matrix.

TABLE 13.14a   Entry Possibilities

| | | Potential Entrant | |
		Enter	Stay Out
Incumbent	High Price (Accommodation)	50, 10	100, 0
	Low Price (Warfare)	30, −10	40, 0

But what if you can make an irrevocable commitment that would alter your incentives once entry occurred—a commitment that would give you little choice but to charge a low price if entry occurred? In particular, suppose you invest *now*, rather than later, in the extra capacity needed to increase output and engage in competitive warfare should entry occur. We'll assume that this extra capacity will cost $30 million to build, maintain, and operate. Of course, if you later maintain a high price (whether or not X enters), this added cost will reduce your payoffs.

We now have a new payoff matrix, as shown in Table 13.14b. Now your threat to engage in competitive warfare if entry occurs is *completely credible*, as a result of your decision to invest in additional capacity. Because you have the additional capacity, you will do better in competitive warfare, if entry occurs, than you would by maintaining a high price. The potential competitor now knows that entry will result in warfare, so it is rational for it to stay out of the market. You can therefore maintain a high price, and earn a profit of $70 million, having deterred entry.[17]

Might an incumbent monopolist deter entry without making the costly move of installing additional production capacity? Earlier we saw that a reputation for irrationality can bestow a strategic advantage. Suppose the incumbent firm has such a reputation. Suppose also that with vicious price-cutting this firm has eventually driven out every entrant in the past, even though it incurred (rationally unwarranted) losses in doing so. Its threat might then indeed be credible. In this case the incumbent's irrationality suggests to the potential competitor that it might be better off staying away.

Of course, if the game described above were to be *indefinitely repeated*, then the incumbent might have a *rational* incentive to carry out the threat of warfare whenever entry actually occurs. The reason is that short-term losses from warfare might be outweighed by longer-term gains from preventing entry. Furthermore, the potential competitor, making the same calculations, might find the incumbent's threat of warfare credible and decide to stay out of the market. Now the incumbent relies on its reputation for being rational—and

TABLE 13.14b Entry Deterrence

| | | Potential Entrant | |
		Enter	Stay Out
Incumbent	High Price (Accommodation)	20, 10	70, 0
	Low Price (Warfare)	30, −10	40, 0

[17] This use of investment to deter entry is discussed in more detail in Jean Tirole, *The Theory of Industrial Organization* (Cambridge, Mass.: MIT Press, 1988), and Marvin B. Lieberman, "Strategies for Capacity Expansion," *Sloan Management Review* (Summer 1987): 19–27.

in particular for being far-sighted—to provide the credibility needed to deter entry. But whether this works depends on the time horizon and the relative gains and losses associated with accommodation and warfare.

We have seen that the attractiveness of entry depends largely on how incumbents can be expected to react. In general, incumbents cannot be expected to maintain output at the preentry level once entry has occurred. Eventually, incumbents may back off and reduce output, raising price to a new joint profit-maximizing level. Because potential entrants know this, incumbent firms must create a credible threat of warfare to deter entry. A reputation for irrationality can help do this. Indeed, this seems to be the basis for much of the entry-preventing behavior that goes on in actual markets. The potential entrant must consider that *rational* industry discipline can break down after entry occurs. By fostering an image of irrationality and belligerence, an incumbent firm might convince potential entrants that the risk of warfare is too high.[18]

Strategic Trade Policy and International Competition

We have seen how a preemptive investment can give a firm an advantage by creating a credible threat to potential competitors. In some situations a preemptive investment—subsidized or otherwise encouraged by the government—can give a *country* an advantage in international markets, and be an important instrument of trade policy.

Does this conflict with what you have learned about the benefits of free trade? In Chapter 9, for example, we saw how trade restrictions such as tariffs or quotas lead to deadweight losses. In Chapter 16 we go further and show how, in a general way, free trade between people (or between countries) is mutually beneficial. Given the virtues of free trade, how could government intervention in an international market ever be warranted? An emerging literature in international trade theory suggests that in certain situations a country can benefit by adopting policies that give its domestic industries a competitive advantage.[19]

To see how this might occur, consider an industry with substantial economies of scale, so that a few large firms can produce much more efficiently than

---

[18] There is an analogy here to *nuclear deterrence*. Consider the use of a nuclear threat to deter the former Soviet Union from invading Western Europe during the cold war. If they invaded, would the United States actually react with nuclear weapons, knowing that the Soviets would then respond in kind? It is not rational for the United States to react this way, so a nuclear threat might not seem credible. But this assumes that everyone is rational; there is a reason to fear an *irrational* response by the United States. Even if an irrational response is viewed as very improbable, it can be a deterrent, given the costliness of an error. The United States can thus gain by promoting the idea that it might act irrationally, or that events might get out of control once an invasion occurs. This is the "rationality of irrationality." See Thomas C. Schelling, *The Strategy of Conflict*.

[19] For a good overview of this literature, see Paul R. Krugman, "Is Free Trade Passé?" *Journal of Economic Perspectives* 1 (Fall 1987): 131–144; and Elhanan Helpman and Paul R. Krugman, *Trade Policy and Market Structure* (Cambridge, Mass.: MIT Press, 1989).

many small ones. Suppose that by granting subsidies or tax breaks, the government can encourage domestic firms to expand faster than they would otherwise. This might prevent firms in other countries from entering the world market, so that the domestic industry can enjoy higher prices and greater sales. Such a policy would work by creating a credible threat to potential entrants; large domestic firms, taking advantage of scale economies, would be able to satisfy world demand at a low price, so that if other firms entered price would be driven below the point at which they could make a profit.

For example, consider the international market for commercial aircraft. The development and production of a new line of aircraft are subject to substantial economies of scale; it wouldn't pay to develop a new aircraft unless a firm expected to sell many of them. Suppose that Boeing and Airbus (a European consortium that includes France, West Germany, Britain, and Spain) are each considering developing a new aircraft (as indeed they were in the late 1970s and early 1980s). The ultimate payoff to each firm depends in part on what the other firm does. Suppose it is only economical for one firm to produce the new aircraft. Then the payoffs might look like those in Table 13.15a.[20]

If Boeing has a head start in the development process, the outcome of the game is the upper right-hand corner of the payoff matrix. Boeing will produce a new aircraft, and Airbus, realizing that it would lose money if it did the same, will not. Boeing will then earn a profit of 100.

European governments, of course, would prefer that Airbus produce the new aircraft. Could they change the outcome of this game? Suppose they commit to subsidizing Airbus, and make this commitment before Boeing has committed itself to produce. If the European governments committed to pay a subsidy of 20 to Airbus if it produces the plane, *regardless of what Boeing does*, the payoff matrix would change to the one in Table 13.15b.

Now Airbus will make money from a new aircraft whether or not Boeing produces one. Hence, Boeing knows that even if it commits to producing, Airbus will produce as well, and Boeing will lose money. Thus, Boeing will decide not to produce, and the outcome will be the one in the lower left-hand corner. A subsidy of 20, then, changes the outcome from one in which

TABLE 13.15a   Development of a New Aircraft

		Airbus	
		Produce	Don't Produce
Boeing	Produce	−10, −10	100, 0
	Don't Produce	0, 100	0, 0

[20] This example is drawn from Paul Krugman, "Is Free Trade Passé?," *op. cit.*

TABLE 13.15b   Development of Aircraft After European Subsidy

		Airbus	
		Produce	Don't Produce
Boeing	Produce	−10, 10	100, 0
	Don't Produce	0, 120	0, 0

Airbus does not produce and earns 0 to one in which it does produce and earns 120. Of this, 100 is a transfer of profit from the United States to Europe. Thus, from the European point of view, subsidizing Airbus yields a high return.

European governments *did* commit to subsidizing Airbus, and during the 1980s, Airbus successfully introduced several new airplanes. The result, however, was not quite the one in our stylized example. Boeing also introduced new airplanes (the 757 and 767 models) that were extremely profitable. As commercial air travel grew, it became clear that both companies could profitably develop and sell a new generation of airplanes. Nonetheless, Boeing's market share would have been much larger without the European subsidies to Airbus. One study estimated that those subsidies totalled $25.9 billion during the 1980s, and found that Airbus would not have entered the market without them.[21]

The example of Boeing and Airbus shows how strategic trade policy can transfer profits from one country to another. The story, however, is not complete. A country that uses such a policy may provoke retaliation from its trading partners. If a trade war results, all countries could end up much worse off. The possibility of such an outcome must be considered before adopting a strategic trade policy.

EXAMPLE 13.5   DU PONT DETERS ENTRY IN THE TITANIUM DIOXIDE INDUSTRY

Titanium dioxide is a whitener used in paints, paper, and other products. In the early 1970s, Du Pont and National Lead each accounted for about a third of U.S. titanium dioxide sales; another seven firms produced the remainder. In 1972, Du Pont was weighing whether to expand its capacity. The industry was changing, and with the right strategy, those changes might enable Du Pont to capture more of the market and dominate the industry.[22]

---

[21] "Aid to Airbus Called Unfair in U.S. Study," *New York Times*, September 8, 1990.

[22] This example is based on Pankaj Ghemawat, "Capacity Expansion in the Titanium Dioxide Industry," *Journal of Industrial Economics* 33 (Dec. 1984): 145–163; and P. Ghemawat, "Du Pont in Titanium Dioxide," Harvard Business School, Case No. 9–385–140, June 1986.

Three factors had to be considered. First, although the future demand for titanium dioxide was uncertain, it was expected to grow substantially. Second, the government had announced that new environmental regulations would be imposed. And third, the prices of raw materials used to make titanium dioxide were rising. The new regulations and the higher input prices would have a major effect on production cost, and give Du Pont a cost advantage, both because its production technology was less sensitive to the change in input prices and because its plants were in areas that made disposal of corrosive wastes much less difficult than it would be for other producers. Because of these cost changes, Du Pont anticipated that National Lead and some of the other producers would have to shut down part of their capacity. Du Pont's competitors would in effect have to "reenter" the market by building new plants. Could Du Pont deter them from doing this?

In 1972, Du Pont's Executive Committee considered the following strategy: invest nearly $400 million in increased production capacity to try to capture 64 percent of the market by 1985. The production capacity that would be put on line would be much more than what was actually needed. The idea was to *deter Du Pont's competitors from investing*. Scale economies and movement down the learning curve would give Du Pont a cost advantage. This would make it hard for other firms to compete, and would make credible the implicit threat that Du Pont would fight in the future, rather than accommodate.

The strategy was sensible, and it seemed to work for a few years. By 1975, however, things began to go awry. First, demand grew much less than expected, so that there was excess capacity industrywide. Second, the environmental regulations were only weakly enforced, so that Du Pont's competitors did not have to shut down capacity as expected. And finally, Du Pont's strategy led to antitrust action by the Federal Trade Commission in 1978. (The FTC claimed that Du Pont was attempting to monopolize the market. Du Pont won the case, but the decline in demand made its victory moot.)

For more than a decade, the disposable diaper industry in the United States has been dominated by just two firms: Procter & Gamble, with an approximately 50–60 percent market share, and Kimberly-Clark, with another 30 percent.[23] How do these firms compete? And why haven't other firms been able to enter and take a significant share of this $4 billion per year market?

Even though there are only two major firms, competition is intense. The competition occurs mostly in the form of *cost-reducing innovation*. The key to success is to perfect the manufacturing process, so that a plant can manufac-

[23] Procter & Gamble makes Pampers, Ultra Pampers, and Luvs. Kimberly-Clark has only one major brand, Huggies.

ture diapers in high volume and at low cost. This is not as simple as it might seem. Packing cellulose fluff for absorbency, adding an elastic gatherer, and binding, folding, and packaging the diapers—at a rate of about 3000 diapers per minute and at a cost of about 6 to 8 cents per diaper—requires an innovative, carefully designed, and finely tuned process. Furthermore, small technological improvements in the manufacturing process can result in a significant competitive advantage. If a firm can shave its production cost even slightly, it can reduce price and capture market share. As a result, both firms are forced to spend heavily on research and development (R&D) in a race to reduce cost.[24]

The payoff matrix in Table 13.16 illustrates this. If both firms spend aggressively on R&D, they can expect to maintain their current market shares. P&G will then earn a profit of 40, and Kimberly (with a smaller market share) will earn 20. If neither firm spends money on R&D, their costs and prices would remain constant, and the money saved would become part of profits. P&G's profit would increase to 60, and Kimberly's to 40. However, if one firm continues to do R&D and the other doesn't, the innovating firm will eventually capture most of its competitor's market share. (For example, if Kimberly does R&D and P&G doesn't, P&G can expect to lose 20, while Kimberly's profit increases to 60.) The two firms are therefore in a Prisoners' Dilemma; spending money on R&D is a dominant strategy for each firm.

Why hasn't cooperative behavior evolved? After all, the two firms have been competing in this market for years, and the demand for diapers is fairly stable. For several reasons, a Prisoners' Dilemma involving R&D is particularly hard to resolve. First, it is difficult for a firm to monitor its competitor's R&D activities the way it can monitor price. Second, it can take several years to complete an R&D program that leads to a major product improvement. As a result, tit-for-tat strategies, in which both firms cooperate until one of them "cheats," are less likely to work. A firm may not find out that its competitor has been secretly doing R&D until the competitor announces a new and improved product, and by then it may be too late for the firm to gear up an R&D program of its own.

| | | Kimberly-Clark | |
		R&D	No R&D
P&G	R&D	40, 20	80, −20
	No R&D	−20, 60	60, 40

[24] See Michael E. Porter, "The Disposable Diaper Industry," Harvard Business School Case 9–380–175, July 1981; "Innovation Key to Diaper War," New York Times, Nov. 25, 1986; and "P&G Moves to Revamp Its Pampers," Wall Street Journal, August 9, 1989. P&G developed a superabsorbent chemical to replace the cellulose fluff, allowing for a thinner and lighter diaper.

The ongoing R&D expenditures by P&G and Kimberly-Clark also serve to deter entry. In addition to brand name recognition, these two firms have accumulated so much technological know-how and manufacturing proficiency that they would have a substantial cost advantage over any firm just entering the market. Besides building new factories, an entrant would have to spend a considerable amount on R&D to capture even a small share of the market. After it began producing, a new firm would have to continue to spend heavily on R&D to reduce its costs over time. Entry would be profitable only if P&G and Kimberly-Clark stop doing R&D, so that the entrant could catch up and eventually gain a cost advantage. But as we have seen, no rational firm would expect this to happen.[25]

13.8 *Bargaining Strategy*

In looking at the Prisoners' Dilemma and related problems, we have assumed that collusion was limited by an inability to make an enforceable agreement. Clearly, alternative outcomes are possible (and likely) if firms or individuals can make promises that can be enforced. The Prisoners' Dilemma illustrated by the pricing problem shown in Table 13.8 is a good example of this. If there were no antitrust laws and both firms could make an enforceable agreement about pricing, they would both charge a high price and make profits of 50. Here, the bargaining problem is simple.

Other bargaining situations are more complicated, however, and the outcome can depend on the ability of either side to make a strategic move that alters its relative bargaining position. For example, consider two firms that are each planning to introduce one of two products, which happen to be complementary goods. As the payoff matrix of Table 13.17 shows, Firm 1 has an

TABLE 13.17   Production Decision

| | | Firm 2 | |
		Produce A	Produce B
Firm 1	Produce A	40, 5	50, 50
	Produce B	60, 40	5, 45

---

[25] Example 15.3 in Chapter 15 examines in more detail the profitability of capital investment by a new entrant in the diaper market.

advantage in producing *A*, so that if both firms produce *A*, Firm 1 will be able to maintain a lower price and will make much higher profits. Similarly, Firm 2 has an advantage in producing product *B*. As should be clear from the payoff matrix, if the two firms could agree about who will produce what, the only rational outcome would be that in the upper right-hand corner. Firm 1 produces *A*, Firm 2 produces *B*, and both firms make profits of 50. Indeed, even *without cooperation* this outcome will result, whether Firm 1 or Firm 2 moves first or both firms move simultaneously. The reason is that producing *B* is a dominant strategy for Firm 2, so (*A*, *B*) is the only Nash equilibrium.

Firm 1 would, of course, prefer the outcome in the lower left-hand corner of the payoff matrix. But in the context of this limited set of decisions, it cannot achieve that outcome. Suppose, however, that Firms 1 and 2 are also bargaining over a second issue—whether to join a research consortium that a third firm is trying to form. Table 13.18 shows the payoff matrix for this decision problem. Clearly, the dominant strategy is for both firms to enter the consortium, thereby obtaining increased profits of 40.

Now suppose that Firm 1 *links the two bargaining problems* by announcing that it will join the consortium *only* if Firm 2 agrees to produce product *A*. (How can Firm 1 make this threat credible?) In this case it is indeed in Firm 2's interest to agree to produce *A* (with Firm 1 producing *B*), in return for Firm 1's participation in the consortium. This example illustrates how a strategic move can be used in bargaining, and why combining issues in a bargaining agenda can sometimes benefit one side at the other's expense.

Two people bargaining over the price of a house is another example of this. Suppose I, as a potential buyer, do not want to pay more than $200,000 for a house that is actually worth $250,000 to me. The seller is willing to part with the house at any price above $180,000 but would like to receive the highest price she can. If I am the only bidder for the house, how can I make the seller think I will walk away rather than pay more than $200,000?

I might declare that I will never, ever pay more than $200,000 for that house. But is such a promise credible? It is if the seller knows that I have a *strong reputation* for toughness and steadfastness and that I have never broken my word on a promise of this sort. But suppose I have no such reputation. Then the seller knows that I have every incentive to make the promise (making it costs nothing), but little incentive to keep it (since this will probably be our

		Firm 2	
		Work Alone	Enter Consortium
Firm 1	Work Alone	10, 10	10, 20
	Enter Consortium	20, 10	40, 40

TABLE 13.18   Decision to Join Consortium

only business transaction together). As a result, this promise by itself is not likely to improve my bargaining position.

The promise can work, however, if it is combined with a strategic move that gives it credibility. Such a strategic move must reduce my flexibility—limit my options—so that I have no choice but to keep the promise. A possible move would be to make an enforceable bet with a third party—for example, "If I pay more than $200,000 for that house, I'll pay you $60,000." Alternatively, if I am buying the house on behalf of my company, the company might insist on authorization by the Board of Directors for a price above $200,000, and announce that the board will not meet again for several months. In both cases, my promise becomes credible because I have destroyed my ability to break it. The result is less flexibility—and more bargaining power.

Summary

1. A game is cooperative if the players can communicate and arrange binding contracts; otherwise it is noncooperative. In either kind of game, the most important aspect of strategy design is understanding your opponent's position, and (if your opponent is rational) correctly deducing the likely response to your actions. Misjudging an opponent's position is a common mistake, as Example 13.1, "Acquiring a Company," illustrates.[26]

2. A Nash equilibrium is a set of strategies such that each player is doing the best it can, given the strategies of the other players. An equilibrium in dominant strategies is a special case of a Nash equilibrium; a dominant strategy is optimal no matter what the other players do. A Nash equilibrium relies on the rationality of each player. A maximin strategy is more conservative because it maximizes the minimum possible outcome.

3. Some games have no Nash equilibria in pure strategies, but have one or more equilibria in mixed strategies. A mixed strategy is one in which the player makes a random choice among two or more possible actions, based on a set of chosen probabilities.

4. Strategies that are not optimal for a one-shot game may be optimal for a repeated game. Depending on the number of repetitions, a "tit-for-tat" strategy, in which one plays cooperatively as long as one's competitor does the same, may be optimal for the repeated Prisoners' Dilemma.

5. In a sequential game, the players move in turn. In some cases, the player who moves first has an advantage. Players may then have an incentive to try to precommit themselves to particular actions before their competitors can do the same.

---

[26] Here is the solution to Company A's problem: *It should offer nothing for Company T's stock.* Remember that Company T will accept an offer only if it is greater than the per share value under current management. Suppose you offer $50. Thus, Company T will accept this offer only if the outcome of the exploration project results in a per share value under current management of $50 or less. Any values between $0 and $100 are equally likely. Therefore the *expected value* of Company T's stock, *given that it accepts the offer*, i.e., given that the outcome of the exploration project leads to a value less than $50, is $25, so that under the management of Company A the value would be (1.5)($25) = $37.5, which is less than $50. In fact, for any price P, if the offer is accepted, Company A can expect a value of only $(\frac{3}{4})P$.

6. An empty threat is a threat that one would have no incentive to carry out. If one's competitors are rational, empty threats are of no value. To make a threat credible, it is sometimes necessary to make a strategic move by constraining one's later behavior, so that there would be an incentive to carry out the threat.

7. To deter entry, an incumbent firm must convince any potential competitor that entry will be unprofitable. This may be done by investing, and thereby giving credibility to the threat that entry will be met by price warfare. Strategic trade policies by governments sometimes have this objective.

8. Bargaining situations are examples of cooperative games. As with noncooperative games, in bargaining one can sometimes gain a strategic advantage by limiting one's flexibility.

Questions for Review

1. What is the difference between a cooperative and a noncooperative game? Give an example of each.

2. What is a dominant strategy? Why is an equilibrium stable in dominant strategies?

3. Explain the meaning of a Nash equilibrium. How does it differ from an equilibrium in dominant strategies?

4. How does a Nash equilibrium differ from a game's maximin solution? In what situations is a maximin solution a more likely outcome than a Nash equilibrium?

5. What is a "tit-for-tat" strategy? Why is it a rational strategy for the infinitely repeated Prisoners' Dilemma?

6. Consider a game in which the Prisoners' Dilemma is repeated 10 times, and both players are rational and fully informed. Is a tit-for-tat strategy optimal in this case? Under what conditions would such a strategy be optimal?

7. Suppose you and your competitor are playing the pricing game shown in Table 13.8. Both of you must announce your prices at the same time. Might you improve your outcome by promising your competitor that you will announce a high price?

8. What is meant by "first-mover advantage"? Give an example of a gaming situation with a first-mover advantage.

9. What is a "strategic move"? How can the development of a certain kind of reputation be a strategic move?

10. Can the threat of a price war deter entry by potential competitors? What actions might a firm take to make this threat credible?

11. A strategic move limits one's flexibility and yet gives one an advantage. Why? How might a strategic move give one an advantage in bargaining?

Exercises

1. In many oligopolistic industries, the same firms compete over a long period of time, setting prices and observing each other's behavior repeatedly. Given that the number of repetitions is large, why don't collusive outcomes typically result?

2. Many industries are often plagued by overcapacity—firms simultaneously make major investments in capacity expansion, so that total capacity far exceeds demand. This happens in industries in which demand is highly volatile and unpredictable,

but also in industries in which demand is fairly stable. What factors lead to overcapacity? Explain each briefly.

3. Two computer firms, A and B, are planning to market network systems for office information management. Each firm can develop either a fast, high-quality system (H), or a slower, low-quality system (L). Market research indicates that the resulting profits to each firm for the alternative strategies are given by the following payoff matrix:

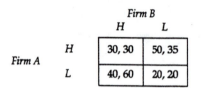

		Firm B	
		H	L
Firm A	H	30, 30	50, 35
	L	40, 60	20, 20

a. If both firms make their decisions at the same time and follow *maximin* (low-risk) strategies, what will the outcome be?
b. Suppose both firms try to maximize profits, but Firm A has a head start in planning, and can commit first. Now what will the outcome be? What will the outcome be if Firm B has the head start in planning and can commit first?
c. Getting a head start costs money (you have to gear up a large engineering team). Now consider the *two-stage* game in which *first*, each firm decides how much money to spend to speed up its planning, and *second*, it announces which product (H or L) it will produce. Which firm will spend more to speed up its planning? How much will it spend? Should the other firm spend *anything* to speed up its planning? Explain.

4. Two firms are in the chocolate market. Each can choose to go for the high end of the market (high quality) or the low end (low quality). Resulting profits are given by the following payoff matrix:

		Firm 2	
		Low	High
Firm 1	Low	−20, −30	900, 600
	High	100, 800	50, 50

a. What outcomes, if any, are Nash equilibria?
b. If the manager of each firm is conservative and each follows a maximin strategy, what will be the outcome?
c. What is the cooperative outcome?
d. Which firm benefits most from the cooperative outcome? How much would that firm need to offer the other to persuade it to collude?

5. Two major networks are competing for viewer ratings in the 8:00–9:00 P.M. and 9:00–10:00 P.M. slots on a given weeknight. Each has two shows to fill this time period and is juggling its lineup. Each can choose to put its "bigger" show first or to place it second in the 9:00–10:00 P.M. slot. The combination of decisions leads to the following "ratings points" results:

		Network 2	
		First	Second
Network 1	First	18, 18	23, 20
	Second	4, 23	16, 16

a. Find the Nash equilibria for this game, assuming that both networks make their decisions at the same time.
b. If each network is risk averse and uses a maximin strategy, what will be the resulting equilibrium?
c. What will be the equilibrium if Network 1 makes its selection first? If Network 2 goes first?
d. Suppose the network managers meet to coordinate schedules, and Network 1 promises to schedule its big show first. Is this promise credible, and what would be the likely outcome?

6. We can think of U.S. and Japanese trade policies as a Prisoners' Dilemma. The two countries are considering policies to open or close their import markets. Suppose the payoff matrix is:

		Japan	
		Open	Close
U.S.	Open	10, 10	5, 5
	Close	−100, 5	1, 1

a. Assume that each country knows the payoff matrix and believes that the other country will act in its own interest. Does either country have a dominant strategy? What will be the equilibrium policies if each country acts rationally to maximize its welfare?

b. Now assume that Japan is not certain that the U.S. will behave rationally. In particular, Japan is concerned that U.S. politicians may want to penalize Japan even if that does not maximize U.S. welfare. How might this affect Japan's choice of strategy? How might this change the equilibrium?

7. You are a duopolist producer of a homogeneous good. Both you and your competitor have *zero* marginal costs. The market demand curve is

$$P = 30 - Q$$

where $Q = Q_1 + Q_2$. Q_1 is your output, and Q_2 is your competitor's output. Your competitor has also read this book.

a. Suppose you are to play this game only once. If you and your competitor must announce your outputs at the same time, how much will you choose to produce? What do you expect your profit to be? Explain.

b. Suppose you are told that you must announce your output before your competitor does. How much will you produce in this case, and how much do you think your competitor will produce? What do you expect your profit to be? Is announcing first an advantage or a disadvantage? Explain briefly. *How much would you pay* to be given the option of announcing either first or second?

c. Suppose instead that you are to play the first round of a *series of ten rounds* (with the same competitor). In each round you and your competitor announce your outputs at the same time. You want to maximize the sum of your profits over the ten rounds. How much will you produce *in the first round*? How much would you expect to produce in the tenth round? The ninth round? Explain briefly.

d. Once again you will play a series of ten rounds. This time, however, in each round your competitor will announce its output before you announce yours. How will your answers to (c) change in this case?

*8. Defendo has decided to introduce a revolutionary video game, and as the first firm in the market, it will have a monopoly position for at least some time. In deciding what type of manufacturing plant to build, it has the choice of two technologies. Technology A is publicly available, and will result in annual costs of:

$$C^A(q) = 10 + 8q$$

Technology B is a proprietary technology developed in Defendo's research labs. It involves higher fixed cost of production, but lower marginal costs:

$$C^B(q) = 60 + 2q$$

Defendo's CEO must decide which technology to adopt. Market demand for the new product is $P = 20 - Q$, where Q is total industry output.

a. Suppose Defendo were certain that it would maintain its monopoly position in the market for the entire product lifespan (about five years) without threat of entry. Which technology would you advise the CEO to adopt? What would be Defendo's profit given this choice?

b. Suppose Defendo expects its archrival, Offendo, to consider entering the market shortly after Defendo introduces its new product. Offendo will have access only to Technology A. If Offendo does enter the market, the two firms will play a Cournot game (in quantities) and arrive at the Cournot–Nash equilibrium.

(i) If Defendo adopts Technology A and Offendo enters the market, what will be the profits of both firms? Would Offendo choose to enter the market given these profits?

(ii) If Defendo adopts Technology B and Offendo enters the market, what will be the profit of each firm? Would Offendo choose to enter the market given these profits?

(iii) Which technology would you advise the CEO of Defendo to adopt given the threat of possible entry? What will be Defendo's profit given this choice? What will be consumer surplus given this choice?

c. What happens to social welfare (the sum of consumer surplus and producer profit) as a result of the threat of entry in this market? What happens to equilibrium price? What might this imply about the role of *potential* competition in limiting market power?

9. Three contestants, A, B, and C, each have a balloon and a pistol. From fixed positions, they fire at

each other's balloon. When a balloon is hit, its owner is out. When only one balloon remains, its owner is the winner, and receives a $1000 prize. At the outset, the players decide by lot the order in which they will fire, and each player can choose any remaining balloon as his target. Everyone knows that A is the best shot and always hits the target, that B hits the target with probability .9, and that C hits the target with probability .8. Which contestant has the highest probability of winning the $1000? Explain why.

CHAPTER 17

Markets with Asymmetric Information

For most of this book, we have assumed that consumers and producers have complete information about the economic variables that are relevant for the choices they face. Now we will see what happens when some parties know more than others—i.e., when there is *asymmetric information.*

Asymmetric information is characteristic of many business situations. Frequently, a seller of a product knows more about its quality than the buyer does. Workers usually know their own skills and abilities better than employers. And business managers know more about their firm's costs, competitive position, and investment opportunities than do the owners of the firm.

Asymmetric information explains many institutional arrangements in our society. It is a reason why automobile companies offer warranties on parts and service for new cars; why firms and employees sign contracts that include incentives and rewards; and why the shareholders of corporations need to monitor the behavior of the firm's managers.

We begin by examining a situation in which the sellers of a product have better information about its quality than buyers have. We will see how this kind of asymmetric information can lead to market failure. In the second section, we see how sellers can avoid some of the problems associated with asymmetric information by giving potential buyers signals about the quality of their product. Product warranties provide a type of insurance that can be helpful when buyers have less information than sellers. But as the third section shows, the purchase of insurance entails difficulties of its own when buyers have better information than sellers.

In the fourth section, we show that managers may pursue goals other than profit maximization when it is costly for the owners of private corporations to monitor the managers' behavior. (In other words, managers have better information than owners.) We also show how firms can give managers an incentive to maximize profits even when monitoring their behavior is costly. Finally, we show that labor markets may operate inefficiently when employees have better information about their productivity than employers have.

17.1 *Quality Uncertainty and the Market for "Lemons"*

Suppose you bought a new car for $10,000, drove it 100 miles, and then decided you really didn't want it. There was nothing wrong with the car—it performed beautifully and met all your expectations. You simply felt that you could do just as well without it and would be better off saving the money for other things. So you decide to sell the car. How much should you expect to get for it? Probably not more than $8000—even though the car is brand new, has been driven only 100 miles, and has a warranty that is transferable to a new owner. And if you were a prospective buyer, you probably wouldn't pay much more than $8000 yourself.

Why does the mere fact that the car is second hand reduce its value so much? To answer this question, think about your own concerns as a prospective buyer. Why, you would wonder, is this car for sale? Did the owner really change his or her mind about the car just like that, or is there something wrong with it? Perhaps this car is a "lemon."

Used cars sell for much less than new cars because *there is asymmetric information about their quality*: The seller of a used car knows much more about the car than the prospective buyer does. The buyer can hire a mechanic to check the car, but the seller has had experience with it, and will know more about it. Furthermore, the very fact that the car is for sale indicates that it may be a "lemon"—why sell a reliable car? As a result, the prospective buyer of a used car will always be suspicious of its quality—and with good reason.

The implications of asymmetric information about product quality were first analyzed by George Akerlof in a classic paper.[1] Akerlof's analysis goes far beyond the market for used cars. The markets for insurance, financial credit, and even employment are also characterized by asymmetric quality information. To understand its implications, we will start with the market for used cars and then see how the same principles apply to other markets.

The Market for Used Cars

Suppose two kinds of used cars are available—high-quality cars and low-quality cars. Also, *suppose that both sellers and buyers can tell which kind of car is*

---

[1] George A. Akerlof, "The Market for 'Lemons': Quality Uncertainty and the Market Mechanism," *Quarterly Journal of Economics* (Aug. 1970): 488–500.

which. There will then be two markets, as illustrated in Figures 17.1a and 17.1b. In Figure 17.1a, S_H is the supply curve for high-quality cars, and D_H is the demand curve. Similarly, S_L and D_L in Figure 17.1b are the supply and demand curves for low-quality cars. Note that S_H is higher than S_L because owners of high-quality cars are more reluctant to part with them and must receive a higher price to do so. Similarly, D_H is higher than D_L because buyers are willing to pay more to get a high-quality car. As the figure shows, the market price for high-quality cars is $10,000, for low-quality cars $5000, and 50,000 cars of each type are sold.

In reality, the seller of a used car knows much more about its quality than a buyer does. Consider what happens, then, if sellers know the quality of cars, but buyers do not. (Buyers discover the quality only after they buy a car and drive it for a while.) Initially, buyers might think that the odds are 50-50 that a car they buy will be high quality. (The reason is that when both sellers *and* buyers knew the quality, 50,000 cars of each type were sold.) When making a

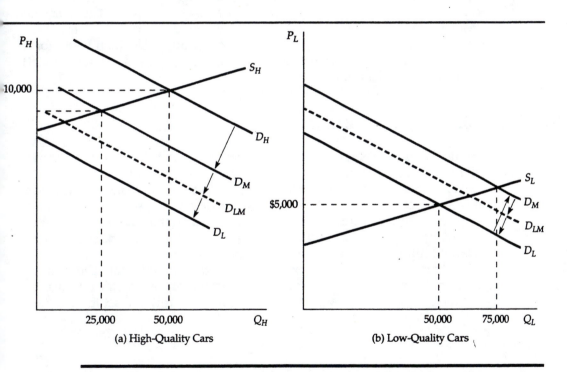

FIGURE 17.1 The Lemons Problem. When sellers of products have better information about product quality than buyers, a lemons market may develop in which low-quality goods drive out high-quality goods. In (a) the demand curve for high-quality cars shifts from D_H to D_M as buyers lower their expectations about the average quality of cars on the market. Likewise, in (b) the demand curve for low-quality cars shifts from D_L to D_M. As a result, the quantity of high-quality cars sold falls from 50,000 to 25,000, and the quantity of low-quality cars increases from 50,000 to 75,000. Eventually, only low-quality cars are sold.

purchase, buyers would therefore view all cars as being of "medium" quality. (Of course, after buying the car, they will learn its true quality.) The demand for medium-quality cars, denoted by D_M in Figure 17.1, is below D_H but above D_L. As the figure shows, *fewer high-quality cars (25,000) and more low-quality cars (75,000) will now be sold.*

As consumers begin to realize that most cars sold (about three-fourths of the total) are low quality, their demands shift. As Figure 17.1 shows, the new demand curve might be D_{LM}, which means that on average cars are of low to medium quality. However, the mix of cars then shifts even more heavily to low quality. As a result, the demand curve shifts further to the left, pushing the mix of cars even further to low quality. *This shifting continues until only low-quality cars are sold.* At that point the market price would be too low to bring forth any high-quality cars for sale, so consumers correctly assume that any car they buy will be low quality, and the demand curve will be D_L.

The situation in Figure 17.1 is extreme. The market may come into equilibrium at a price that brings forth at least some high-quality cars. *But the fraction of high-quality cars will be smaller than it would be if consumers could identify quality before making the purchase.* That is why I should expect to sell my brand new car, which *I know* is in perfect condition, for much less than I paid for it. Because of asymmetric information, low-quality goods drive high-quality goods out of the market.

Implications of Asymmetric Information

Our used cars example shows how asymmetric information can result in market failure. In an ideal world of fully functioning markets, consumers would be able to choose between low-quality and high-quality cars. Some would choose low-quality cars because they cost less, while others would prefer to pay more for high-quality cars. Unfortunately, consumers cannot in fact easily determine the quality of a used car until after they purchase it, so the price of used cars falls, and high-quality cars are driven out of the market.

Used cars are just a stylized example to illustrate an important problem that affects many markets. Let's look at other examples of asymmetric information, and then see how the government or private firms might react to it.

Insurance

Why do people over age 65 have difficulty buying medical insurance at almost any price? Older people do have a much higher risk of serious illness, but why doesn't the price of insurance rise to reflect that higher risk? The reason is asymmetric information. People who buy insurance know much more about their general health than any insurance company can hope to know, even if it insists on a medical examination. As a result, there is *adverse selection*, much as with used cars. Because unhealthy people are more likely to want insurance, the proportion of unhealthy people in the pool of insured people increases. This forces the price of insurance to rise, so that more healthy people, realizing their low risks, elect not to be insured. This further increases the proportion of unhealthy people, which forces the price of insurance up more, and so on, until nearly all people who want to buy insurance are unhealthy. At that point selling insurance becomes unprofitable.

Adverse selection can make the operation of insurance markets problematic in other ways. Suppose an insurance company wants to offer a policy for a particular event, such as an auto accident that results in property damage. It selects a target population—say, men under age 25—to whom it plans to market this policy, and it estimates the frequency of accidents within this group. For some of these people, the probability of being in an accident is low, much less than .01; for others it is high, much more than .01. If the insurance company cannot distinguish between high- and low-risk men, it will base the premium for all men on the average experience, i.e., an accident probability of .01. With better information some people (those with low probabilities of an accident) will choose not to insure, while others (those with high probabilities of an accident) will purchase the insurance. This in turn raises the accident probability of those who are insured above .01, forcing the insurance company to raise its premium. In the extreme, only those who are likely to suffer a loss will choose to insure, making it impractical to sell insurance.

These kinds of market failure create a role for government. For health insurance, it provides an argument in favor of Medicare or related forms of government health insurance for the elderly. By providing insurance for *all* people over age 65, the government eliminates the problem of adverse selection.[2]

The Market for Credit

By using a credit card, many of us borrow money without providing any collateral. Most credit cards allow the holder to run a debit of several thousand dollars, and many people hold several credit cards. Credit card companies earn money by charging interest on the debit balance. But how can a credit card company or bank distinguish high-quality borrowers (who pay their debts) from low-quality borrowers (who don't)? Clearly, borrowers know more about whether they will pay than the company does. Again, the "lemons" problem arises. Credit card companies and banks must charge the same interest rate to *all* borrowers, which attracts more low-quality borrowers, which forces the interest rate up, which increases the number of low-quality borrowers, which forces the interest rate up further, and so on.

In fact, credit card companies and banks *can*, to some extent, use computerized credit histories, which they often share with one another, to distinguish "low-quality" from "high-quality" borrowers. Many people think that com-

---

[2] The same general argument applies to all age groups. That is one reason that insurance companies avoid adverse selection by offering group health insurance policies at places of employment.

puterized credit histories are an invasion of privacy. Should companies be allowed to keep these credit histories and share them with other companies? We can't answer this question for you, but we can point out that credit histories perform an important function. They eliminate, or at least greatly reduce, the problem of asymmetric information and adverse selection, which might otherwise prevent credit markets from operating. Without these histories, even the creditworthy would find it extremely costly to borrow money.

The Importance of Reputation and Standardization

Asymmetric information is also present in many other markets. Here are just a few examples: *retail stores* (Will the store repair or allow you to return a defective product? The store knows more about its policy than you do.); *dealers of rare stamps, coins, books, and paintings* (Are the items real or counterfeit? The dealer knows much more about their authenticity than you do.); *roofers, plumbers, and electricians* (When a roofer repairs or renovates the roof of your house, do you climb up to check the quality of the work?); *restaurants* (How often do you go into the kitchen to check if the chef is using fresh ingredients and obeying the health laws?).

In all these cases, the seller knows much more about the quality of the product than the buyer does. Unless sellers can provide information about quality to buyers, low-quality goods and services will drive out high-quality ones, and there will be market failure. Sellers of high-quality goods and services, therefore, have a big incentive to convince consumers that their quality is indeed high. In the examples cited above, this is done largely by *reputation*. You shop at a particular store because it has a reputation for servicing its products; you hire a particular roofer and plumber because they have a reputation for doing good work; and you go to a particular restaurant because it has a reputation for using fresh ingredients, and nobody you know became sick after eating there.

Sometimes it is impossible for a business to develop a reputation. For example, most of the customers of a diner or a motel on a highway go there only once, or infrequently, while on a trip, so that the business has no opportunity to develop a reputation. How, then, can these diners and motels deal with the "lemons" problem? One way is by *standardization*. In your hometown, you may not prefer to eat regularly at McDonald's. But a McDonald's may look more attractive when you are driving along a highway and want to stop for lunch. The reason is that McDonald's provides a standardized product; the same ingredients are used and the same food is served in every McDonald's anywhere in the country. Who knows? Joe's Diner might serve better food, but you *know* exactly what you will be buying at McDonald's.

EXAMPLE 17.1   LEMONS IN MAJOR LEAGUE BASEBALL

How can we test for the presence of a lemons market? One way is to compare the performance of products that are resold with similar products that are seldom put up for resale. In a lemons market, purchasers of second-hand products will have limited information, and resold products should be lower in quality than products that rarely appear on the market. One such "second-hand" market has been created in recent years by a change in the rules governing contracts in major league baseball.[3]

Before 1976, major league baseball teams had the exclusive right to renew their players' contracts. After a 1976 ruling declared this system illegal, a new contracting arrangement was created. After six years of major league service, players can now sign new contracts with their original team or become free agents and sign with new teams. Having many free agents creates a second-hand market in baseball players. The original team can make an offer that will either retain a player or lose him to the free-agent market.

Asymmetric information is prominent in the free-agent market. One potential purchaser, the player's original team, has better information about the player's abilities than other teams have. If we were looking at used cars, we could test for the existence of asymmetric information by comparing their repair records. In baseball we can compare player disability records. If players are working hard and following rigorous conditioning programs, we would expect a low probability of injury and a high probability that they will be able to perform if injured. In other words, more motivated players will spend less time on the bench owing to disabilities. If a lemons market exists, we would expect free agents to have higher disability rates than players who are renewed. Players may also have preexisting physical conditions that their original teams know about that make them less desirable candidates for contract renewal. Because more such players would become free agents, free agents would experience higher disability rates for health reasons.

Table 17.1, which lists the postcontract performance of all players who have signed multiyear contracts, makes two points. First, both free agents and renewed players have increased disability rates after signing contracts. The disabled days per season increase from an average of 4.73 to an average of 12.55. Second, the postcontract disability rates of renewed and not-renewed players are significantly different. On average, renewed players are disabled 9.68 days, free agents 17.23 days.

TABLE 17.1   Player Disability

	Days Spent on Disabled List per Season		
	Precontract	Postcontract	Percent Change
All players	4.73	12.55	165.4
Renewed players	4.76	9.68	103.4
Free agents	4.67	17.23	268.9

[3] This example is based on Kenneth Lehn's study of the free-agent market. See "Information Asymmetries in Baseball's Free Agent Market," *Economic Inquiry* (1984): 37–44.

These two findings suggest a lemons market in free agents that exists because baseball teams know their own players better than the other teams with which they compete.

17.2 *Market Signaling*

We have seen that asymmetric information can sometimes lead to a "lemons problem": Because sellers know more about the quality of a good than buyers do, buyers may assume that quality is low, so that price falls, and only low-quality goods are sold. We also saw how government intervention (in the market for health insurance, for example) or the development of a reputation (in service industries, for example) can alleviate this problem. Now we will examine another important mechanism through which sellers and buyers deal with the problem of asymmetric information: *market signaling*. The concept of market signaling was first developed by Michael Spence, who showed that in some markets sellers send buyers *signals* that convey information about a product's quality.[4]

To see how market signaling works, let's look at a *labor market*, which is a good example of a market with asymmetric information. Suppose a firm is thinking about hiring some new people. The new workers (the "sellers" of labor) know much more about the quality of the labor they can provide than the firm (the buyer of labor). For example, they know how hard they tend to work, how responsible they are, what their skills are, and so forth. The firm will find these things out only after workers have been hired and have been working for some time. At the time they are hired, the firm knows little about how productive they will turn out to be.

Why don't firms simply hire workers, see how well they work, and then fire those with low productivity? Because this is often very costly. In many countries, and in many firms in the United States, it is difficult to fire someone who has been working more than a few months. (The firm may have to show just cause or pay severance pay.) Also, in many jobs workers do not become fully productive for at least six months. Before that time, considerable on-the-job training may be required, for which the firm must invest substantial resources. Thus the firm might not learn how good workers are for six months to a year. As a result, firms would be much better off if they knew how productive potential employees are *before* they hired them.

What characteristics can a firm examine to obtain information about people's productivity before it hires them? Can potential employees convey informa-

---

[4] See Michael Spence, *Market Signaling* (Cambridge, MA: Harvard University Press, 1974).

tion about their productivity? Dressing well for the job interview might convey some information, but even unproductive people sometimes dress well to get a job. Dressing well is thus a weak signal—it doesn't do much to distinguish high-productivity from low-productivity people. *To be strong, a signal must be easier for high-productivity people to give than for low-productivity people to give, so that high-productivity people are more likely to give it.*

For example, *education* is a strong signal in labor markets. A person's educational level can be measured by several things—the number of years of schooling, degrees obtained, the reputation of the university or college that granted the degrees, the person's grade point average, and so on. Of course, education can directly and indirectly improve a person's productivity by providing information, skills, and general knowledge that are helpful in work. But even if education did *not* improve one's productivity, it would still be a useful *signal* of productivity because more productive people will find it easier to attain a high level of education. (Productive people tend to be more intelligent, more motivated, and more energetic and hard-working—characteristics that are also helpful in school.) More productive people are therefore more likely to attain a high level of education *to signal their productivity to firms and thereby obtain better-paying jobs.* And firms are correct in considering education a signal of productivity.

A Simple Model of Job Market Signaling

To understand how signaling works, it will be useful to discuss a simple model.[5] Let's assume there are only low-productivity workers (Group I), whose average and marginal product is 1, and high-productivity workers (Group II), whose average and marginal product is 2. Workers will be employed by competitive firms whose products sell for $10,000, and who expect an average of 10 years of work from each employee. We also assume that half the workers in the population are in Group I and the other half in Group II, so that the *average* productivity of all workers is 1.5. Note that the revenue expected to be generated from Group I workers is $100,000 ($10,000/year × 10 years) and from Group II workers is $200,000 ($20,000/year × 10 years).

If firms could identify people by their productivity, they would offer them a wage equal to their marginal revenue product. Group I people would be paid $10,000 per year, Group II people $20,000. On the other hand, if firms could not identify people's productivity before they hired them, they would pay all workers an annual wage equal to the average productivity, $15,000. Group I people would then earn more ($15,000 instead of $10,000), at the expense of Group II people (who would earn $15,000 instead of $20,000).

Now let's consider what can happen with signaling via education. Suppose all the attributes of an education (degrees earned, grade point average, etc.)

---
[5] This is essentially the model developed in Spence, *Market Signaling*.

can be summarized by a single index y that represents years of higher education. All education involves a cost, and the higher the educational level y, the higher the cost. This cost includes tuition and books, the opportunity cost of foregone wages, and the psychic cost of having to work hard to obtain high grades. What is important is that *the cost of education is greater for the low-productivity group than for the high-productivity group.* We might expect this for two reasons. First, low-productivity workers may simply be less studious. Second, low-productivity workers may progress more slowly through degree programs in which they enroll. In particular, suppose that for Group I people the cost of attaining educational level y is given by

$$C_I(y) = \$40,000y$$

and for Group II people it is

$$C_{II}(y) = \$20,000y$$

Now suppose (to keep things simple and to dramatize the importance of signaling) that *education does nothing to increase one's productivity; its only value is as a signal.* Let's see if we can find a market equilibrium in which different people obtain different levels of education, and firms look at education as a signal of productivity.

Consider the following possible equilibrium. Suppose firms use this decision rule: *Anyone with an education level of y^* or more is a Group II person and is offered a wage of $20,000, and anyone with an education level below y^* is a Group I person and is offered a wage of $10,000.* The particular level y^* that the firms choose is arbitrary, but for this decision rule to be part of an equilibrium, firms must have identified people correctly, or else the firms will want to change the rule. Will this rule work?

To answer this, we must determine how much education the people in each group will obtain, *given that firms are using this decision rule.* To do this, remember that education allows one to get a better-paying job. The benefit of education $B(y)$ is the *increase* in the wage associated with each level of education, as shown in Figure 17.2. Observe that $B(y)$ is 0 initially, which represents the $100,000 base 10-year earnings that are earned without any college education. But when the education level reaches y^* or greater, $B(y)$ jumps to $100,000.

How much education should a person obtain? Clearly the choice is between *no* education (i.e., $y = 0$) and an education level of y^*. The reason is that any level of education less than y^* results in the same base earnings of $100,000, so there is no benefit from obtaining an education at a level above 0, but below y^*. Similarly, there is no benefit from obtaining an educational level above y^* because y^* is sufficient to allow one to enjoy the higher total earnings of $200,000.

In deciding how much education to obtain, people compare the benefit of education with the cost. People in each group make the following cost-benefit calculation: *Obtain the education level y^* if the benefit (i.e., the increase in earnings) is at least as large as the cost of this education.* For both groups, the ben-

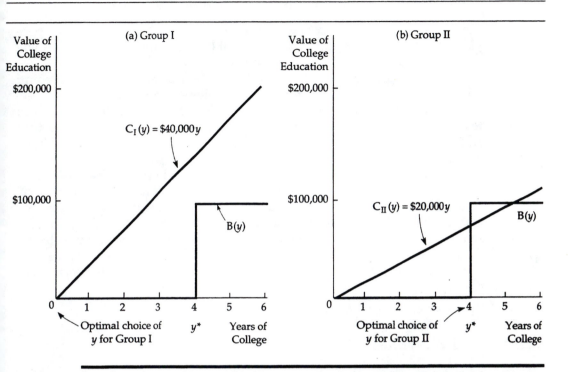

FIGURE 17.2 **Signaling.** Education can be a useful signal of the high productivity of a group of workers if education is easier to obtain for this group than for the low-productivity group. In (a) the low-productivity group will choose an education level of $y = 0$ because the cost of education is greater than the increased earnings. However, in (b), the high-productivity group will choose an education level of $y^* = 4$ because the gain in earnings is greater than the cost.

efit (the increase in earnings) is $100,000. The costs, however, differ for the two groups. For Group I, the cost is $40,000y$, but for Group II the cost is only $20,000y$. Therefore, Group I people will obtain *no* education as long as

$$\$100,000 < \$40,000y^* \text{ or } y^* > 2.5$$

and Group II people will obtain an education level y^* as long as

$$\$100,000 > \$20,000y^* \text{ or } y^* < 5$$

These results give us an equilibrium *as long as y^* is between 2.5 and 5.* Suppose, for example, that y^* is 4.0, as in Figure 17.2. Then people in Group I will find that education does not pay, and they will not obtain any, whereas people in Group II will find that education does pay, and they will obtain the level $y = 4.0$. Now, when a firm interviews job candidates who have no college education, it correctly assumes they have low productivity and offers them a wage of $10,000. Similarly, when the firm interviews people who have four years of college, it correctly assumes their productivity is high, and their wage should be $20,000. We therefore have an equilibrium; high-productivity people will obtain a college education to signal their productivity, and firms will read this signal and offer them a high wage.

This is a simple, highly stylized model, but it illustrates a significant point: Education can be an important signal that allows firms to sort workers according to productivity. Some workers (those with high productivity) will want to obtain a college education, *even if that education does nothing to increase their productivity*. These workers simply want to identify themselves as being highly productive, so they obtain the education to send a signal.

Of course, in the real world, education *does* provide useful knowledge and does increase one's ultimate productivity. (We wouldn't have written this book if we didn't believe that.) But education also serves a signaling function. For example, many firms insist that a prospective manager have an MBA. One reason for this is that MBAs learn economics, finance, and other useful subjects. But there is a second reason—to complete an MBA program takes intelligence, discipline, and hard work, and people with those qualities tend to be very productive.

Guarantees and Warranties

We have stressed the role of signaling in labor markets, but signaling can also play an important role in many other markets in which there is asymmetric information. Consider the markets for such durable goods as televisions, stereos, cameras, and refrigerators. Many firms produce these items, but some brands are more dependable than others. If consumers could not tell which brands tend to be more dependable, the better brands couldn't be sold for higher prices. Firms that produce a higher-quality, more dependable product would therefore like to make consumers aware of this, but how can they do it in a convincing way? The answer is through *guarantees and warranties*.

Guarantees and warranties effectively signal product quality because an extensive warranty is more costly for the producer of a low-quality item than for the producer of a high-quality item. (The low-quality item is more likely to require servicing under the warranty, which the producer will have to pay for.) As a result, in their own self-interest, producers of low-quality items will not offer an extensive warranty. Consumers can therefore correctly view an extensive warranty as a signal of high quality, and they will pay more for products that offer one.

17.3 *Moral Hazard*

When one party is fully insured and cannot be accurately monitored by an insurance company with limited information, its behavior may change *after* the insurance has been purchased. This is the problem of *moral hazard. Moral haz-*

ard occurs when the party to be insured can affect the probability or magnitude of the event that triggers payment. For example, if I have complete medical insurance coverage, I may visit the doctor more often than I would if my coverage were limited. If the insurance provider can monitor its insurees' behavior, it can charge higher fees for those who make more claims. But if the company cannot monitor behavior, it may find its payments to be larger than expected. With moral hazard, insurance companies may be forced to increase their premiums or even to refuse to sell insurance at all.

Consider, for example, the decisions faced by the owners of a warehouse worth $100,000 and by their insurance company. Suppose that if the owners run a $50 fire prevention program for their employees, the probability of a fire is .005. Without this program, the probability of a fire increases to .01. Knowing this, the insurance company faces a dilemma if it cannot monitor whether there will be a fire prevention program. The policy that the insurance company offers cannot include a clause stating that payments will be made only if there is a fire prevention program. If the program were in place, the company could insure the warehouse for a premium equal to the expected loss from a fire, which is $500 (.005 × $100,000). Once the insurance policy is purchased, however, the owners no longer have an incentive to run the program. If there is a fire, they will be fully compensated for their financial loss. Thus, if the insurance company sells a policy for $500, it will incur losses because the expected loss from fire will be $1000 (.01 × $100,000).

Moral hazard is not only a problem for insurance companies. It also alters the ability of markets to allocate resources efficiently. In Figure 17.3, for example, *D* gives the demand for automobile driving in miles per week. The

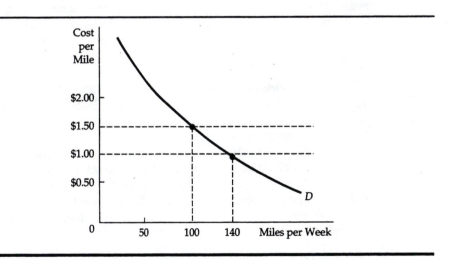

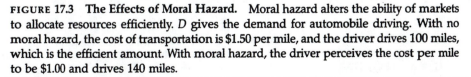

FIGURE 17.3   **The Effects of Moral Hazard.**   Moral hazard alters the ability of markets to allocate resources efficiently. *D* gives the demand for automobile driving. With no moral hazard, the cost of transportation is $1.50 per mile, and the driver drives 100 miles, which is the efficient amount. With moral hazard, the driver perceives the cost per mile to be $1.00 and drives 140 miles.

demand curve is downward sloping because some people switch to alternative transportation as the cost of driving increases. Suppose initially that the cost of driving includes the insurance cost, and that insurance companies can accurately measure miles driven. In this case, there is no moral hazard. Drivers know that more driving will increase their insurance premium and hence increase their total cost of driving (the cost per mile is assumed to be constant). For example, if the cost of driving is $1.50 per mile (50 cents of which is insurance cost), the driver will go 100 miles per week.

A moral hazard problem arises because it is difficult for insurance companies to monitor individual driving habits; the insurance premium does not depend on miles driven. As a result, drivers assume that any additional accident costs that they incur will be spread over a large group, with only a negligible portion accruing to each of them individually. Since their insurance premium does not vary with the number of miles that they drive, an additional mile of transportation will cost $1.00, rather than $1.50. The number of miles driven will increase from 100 to the socially inefficient level of 140.

EXAMPLE 17.2   REDUCING MORAL HAZARD—WARRANTIES OF ANIMAL HEALTH

For buyers of livestock, information about the animals' health is very important.[6] Unhealthy animals gain weight more slowly than healthy animals, and are less likely to reproduce. Because of asymmetric information in the livestock market (sellers know the health of an animal better than buyers do), most states require warranties on the sale of livestock. Under these laws sellers promise (warrant) that their animals are free from hidden diseases and are responsible for all costs arising from any diseased animals.

Although warranties solve the problem of the seller's having better information than the buyer, they also create a form of moral hazard. Guaranteeing reimbursement to the buyer for all costs associated with diseased animals means that insurance rates are not tied to the level of care that buyers or their agents take to protect their livestock against disease. As a result of these warranties, livestock buyers tend to avoid early diagnosis of diseased livestock, and losses increase.

In response to the moral hazard problem, half the states have modified their animal warranty laws by requiring sellers to tell buyers whether livestock are diseased at the time of sale. Some states also require sellers to comply with state and federal animal health regulations, thereby reducing disease. Beyond this, however, warranties that animals are free from hidden disease must be an explicit written or oral guarantee to buyers.

---

[6] This example is based on Terence J. Centner and Michael E. Wetzstein, "Reducing Moral Hazard Associated with Implied Warranties of Animal Health," *American Journal of Agricultural Economics* 69 (1987): 143–150.

EXAMPLE 17.3   CRISIS IN THE SAVINGS AND LOAN INDUSTRY

In 1934, during the Great Depression, the U.S. government introduced a broad-based system of financial insurance. The Federal Deposit Insurance Corporation provided insurance for deposits at commercial banks, and the Federal Savings and Loan Insurance Corporation did the same (up to $100,000 per account) for deposits at savings and loans. These insurance programs created the seeds of moral hazard on the part of depositors, since a depositor could lend money to any financial institution, no matter how risky that institution's loans, without bearing any risk.

Later, depositor moral hazard was coupled with moral hazard by owners of savings and loans. Beginning in 1982, new participants in the business found that they could attract large sums of government-insured capital and invest the money virtually without restriction in highly speculative investments. Because the deposits were insured, they had little incentive to evaluate the risks involved.

Essentially, deposit insurance enabled savings and loans to make riskier loans on a larger scale than they would otherwise. The adverse incentives created by moral hazard coupled with the collapse of the real estate boom in the sun belt and energy-producing states led to the failure of many savings and loans.

In 1990 the cost of bailing out depositors whose money was lost when over 1000 savings and loans failed was estimated conservatively to be over $200 billion.[7] The biggest losses were in Texas, where over $42 billion had been spent by October 1990. The total outlays by the agencies responsible for deposit insurance were nearly $100 billion just through 1990.

While the prospects for the future are not bright, there are some hopeful signs. Aware of the adverse incentives that were created by moral hazard, the government has modified its insurance system. Today, the Federal Deposit Insurance Corporation regulates the savings and loan and banking industries, and savings and loans now face stiff capital requirements that force managers to bear a stake in the outcome of their investment policies. With a good deal of their own money at risk, managers are less inclined to invest speculatively.

A number of additional reforms could help to remove the moral hazard problem on the part of depositors and savings and loan owners. Proposals that would affect depositors include (i) lowering the amount of insurance coverage; (ii) making the maximum coverage apply to each individual, no matter how many accounts that individual has; and (iii) allowing for coinsurance, whereby the deposit insurance reimburses losses on less than a dollar-for-dollar basis. Proposals directed towards owners include (i) charging savings and loans insurance premiums that are based on the riskiness of the savings and loan portfolio—the greater the risk, the higher the premium; and (ii) restricting the investment opportunities available to savings and loan owners.

---

[7] *American Banker*, October 9, 1990.

17.4 *The Principal–Agent Problem*

If monitoring the productivity of workers were costless, the owners of a business could ensure that their managers and workers were working effectively. In most firms, however, owners can't monitor everything that employees do—employees are better informed than owners. This information asymmetry creates a *principal–agent* problem.

An *agency relationship* exists whenever there is an employment arrangement in which one person's welfare depends on what another person does.[8] The *agent* is the person who acts, and the *principal* is the party whom the action affects. In our example, the manager and the workers are agents, and the owner is the principal. *The principal–agent problem is that managers may pursue their own goals, even at the cost of obtaining lower profits for owners.*

Agency relationships are widespread in our society. For example, doctors serve as agents for hospitals, and as such, may select patients and do procedures consistent with their personal preferences, but not necessarily with the objectives of the hospital. Similarly, managers of housing properties may not maintain the property the way that the owners would like.

How does incomplete information and costly monitoring affect how agents act? And what mechanisms can give managers the incentive to operate in the owner's interest? These questions are central to any principal–agent analysis. In this section we study the principal–agent problem from several perspectives. First, we look at the owner–manager problem within private and public enterprises. Second, we discuss how owners can use contractual relationships with their employees to deal with the principal–agent problems.

The Principal–Agent Problem in Private Enterprises

An individual family or financial institution owns more than 10 percent of the shares of only 16 of the 100 largest industrial corporations.[9] Clearly, most large firms are controlled by management. The fact that most stockholders have only a small percentage of the firm's total equity makes it difficult for them to obtain information about how well the firm's managers are performing. One function of owners (or their representatives) is to monitor the behavior of man-

---

[8] For more discussion of agency costs, see Richard Jensen and William Meckling, "Theory of the Firm: Managerial Behavior, Agency Costs, and Ownership Structure," *Journal of Financial Economics* 11 (1976): 305–360; and Eugene Fama, "Agency Problems and the Theory of the Firm," *Journal of Political Economy* 88 (1980): 288–307. See also Oliver Williamson, *The Economic Institutions of Capitalism* (New York: Free Press, 1985).

[9] See Merritt B. Fox, *Finance and Industrial Performance in a Dynamic Economy* (New York: Columbia University Press, 1987).

agers. But monitoring is costly, and information is expensive to gather and use, especially for an individual.[10]

Managers of private enterprises can thus pursue their own objectives. But what are these objectives? One view is that managers are more concerned with growth than with profit per se; more rapid growth and larger market share provide more cash flow, which in turn allows managers to enjoy more perks. Another view deemphasizes growth but does emphasize the utility that managers get from their jobs, not only from profit but also from the respect of their peers, the power to control the corporation, the fringe benefits and other perks, and a long tenure on the job.

However, there are important limitations to managers' ability to deviate from the objectives of owners. First, stockholders can complain loudly when they feel that managers are behaving improperly, and in exceptional cases they can oust the current management (perhaps with the help of the board of directors of the corporation, whose job it is to monitor managerial behavior). Second, a vigorous market for corporate control can develop. If a takeover bid becomes more likely when the firm is poorly managed, managers will have a strong incentive to pursue the goal of profit maximization. Third, there can be a highly developed market for managers. If managers who maximize profit are in great demand, they will earn high wages, which in turn will give other managers an incentive to pursue the same goal.

Unfortunately, the means by which stockholders control managers' behavior are limited and imperfect. Corporate takeovers may be motivated by personal and economic power, for example, instead of economic efficiency. The managers' labor market may also not work perfectly, given that top managers are frequently near retirement and have long-term contracts. As a result, it is important to look for solutions to the principal–agent problem in which owners alter the incentives that managers face, without resort to government intervention. We consider some of these solutions in the next section.

The Principal–Agent Problem in Public Enterprises

The principal–agent framework can also help us understand the behavior of the managers of public organizations. There managers may be interested in power and perquisites, both of which can be obtained by expanding their organization beyond its "efficient" level. Because it is also costly to monitor the behavior of public managers, there are no guarantees that they will produce the efficient output. Legislative checks on a government agency are not likely to be effective as long as the agency has better information about its costs than the legislature has.

Although the public sector lacks some of the market forces that keep private managers in line, government agencies can still be effectively monitored.

---

[10] There are economies of scale in gathering information but there is no obvious way in which the information can be sold.

First, managers of government agencies care about more than just the size of their agency. Indeed, many choose lower-paying public jobs because they are concerned about the "public interest." Second, public managers are subject to the rigors of the managerial job market, much the way private managers are. If public managers are perceived to be pursuing improper objectives, their ability to obtain high salaries in the future might be impaired. Third, the legislature and other government agencies perform an oversight function. For example, the Government Accounting Office and the Office of Management and Budget spend much of their energy monitoring other agencies.

At the local rather than the federal level, public managers are subject to even more checks. Suppose, for example, that a city transit agency has expanded bus service beyond the efficient level. Then, the citizens can vote the transit managers out of office, or, if all else fails, use alternative transportation or even move. And competition among agencies can be as effective as competition among private firms in constraining the non-profit-maximizing behavior of managers.

EXAMPLE 17.4   THE MANAGERS OF NONPROFIT HOSPITALS AS AGENTS

Do the managers of nonprofit organizations have the same goals as those of for-profit organizations? Are nonprofit organizations more or less efficient than for-profit firms? We can get some insight into these issues by looking at the provision of health care. In a study of 725 hospitals, from 14 major hospital chains, the return on investment and average costs of nonprofit and for-profit were compared to determine if they performed differently.[11]

The study found that for 1977 and 1981 the rate of returns between the two types of hospitals did indeed differ. For example, in 1977 for-profits earned an 11.6 percent return, while nonprofits earned 8.8 percent. In 1981, for-profits earned 12.7 percent and nonprofits only 7.4 percent. A straight comparison of returns and costs of these hospitals is not appropriate, however, because the hospitals perform different functions. For example, 24 percent of the nonprofit hospitals provide medical residency programs as compared with only 6 percent of the for-profit hospitals. Similar differences can be found in the provision of speciality care, where 10 percent of the nonprofits have open-heart units as compared with 5 percent of the for-profits. In addition, 43 percent of nonprofits had premature infant units, while only 29 percent of the for-profits had the equivalent units.

Using a statistical regression analysis, which controls for differences in the services performed, one can determine whether differences in services account for the higher costs. The study found that after adjusting for services performed, the average cost of a patient day in nonprofit hospitals was 8 percent

[11] Regina E. Herzlinger and William S. Krasker, "Who Profits from Nonprofits?" *Harvard Business Review* 65 (Jan.–Feb. 1987): 93–106.

higher than in for-profit hospitals. This implies that the profit status of the hospital affects its performance in the way principal-agent theory predicts: Without the competitive forces faced by for-profit hospitals, nonprofit hospitals may be less cost-conscious and therefore less likely to serve appropriately as agents for their principals, society at large.

Of course, nonprofit hospitals provide services that society may well wish to subsidize. But the added cost of running a nonprofit hospital should be considered when determining whether it should be granted tax-exempt status.

Incentives in the Principal–Agent Framework

We have seen why managers' and owners' objectives are likely to differ within the principal–agent framework. How, therefore, can owners design reward systems so that managers and workers can come as close as possible to meeting the owners' goals? To answer this question, let's study a specific problem.[12]

A small manufacturer uses labor and machinery to produce watches. The owners want to maximize their profit. They must rely on a machine repairperson whose effort will influence the likelihood that the machines break down, and thus affect the firm's level of profit. Profit also depends on other random factors, such as the quality of parts and the reliability of other labor. As a result of high monitoring costs, the owners can neither measure the effort of the repairperson directly nor be sure that the same effort will always generate the same profit level. Table 17.2 describes these circumstances.

The table shows that the repairperson can work with either a low or high amount of effort. Low effort generates either $10,000 or $20,000 profit (with equal probability), depending on the random factors that we mentioned. We've labeled the lower of the two profit levels "poor luck," and the higher profit level "good luck." When the repairperson makes a high effort, the profit will be either $20,000 (when there is poor luck) or $40,000 (when there is good luck). These numbers highlight the problem of incomplete information, because the owners cannot know whether the repairperson has made a low or high effort when the firm's profit is $20,000.

TABLE 17.2   The Profit from Making Watches

	Poor Luck	Good Luck
Low effort ($a = 0$)	$10,000	$20,000
High effort ($a = 1$)	$20,000	$40,000

[12] This discussion is motivated in part by Bengt Holmstrom, "Moral Hazard and Observability," *Bell Journal of Economics* 10 (1979): 74–91.

Suppose the repairperson's goal is to maximize the wage payment that he receives, net of the cost of lost leisure and unpleasant work time associated with any effort that he makes. To simplify, we'll suppose that the cost of effort is 0 for low effort and $10,000 for high effort. (Formally, $c = \$10,000a$.)

Now we can state the principal–agent problem from the owners' perspective. The owners' goal is to maximize expected profit, given the uncertainty of outcomes and given that the repairperson's behavior cannot be monitored. The owners can contract to pay the repairperson for his work, but the payment scheme must be based entirely on the measurable output (profit) of the manufacturing process, not on the repairperson's effort. To signify this link, we describe the payment scheme as $w(\pi)$, stressing that payments can depend only on measured profit.

What is the best payment scheme? And can that scheme be as effective as one based on effort rather than output? We can only begin to study the answers here. The best payment scheme depends on the nature of production, the degree of uncertainty, and the objectives of both owners and managers. The arrangement will not always be as effective as an ideal scheme that is directly tied to effort. A lack of information can lower economic efficiency because both the owners' profit and the repairperson's payment may fall at the same time.

Let's see how to design a payment scheme when the repairperson wishes to maximize his payment received net of the cost of effort made.[13] Suppose first that the owners offer a fixed wage payment to the repairperson. Any wage will do, but we can see things most clearly if we assume that the wage is 0. (Here, 0 could represent a wage no higher than the wage rate paid in other comparable jobs.) Facing a wage of 0, the repairperson has no incentive to make a high level of effort. The reason is simple: The repairperson does not share in any of the gains that the owners enjoy from the increased effort. It follows, therefore, that a fixed payment will lead to an inefficient outcome. When $a = 0$, and $w = 0$, the owner will earn an expected profit of $15,000, and the repairperson a net wage of 0.

Both the owners and the repairperson will be better off if the repairperson is rewarded for his productive effort. Suppose, for example, that the owners offer the repairperson the following payment scheme:

$$\text{If } \pi = \$10,000 \text{ or } \$20,000, w = 0 \tag{17.1}$$

$$\text{If } \pi = \$40,000, w = \$24,000$$

Under this bonus arrangement, a low effort generates no payment. A high effort, however, generates an expected payment of $12,000, and a payment net of the cost of effort of $2,000. Now, the repairperson will choose to make a high level of effort. This makes the owners better off than before because they get an expected profit of $30,000, and a net profit of $18,000.

---

[13] We assume that the repairperson is risk neutral, so that no efficiency is lost. If, however, the repairperson were risk averse, there would be an efficiency loss.

This isn't the only payment scheme that will work for the owners, however. Suppose they contract to have the worker participate in the following profit-sharing arrangement. When profits are greater than $18,000:

$$w = \pi - \$18,000 \qquad (17.2)$$

(Otherwise the wage is zero.) Now if the repairperson offers low effort, he receives an expected payment of $1000. But if he offers a high level of effort, his expected payment is $12,000, and his expected payment net of the cost of effort is $2,000. (The owners' net profit is $18,000 as before.)

Thus, in our example, a profit-sharing arrangement achieves the same outcome as a bonus payment system. In more complex situations, the incentive effects of the two types of arrangements will differ. However, the basic idea illustrated here applies to all principal–agent problems. When it is impossible to measure effort directly, an incentive structure that rewards the outcome of high levels of effort can induce agents to aim for the goals that the owners set.

*17.5 Managerial Incentives in an Integrated Firm

We have seen that owners and managers of firms can have asymmetric information about demand, cost, and other variables. We've also seen how owners can design a reward structure to encourage managers to make the appropriate effort. Now we focus our attention on firms that are *integrated*—that consist of several divisions, each with its own managers. Some firms are *horizontally integrated*—several plants produce the same or related products. Others are also *vertically integrated*—"upstream" divisions produce materials, parts, and components that "downstream" divisions use to produce final products. Integration creates organizational problems. We addressed some of these problems in the Appendix to Chapter 11, where we discussed *transfer pricing* in the vertically integrated firm, that is, how the firm sets prices for parts and components that upstream divisions supply to downstream ones. Here we will examine problems that stem from asymmetric information.

Asymmetric Information and Incentive Design in the Integrated Firm

In an integrated firm, the managers of the different divisions are likely to have better information about their operating costs and production potential than central management has. This asymmetric information causes two problems.

First, how can central management elicit accurate information about divisional operating costs and production potential from the divisional managers?

This is important because the inputs to some divisions may be the outputs of other divisions, because deliveries must be scheduled to customers, and because prices cannot be set without knowing overall production capacity and costs. Second, what reward or incentive structure should central management use to encourage the divisional managers to produce as efficiently as possible? Should the divisional managers be given a bonus based on how much they produce, and if so, how should it be structured?

To understand these problems, consider a firm with several plants that all produce the same product. Each plant's manager has much better information about its production capacity than central management has. The firms' central management wants to learn more about how much each plant can produce, so that it can avoid bottlenecks and schedule deliveries reliably. It also wants each plant to produce as much as possible. Let's examine how central management can obtain the information it wants and also encourage the plant managers to run the plants as efficiently as possible.

One way is to give the plant managers a bonus based on either the total output of their plant or its operating profit. While this would encourage the plant managers to maximize their plant's output, it would penalize managers whose plants have higher costs and lower capacity. (Even if these plants produced efficiently, their output and operating profit—and hence their bonus—would be lower than that of plants with lower costs and higher capacities.) The plant managers would also have no incentive to obtain and reveal accurate information about cost and capacity.

A second way is to ask the plant managers about their costs and capacities, and *then* to base their bonus on how well they do relative to their answer. For example, each manager might be asked how much his or her plant can produce each year. Then at the end of the year, the manager would receive a bonus based on how close the plant's output was to this target. For example, if the manager's estimate of the feasible production level is Q_f, the annual bonus in dollars, B, might be

$$B = 10,000 - .5(Q_f - Q) \qquad (17.3)$$

where Q is the plant's actual output, 10,000 is the bonus when output is at capacity, and .5 is a factor chosen to reduce the bonus if Q is below Q_f.

With this scheme, however, the plant managers would have an incentive to *underestimate* the capacity of their plant. By claiming a capacity below what they know to be true, they can more easily earn a large bonus, even if they do not operate efficiently. For example, if a manager estimates the capacity of her plant to be 18,000 rather than 20,000, and the plant actually produces only 16,000, her bonus increases from $8,000 to $9,000. Thus, this scheme fails to elicit accurate information about capacity, and does not ensure that the plants will be run as efficiently as possible.

Now let's modify this scheme. We will still ask the plant managers how much their plants can feasibly produce and tie their bonuses to this estimate. However, we will use a slightly more complicated formula than (17.3) to calculate the bonus:

$$\text{If } Q > Q_f, \quad B = .3Q_f + .2(Q - Q_f)$$
$$\text{If } Q \leq Q_f, \quad B = .3Q_f - .5(Q_f - Q) \tag{17.4}$$

The parameters (.3, .2, and .5) have been chosen so that each plant manager has the incentive to reveal the *true* feasible production level, *and* to make Q, the actual output of the plant, as large as possible.

To see that this scheme does the job, look at Figure 17.4. Assume that the true production limit is $Q^* = 20{,}000$ units per year. The bonus that the manager will receive if she states the feasible capacity to be the true production limit is given by the line $Q_f = 20{,}000$. The line is continued for outputs beyond 20,000 to illustrate the bonus scheme, but dashed to signify the infeasibility of such production. Note that the manager's bonus is maximized when the firm produces at its limit of 20,000 units; the bonus is then $6,000.

Suppose, however, that the manager reports a feasible capacity of only 10,000. Then the bonus she receives is given by the line $Q_f = 10{,}000$. The maximum bonus is now $5,000, which is obtained by producing an output of 20,000. But note that this is less than the bonus the manager would receive if she correctly stated the feasible capacity to be 20,000.

The same line of argument applies when the manager exaggerates available capacity. If the manager states the feasible capacity to be 30,000 units per year,

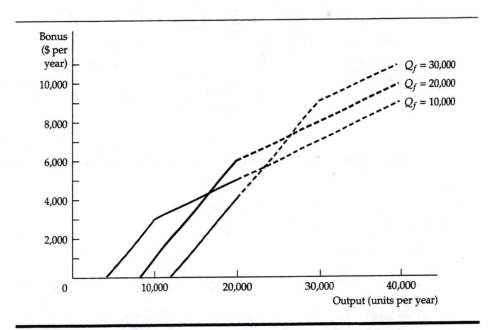

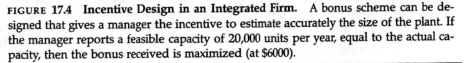

FIGURE 17.4 **Incentive Design in an Integrated Firm.** A bonus scheme can be designed that gives a manager the incentive to estimate accurately the size of the plant. If the manager reports a feasible capacity of 20,000 units per year, equal to the actual capacity, then the bonus received is maximized (at $6000).

the bonus is given by the line $Q_f = 30,000$. The maximum bonus of $4,000, which is achieved at an output of 20,000, is less than the bonus she could have received had she reported feasible capacity correctly.[14]

Applications

This problem of asymmetric information and incentive design comes up often in managerial settings, so incentive schemes like the one described above arise in many contexts. One example is how to encourage salespeople to set and reveal realistic sales targets, and then work as hard as possible to meet them.

Most salespeople cover specific territories. A salesperson assigned to an urban and densely populated territory can usually sell more product each month than a salesperson assigned to a sparsely populated area. The company, however, wants to reward all its salespeople equitably. It also wants to give them the incentive to work as hard as possible and to report realistic sales targets, so that it can plan production and delivery schedules. Companies have always used bonuses and commissions to reward salespeople, but the incentive schemes have often been poorly designed. Typically, salespeople's commissions were proportional to their sales. This elicited neither accurate information about feasible sales targets nor maximum performance.

Now companies are learning that bonus schemes of the sort given by equation (17.4) provide better results. The salesperson can be given a matrix of numbers that shows the bonus as a function of both the sales target (chosen by the salesperson) and the actual level of sales. (The numbers would be calculated from equation (17.4) or some similar formula.) Salespeople will quickly figure out that they do best by reporting a feasible sales target, and then working as hard as possible to meet it.[15]

17.6 *Asymmetric Information in Labor Markets: Efficiency Wage Theory*

When the labor market is competitive, all who wish to work will find jobs for a wage equal to their marginal product. Yet most countries have substantial unemployment even though many people are aggressively seeking work.

[14] Any bonus of the form $B = \beta Q_f + \alpha(Q - Q_f)$ for $Q > Q_f$, and $B = \beta Q_f - \gamma(Q_f - Q)$ for $Q \leq Q_f$, with $\gamma > \beta > \alpha > 0$ will work. See Martin L. Weitzman, "The New Soviet Incentive Model," *Bell Journal of Economics* VII (Spring 1976): 251–256. There is a dynamic problem with this scheme that we have ignored: Managers must weigh a large bonus for good performance this year against being assigned more ambitious targets in the future. This is discussed in Martin Weitzman, "The 'Ratchet Principle' and Performance Incentives," *Bell Journal of Economics* 11 (Spring 1980): 302–308.

[15] See Jacob Gonik, "Tie Salesmen's Bonuses to their Forecasts," *Harvard Business Review* (May–June 1978): 116–123.

Many of the unemployed would presumably work even for a lower wage rate than that being received by employed people. Why don't we see firms cutting wage rates, increasing employment levels, and thereby increasing their profit? Can our models of competitive equilibrium explain persistent unemployment?

In this section we show how the *efficiency wage theory* can explain the presence of unemployment and wage discrimination.[16] We have thus far determined labor productivity according to workers' abilities and firms' investment in capital. Efficiency wage models recognize that labor productivity also depends on what wage rate is paid.[17] There are various explanations for this relationship. In developing countries, economists have suggested that the productivity of workers depends on the wage rate for nutritional reasons. Better-paid workers can afford to buy more and better food and are therefore healthier and can work harder.

A better explanation for the United States is found in the *shirking model*. Because monitoring workers is costly or impossible, firms have imperfect information about worker productivity, and there is a principal-agent problem. In its simplest form, the shirking model assumes perfectly competitive markets, so all workers are equally productive and earn the same wage. Once hired, workers can either work productively or slack off (shirk). But because information about their performance is limited, workers may not get fired for shirking.

The model works as follows. If a firm pays its workers the market clearing wage w^*, they have an incentive to shirk. Even if they get caught and are fired (and they might not be), they can immediately get hired somewhere else for the same wage. In this situation, the threat of being fired does not impose a cost on workers, so they have no incentive to be productive. As an incentive not to shirk, a firm must offer workers a higher wage. At this higher wage, workers who are fired for shirking will have to face a decrease in wages if they get hired by another firm at w^*. If the difference in wages is large enough, workers will be induced to be productive, and this firm will not have a problem with shirking. The wage at which no shirking occurs is the *efficiency wage*.

Up to this point, we have looked at only one firm. But all firms face the problem of shirking. This means that all firms will offer wages greater than the market clearing wage w^*, say, w_e (efficiency wage). Does this remove the incentive for workers not to shirk because they will be hired at the higher wage by other firms if they get fired? No; because all firms are offering wages greater than w^*, the demand for labor is less than the market-clearing quantity, and there is unemployment. This means that workers fired for shirking will face a spell of unemployment before earning w_e at another firm.

---

[16] See Janet L. Yellen, "Efficiency Wage Models of Unemployment," *American Economic Review* 74 (May 1984): 200–205. The graphical analysis relies on Joseph E. Stiglitz, "The Causes and Consequences of the Dependence of Quality on Price," *Journal of Economic Literature* 25 (March 1987): 1–48.

[17] This linkage between productivity and wages has been discussed by economists before the development of efficiency wage theory, most notably by Karl Marx.

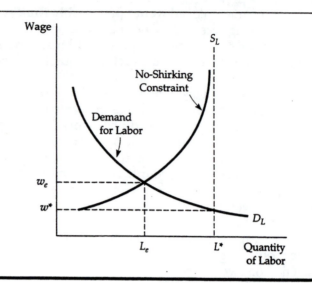

FIGURE 17.5   Unemployment in a Shirking Model.   Unemployment can arise in otherwise competitive labor markets when employers cannot accurately monitor workers. Here the "no shirking constraint" gives the wage necessary to keep workers from shirking on the job. The firm hires L_e workers (at a higher than competitive efficiency wage w_e), creating $L^* - L_e$ of unemployment.

Figure 17.5 shows shirking in the labor market. The demand for labor D_L is downward-sloping for the traditional reasons. If there were no shirking, the intersection of D_L with the supply of labor (S_L) would set the market wage at w^*, and full employment would result (L^*). With shirking, however, individual firms are unwilling to pay w^*. Rather, for every level of unemployment in the labor market, firms need to pay some wage greater than w^* to induce workers to be productive. This wage is shown as the no-shirking constraint (NSC) curve. This curve shows the minimum wage workers need earn in order not to shirk, for each level of unemployment. Note that the greater the level of unemployment, the smaller the difference between the efficiency wage and w^*. This is because with high levels of unemployment, people who shirk risk long periods of unemployment and therefore don't need much inducement to be productive.

In Figure 17.5, the equilibrium wage will be at the intersection of the NSC curve and D_L curves, with L_e workers earning w_e. This is because the NSC curve gives the lowest wage that firms can pay and still avoid shirking. Firms do not need to pay more than this to get the number of workers they need, and they will not pay less than this because of shirking. Note that the NSC curve never crosses the labor supply curve. This means that there will always be some unemployment in equilibrium.

EXAMPLE 17.5   EFFICIENCY WAGES AT FORD MOTOR COMPANY

One of the early examples of the payment of efficiency wages can be found in the history of Ford, one of America's major automobile producers.[18] Before 1913 automobile production had depended heavily on skilled workers. But the introduction of the assembly line drastically changed the workplace. Now jobs demanded much less skill, and production depended on maintaining the assembly-line equipment. As the automobile plants changed, workers became increasingly disenchanted. In 1913, turnover at Ford was 380 percent. The following year, it rose to 1000 percent, and profit margins fell sharply.

Ford needed to maintain a stable work force, and Henry Ford (and his business partner James Couzens) provided it. In 1914, when the going wage for a day's work in industry averaged between $2 and $3, Ford Motor Company introduced a pay policy of $5 a day for its workers. Improved labor efficiency (not generosity) was behind this policy. The goal was to attract better workers who would stay with their jobs, and eventually to increase profits.

Although Henry Ford was attacked for it, this policy succeeded. The work force did become more stable, and the publicity helped Ford's sales. And because Henry Ford had his pick of workers, he could hire a group that was on average more productive. Ford stated that the wage increase did in fact increase the loyalty and personal efficiency of his workers, and quantitative estimates support his statements. According to calculations by Ford's chief of labor relations, productivity increased by 51 percent. Another study found that absenteeism had been halved, and discharges for cause had declined sharply. So the productivity increase more than offset the increase in wages. As a result, Ford's profitability rose from $30 million in 1914 to $60 million in 1916.

Summary

1. The seller of a product often has better information about its quality than the buyer. Asymmetric information of this type creates a market failure in which bad products tend to drive good products out of the market. The market failure can be eliminated if sellers offer standardized products, provide guarantees or warranties, or find other ways to maintain a good reputation for their product.

---

[18] See J.R. Lee, "So-called Profit Sharing System in the Ford Plant," *Annals of the American Academy of Political and Social Science* (May 1915): 297–310; David Halberstam, *The Reckoning* (New York: William Morrow, 1986), pp. 91–92; and Daniel M.G. Raff and Lawrence H. Summers, "Did Henry Ford Pay Efficiency Wages?" *Journal of Labor Economics* (1987): 557–586.

2. Insurance markets frequently involve asymmetric information because the insuring party has better information about the risk involved than the insurance company. This can lead to adverse selection, in which the poorer risks choose to insure, and the good risks do not. Another problem for insurance markets is moral hazard, in which the insuring party takes less care to avoid losses after insuring than before.

3. Sellers can deal with the problem of asymmetric information by sending buyers signals about the quality of their product. For example, workers can signal their high productivity by obtaining a high level of education.

4. Asymmetric information may make it costly for the owners of firms (the principal) to monitor accurately the behavior of the firm's manager (the agent). Managers may seek higher fringe benefits for themselves, or a goal of sales maximization, even though the shareholders would prefer to maximize profit.

5. Owners can avoid some of the principal–agent problems by designing contracts that give their agents the incentive to perform productively.

6. Asymmetric information can explain why labor markets have substantial unemployment when some workers are actively seeking work. According to efficiency wage theory, a wage higher than the competitive wage (the efficiency wage) increases worker productivity by discouraging workers from shirking on the job.

Questions for Review

1. Why can asymmetric information between buyers and sellers lead to market failure when a market is otherwise perfectly competitive?

2. If the used car market is a "lemons" market, how would you expect the repair record of used cars that are sold to compare with the repair record of those not sold?

3. Explain the difference between adverse selection and moral hazard in insurance markets. Can one exist without the other?

4. Describe several ways in which sellers can convince buyers that their products are of high quality. Which methods apply to the following products: Maytag washing machines, Burger King hamburgers, large diamonds?

5. Why might a seller find it advantageous to signal the quality of her product? How are guarantees and warranties a form of market signaling?

6. Why might managers of firms be able to achieve objectives other than profit maximization, the goal of the firm's shareholders?

7. How can the principal–agent model be used to explain why public enterprises, such as post offices, might pursue goals other than profit maximization?

8. Why are bonus and profit-sharing payment schemes likely to resolve principal–agent problems, whereas a fixed wage payment will not?

9. What is an efficiency wage? Why is it profitable for the firm to pay an efficiency wage when workers have better information about their productivity than firms do?

Exercises

1. Many consumers view a well-known brand name as a signal of quality and will pay more for a brand-name product (e.g., Bayer aspirin instead of generic aspirin, or Birds Eye frozen vegetables instead of the supermarket's own brand). Can a brand name provide a useful signal of quality? Why or why not?

2. Gary is a recent college graduate. After six months at his new job, he has finally saved enough to buy his first car.

a. Gary knows very little about the differences between makes and models of cars. How could he use market signals, reputation, or standardization to make comparisons?

b. You are a loan officer in a bank. After selecting a car, Gary comes to you seeking a loan. Since he has only recently graduated, he does not have a long credit history. Despite this, the bank has a long history of financing cars of recent college graduates. Is this information useful in Gary's case? If so, how?

3. A major university bans the assignment of D or F grades. It defends its action by claiming that students tend to perform above average when they are free from the pressures of flunking out. The university states that it wants all its students to get As and Bs. If the goal is to raise overall grades to the B level or above, is this a good policy? Discuss with respect to the problem of moral hazard.

4. Professor Jones has just been hired by the economics department at a major private university. The president of the board of regents has stated that the university is committed to providing top-quality education for its undergraduates. Two months into the semester, Professor Jones fails to show up for his classes. It seems he is devoting all his time to economic research rather than to teaching. Professor Jones argues that his research will bring additional prestige to the department and the university. Should he be allowed to continue exclusively with research? Discuss with reference to the principal-agent problem.

5. Faced with a reputation for producing automobiles with poor repair records, a number of American automobile companies have offered extensive guarantees to car purchasers (e.g., a seven-year warranty on all parts and labor associated with mechanical problems).

a. In light of your knowledge of the lemons market, why is this a reasonable policy?

b. Is the policy likely to create a moral hazard problem? Explain.

6. To promote competition and consumer welfare, the Federal Trade Commission requires firms to advertise truthfully. How does truth in advertising promote competition? Why would a market be less competitive if firms advertised deceptively?

7. An insurance company is considering issuing three types of fire insurance policies: (i) complete insurance coverage, (ii) complete coverage above and beyond a $10,000 deductible, and (iii) 90 percent coverage of all losses. Which policy is more likely to create moral hazard problems?

8. You have seen how asymmetric information can reduce the average quality of the products sold in a market, as low-quality products drive out the high-quality ones. For those markets where asymmetric information is prevalent, would you agree or disagree with each of the following? Explain briefly:

a. The government should subsidize *Consumer Reports*.

b. The government should impose quality standards; e.g., firms should not be allowed to sell low-quality items.

c. The producer of a high-quality good will probably want to offer an extensive warranty.

d. The government should require *all* firms to offer extensive warranties.

9. Two used car dealerships compete side by side on a main road. The first, Harry's Cars, sells high-quality cars that it carefully inspects and, if necessary, services. It costs Harry's, on average, $8,000 to buy and service each car that it sells. The second dealership, Lew's Motors, sells lower-quality cars. It costs Lew's on average only $5,000 for each car that it sells. If consumers knew the quality of the used cars they were buying, they would gladly pay $10,000 on average for cars Harry's sells and pay only $7,000 on average for the cars Lew's sells.

Unfortunately, the dealerships are too new to have established reputations, so consumers don't know the quality of each dealership's cars. Consumers shopping at these dealerships figure that they have a 50–50 chance of ending up with a high-quality car, no matter which dealership they go to, and hence are willing to pay $8,500 on average for a car.

Harry's has an idea—it will offer a bumper-to-bumper warranty for all the cars it sells. It knows that a warranty lasting Y years will cost $500Y on average, and it also knows that if Lew's tries to offer the same warranty, it will cost Lew's $2000Y on average.

a. Suppose Harry's offers a one-year warranty on all the cars it sells. Will this generate a credible signal of quality? Will Lew's match the offer, or will it fail to match it so that consumers can correctly assume that because of the warranty, Harry's cars are high quality and hence worth $10,000 on average?

b. What if Harry's offers a two-year warranty on its cars? Will this generate a credible signal of quality? What about a three-year warranty?

c. If you were advising Harry's, how long a warranty would you urge it to offer? Explain why.

10. A firm's short-run revenue is given by $R = 10e - e^2$, where e is the level of effort by a typical worker (all workers are assumed to be identical). A worker chooses his level of effort to maximize his wage net of effort $w - e$ (the per-unit cost of effort is assumed to be 1). Determine the level of effort and the level of profit (revenue less wage paid) for each of the following wage arrangements. Explain why these different principal–agent relationships generate different outcomes.

a. $w = 2$ for $e \geq 1$; otherwise $w = 0$.

b. $w = R/2$.

c. $w = R - 12.5$.

Glossary

Accounting Cost *(page 194)* Actual expenses plus depreciation charges for capital equipment. (These charges are determined by the Internal Revenue Service.)

Adverse Selection *(page 596)* A form of market failure resulting from asymmetric information: If insurance companies must charge a single premium because they cannot distinguish between high-risk and low-risk individuals, more high-risk individuals will insure, making it unprofitable to sell insurance.

Agent *(page 608)* An individual employed by a principal to implement the objective of the principal.

Antitrust Laws *(page 353)* Regulations intended to promote a competitive economy by prohibiting actions that restrain competition.

Arc Elasticity of Demand *(page 110)* Used when dealing with a relatively large price change, the arc elasticity is equal to $(\Delta Q/\Delta P)\,(\bar{P}/\bar{Q})$ where $\bar{P}$ and $\bar{Q}$ are the averages of the prices and quantities before and after the price change.

Asymmetric Information *(page 593)* A situation in which a buyer and a seller have different information about a transaction.

Average Cost *(page 198)* Production cost per unit of output.

Average Expenditure *(page 345)* The price per unit paid by a buyer.

Average Product *(page 171)* Total output per unit of a particular input.

Average Revenue *(page 321)* Revenue divided by the number of units sold, i.e., price per unit.

Backward-Bending Labor Supply Curve *(page 502)* The portion of the labor supply curve at which the wage rate increases and the hours of work supplied decrease, giving the curve a negative slope.

Bandwagon Effect *(page 118)* A positive network externality in which an individual demands a good in part because many other people have the good.

Barrier to Entry *(page 419)* Anything that makes it prohibitive for new firms to enter a market; it is necessary if incumbent firms are to maintain monopoly power.

Bilateral Monopoly *(page 352)* A market with one buyer and one seller.

Budget Line *(page 69)* All combinations of goods that can be purchased with an individual's income.

Bundling *(page 384)* A pricing strategy that involves selling two or more products as a package.

CAPM (Capital Asset Pricing Model) *(page 538)* A model in which the risk premium for a capital investment depends on the correlation of the investment's return with the return on the entire stock market.

Cardinal Ranking *(page 63)* A quantitative measure of the value of a good in terms of a basic unit of utility.

Cartel *(page 414)* A group of firms that explicitly agree to set prices and/or to limit output.

Ceiling Price *(page 49)* A maximum price that firms are allowed by the government to charge for a good.

Clayton Act *(page 354)* As amended by the Robinson-Patman Act, a law that makes it illegal to discriminate by charging buyers of essentially the same product different prices.

Coase Theorem *(page 643)* When parties can bargain without cost and to their mutual advantage,

669

the resulting outcome will be efficient, regardless of how the property rights are specified.

Common Property Resource *(page 645)* A resource, such as air and water, to which anyone has free access.

Comparative Advantage *(page 582)* A country A has a comparative advantage over another country B in producing a good if the cost of producing the good in A, relative to the cost of producing other goods in A, is lower than the cost of producing the good in B, relative to the cost of producing other goods in B.

Competitive Markets *(page 11)* Markets in which buyers and sellers individually have little or no ability to affect prices.

Complements *(page 101)* Goods that tend to be used together, so that an increase in the price of one good tends to decrease the demand for its complement.

Constant Cost Industry *(page 264)* An industry whose long-run supply curve is horizontal.

Constant Returns to Scale *(page 187)* When a doubling of inputs causes output to double.

Consumer Price Index *(page 13)* A measure of the aggregate price level based on a large market basket of goods; calculated by the U.S. Bureau of Labor Statistics.

Consumer Surplus *(page 113)* The difference between the amount consumers are willing to pay for a good and the amount they actually pay.

Contestable Market *(page 272)* A market that firms can freely enter or exit without incurring sunk costs.

Contract Curve *(page 566)* A curve that includes all efficient allocations of two goods between two consumers, or two inputs between two production functions, in an Edgeworth box.

Cooperative Game *(page 454)* A game in which players can negotiate binding contracts that allow them to plan joint strategies.

Cost Function *(page 224)* A relationship between the cost of production and the level of output of a firm or firms.

Cournot Equilibrium *(page 424)* The Nash equilibrium that occurs when firms simultaneously choose the quantities they will produce.

Cournot Model *(page 421)* An oligopoly model in which firms assume that their competitors' outputs are fixed, and simultaneously decide how much to produce.

Cross-Price Elasticity of Demand *(page 31)* The percentage change in the quantity demanded of a good that results from a 1 percent increase in the price of another good.

Deadweight Loss *(page 280)* A measure of efficiency loss, given by the sum of lost consumer and producer surplus, less revenues to the government.

Decreasing Cost Industry *(page 267)* An industry whose long-run supply curve is downward sloping.

Decreasing Returns to Scale *(page 187)* When a doubling of inputs causes output to increase by less than a factor of two.

Demand Curve *(page 95)* The amount of a good consumers are willing to purchase as a function of its price.

Depreciation *(page 195)* The decline in value of a capital asset as it is used over time.

Discount Rate *(page 535)* A rate used to compare the value of a dollar received in the future to a dollar received today.

Diseconomies of Scale *(page 212)* When a firm's costs more than double in response to a doubling of output.

Diseconomies of Scope *(page 218)* When one firm produces less of two outputs than two separate specialized firms could produce.

Diversifiable Risk (also Nonsystematic Risk) *(page 537)* Risk that can be eliminated by diversifying, e.g., by investing in many projects or by holding the stocks of many companies.

Dominant Firm Model *(page 442)* A model of oligopoly in which one firm sets price, knowing that other firms will produce as much as they want at that price.

Dominant Strategy *(page 456)* A strategy that is optimal regardless of how one's competitors behave.

Duality in Consumer Theory *(page 134)* The optimum allocation of income between two goods may be determined by choosing the highest indifference curve that is tangent to the budget line, or by choosing the lowest budget line that touches a given indifference curve.

Durable Good *(page 33)* A consumption or capital good bought to provide services for a long time.

Economic Profit *(page 258)* The difference between a firm's revenues and costs, including any opportunity costs.

Economic Rent *(page 261)* The difference between the payments made to a factor of production and the minimum amount that must be spent to obtain the use of that factor.

Economies of Scale *(page 212)* When a firm's costs less than double in response to a doubling of output.

Economies of Scope *(page 218)* When one firm produces more of two outputs than two specialized firms could produce.

Edgeworth Box Diagram *(page 564)* A diagram that shows all possible allocations of two goods between two people, or of two inputs between two production processes.

Effective Yield *(page 529)* The interest rate that equates the price of a bond with the present discounted value of its expected future payments. Also called the *rate of return* on the bond.

Efficiency Wage *(page 617)* The wage a firm will pay to an employee as an incentive not to shirk.

Elastic Demand *(page 29)* When the percentage change in quantity demanded of a good in response to a 1 percent change in price is greater than one in magnitude.

Elasticity *(page 28)* A measure of the percentage change in one variable resulting from a 1 percent increase in the other variable.

Emissions Fee *(page 630)* A charge per unit of emissions imposed on a polluter.

Emissions Standard *(page 630)* A legal limit on how much pollutant a firm may emit.

Engel Curve *(page 99)* The quantity of a good consumed as a function of income.

Equal Marginal Principle *(page 88)* A rule for optimization when two or more options are available, i.e., to maximize utility, a consumer should equalize the marginal utility of each dollar spent on each good consumed.

Equilibrium Price (also Market-Clearing Price) *(page 19)* The price at which the quantity supplied and quantity demanded are equal.

Excess Demand *(page 49)* Demand that results when the quantity demanded exceeds the quantity supplied because a price ceiling keeps the price of a good below its equilibrium price.

Expansion Path *(page 209)* A curve that describes the combinations of labor and capital a firm will choose to minimize costs for every level of output.

Expected Value *(page 140)* The average value of a set of uncertain outcomes.

Explicit Cost *(page 194)* The actual outlays by a firm, including wages, salaries, costs of materials, and property rentals.

Externality *(page 623)* An action by either a producer or a consumer that affects other producers or consumers, yet is not accounted for in the market price.

Feedback Effect *(page 558)* A price or quantity adjustment in one market that is caused by price and quantity adjustments in related markets.

First-Degree Price Discrimination *(page 364)* Charging each person her reservation price for a good.

Fixed Cost *(page 198)* A cost that does not vary with the level of production, such as plant maintenance and insurance.

Fixed Inputs *(page 170)* Factors that cannot be changed in the short run.

Fixed-Proportions Production Function *(page 183)* When the production isoquants are L-shaped, so that only one combination of labor and capital can be used to produce each level of output.

Free Entry (Exit) *(page 415)* When firms may enter (exit) an industry without incurring a sunk cost.

Free Rider *(page 652)* A consumer or producer that does not pay for a nonexclusive good in the expectation that others will.

General Equilibrium Analysis *(page 558)* A method of analysis that simultaneously determines the prices and quantities in several markets.

Giffen Good *(page 104)* A good whose demand curve slopes upward as a result of a large income effect.

Income-Consumption Curve *(page 97)* A curve that includes the utility-maximizing combinations of goods associated with every income level.

Income Effect *(page 104)* The increase in consumption brought about by an increase in income, when the prices of goods are held constant.

Income Elasticity of Demand *(page 31)* The percentage change in the quantity demanded of a good resulting from a 1 percent increase in income.

Increasing Cost Industry *(page 265)* An industry whose long-run supply curve is upward sloping.

Increasing Returns to Scale *(page 187)* When a doubling of inputs causes output to more than double.

Indifference Curve *(page 59)* A graphical representation of all combinations of market baskets that provide the same level of satisfaction.

Indifference Map *(page 62)* A set of indifference curves that describes the consumer's preferences among various combinations of market baskets.

Inelastic Demand *(page 29)* When the percentage change in the quantity demanded of a good in response to a 1 percent change in price is less than one in magnitude.

Inferior Good *(page 98)* A good for which consumption falls as an individual's income rises.

Intertemporal Price Discrimination *(page 375)* Separating consumers into groups with varying demand functions and charging them different prices at different points in time.

Isocost Line *(page 204)* A line that includes all possible combinations of inputs that can be purchased for a given amount of money.

Isoquant *(page 168)* A curve that shows all the possible combinations of inputs that yield the same output.

Isoquant Map *(page 169)* A set of isoquants, each of which shows the maximum output that can be achieved for any set of inputs.

Kinked Demand Curve *(page 438)* The demand curve oligopolistic firms face due to the rigidity of prices, where the price elasticity of demand is higher for price increases than for decreases.

Labor Productivity *(page 177)* The average product of labor as applied to an industry or to the economy as a whole.

Law of Diminishing Returns *(page 174)* As the use of an input increases (while other inputs remain constant), the additional output produced will eventually decrease.

Learning Curve *(page 220)* The relationship between a firm's cumulative output and the (declining) amount of inputs needed to produce a unit of output.

Lerner Index *(page 334)* A measure of monopoly power calculated as the excess of price over marginal cost as a fraction of marginal cost.

Marginal Cost (or Incremental Cost) *(page 198)* The increase in cost from producing one additional unit of output.

Marginal Expenditure *(page 345)* The incremental cost of purchasing one additional unit of a good.

Marginal External Cost *(page 624)* The increase in cost imposed externally as a firm (or firms) increases its output by one unit.

Marginal Product of Inputs *(page 171)* The additional output produced as the input is increased by one unit.

Marginal Rate of Substitution *(page 64)* The amount of one good an individual will give up to gain one more unit of another good.

Marginal Rate of Technical Substitution *(page 181)* The amount by which one input can be reduced when one extra unit of another input is used, so that output remains constant.

Marginal Rate of Transformation *(page 578)* A measure of how much of one good must be given up to produce an additional unit of another good.

Marginal Revenue *(page 240)* The change in revenue resulting from a one-unit increase in output.

Marginal Revenue Product *(page 492)* The additional revenue resulting from the sale of output created by the use of one additional unit of an input.

Marginal Social Cost *(page 624)* The sum of marginal cost and marginal external cost (for each level of output).

Marginal Utility *(page 87)* A measure of the additional satisfaction obtained from consuming one additional unit of a good.

Market *(page 10)* A collection of buyers and sellers who interact, resulting in the possibility of exchange.

Market Demand Curve *(page 107)* The horizontal summation of all individual consumers' demand curves.

Market Power *(page 322)* The ability to profitably affect price. Refers to either monopoly or monopsony power.

Market Signaling *(page 600)* The process by which sellers send buyers information about a product's quality.

Markup Pricing *(page 334)* Increasing the production cost of a good by a fixed percentage to determine a sales price.

Maximin Strategy *(page 460)* A gaming strategy that maximizes the minimum gain that can result.

Median Voter *(page 655)* The individual with the median preferred outcome among all voters.

Mixed Bundling *(page 389)* When two or more goods are sold both as a package and individually.

Mixed Strategy *(page 461)* A gaming strategy in which a player makes a random choice among two or more possible actions, based on a set of chosen probabilities.

Monopolistic Competition *(page 413)* A market in which firms compete by selling differentiated products that are highly substitutable for one another, and there is free entry and exit.

Monopoly *(page 319)* A market with only one seller.

Monopoly Power *(page 319)* The ability of a firm to profitably charge a price higher than marginal cost.

Monopsony *(page 319)* A market with only one buyer.

Monopsony Power *(page 320)* The ability of a buyer to purchase a good at a price below its marginal value.

Moral Hazard *(page 604)* When an insured party can affect the probability or magnitude of an event against the occurrence of which it is insured.

Nash Equilibrium *(page 421)* A set of strategies or actions in which each player is doing the best it can, given the actions of its opponents.

Natural Monopoly *(page 343)* An industry in which economies of scale are so great that the efficient level of production for one firm satisfies the entire market demand.

Net Present Value *(page 532)* The present discounted value of expected future cash flows from an investment, less the cost of the investment.

Network Externality *(page 118)* The dependence of an individual's demand on the consumption levels of other people.

Nominal Discount Rate *(page 535)* A discount rate that includes the effects of inflation.

Nominal Price *(page 13)* The price actually quoted for a good at a given point in time; also called the "current dollar" price.

Noncooperative Game *(page 454)* A game in which negotiation and enforcement of a binding contract are not possible.

Nonexclusive Good *(page 648)* A good that people cannot be excluded from consuming, and for the use of which it is difficult to charge them.

Nonrival Good *(page 648)* A good for which the marginal cost of provision to an additional consumer is zero.

Normal Good *(page 98)* A good for which consumption increases when income rises.

Normative Analysis *(page 6)* An analysis leading to a recommendation or a prescription.

Oligopoly *(page 419)* A market with few sellers.

Oligopsony *(page 345)* A market with few buyers.

Opportunity Cost *(page 194)* The cost associated with opportunities that are foregone by not putting the firm's resources to their highest value use.

Opportunity Cost of Capital *(page 533)* The rate of return that one could earn by investing in a different project with similar risk.

Ordinal Ranking of Utility *(page 63)* Values that denote relative levels of satisfaction, assigned when the particular unit of utility is unimportant.

Pareto Efficiency *(page 567)* An allocation of goods in which one person must be made worse off in order to make another person better off.

Partial Equilibrium Analysis *(page 558)* A determination of the equilibrium prices and quantities in a particular market that ignores effects from other markets.

Peak-Load Pricing *(page 376)* A form of intertemporal price discrimination in which peak users pay more than off-peak users because marginal cost is higher during peak periods.

Perfect Competition *(page 271)* A market in which all goods are perfect substitutes, there are no barriers to entry, and no firm can affect the market price.

Positive Analysis *(page 5)* An explanation or prediction of an economic activity.

Predatory Pricing *(page 354)* A pricing policy designed to drive one or more competitors out of business and/or discourage new entrants to a market.

Present Discounted Value *(page 524)* The current value of an expected future cash flow.

Price-Consumption Curve *(page 95)* A curve derived by tracing the utility-maximizing combinations of two goods as the price of one changes.

Price Discrimination *(page 363)* Charging different prices to different customers for similar goods.

Price Elasticity of Demand *(page 110)* The percentage change in the quantity demanded of a good resulting from a 1 percent increase in the price of that good.

Price Elasticity of Supply *(page 32)* The percentage change in the quantity supplied of a good resulting from a 1 percent increase in the price of that good.

Price Leadership *(page 439)* A form of implicit collusion, where one firm in the market sets the price and other firms follow suit.

Price Support *(page 292)* A policy by which the government sets the market price of a good, usually an agricultural product, above the free-market level and buys up whatever output is needed to maintain that price.

Price Taker *(page 242)* A firm with no influence over the market price.

Principal *(page 608)* An individual who employs one or more agents to achieve his or her objective.

Principal–Agent Problem *(page 608)* The problem that arises when managers (agents) pursue their own goals, even if that entails lower profits for the owners of the firm (the principals).

Prisoners' Dilemma *(page 435)* A game in which two prisoners must decide separately whether to confess to a crime; it is a parable for competition in which all firms would do better if they cooperated, but each has a strong incentive to undercut its competitors.

Producer Surplus *(page 255)* The sum over all units of production of the difference between the market price of the good and the marginal cost of production.

Production Possibilities Frontier *(page 577)* A curve that describes the various combinations of two goods that can be produced given fixed quantities of inputs.

Profit Maximization *(page 239)* The goal of a firm; it is achieved when the marginal revenue of the firm is equal to the marginal cost of production.

Public Good *(page 648)* A nonexclusive and non-rival good.

Pure Bundling *(page 385)* When a firm sells two or more goods only as a package.

Rate of Return *(page 529)* The discount rate that makes the net present value of an investment equal to zero.

Rate-of-Return Regulation *(page 344)* Setting a price that gives a monopoly a competitive return on its assets.

Reaction Curve *(page 423)* The profit-maximizing production choices of one firm in a duopoly as a function of the other firm's output.

Real Discount Rate *(page 535)* The discount rate that applies when cash flows are in real terms, i.e., after netting out inflation.

Real Price *(page 13)* The price of a good relative to the aggregate price level; also called the "constant dollar" price.

Regulatory Lag *(page 344)* Delays that are usually required to change a regulated price.

Reservation Price *(page 364)* The maximum amount that a customer is willing to pay for a good.

Return *(page 157)* The total monetary flow an asset yields as a fraction of its price.

Revealed Preference *(page 81)* An approach to consumer theory in which preferences are determined by observing the choices consumers make.

Risk *(page 139)* The possibility of several different outcomes occurring when the probability of each outcome is known.

Risk-Averse Individual *(page 146)* A person who prefers a certain income to a risky alternative with the same expected income.

Risk-Free Return *(page 159)* A return which is free of risk, whether of default or interest rate fluctuations. An example is the return on U.S. Treasury bills.

Risk-Loving Individual *(page 146)* A person who prefers a risky alternative to a certain one even though both offer the same expected income.

Risk-Neutral Individual *(page 146)* A person who is indifferent between earning a certain income and earning a risky one with the same expected income.

Risk Premium *(page 147)* The amount of money that a risk-averse individual will pay to avoid taking a risk.

Secondary Supply *(page 39)* The supply from recycled scrap material.

Second-Degree Price Discrimination *(page 367)* Charging different prices for different quantities of the same good.

Sequential Game *(page 469)* A game in which players move in order, rather than simultaneously.

Sherman Act *(page 354)* A law that prohibits contracts, combinations, or conspiracies that restrain trade, and makes monopolizing or attempting to monopolize illegal.

Slutsky Equation *(page 136)* An equation that separates the effect of a price change on quantity demanded into an income and a substitution effect.

Snob Effect *(page 120)* A negative network externality in which an individual's demand for a good is higher the fewer are the other people who have it.

Stackelberg Model *(page 427)* A model of oligopoly in which one firm sets output before the other firms do.

Strategic Move *(page 420)* An action that constrains one's own behavior in a way that yields a strategic advantage.

Substitutes *(page 101)* Goods that compete in the market, so that if the price of one good increases, the quantity demanded of the substitute will also increase.

Substitution Effect *(page 103)* The change in consumption of a good that is associated with a change in its price, while the level of satisfaction is held constant.

Sunk Cost *(page 195)* An expenditure that when made cannot be recovered.

Supply Curve *(page 18)* The amount producers are willing to sell as a function of the market price.

Technical Efficiency *(page 167)* When firms combine their inputs to produce a given output as inexpensively as possible.

Third-Degree Price Discrimination *(page 368)* Dividing consumers into two or more groups with different demands for a product in order to charge different prices to each group.

Tit-for-Tat Strategy *(page 464)* In a repeated game, a strategy that responds in kind to an opponent's previous play. The strategy cooperates with cooperative opponents and retaliates against uncooperative ones.

Total Cost *(page 198)* The total cost of production, composed of fixed and variable costs.

Transfer Prices *(page 402)* The internal prices at which the parts and components from a firm's upstream divisions are "sold" to downstream divisions.

Transferable Emissions Permits *(page 633)* Marketable permits, allocated among firms, that specify the maximum level of emissions that can be generated.

Transitivity of Preferences *(page 59)* If a consumer prefers basket A to basket B, and also prefers basket B to basket C, then he will prefer basket A to basket C.

Two-Part Tariff *(page 379)* A form of pricing in which consumers are charged both an entry fee and a usage fee.

Tying *(page 392)* Requiring the purchaser of a product to also purchase a second product from the same firm.

Uncertainty *(page 139)* The possibility of several different outcomes occurring when the probability of each is unknown.

User Cost *(page 545)* The opportunity cost of depletion when producing a unit of an exhaustible resource.

Utility *(page 85)* The level of satisfaction that a person gets from consuming a good or undertaking an activity.

Utility Possibilities Frontier *(page 571)* A curve that includes all efficient allocations of resources measured in terms of the utility levels of two individuals.

Variable Cost *(page 198)* A cost that varies with the level of output, such as expenditures on wages and raw materials.

Welfare Effects *(page 276)* Gains and losses brought about by government policy.

Index

Nagle, Thomas, 246
Narasimhan, Chakravarthi, 373
Nash equilibrium, 421, 424, 458
   and Cournot equilibrium, 424, 458
   and games, 458–463
   maximin strategies, 460–461
   mixed strategies, 461–463
   as noncooperative equilibrium, 433
   in prices, 429, 431
   for Prisoners' Dilemma, 461
Nash, John, 421
Natural gas
   ceiling price, 50–51
   price controls, 50–51, 281–283
Natural monopoly, 339, 343
Negative externalities, 624–626
Net present value, 532–536,
   540–541
Network externalities, 118–122
   bandwagon effect, 118–120
   negative, 118, 120
   positive, 118, 119–120
   snob effect, 120–121
Nevin, John R., 418
Noll, Roger, 513
Nominal price, 13–14
Noncompetitive market, 11
Noncooperative games, 433–435
Nondiversifiable risk, 537–538
Nonprofit hospitals, returns from,
   610–611
Normative analysis, 6
Nozick, Robert, 572
Nuclear deterrence, 479

Oates, Wallace E., 634
Oi, Walter, 379, 509
Oil
   and OPEC, 444–446
   petroleum products, short-run
      production of, 250–251
   production decisions, 543–547
   supply and demand curves for,
      46–48
Okun, Arthur M., 6, 573
Oligopoly, 272, 419–428
   banks, 440–442
   competition versus collusion,
      433–436
   Cournot model, 421–427
   dominant firm model, 442–443
   equilibrium in, 420–421
   kinked demand curve model,
      438–439
   price competition, 428–432
   price leadership, 439–440

price rigidity, 438
price signaling, 439–440
Prisoners' dilemma, 433–438
Stackelberg model, 428–429
Oligopsony, 345
Olson, C. Vincent, 292
OPEC, 36–37, 46
   oil cartel, 444–446
   pricing analysis, 445–446
Opportunity cost, 194
   of capital, 533
   of time, 196–197
Optimization problem, 131
Ordinal ranking, indifference
   curves, 63
Output
   cost-minimization and output
      level, 209
   and isoquants, 169
   in long run, 256–263
   measurement as low, 203
   and production function, 167
   in short run, 243–246
Output efficiency, 579–580
Output markets, 491
   production efficiency in,
      580–581, 588
Output tax, 267–270

Panzar, John C., 217, 272
Parallel pricing, 354
Partial equilibrium analysis, 558
Payment-in-kind program, 296
Payment streams, present value of,
   525–526
Payoff matrix, 434–435, 456–457,
   474
Peak-load pricing, 376–378
Perfect complements, indifference
   curves, 66–67
Perfect substitutes, indifference
   curves, 66–67
Perfectly competitive market, 11,
   271–272
Perfectly elastic supply, 253
Perfectly inelastic supply, 253
Perpetuity, bond, 529
Pindyck, Robert S., 36, 50, 444, 446,
   533, 547, 659, 665
Point elasticity of demand, 109
Polaroid, 383–384
Polinsky, A. Mitchell, 149
Porter, Michael E., 472, 483, 540
Porter, Richard, 638
Positive analysis, 5–6
Positive externalities, 626–627

Predatory pricing, 354
Present value
   of cash flow from bond, 528–529
   net present value, 532–536,
      540–541
   present discounted value,
      524–526
   of stream of payments, 525–526
Price
   constant, and income effect, 104
   market price, 11–12, 241–242
   minimum prices, 288–290
   nominal price, 13–14
   real price, 13–14
Price changes
   effects on budget line, 72–73
   fall in price, effects of, 101–102
   and individual demand, 94–95
   input price, firm's response to,
      249–250
   and substitution effect, 103–104
Price competition
   Bertrand model, 428–429
   with differentiated products,
      430–431
   with homogeneous products,
      428–429
   oligopoly, 428–432
Price-consumption curve, 95–97
   and complement/substitute
      goods, 101
Price controls, 49–51
   ceiling price, 49
   changes in surplus from,
      279–281
   and deadweight loss, 280–281
   gasoline, 88
   and natural gas shortage, 50–51,
      281–283
Price discrimination, 361–363
   and airlines, 374
   coupons and rebates as, 372–373
   first-degree, 364–366
   intertemporal, 375–378
   peak-load pricing, 376–378
   publishing industry, 378–379
   second-degree, 366–367
   third-degree, 368–371
   and tying, 392
Price elasticity
   cross-price elasticity of demand,
      31–32
   of demand, 29–30, 125–126
   and expenditure, 110–111
   of supply, 32
Price fixing, 356–357